thomson ● com

changing the way the world learns

To get extra value from this book for no additional cost, go to:

http://www.thomson.com/wadsworth.html

thomson.com is the World Wide Web site for Wadsworth/ITP and is your direct source to dozens of on-line resources. *thomson.com* helps you find out about supplements, experiment with demonstration software, search for a job, and send e-mail to many of our authors. You can even preview new products and exciting new technologies.

thomson.com Visit us soon, it's changing the way the world learns about our future.

D1042667

The problem of

Abortion Third Edition

edited by

Susan Dwyer
McGill University

Joel Feinberg
The University of Arizona

Wadsworth Publishing Company
I(T)P® An International Thomson Publishing Company

Belmont, CA • Albany, NY • Bonn • Boston • Cincinnati • Detroit •
Johannesburg • London • Madrid • Melbourne • Mexico City • New York •
Paris • San Francisco • Singapore • Tokyo • Toronto • Washington

Philosophy Editor: *Peter Adams*
Assistant Editor: *Clay Glad*
Editorial Assistant: *Greg Brueck*
Production: *Scratchgravel Publishing Services*
Print Buyer: *Barbara Britton*

Permissions Editor: *Jeanne Bosschart*
Copy Editor: *Robin Whitaker*
Cover Designer: *Laurie Anderson*
Compositor: *Scratchgravel Publishing Services*
Printer: *Malloy Lithographing, Inc.*

Printed in the United States of America
1 2 3 4 5 6 7 8 9 10

For more information, contact Wadsworth Publishing Company, 10 Davis Drive, Belmont, CA 94002,
or electronically at http://www.thomson.com/wadsworth.html

International Thomson Publishing Europe
Berkshire House 168-173
High Holborn
London, WC1V 7AA, England

International Thomson Editores
Campos Eliseos 385, Piso 7
Col. Polanco
11560 México D.F. México

Thomas Nelson Australia
102 Dodds Street
South Melbourne 3205
Victoria, Australia

International Thomson Publishing Asia
221 Henderson Road
#05-10 Henderson Building
Singapore 0315

Nelson Canada
1120 Birchmount Road
Scarborough, Ontario
Canada M1K 5G4

International Thomson Publishing Japan
Hirakawacho Kyowa Building, 3F
2-2-1 Hirakawacho
Chiyoda-ku, Tokyo 102, Japan

International Thomson Publishing GmbH
Königswinterer Strasse 418
53227 Bonn, Germany

International Thomson Publishing Southern Africa
Building 18, Constantia Park
240 Old Pretoria Road
Halfway House, 1685 South Africa

Library of Congress Cataloging-in-Publication Data
The problem of abortion / edited by Susan Dwyer, Joel Feinberg. — 3rd
  ed.
      p.   cm.
  Includes bibliographical references.
  ISBN 0-534-50514-7 (alk. paper)
    1. Abortion—North America.   2. Abortion—Moral and ethical
aspects.   I. Dwyer, Susan.   II. Feinberg, Joel, 1926–   .
179'.76—dc20   96-19686

Contents

Legal Appendix:

Preface

There has been no diminution of interest in the problem of abortion in the twenty-three years since the publication of the first edition of *The Problem of Abortion*. Since the appearance of the second edition in 1984, abortion has assumed, for better or worse, a central place in politics and public policy discussion around the world. In recent years, disagreement about abortion has even led to extreme violence, especially in the United States.

As Joel Feinberg noted in his introduction to the second edition, most of the problems raised by abortion are fundamentally philosophical. So it is not surprising that philosophers have been as busy as ever with the problem of abortion. Indeed, given the importance that the problem of abortion has assumed in these times, it is arguable that philosophers have an obligation to think harder and more clearly about the philosophical issues at stake.

The central philosophical question is, When, if ever, is abortion morally justifiable? Traditionally, this question has been approached in one of the two ways exemplified in the second edition. First, there is the issue of determining the moral status of the unborn. Second, there is the matter of how to resolve conflicting claims, namely, the claims of the pregnant woman and those of the fetus. But in recent years, some philosophers have turned to new ways of thinking about abortion. In particular, many believe that the apparent intractability of the moral problem of abortion results from certain inadequacies in the traditional formulations of that problem. For example, the appropriateness of construing the permissibility of abortion in terms of competing rights (those of the pregnant woman versus those of the fetus) has been criticized from a number of different quarters. Claiming that the relation between a pregnant woman and the fetus she carries is morally unique, some feminist philosophers urge that we jettison the language of rights in favor of talk about the care and responsibility involved in pregnancy and parenthood. In a recent book, *Life's Dominion*, Ronald Dworkin argues that the fundamental disagreement about abortion is not about rights at all, but rather it concerns different views about how best to respect the sanctity of human life.

In compiling this new edition, we have attempted to retain some of the best examples of traditional approaches to the moral problem of abortion and to include some examples of newer work that is critical of these approaches. We have also tried to provide a sense of the scope of positions one may take with respect to the problem of abortion. Among the additions are: two papers that argue against the moral permissibility of abortion (Marquis, Brody); a discussion of abortion from the perspective of virtue ethics (Hursthouse); and several papers that take up a variety of feminist concerns about abortion (Mackenzie, Wolf-Devine, Markowitz). This new edition also stands out for its inclusion of a substantial excerpt from Ronald Dworkin's *Life's Dominion*. No doubt, there are some perspectives that are not represented. Readers seeking guidance to this literature are invited to consult the extensive, thematically arranged Bibliography.

In addition to changes in philosophical thinking about abortion, the last decade has seen a considerable amount of judicial activity concerning abortion. The landmark decision of the U.S. Supreme Court, *Roe v. Wade* (1973), which granted women a constitutional right to abortion, has come under fire. During the 1980s and 1990s several states introduced legislation that restricts access to abortion, and in a series of decisions, the U.S. Supreme Court has upheld the withdrawal of federal funding for abortions. The legal status of abortion in Canada remains essentially unresolved. Although most Canadian women have access to abortion services, there is no explicit legislation governing abortion. In order to provide instructors and students with a sense of the legal debate about abortion, we have included a Legal Appendix. Dwyer's essay "A Short Legal History of Abortion in the United States and Canada" is followed by an annotated comparative chronology of relevant U.S. and Canadian Supreme Court decisions on abortion. Excerpts from *Roe v. Wade* and *Planned Parenthood of Southeastern Pennsylvania v. Casey* (1992) are also included.

Students are representative of the population at large, so the discussion of abortion in the classroom can be expected to be lively and passionate. The topic of abortion excites and puzzles students and provides instructors with ample opportunity to introduce students to some central concepts and theories in moral philosophy, as well as to the tools the philosopher can bring to bear on the discussion of public policy. Given that *everyone* who thinks about the problem of abortion judges that there is much at stake, we have all the more reason to think critically and carefully about this extremely divisive issue.

Acknowledgments

We would like to thank the following reviewers for their suggestions: Tracy Isaacs, University of Western Ontario; Mary Mahowald, University of Chicago; John Reeder, Brown University; Jeffrey Reiman, The American University; Russ Schafer-Landau, University of Kansas; Larry S. Temkin, Harvard University; and Douglas M. Weber, Creighton University. Paul Kershaw's diligent help with the bibliography and with the compilation of the manuscript is especially appreciated. Janet Michelin provided exceptional research assistance for the Legal Appendix. Finally, special thanks are due to Paul Pietroski for his comments on the introductory essay and the Legal Appendix, and to Ken O'Day.

Susan Dwyer
Joel Feinberg

The problem of

Abortion

Understanding the Problem of Abortion

Susan Dwyer

1. The Problems of Abortion

Abortion raises a number of difficult questions for morality, law, and public policy. When, if ever, is abortion morally permissible? Do women have a legal right to abortion, and how is that right to be justified? Ought abortions for poor women be funded by the state? These questions are related in the sense that answers to any one of them have implications for answers to the others. But it is crucial to remember that they are different questions. For example, suppose abortion is never morally permissible. It would not follow from that alone that the government ought to prohibit abortion, for we recognize that not all immoral behavior should be made be illegal. Whether the state ought to prohibit abortion depends upon *why* abortion is thought to be morally impermissible: contrast the idea that abortion is morally wrong because abortion is murder with the view that abortion is wrong because it is a waste of resources. Or suppose, as is the case in the United States, that women have a legal right to abortion. That fact does not, by itself, entail that the state ought to fund such procedures. You may have a legal right to drive a motor vehicle, but the state is not obliged to buy you a car.

There is, then, no *single* problem of abortion. When we think about abortion, we must be precise about which particular set of questions—moral or legal—we are attempting to address. Many philosophers have contributed to discussions about abortion law and public policy, but their contributions have generally been grounded in arguments either for or against the moral permissibility of abortion. Indeed, most philosophers agree that the moral question—When, if ever, is abortion morally justifiable?—is central. To say this question is central is to say that, even if one is immediately concerned with arguing for a particular policy on abortion, one cannot completely ignore the matter of the moral permissibility of abortion. For the most part, the essays in this collection reflect this approach.

So, when, if ever, is abortion permissible? It is tempting to think that we can answer this question simply by determining the moral status of the fetus. Some people believe, for example, that the moral permissibility of abortion depends almost entirely on whether or not the fetus has a right to life: if the fetus has a right to life, abortion is rarely, if ever, justified; if the fetus does not have such a right, then abortion is permissible in most cases. But fetuses develop in, and only in, the bodies of individual women. Thus, in considering whether abortion is ever justifiable, we must also examine the rights and responsibilities of the pregnant woman. Do women have rights over their bodies that outweigh any right to life fetuses might have? Or does a pregnant woman, in virtue of her special connection to the fetus, have particular responsibilities to bring the fetus to term?

Arguably, additional considerations are introduced when we reflect on the fact that pregnancy, childbearing, and childrearing occur in particular social and political contexts. There is ample evidence to support the view that women do not enjoy full equality with men in contemporary North American society. One might argue that this fact, together with the idea that women have a moral right to equality, bears on the moral question of abortion. As we shall see below, however, it is a complicated matter to determine what relevance these social and political considerations have for the moral justifiability of abortion.

The following five sections provide a brief sketch of some of the main issues discussed in the papers in this collection. In section 2, a variety of positions concerning the moral status of the fetus are examined. Section 3 explores some of the implications of taking women into account in our reasoning about the moral permissibility of abortion. Section 4 deals with abortion from the perspective of virtue ethics, and section 5 outlines a recent suggestion of Ronald Dworkin's about how best to understand disagreement over abortion. The relation between philosophical arguments for the moral (im)permissibility of abortion and arguments about what sort of policy the state ought to deploy regarding abortion is the topic of section 6.

2. The Moral Status of the Fetus

Solving the moral problem of abortion can appear to be relatively simple: all we need to do is determine the moral status of the fetus.[1] If a fetus is, in all morally relevant respects, identical to a normal adult human being, then abortion is morally on a par with murder. For at least as it is currently practiced, abortion entails the death of the fetus. However, if a fetus is properly thought of as a mere parasite, say, then abortion will hardly raise any moral issue at all. But appearances can be deceiving. First, determining the moral status of the fetus is notoriously difficult. Second, and more important, no

---

[1]As noted in the introduction to the previous edition of this book, the generalized use of *fetus* to denote any stage of prenatal development can be misleading. Embryologists employ a variety of terms to distinguish between the different developmental stages of an unborn entity: the earliest product of the fertilization is a *single-celled zygote;* during the first week of its existence, including its implantation in the uterine wall, the unborn entity is called a *conceptus; embryo* refers to the entity between the second and eighth weeks; and *fetus* is reserved to refer to the entity from the eighth week of gestation until birth. Since many people believe that the moral permissibility of abortion depends upon the stage of pregnancy at which it occurs, it might be better to employ the more neutral expression *product of conception* to refer to the unborn. But this expression is too cumbersome, so the term *fetus* will be used throughout; however, it should be interpreted to mean *product of conception.*

particular conclusion concerning the permissibility of abortion follows directly from a premise about the moral status of the fetus; additional premises are required to derive any such conclusion. Indeed, most of us take factors other than the status of the fetus into account in our reasoning about the moral permissibility of abortion.

2.1 Human Beings and Persons

Claims about the moral status of the fetus are often couched in terms of whether or not the fetus is a person. In everyday discourse, the expressions *person* and *human being* are used synonymously. However, philosophers generally distinguish between persons and human beings. In moral discourse, the term *person* has a technical meaning. *Person* is used to refer to a member of a particular class of beings to whom is owed a special kind of treatment; for example, persons are those creatures with rights and duties, including the right to life,[2] whereas to be a human being is to be a member of the species *Homo sapiens*. Now, figuring out whether a creature is a human being in this latter sense is a scientific matter; being a member of a particular species depends upon certain facts of evolutionary biology. In contrast, it is a philosophical matter which creatures get to count as persons; in particular, an analysis of the concept of personhood is required before we can determine whether some creature is a person or not. There can be no doubt that the fetus is a human being in the biological sense. So when philosophers ask whether the fetus is a person, in order to determine whether the fetus has a right to life, they have something else in mind. To see what that something else might be, let us consider what some of the authors in this volume have to say about personhood.

Mary Anne Warren's and Michael Tooley's suggestions are typical. They each specify some property or properties as necessary for personhood (having a right to life). To say that a property is necessary for being a person (having a right to life) is to say that any being that lacks that property is not a person (does not have a right to life). Warren takes the following traits to be central to the concept of personhood: consciousness; sentience; the presence of self-concepts and self-awareness; and developed capacities to reason, to communicate, and to engage in self-motivated activity. According to Warren, any creature that lacks all these traits is not a person. Warren argues that fetuses are not persons, on the grounds that they do not possess any of these traits to a significant degree. Michael Tooley provides a more specific condition necessary for being a person. He argues that a creature has a right to life only if it possesses a concept of itself as a continuing subject of experiences. He concludes that, because a fetus cannot have a concept of itself as such a subject, a fetus does not have a right to life.

We can imagine other accounts of personhood according to which fetuses are persons and so have a right to life. For example, if being human—that is, being a member of the species *Homo sapiens*—were sufficient for being a person, fetuses would clearly be persons. Something like this appears to be the official view of the Catholic church, as expressed in the excerpt from Pope John Paul II's Encyclical Letter, *Evangelium Vitae*.

---

[2] It is, of course, arguable whether only persons have a right to life. Some people believe that certain animals have a right to life even if they are not persons. For the sake of simplicity here, *person* shall mean, at least, "creature with a right to life."

Alternatively, one might propose a different condition sufficient for qualifying as a person, for instance, having the capacity to feel pain. What we know about fetal brain development suggests that fetuses have the capacity to feel pain at thirty weeks of gestation. According to this account of personhood, we should have to say that a fetus becomes a person at thirty weeks of gestation. But notice that, on this view, all sorts of creatures, including iguanas and cows, are persons and have a right to life.[3] Thus, depending on what are the necessary or sufficient conditions for being a person, the set of persons can be very large (that is, include all human beings as well as iguanas and cows), or it can be very small (that is, include only some human beings).

There is plenty of room for disagreement about whether or not the fetus is a person. But even if we could agree on the metaphysical question about the necessary and sufficient conditions for personhood, and we could agree on the factual question about whether a fetus satisfies those conditions or not, we still could not conclude that abortion is or is not morally permissible. Notice that neither of the following arguments is valid:

A. A fetus is a person from the moment of conception.
Therefore, abortion is always morally impermissible.

B. A fetus is not a person at any stage of its development.
Therefore, abortion is always morally permissible.

In order to be valid, both arguments A and B need to be supplemented with other premises. An obvious addition to argument A would be the assumption that it is always morally impermissible to kill a person; and argument B might be augmented with a premise stating that there is no factor apart from the fetus' personhood that is relevant to the moral permissibility of abortion.[4] However, even the truth of these additional premises can be disputed.

First, some philosophers hold that it *is* sometimes permissible to kill a person, for example, in self-defense. On this view, someone might argue that, even if the fetus is a person, abortion is morally permissible in those cases where the continued existence of the fetus seriously threatens the pregnant woman's life or health.[5] Judith Jarvis Thomson advances a different argument for the conclusion that abortion is sometimes permissible, even on the assumption that the fetus has a right to life from the moment of conception. Thomson's argument depends on an examination of what the right to life consists in. We need to know what the right to life consists in in order to determine under what conditions this right is violated—that is, in order to determine which killings

---

[3]This indicates one way in which philosophical reflections about abortion are related to philosophical reflections on the permissibility of killing animals.

[4]Michael Tooley is explicit about this. He argues that fetuses and neonates lack a necessary property for having a right to life. But his conclusion is that, *if* there are no other reasons against abortion and infanticide, then these practices are morally acceptable.

[5]But see Baruch Brody's paper "Against an Absolute Right to Abortion" (in this volume), in which he argues that abortion cannot be justified on grounds of self-defense, because the fetus cannot be thought of as an agent whose intent is to threaten the pregnant woman's life.

are unjust (that is, impermissible) killings. Thomson argues that "having a right to life does not guarantee having either a right to be given the use of or a right to be allowed continued use of another person's body—even if one needs it for life itself." It does not follow from this that all abortions are morally permissible. Thomson concedes that "there are *some* cases in which the unborn person has a right to the use of its mother's body, and therefore *some* cases in which abortion is unjust killing."

A second point of contention concerns the sort of additional premise required by argument B: Is being a person all that matters in determining whether it is impermissible to kill a particular creature? L. W. Sumner and Don Marquis appear to think not, but for very different reasons, as we shall now see.

2.2. The Gradualist View, Viability, and Futures Like Ours

Sumner agrees that "the central issue in the morality of abortion is the moral status of the fetus." However, instead of characterizing the moral status of the fetus in terms of personhood, Sumner suggests that we employ the more general concept of *moral standing,* where "a creature has *moral standing* if, for the purpose of moral decisionmaking, it must be counted for something in its own right." Unlike the property of being a person, the property of having moral standing is a matter of degree: "To count for nothing is to have no moral standing; to count for as much as possible (as much, that is, as any creature does) is to have full moral standing." Moreover, having some moral standing entails having some right to life. Sumner claims that the notion of moral standing better fits the *developmental* facts of pregnancy.[6] The physical properties of the fetus change dramatically over the course of pregnancy, and it seems plausible to attribute moral significance to these changes. Let us call this view the *gradualist* view. Many people apparently hold some version of the gradualist view. For example, it is a common intuition that a late-term abortion is morally worse than an early-term abortion. One explanation of this widely held view is that people believe that, as the fetus matures, its moral standing increases and it is owed more by way of moral consideration.

If the gradualist account of the moral status of the fetus is to help us resolve the problem of abortion, it needs to specify both the properties a creature must possess in order to have any moral standing at all and the stage in its development at which the average fetus acquires those properties.[7] For (at least) two reasons, Sumner favors sentience as the criterion of having moral standing, where sentience is the "capacity for feeling or

---

[6]The philosophers represented in this volume disagree about the moral significance of fetal development. Warren and Tooley explicitly downplay its relevance; Thomson mentions it only in passing. To varying degrees, Brody and Sumner take developmental facts into account in assessing the moral permissibility of abortion. However, developmental facts are beside the point according to the official Catholic view and to Don Marquis' view, both of which have it that abortion is always seriously morally wrong. By contrast, Catriona Mackenzie insists that we grant moral significance not only to fetal development but also to the changes a woman undergoes during pregnancy.

[7]It is worth noting here that not all philosophers think that the moral standing of the fetus is determined by the fetus' *intrinsic* properties. Some argue that the fetus' moral status is also a function of its *relational* properties. This matter is discussed in section 3.2, below.

affect." First, like moral standing, sentience comes in degrees: "In its most primitive form it is the ability to experience sensations of pleasure and pain, and thus the ability to enjoy and suffer. Its more developed forms include wants, aims, and desires . . . ; attitudes, tastes, and values; and moods, emotions, sentiments, and passions." Second, we have some understanding of the physiological basis of sentience; in particular, we know that some cortical activity is a necessary condition for being minimally sentient. Thus, Sumner holds that we can determine when the fetus acquires moral standing by examining fetal brain development. Sumner is doubtful that we can point to a *precise* time at which the fetus acquires some right to life. Rather he suggests that the threshold of sentience falls sometime in the second trimester.

Again, it is important to be clear about the implications of gradualist accounts of the moral status of the fetus for the moral permissibility of abortion. Like arguments A and B above, the following argument is not valid:

C.   A fetus acquires some moral standing at *n* weeks of gestation.
     Therefore, abortion is always morally permissible prior to *n* weeks of gestation, and abortion is always morally impermissible after *n* weeks of gestation.

In order to derive a conclusion about the permissibility of abortion from a premise about when a fetus acquires some moral standing, we need to say what degree of moral standing is sufficient to make abortion impermissible.

Sumner does not explicitly appeal to the notion of viability in his argument concerning the morality of abortion, but his approach is likely to be of interest to people who do believe that viability marks a morally significant stage in pregnancy. *Viability* refers to the earliest point during pregnancy at which the fetus can be removed from the woman's body and be kept alive. (Viability depends upon prevailing medical technology and is currently placed at some point during the second trimester.) Some people hold that abortion is morally permissible prior to viability, but that it is impermissible after viability.[8] The underlying idea appears to be that the fetus develops substantial moral standing when it acquires the ability to live independently of its biological mother. This is an initially attractive idea. But as Heather Gert argues, when we couple it with the widely held belief that late-term abortions are morally worse than early-term abortions, we get an odd result. Gert holds that, if we say previability abortion is permissible while postviability abortion is impermissible, "we seem to be saying that a woman is free to withdraw support from a fetus as long as this fetus is wholly dependent on her, but that as soon as it gains the ability to survive on its own . . . , she is no longer permitted to withdraw that support."

Don Marquis advances another argument about the moral permissibility of abortion that does not appeal to the personhood (or lack thereof) of the fetus. He claims that we can solve the problem of abortion only when we have to hand a theoretical account of what makes killing morally wrong. Marquis begins by considering what makes killing

---

[8]The notion of viability also has legal significance. In *Roe v. Wade*, 410 U.S. 113 (1973), and more recently in *Planned Parenthood of Southeastern Pennsylvania v. Casey*, 120 L.Ed. 2d 674 (1992), the U.S. Supreme Court argued that the state's interest in protecting fetal life becomes compelling after viability. See the Legal Appendix for details.

adult human beings wrong. He says, "The loss of one's life is one of the greatest losses one can suffer. The loss of one's life deprives one of all the experiences, activities, projects, and enjoyments that would otherwise have constituted one's future," where these experiences, activities, and so on, are valuable either for their own sakes or as a means to something else that is valuable for its own sake. Killing is wrong, Marquis claims, because death deprives us of a valuable future. Put another way, Marquis' central point is that having a valuable future—that is, a future like that of a normal adult human being, a "future like ours"—is sufficient to make the killing of any creature that has this property *prima facie* seriously morally wrong. He argues that, because standard fetuses have futures like ours, abortion is always *prima facie* seriously morally wrong. Marquis thus appears to be able to avoid many of the difficulties associated with arguments about the morality of abortion that appeal to the notion of a person. Moreover, on his view, we need not specify any particular stage during pregnancy after which abortion is impermissible. For Marquis, abortion is *prima facie* seriously morally wrong at *all* stages of pregnancy. It is worth noting, however, the force of the modifier *prima facie*. To say that some action A is *prima facie* seriously morally wrong is to say that, *other things equal*, A is seriously morally wrong. Marquis' account leaves open the possibility that *some* abortions are morally permissible, for there might be occasions on which other things are *not* equal.[9]

2.3. Summary

We have seen that the fact (if it is a fact) that fetuses are persons does not entail that abortion is always morally impermissible. Neither does the fact (if it is a fact) that fetuses are not persons entail that abortion is always morally permissible; there may well be *other* reasons why abortion is morally wrong. Hence, settling the moral status of the fetus does not, by itself, answer the question of when, if ever, abortion is morally permissible. This is not to say that determining the moral status of the fetus is of *no* consequence in considering the justifiability of abortion. But it does show that we must exercise caution in evaluating arguments about abortion that appear to rely solely on claims about the status of the fetus; other assumptions, explicit or not, are sure to be at work as well. For example, people at all points on the spectrum regarding the moral permissibility of abortion, from the most conservative to the most liberal, appear to take factors other than the moral status of the fetus into account in their reasoning. Most people are inclined to allow that abortion is morally permissible when pregnancy is a result of rape or incest or when its continuation poses a serious threat to the pregnant woman's health or life. Others think that abortion is permissible for a wider range of reasons—for example, that becoming a parent at a particular time would make it impossible for a woman to finish her college education. All these considerations would be irrelevant if the moral justifiability of abortion were to depend entirely on the moral status of the fetus.

---

[9]It is interesting to compare Marquis' argument about the morality of abortion with that of Jonathan Glover, presented in his *Causing Death and Saving Lives* (Harmondsworth, Middlesex: Penguin Books, 1977). Glover adopts a similar account of what makes killing wrong, but he reaches a conclusion about the permissibility of abortion which is very different from Marquis'.

3. Taking Women into Account

The need to consider matters other than the moral standing of the fetus is made obvious by an undeniable fact about pregnancy: pregnancy occurs in women's bodies. Thus any discussion of abortion must take into account the pregnant woman herself. Again, we must not be misled into thinking that certain claims about the rights and duties of pregnant women, alone, entail conclusions about the moral permissibility of abortion. As we shall see in this section, the fact (if it is a fact) that women have a right to determine what happens in and to their bodies does not entail that abortion is always morally permissible. But neither does the fact (if it is a fact) that a pregnant woman has special duties to the fetus she carries entail that abortion is always morally impermissible.

Typically, philosophers have taken the interests of women into account in arguments concerning the moral permissibility of abortion by arguing that women have a *right to bodily integrity,* that is, a right to determine what happens in and to their bodies. Such approaches invite us to think of the moral problem of abortion in terms of a *conflict* between the rights of the fetus and the rights of the pregnant woman. On this view, the permissibility of abortion depends upon the relative stringency or strength of those rights. However, in recent years, some feminist philosophers have argued that pregnancy is a morally unique human relation and that this renders implausible the idea that a pregnant woman could stand in an adversarial relationship to the fetus she carries.

3.1. The Right to Bodily Integrity

It seems unproblematic to say that all (adult) human beings have a right to bodily integrity, that is, a right to determine what will happen in and to their bodies. The right to bodily integrity should not be confused with an absolute right to do whatever one wishes with one's body. None of us has such a right; for example, it is impermissible for you sit in the lap of a classmate during lectures unless that person explicitly gives you leave to do so. The right to bodily integrity is best understood negatively, that is, in terms of what having the right protects us from. So, for example, your classmate's right to bodily integrity entails that you may not sit in his or her lap uninvited. More seriously, a surgeon would violate your right to bodily integrity were she to perform some operation on you without your (informed) consent.‹Applied to the topic at hand, one might attempt to establish the moral permissibility of abortion on the grounds that a woman's right to bodily integrity is violated if she is forced to continue with an unwanted pregnancy. However, notice that the following argument is *not* valid:

> **D.** Pregnancy is a state of a woman's body.
> A (pregnant) woman has the right to determine what happens in and to her body.
> *Therefore,* abortion is always morally permissible.

To see why argument D is invalid we need only recall the several views concerning the moral status of the fetus examined in the previous section. Suppose the fetus has a right to life. Do we think that the right to bodily integrity is stronger than the right to life, such that when these rights conflict we ought always respect the former at the expense of the latter? Clearly, we do not. To return to our earlier example, we would not judge it permissible for your classmate to kill you in order to get you off his or her lap. At the very most, then, a woman's right to bodily integrity would justify the removal of the fetus from her uterus but not its death.[10] However, it is arguable that many women choose abortion because they do not want a particular entity to exist at all. The decision to continue a pregnancy is a decision to assume the responsibility for the present well-being of the fetus and for the future well-being of the child it will become. When a woman chooses abortion, she is not simply choosing to have the fetus removed; she is choosing, as Catriona Mackenzie puts it, "that there be no *being at all* in relation to whom she is in a situation of such responsibility."[11]

Alternatively, suppose that the fetus has no moral standing. Then a woman's right to bodily integrity might justify abortion, at least if there were no other stronger morally relevant considerations at stake, for example, that the birth of a particular child would guarantee the end of an especially awful war. In between the extremes of granting full moral standing and no moral standing to the fetus there are a variety of positions, such that a woman's right to bodily integrity might be strong enough to justify abortion only up to a specified time during pregnancy. In any case, the assumption that every woman has a right to determine what happens in and to her own body does not imply that abortion is always morally permissible.

3.2. The Moral Uniqueness of Pregnancy

Feminist philosophers have voiced additional worries about the appeal to a right to bodily integrity in discussion about abortion. Mary Anne Warren suggests that the alleged right to bodily integrity is premised on a false view about the relation persons bear to their bodies, namely, that persons *own* their bodies.[12] More important, Catriona Mackenzie holds that the attempt to justify abortion in terms of a woman's right to bodily integrity seriously misconstrues the unique moral nature of human pregnancy. Mackenzie does not provide an argument for or against the moral permissibility of abortion. Rather her primary aim is to persuade us to approach the moral problem of abortion in a new way.

---

[10]Michael Tooley points out that a woman's right to bodily integrity might not even justify the removal of the fetus from her body. Let us assume that the pregnant woman has a right to bodily integrity that is stronger than the fetus' right to life. Tooley writes, "One can still argue that abortion ought not to be permitted. For if A's right is stronger than B's, and it is impossible to satisfy both, it does not follow that A's should be satisfied rather than B's. It may be possible to compensate A if his right isn't satisfied, but impossible to compensate B if his right isn't satisfied. . . . If the fetus has a right to life and the right is not satisfied, there is certainly no way the fetus can be compensated. On the other hand, if the woman's right to rid her body of harmful and annoying parasites is not satisfied, she can be compensated" (p. 48).

[11]This point is developed in more detail by Steven Ross in "Abortion and the Death of the Fetus," *Philosophy & Public Affairs* 11 (1982): 232–245.

[12] Traditionally, the right to bodily integrity derives from considerations of *self-ownership* and encourages us to think of our bodies as pieces of private property. But when we reflect more deeply on the relation a person bears to his body, we may recognize the inadequacy of the idea that a person stands to his body as he stands to his car or bicycle: when someone breaks his own arm, we do not say that he has damaged his property; we say that he has hurt *himself*. Similar questions regarding the appropriateness of body ownership arise in discussions about the morality of organ sale and donation.

Arguments for and against the moral permissibility of abortion that rely on claims about the rights of the pregnant woman and the rights of the fetus, as well as on the relative stringency of those rights, appear to assume that it makes sense to think of a pregnant woman as standing in an adversarial relation to the fetus she carries. This in turn depends on the plausibility of construing the pregnant woman and the fetus as wholly distinct entities. Focusing on certain biological and psychological facts of pregnancy, Mackenzie argues that women's *experience* of pregnancy undermines the proposition that the woman and the fetus are separate entities in any ordinary understanding of 'separate.'[13] She contends that "the physical processes which occur during pregnancy, give rise to a unique bodily perspective." Drawing on the ideas of Maurice Merleau-Ponty, Mackenzie suggests that a person's self-concept and her point of view on the world depend in large part on her experience of having a certain body. Changes to a person's body can, then, deeply affect her understanding of herself and the world around her. Mackenzie writes:

> The experience of pregnant embodiment, that is, the gradual differentiation and development from within her own body of another being which is now part of herself, . . . affects a woman's mode of being-in-the-world both physically and morally and, as a consequence, re-shapes her sense of self. She is now no longer just herself but herself and another, but this other is not yet separate from herself.[14]

Furthermore, Mackenzie argues that, if we adopt a view of pregnancy that respects the deep interconnection between the woman and the fetus, we will see that the moral status of the fetus is determined not only by features it lacks or possesses but also by the relations in which it stands to others. In other words, the moral standing of the fetus is as much a matter of its *relational* properties as it is of its *intrinsic* properties.[15] As we saw in section 2 above, philosophers tend to address the question of the moral status of the fetus solely in terms of the fetus' intrinsic properties. For example, in their attempts

---

[13]See also Eugenie Gatens-Robinson, "A Defense of a Woman's Choice: Abortion and the Ethics of Care," *Southern Journal of Philosophy* 30 (1992): 39–66, who discusses the morally relevant biological aspects of pregnancy; and Iris Marion Young, "Pregnant Embodiment: Subjectivity and Alienation" in *Throwing Like a Girl and Other Essays in Feminist Philosophy and Social Theory* (Bloomington, Ind.: Indiana University Press, 1990), who examines the subjective experience of pregnancy.

[14]The cultural significance of pregnancy also affects the ways in which a woman's identity (that is, her self-understanding) is changed in the experience of pregnancy. The pregnant woman is treated differently from the nonpregnant woman, and she comes to think of herself as a *mother,* where "to become a mother is to take on a particular moral task and to simultaneously render oneself vulnerable in a variety of ways for perhaps a lifetime" (Eugenie Gatens-Robinson, "A Defense of a Woman's Choice: Abortion and the Ethics of Care," 57–58).

[15]See, for example, Susan Sherwin, "Abortion through a Feminist Ethics Lens," *Dialogue* 30 (1991): 327–342, who writes: "There is no absolute value that attaches to fetuses apart from their relational status determined in the context of their particular development' (336). Annette Baier makes a similar point in saying that even the property of being a person is a relational property: "A person, perhaps, is best seen as one who was long enough dependent upon other persons to acquire the essential arts of personhood. Persons essentially are *second* persons, who grow up with other persons. . . . Persons come after and before other persons" (*Postures of the Mind: Essays on Mind and Morals* [Minneapolis: University of Minnesota Press, 1985], 84–85).

to argue that the fetus is (or is not) a person, many philosophers employ a two-step procedure: first, they specify what properties are necessary and/or sufficient for being a person; and second, they argue that the average fetus either possesses or lacks those features. According to these theorists, then, whether or not a fetus is a person depends on, and only on, properties of the fetus itself. Mackenzie agrees that, on the grounds of its intrinsic properties alone, the fetus is not a person. Nonetheless, she argues that the fetus has some moral standing in virtue of the relation it bears to the woman who carries it. In particular, the fetus acquires some moral significance when the pregnant woman decides to accept parental responsibility for it, that is, when the woman makes a "a commitment to bringing into existence a future child" with all that that entails. To say that the fetus has this significance is not to say that the fetus has a full-fledged right to life. But it does imply that the fetus has some claim to care and nurture from the woman and to protection from harm from others.

To the extent that Mackenzie emphasizes the moral relevance of the relationship between the pregnant woman and the fetus she carries, her analysis has much in common with some other feminist approaches to the moral problem of abortion. It will be helpful to say just a little about the most influential of those other approaches.

3.3. Feminist Ethics

Some feminist philosophers distinguish between moral theories based on individual rights and moral theories that emphasize the *connections* between people and the responsibilities these relationships generate. Developmental psychologist Carol Gilligan[16] claimed to have discovered that people tend to employ either an *ethic of justice* or an *ethic of care* in their moral reasoning. To employ an ethic of justice is to think about moral problems in terms of individual rights and to solve moral problems by determining whose rights take priority in a given situation. In contrast, to employ an ethic of care is to think about moral problems in terms of responsibility and to solve moral problems with an eye to maintaining whatever ongoing relationships are implicated a particular situation. Furthermore, Gilligan claimed that the ethic of care is associated with women in the following sense: although some men and women manifest both types of moral orientation, and some women manifest a justice perspective exclusively, no men manifest a care perspective exclusively.[17] This gender difference has suggested

---

[16]Carol Gilligan, *In a Different Voice* (Cambridge, Mass.: Harvard University Press, 1982). Gilligan's view is controversial; for works that are critical of Gilligan, see the Bibliography under "Feminist Ethics."

[17]One need not claim that the "different voice" that Gilligan hears in talking about moral problems with women is a manifestation of women's essential nature. Indeed, Gilligan herself appears to think that gender differences in moral reasoning are the result of socialization. Girls' development tends to involve an identification with their primary caretakers—their mothers—whereas boys' development tends to involve the separation from their primary caretakers. Thus, women come to think of themselves as fundamentally in relation to others, and boys come to conceive of themselves as fundamentally separate from others. Finally, the fact that men and women are able to manifest both types of moral orientation suggests that the difference is not likely to be rooted in biology. See, for example, Carol Gilligan, "Women and Moral Orientation," in Eva F. Kittay and Diana E. Meyers, eds., *Women and Moral Theory* (Totowa, N.J.: Rowman and Littlefield, 1987).

to some that a feminine approach to moral problems will (and should) take the form of an ethic of care. Celia Wolf-Devine describes the distinction thus:

> The feminine voice in ethics attends to the particular other, thinks in terms of responsibilities to care for others, is sensitive to our interconnectedness, and strives to preserve relationships. It contrasts with the masculine voice, which speaks in terms of justice and rights, stresses consistency and principles, and emphasizes the autonomy of the individual and impartiality in one's dealings with others.

What implications does an ethic of care have for the moral problem of abortion?

As Wolf-Devine's characterization suggests, to approach a moral problem from the perspective of care is to approach that problem in all its particularity. An ethic of care directs us to think about the connections between all the individuals involved in the moral situation and to resolve whatever moral tensions exist in terms of what responsible action requires. Care theorists resist making generalizations about the permissibility of abortion, for they believe each moral situation is unique, and whether having an abortion is a responsible action for a woman depends upon the particular circumstances of her pregnancy. The central idea is that, when a woman chooses to continue a pregnancy, she chooses to assume particular obligations associated with the nurturance of the fetus and the child it will become. Now, for a variety of reasons, a woman might be unable to meet these obligations. Perhaps she is too young or too poor, or perhaps she is in an abusive relationship and fears for her safety and that of the fetus. The idea is that choosing an abortion in such conditions might well be the responsible course of action for the woman concerned. In choosing abortion, the woman refuses to undertake obligations she has good reason to believe she cannot fulfill.

However, Wolf-Devine is skeptical of such defenses of abortion. She argues that feminist philosophers who adopt the feminine voice in ethics "face a *prima facie* inconsistency between an ethics of care and abortion." An ethic of care emphasizes the interconnections between people; it counsels that moral problems be resolved in ways that are nonharmful and that preserve the relationships at stake. But abortion clearly involves harm, to the fetus and possibly to others. It is also hard to see how abortion respects interconnectedness; indeed, abortion irreversibly severs and terminates a particularly significant connection between the fetus and the pregnant woman. In short, Wolf-Devine claims, "abortion is a failure to care for one living being who exists in a particularly intimate relationship to oneself." Thus it would appear that one cannot justify abortion from the perspective of an ethic of care.

Whether or not Wolf-Devine is right about this, it is important to recognize that an ethic of care does not exhaust the range of positions regarding the moral permissibility of abortion that could be called feminist. Indeed, whether an ethic of care really does represent a feminist approach to the justifiability of abortion is a contested question.[18]

---

[18]So, for example, we might want to distinguish between *feminine* and a *feminist* approach to ethics. Full discussion of this distinction is not possible here. But one way of putting the difference is to say that feminine ethics gives voice to women's unique experience as women, whereas feminist ethics is motivated by certain political commitments having to do with eliminating male dominance. The two are not inconsistent, but someone might pursue a project in feminine ethics without thereby pursuing any particular political agenda. For a detailed discussion of each type of ethics as well as the differences and

For example, some feminists want to maintain the centrality of rights in moral discourse. Moreover, it is not self-evident that feminists, just in virtue of being feminists, believe that abortion is morally permissible. Indeed, not all women who call themselves feminists agree that abortion is morally permissible.[19]

To avoid any confusion here, it is worth emphasizing that we are presently discussing arguments for the moral permissibility of abortion, not arguments for particular public policies regarding the availability of abortion. Most feminists argue that justice demands that women ought to have access to safe and legal abortions. So it might be true that feminists, just in virtue of being feminists, are committed to the existence of liberal abortion laws. But arguments for liberal abortion laws, although they certainly embody some *assumptions* about the moral permissibility of abortion, are not themselves arguments for the moral permissibility of abortion. We shall return to this matter in section 6.

4. Virtue Ethics

Feminists are not alone in their skepticism about the fruitfulness of thinking of the moral problem of abortion in terms of competing rights. Proponents of *virtue ethics* also doubt that the problem of abortion is best addressed in terms of resolving competing rights claims. What is distinctive about virtue ethics is that it takes the notion of the virtuous agent as its central normative notion.[20] A virtuous agent is one who acts virtuously, that is, one who has and exercises virtues, where virtues are those character traits a human being needs to flourish or live well. Among these character traits are strength, independence, resoluteness, decisiveness, self-confidence, responsibility, serious-mindedness, and self-determination. According to virtue ethics, a particular action is right if and only if it is an action that a virtuous agent would perform in the given circumstances.

When we consider the problem of abortion from the perspective of virtue ethics, we ask whether, in any given set of circumstances, a virtuous agent would choose abortion. If, in circumstances C, a virtuous agent would choose abortion, then abortion-in-circumstances-C is the right of course of action; if, in circumstances C, a virtuous agent would not choose abortion, then abortion-in-circumstances-C is not the right action.

---

connections between them, see Rosemarie Tong, *Feminine and Feminist Ethics* (Belmont, Calif.: Wadsworth Publishing Company, 1993). See also Judith Jarvis Thomson, *The Realm of Rights* (Cambridge, Mass.: Harvard University Press, 1990), 288, n. 3, who suggests that feminists make a philosophical and a political mistake when they reject a rights-based approach to abortion in favor of a care-based approach.

[19]For an account of prolife feminism, see Sidney Callahan, "Abortion and the Sexual Agenda: A Case for Prolife Feminism," *Commonweal* 123 (1986): 232–238.

[20]Virtue ethics is typically contrasted with two main types of ethical theory: *deontological* and *consequentialist*. A deontological theory takes the notions of rights and duties as central, and it provides an account of right action in terms of those rights and duties. A consequentialist theory, as its name suggests, takes the consequences of actions as determinative of the rightness of those actions.

But how are we to know what a virtuous agent would do in any given situation? Virtue theorists must provide some account here if their theory is going to be of practical assistance.

Virtue theorists attempt to answer this question in terms of what the appropriate attitude toward pregnancy and abortion is: a virtuous agent would perform whatever action or actions are consistent with adopting that attitude. Rosalind Hursthouse suggests that pregnancy (and thus abortion) implicates the very weighty issues of life and death and the value of the family. Adopting the appropriate attitude toward pregnancy and abortion, then, requires taking into account the value of families, the significance of particular lives, and the meaning of death. At the very least, a virtuous agent will always think that abortion is a morally loaded matter. But notice that virtue theory does not make any general claims about the permissibility or impermissibility of abortion. Adopting the appropriate attitude toward abortion, in a given set of circumstances, might be perfectly consistent with choosing abortion and being right in doing so. Hursthouse imagines that a woman might act rightly in having an abortion if she has good reason to believe that continuing with her current pregnancy would make life intolerable for her and her already existing children. On the other hand, consider a woman who chooses abortion as a matter of mere convenience—say, she wants to go on a vacation. According to virtue theory, such a woman would not manifest the appropriate attitude toward (heterosexual) sex, pregnancy, or abortion, and so would act wrongly (viciously) in having an abortion.

Several points are worth noting about the virtue-theory approach to the problem of abortion. First, for the virtue theorist, the existence and strength of rights are morally beside the point. Hence, considerations about the moral status of the fetus or about the pregnant woman's rights are largely irrelevant to the rightness or wrongness of abortion. The virtue theorist holds that it is perfectly possible for someone to exercise his rights viciously, that is, to exercise his rights and thereby do something cruel, stupid, et cetera. "So," says Hursthouse, "whether women have a moral right to terminate their pregnancies is irrelevant within virtue theory, for it is irrelevant to the question 'In having an abortion in these circumstances, would the agent be acting virtuously or viciously or neither?' " Second, virtue theorists, like Catriona Mackenzie, emphasize the moral uniqueness of pregnancy. Hence, no generalizations about the moral (im)-permissibility of abortion are forthcoming from virtue theory. The permissibility or impermissibility of a particular abortion will be contingent on a range of factors in the case at hand. Whether either of these features of virtue ethics—the irrelevance of rights, or the ethics' inability to support a general claim about the moral permissibility of abortion—represents the advantages or disadvantages of virtue theory is a matter for further discussion.

5. The Sanctity of Life

The moral relevance of adopting an appropriate attitude toward pregnancy is also at issue in the analysis of the morality of abortion advanced by Ronald Dworkin. Dworkin's aim is not to provide an argument either for or against the moral permissibility of abortion. Rather, his intention is to explain why people (at least in North America) hold such conflicting views about the morality of abortion. Dworkin's hypothesis is that, while liberals and conservatives alike believe that human life is sacred, they disagree about what respect for the intrinsic value of human life requires.

Dworkin distinguishes two grounds on which a person might oppose abortion. On the one hand, as we have already seen above, one might hold that the fetus has rights and interests that are unjustly violated by abortion. On the other, one might hold that what makes abortion wrong is that it fails to respect the sanctity of human life. Dworkin calls the first approach the *derivative* objection to abortion, because it posits that the wrongness of abortion derives from the rights and interests of the fetus; he calls the second approach the *detached* objection to abortion, because, according to it, the wrongness of abortion is independent of whether or not the fetus has rights and interests. Dworkin argues that we cannot explain people's disagreement about the morality of abortion in terms of the derivative objection. For example, Dworkin points out that some people who claim that abortion is generally impermissible still believe that abortion is justifiable in the case of pregnancy due to rape. But one could not hold this position if one were to believe the reason that abortion is generally impermissible is that fetuses have a full right to life. The moral standing of a fetus is not dependent on how it came into existence. Moreover, Dworkin claims that the idea that "an organism that has never had a mental life can still have interests," and so have rights, is "scarcely comprehensible."[21] Hence, he argues that the detached objection best captures what it is that people disagree about when they disagree about the morality of abortion. Dworkin thus owes an account of what it means to say that human life is sacred.

Very briefly, Dworkin's account of the sanctity of human life is this: Human life has *intrinsic value,* where something is intrinsically valuable "if its value is *independent* of what people happen to enjoy or want or need or what is good for them." So, for example, some people think that knowledge and certain artworks are valuable whether or not anyone happens to like them and whether or not their existence furthers some other end that is valuable in itself. However, the intrinsic value of human life differs in one crucial respect from the intrinsic value of art and knowledge. Arguably, knowledge is also *incrementally* valuable, that is, the more we have of it the better. But, Dworkin says,

> we do not value human life that way. Instead we treat human life as sacred or inviolable. . . . The hallmark of the sacred as distinct from the incrementally valuable is that the sacred is intrinsically valuable because—and therefore only once—it exists. It is inviolable because of what it represents or embodies. It is not important that there be more people. But once a human life has begun, it is very important that it flourish and not be wasted.

The idea that human life is sacred is often taken to be the product of a particular religious view. Nonetheless, although many of the world's religions do posit the sanctity of human life, Dworkin holds that a person can believe in the sacredness and inviolability

---

[21]For a critique of Dworkin's outright rejection of the idea that fetuses have rights, see Judith Jarvis Thomson, "Abortion," *Boston Review* 20 (1995): 11–15.

of human life from a secular perspective. To understand how this can be so, we need to grasp two more of Dworkin's important distinctions.

In the first place, Dworkin contends that things come to be sacred in two ways: either by association or through their history. So, for example, in some cultures certain animals are held sacred because of their association with particular gods; in contrast, we tend to value a painting by Rembrandt not because of what it depicts but because of how it came about. With respect to the sacredness of human life, the historical dimension is the most salient. In the second place, the history of a particular human life encompasses two types of creative processes: natural and human. If we are religious, we might understand the natural processes of our creation as God's will; a secular variant would hold that evolution is the natural creative force that brings about a human life. However, although human beings are certainly natural creations (in some sense), they are also human creations.

> [E]ach developed human being is the product not just of natural creation, but also of the kind of deliberative human creative force that we honor in honoring art. A mature woman, for example, is in her personality, training, capacity, interests, ambitions, and emotions, something like a work of art because in those respects she is the product of human creative intelligence, partly that of her parents and other people, partly that of her culture, and also, through the choices she has made, her *own* creation.

Dworkin holds that each human life is sacred because it is the product of both types of creative investment.

Now let us apply Dworkin's line of thought to the problem of abortion. Abortion is the killing of a fetus and therefore amounts to a waste of human life. Dworkin argues that both liberals and conservatives recognize this feature of abortion and that this explains why *everyone* takes abortion to be a serious moral matter. Even so, liberals hold that abortion is sometimes morally permissible, whereas conservatives hold that abortion is morally permissible only in a limited range of cases (for example, pregnancy due to rape). How does Dworkin help us understand this disagreement? Indeed, if liberals really do believe that human life is sacred, how can they countenance the moral permissibility of abortion? Dworkin's suggestion is that the division between liberals and conservatives over abortion is the result of the moral weight they give, respectively, to the human and the natural creative investment in a human life. That is, liberals tend to place more emphasis on human investment, whereas conservatives tend to highlight natural investment. Thus conservatives are likely to believe that "the gift of life itself is infinitely more significant than anything the person whose life it is may do for himself." On this ground, they think that abortion is rarely justified. Liberals, in contrast, "assign much greater relative importance to the human contribution to life's creative value," and so are likely to argue that abortion is justified in a wide range of cases, including fetal abnormality, rape, failed contraception, threat to the woman's well-being, and so on.

As we have noted, Dworkin does not himself explicitly advance a view about the moral permissibility of abortion; he does not say whether the appropriate attitude toward human life requires valuing natural over human investments or vice versa. Arguably his view, if right, has interesting implications for public policy on abortion. It is to public policy that we now turn.

6. Abortion and Public Policy

When we turn our attention from arguments having primarily to do with the moral permissibility of abortion to arguments concerning what public policy we ought to adopt with respect to abortion, there are (at least) two errors we should be careful to avoid. In the first place, we cannot, in any straightforward way, "read off" what abortion policy should be from a claim about the moral permissibility or moral impermissibility of abortion. In the second place, we must recognize that an argument for liberal abortion laws, although it may embody certain moral assumptions, need not itself be an argument for the moral permissibility of abortion. (Neither need an argument for restrictive abortion laws be an argument for the moral impermissibility of abortion.) Much of the current public debate about abortion is characterized by confusion over precisely these matters, so it is worthwhile to explore them in a little more detail.

The mere fact that some practice is morally impermissible does not entail that that practice ought to be made illegal. Whether the (alleged) moral impermissibility of abortion is sufficient to justify governmental restriction or prohibition of abortion depends in part upon why abortion is morally impermissible. One might argue that abortion is impermissible because it is murder. If that is so, then governmental prohibition would appear to be in order, perhaps mandatory. On this view, even abortion in cases of pregnancy due to rape should be illegal. But suppose one thinks abortion is morally impermissible because it is a form of self-mutilation, like certain types of tattooing or body piercing. It is considerably more difficult to argue for state prohibition of abortion on these grounds, because we generally hold that people should be free to pursue their lives as they see fit as long as they do not harm others. Nonetheless, certain restrictions might be legitimate—for example, the imposition of mandatory waiting periods to encourage women to consider some of the consequences of having an abortion. In short, if one wants to argue for the prohibition of or the imposition of restrictions on abortion, one will need to do more than simply assert that abortion is morally impermissible.

By the same token, abortion on demand is not justified by the claim that abortion is morally permissible. The mere fact that some practice is morally permissible does not entail that the state is never justified in regulating or restricting that practice in some way. Even if abortion is held to be morally innocuous, the state might be justified in regulating abortion—for example, to the extent that it has an interest in regulating medical treatment generally. Notice, too, that someone who holds that abortion is permissible in most cases might argue that the state is justified in imposing certain restrictions. Given the fact that people disagree so profoundly about the morality of abortion, a liberal might support certain funding restrictions, arguing that public funds should not be used for practices many citizens believe are morally wrong.

As mentioned above, there is a second error we must be careful to avoid when we think about abortion policy: we must not mistake arguments for liberal abortion laws for arguments for the moral permissibility of abortion. This confusion is often manifest in arguments concerning abortion that invoke the idea of *autonomy*. The concept of autonomy, like the concept of a person (discussed in section 2 above), is a central one in moral philosophy. Although there is some disagreement about the details, what philosophers have in mind when they speak of autonomy is roughly this: autonomy consists in the ability to control one's life, which in turn requires a degree of liberty to exercise one's deliberative and moral capacities. The notion of autonomy is often expressed in terms of a person's right to make decisions about the most intimate matters of his or her life without undue interference. Many philosophers believe that human dignity depends upon autonomy and, hence, that we must respect people's autonomy if we are to treat them with proper moral consideration. So if we are to show a woman proper moral consideration, we must respect her autonomy, where this involves allowing her to make decisions about the kind of life she wants to live, about the kind of person she wants to be, and so on. Suppose a woman, who has developed a plan of life in which there is no place for children, becomes pregnant because of rape or failed contraception.[22] In such a case, it might be argued that abortion is justified, because to keep the woman from obtaining an abortion (should she choose one) would be to violate her autonomy. To say that it is impermissible for this woman to have an abortion would seem to assume that her decisions and plans for her life count for *nothing*.

However, the imperative to respect the autonomy of women bears on the moral permissibility of certain *restrictions on obtaining an abortion,* not the moral permissibility of abortion itself. Moreover, even if recognizing women's autonomy renders certain restrictions on abortion morally suspect, nothing in the notion of autonomy implies that *whatever* a person decides to do with her life is morally permissible. Hence, certain laws that restrict women's liberty to make and act on important decisions might not violate their autonomy. Surely we think it permissible to prohibit bank robbers from acting on their decisions to rob banks. In particular, *if* the fetus is a person with a right to life from the moment of conception, then it is not clear that a woman's right to autonomy is sufficient to outweigh the fetus' right to life. Arguably, autonomy is highly relevant in determining what the law regarding abortion should be, but it has no obvious bearing on the morality of abortion itself.[23]

The discussion in sections 2 and 3 above highlights the necessity of taking into account both the fetus and the pregnant woman in our deliberations about the moral permissibility of abortion. Similarly, in determining what abortion policies we ought to adopt, we should think about the social, political, and economic context in which preg-

---

[22]People's intuitions about the moral permissibility of abortion in cases of unwanted pregnancy due to rape or failed contraception appear to be clearer than their intuitions about the moral permissibility of abortion in cases involving voluntary, unprotected heterosexual intercourse. But it is very difficult to explain this divergence of intuitions in a principled way. In particular, one needs an account of the moral relevance of the different causes of unwanted pregnancy. Or, to put the point another way, one needs an account of what sort of moral responsibility tracks what sort of causal responsibility. On this difficult issue, see Holly Smith, "Intercourse and the Moral Responsibility for the Fetus," in William B. Bondeson, H. T. Englehardt, Jr., S. F. Spicker, and D. Winship, eds., *Abortion and the Status of the Fetus* (Dordrecht: D. Reidel, 1983).

[23]The idea of autonomy has indeed played a major role in legal reasoning about abortion. In the United States, access to abortion is justified in terms of an alleged right of privacy, where this right protects individuals in making intimate decisions about their lives. (See *Roe v. Wade,* 410 U.S. 113 [1973]). See also *Thornburgh v. American College of Obstetricians and Gynecologists,* 476 U.S. 747 (1986): "[T]he Constitution embodies a promise that a certain private sphere of individual liberty will be kept largely beyond the reach of government. . . . Few decisions are more personal, more properly private, or more basic to individual dignity and autonomy, than a woman's decision . . . whether to end her pregnancy. A woman's right to make that choice freely is fundamental" (772). In Canada, while the Supreme Court has not recognized a constitutional right to abortion, it did appeal to the idea of decisional autonomy in striking down the law that made abortion a crime. (See *R. v. Morgentaler* [1988] 1 S.C.R. 30.)

nancy, childbearing, and childrearing occur. Pregnancy does not occur in a vacuum. Particular women living in particular social circumstances become pregnant in particular ways, and, if they choose to bring their pregnancies to term, such women are largely responsible for the care and well-being of the child. The ways in which pregnancy comes about, the impact a pregnancy is likely to have on the woman and others, the biological fact that only women can become pregnant, and the burdens and risks that pregnancy entails are all relevant to thinking about abortion policy.

Such considerations are at work in a variety of arguments for liberal abortion laws that are motivated by a concern for women's equality. Some theorists argue that genuine equality between men and women requires that women be able to make and act on their own decisions concerning reproduction, where this includes having access to safe contraception and abortion on demand. An argument of this type is presented by Sally Markowitz.

Markowitz proposes two principles—the Impermissible Sacrifice Principle and the Feminist Proviso. The Impermissible Sacrifice Principle states:

> When one social group in a society is systematically oppressed by another, it is impermissible to require the oppressed group to make sacrifices that will exacerbate or perpetuate this oppression;

and the Feminist Proviso says,

> Women are, as a group, sexually oppressed by men; and this oppression can neither be completely understood in terms of, nor otherwise reduced to, oppressions of other sorts.

She concludes that these two principles "justify abortion on demand for women *because they live in a sexist society*." When women are prohibited from controlling their reproductive lives, they are forced to make certain sacrifices. In our culture, women assume most of the financial and emotional burdens of childbearing and childrearing. Such responsibilities are onerous in themselves, but, arguably, when women disproportionately assume these responsibilities, they are made worse off relative to men. Thus, according to Markowitz, a policy that prevents women from obtaining abortions serves to perpetuate women's oppression and is for that reason impermissible.

It is important to recognize some of the implications of Markowitz's argument. In the first place, one cannot justify liberal abortion laws in the way Markowitz recommends and yet argue (as many liberals do) that late-term abortions may be restricted. For Markowitz holds that all abortions should be allowed. Second, on Markowitz's view, the justice of liberal abortion laws is contingent on prevailing social factors. That is, if social conditions were to change in such a way that women are no longer oppressed, then abortion would not be justified, at least not on the grounds that Markowitz advances in her paper. Perhaps, in a society in which women have achieved full equality, the *need* for abortions would diminish.[24] But that does not alter the point here, namely, that Markowitz's defense of abortion in terms of the Impermissible Sacrifice Principle

---

[24]For fuller discussion of this point see Catharine A. MacKinnon, "Privacy v. Equality: Beyond *Roe v. Wade*" in *Feminism Unmodified: Discourses on Life and Law* (Cambridge, Mass.: Harvard University Press, 1987).

and the Feminist Proviso would be rendered moot. Third, Markowitz's argument, if sound, suggests that abortion services should be readily accessible to all women as a demand of justice. Thus, her argument implies that abortion clinics should be established and funded, by the state if necessary, in all parts of the community.

Finally, it is crucial to reiterate that arguments like Markowitz's for liberal abortion laws are not arguments for the moral permissibility of abortion itself. Indeed, Markowitz appears explicitly to reject the idea that abortion is a moral problem. She writes: "From a feminist perspective, . . . abortion is a political issue, one which essentially concerns the interests of and power relations between men and women." This is not to say that such arguments are morally neutral. It is arguable, for example, that Markowitz believes the moral status of the fetus is irrelevant to abortion law. Whether this assumption is legitimate is a very interesting question.[25]

Only a fraction of the possible positions one can hold with respect to abortion and public policy have been discussed here. But together with the arguments discussed in section 2 about the moral status of the fetus, those in section 3 concerning the rights and responsibilities of pregnant women, and the considerations about appropriate attitudes toward human life examined in sections 4 and 5, they are sufficient to show just how complex the problem of abortion is. In their own way, each of the papers in this volume attempts to steer a course through this complexity. Although the authors often reach very different conclusions, their work provides a stimulus to us all in our own thinking about the problem of abortion.

---

[25]For a discussion about the alleged moral neutrality of arguments for permissive abortion laws, see Nicholas Dixon, "Abortion, Moral Neutrality, and Feminism," *Philosophical Forum* 26 (1995): 315–330.

The Unspeakable Crime of Abortion

Pope John Paul II

Among all the crimes which can be committed against life, procured abortion has characteristics making it particularly serious and deplorable. The Second Vatican Council defines abortion, together with infanticide, as an "unspeakable crime."[1]

But today, in many people's consciences, the perception of its gravity has become progressively obscured. The acceptance of abortion in the popular mind, in behaviour and even in law itself, is a telling sign of an extremely dangerous crisis of the moral sense, which is becoming more and more incapable of distinguishing between good and evil, even when the fundamental right to life is at stake. Given such a grave situation, we need now more than ever to have the courage to look the truth in the eye and *to call things by their proper name,* without yielding to convenient compromises or to the temptation of self-deception. In this regard the reproach of the Prophet is extremely straightforward: "Woe to those who call evil good and good evil, who put darkness for light and light for darkness" (*Is* 5:20). Especially in the case of abortion there is a widespread use of ambiguous terminology, such as "interruption of pregnancy," which tends to hide abortion's true nature and to attenuate its seriousness in public opinion. Perhaps this linguistic phenomenon is itself a symptom of an uneasiness of conscience. But no word has the power to change the reality of things: procured abortion is *the deliberate and direct killing, by whatever means it is carried out, of a human being in the initial phase of his or her existence, extending from conception to birth.*

The moral gravity of procured abortion is apparent in all its truth if we recognize that we are dealing with murder and, in particular, when we consider the specific elements involved. The one eliminated is a human being at the very beginning of life. No one more absolutely *innocent* could be imagined. In no way could this human being ever be considered an aggressor, much less an unjust aggressor! He or she is *weak,* defenseless, even to the point of lacking that minimal form of defence consisting in the poignant power of a newborn baby's cries and tears. The unborn child is *totally entrusted* to the protection and care of the woman carrying him or her in the womb. And yet sometimes

From John Paul II, *Evangelium Vitae,* Encyclical Letter, August 16, 1993. Copyright © Libreria Editrice Vaticana.

[1]Pastoral Constitution on the Church in the Modern World *Gaudium et Spes,* 51: "Abortus necnon infanticidium nefanda sunt crimina."

it is precisely the mother herself who makes the decision and asks for the child to be eliminated, and who then goes about having it done.

It is true that the decision to have an abortion is often tragic and painful for the mother, insofar as the decision to rid herself of the fruit of conception is not made for purely selfish reasons or out of convenience, but out of a desire to protect certain important values such as her own health or a decent standard of living for the other members of the family. Sometimes it is feared that the child to be born would live in such conditions that it would be better if the birth did not take place. Nevertheless, these reasons and others like them, however serious and tragic, *can never justify the deliberate killing of an innocent human being.*

As well as the mother, there are often other people too who decide upon the death of the child in the womb. In the first place, the father of the child may be to blame, not only when he directly pressures the woman to have an abortion, but also when he indirectly encourages such a decision on her part by leaving her alone to face the problems of pregnancy:[2] in this way the family is thus mortally wounded and profaned in its nature as a community of love and in its vocation to be the "sanctuary of life." Nor can one overlook the pressures which sometimes come from the wider family circle and from friends. Sometimes the woman is subjected to such strong pressure that she feels psychologically forced to have an abortion: certainly in this case moral responsibility lies particularly with those who have directly or indirectly obliged her to have an abortion. Doctors and nurses are also responsible, when they place at the service of death skills which were acquired for promoting life.

But responsibility likewise falls on the legislators who have promoted and approved abortion laws, and, to the extent that they have a say in the matter, on the administrators of the health-care centres where abortions are performed. A general and no less serious responsibility lies with those who have encouraged the spread of an attitude of sexual permissiveness and a lack of esteem for motherhood, and with those who should have ensured—but did not—effective family and social policies in support of families, especially larger families and those with particular financial and educational needs. Finally, one cannot overlook the network of complicity which reaches out to include international institutions, foundations and associations which systematically campaign for the legalization and spread of abortion in the world. In this sense abortion goes beyond the responsibility of individuals and beyond the harm done to them, and takes on a distinctly social dimension. It is a most serious *wound* inflicted on society and its culture by the very people who ought to be society's promoters and defenders. As I wrote in my *Letter to Families,* "we are facing an immense threat to life: not only to the life of individuals but also to that of civilization itself."[3] We are facing what can be called a *"structure of sin" which opposes human life not yet born.*

Some people try to justify abortion by claiming that the result of conception, at least up to a certain number of days, cannot yet be considered a personal human life. But in fact, "from the time that the ovum is fertilized, a life is begun which is neither that of the father nor the mother; it is rather the life of a new human being with his own growth. It would never be made human if it were not human already. This has always

---

[2]Cf. John Paul II, Apostolic Letter *Muliens Dignitatem* (15 August 1988), 14: *AAS* 80 (1988), 1686.

[3]No. 21: *AAS* 86 (1994), 920.

been clear, and . . . modern genetic science offers clear confirmation. It has demonstrated that from the first instant there is established the programme of what this living being will be: a person, this individual person with his characteristic aspects already well determined. Right from fertilization the adventure of a human life begins, and each of its capacities requires time—a rather lengthy time—to find its place and to be in a position to act."[4] Even if the presence of a spiritual soul cannot be ascertained by empirical data, the results themselves of scientific research on the human embryo provide "a valuable indication for discerning by the use of reason a personal presence at the moment of the first appearance of a human life: how could a human individual not be a human person?"[5]

Furthermore, what is at stake is so important that, from the standpoint of moral obligation, the mere probability that a human person is involved would suffice to justify an absolutely clear prohibition of any intervention aimed at killing a human embryo. Precisely for this reason, over and above all scientific debates and those philosophical affirmations to which the Magisterium has not expressly committed itself, the Church has always taught and continues to teach that the result of human procreation, from the first moment of its existence, must be guaranteed that unconditional respect which is morally due to the human being in his or her totality and unity as body and spirit: *"The human being is to be respected and treated as a person from the moment of conception;* and therefore from that same moment his rights as a person must be recognized, among which in the first place is the inviolable right of every innocent human being to life."[6] . . .

---

[4]Congregation for the Doctrine of the Faith, *Declaration on Procured Abortion* (18 November 1974), Nos. 12–13: *AAS* 66 (1974), 738.

[5]Congregation for the Doctrine of the Faith, Instruction on Respect for Human Life in Its Origin and on the Dignity of Procreation *Donum vitae* (22 February 1987), I, No. 1: *AAS* 80 (1988), 78-79.

[6]*Ibid., loc. cit.,* 79.

Why Abortion Is Immoral

Don Marquis

The view that abortion is, with rare exceptions, seriously immoral has received little support in the recent philosophical literature. No doubt most philosophers affiliated with secular institutions of higher education believe that the anti-abortion position is either a symptom of irrational religious dogma or a conclusion generated by seriously confused philosophical argument. The purpose of this essay is to undermine this general belief. This essay sets out an argument that purports to show, as well as any argument in ethics can show, that abortion is, except possibly in rare cases, seriously immoral, that it is in the same moral category as killing an innocent adult human being.

The argument is based on a major assumption. Many of the most insightful and careful writers on the ethics of abortion—such as Joel Feinberg, Michael Tooley, Mary Anne Warren, H. Tristram Engelhardt, Jr., L. W. Sumner, John T. Noonan, Jr., and Philip Devine[1]—believe that whether or not abortion is morally permissible stands or falls on whether or not a fetus is the sort of being whose life it is seriously wrong to end. The argument of this essay will assume, but not argue, that they are correct.

Also, this essay will neglect issues of great importance to a complete ethics of abortion. Some anti-abortionists will allow that certain abortions, such as abortion before implantation or abortion when the life of a woman is threatened by a pregnancy or abortion after rape, may be morally permissible. This essay will not explore the casuistry of these hard cases. The purpose of this essay is to develop a general argument for the claim that the overwhelming majority of deliberate abortions are seriously immoral.

From Don Marquis, "Why Abortion Is Immoral," *Journal of Philosophy,* LXXXVI, 4 (April 1989): 183–202. Reprinted by permission of the author and the publisher.

[1]Feinberg, "Abortion," in *Matters of Life and Death: New Introductory Essays in Moral Philosophy,* Tom Regan, ed. (New York: Random House, 1986), pp. 256–293; Tooley, "Abortion and Infanticide," *Philosophy and Public Affairs,* II, 1 (1972):37–65; Tooley, *Abortion and Infanticide* (New York: Oxford, 1984); Warren, "On the Moral and Legal Status of Abortion," *The Monist,* LVII, 1 (1973):43–61; Engelhardt, "The Ontology of Abortion," *Ethics,* LXXXIV, 3 (1974):217–234; Sumner, *Abortion and Moral Theory* (Princeton: University Press, 1981); Noonan, "An Almost Absolute Value in History," in *The Morality of Abortion: Legal and Historical Perspectives,* Noonan, ed. (Cambridge: Harvard, 1970); and Devine, *The Ethics of Homicide* (Ithaca: Cornell, 1978).

I

A sketch of standard anti-abortion and pro-choice arguments exhibits how those arguments possess certain symmetries that explain why partisans of those positions are so convinced of the correctness of their own positions, why they are not successful in convincing their opponents, and why, to others, this issue seems to be unresolvable. An analysis of the nature of this standoff suggests a strategy for surmounting it.

Consider the way a typical anti-abortionist argues. She will argue or assert that life is present from the moment of conception or that fetuses look like babies or that fetuses possess a characteristic such as a genetic code that is both necessary and sufficient for being human. Anti-abortionists seem to believe that (1) the truth of all these claims is quite obvious, and (2) establishing any of these claims is sufficient to show that abortion is morally akin to murder.

A standard pro-choice strategy exhibits similarities. The pro-choicer will argue or assert that fetuses are not persons or that fetuses are not rational agents or that fetuses are not social beings. Pro-choicers seem to believe that (1) the truth of any of these claims is quite obvious, and (2) establishing any of these claims is sufficient to show that an abortion is not a wrongful killing.

In fact, both the pro-choice and the anti-abortion claims do seem to be true, although the "it looks like a baby" claim is more difficult to establish the earlier the pregnancy. We seem to have a standoff. How can it be resolved?

As everyone who has taken a bit of logic knows, if any of these arguments concerning abortion is a good argument, it requires not only some claim characterizing fetuses, but also some general moral principle that ties a characteristic of fetuses to having or not having the right to life or to some other moral characteristic that will generate the obligation or the lack of obligation not to end the life of a fetus. Accordingly, the arguments of the anti-abortionist and the pro-choicer need a bit of filling in to be regarded as adequate.

Note what each partisan will say. The anti-abortionist will claim that her position is supported by such generally accepted moral principles as "It is always prima facie seriously wrong to take a human life" or "It is always prima facie seriously wrong to end the life of a baby." Since these are generally accepted moral principles, her position is certainly not obviously wrong. The pro-choicer will claim that her position is supported by such plausible moral principles as "Being a person is what gives an individual intrinsic moral worth" or "It is only seriously prima facie wrong to take the life of a member of the human community." Since these are generally accepted moral principles, the pro-choice position is certainly not obviously wrong. Unfortunately, we have again arrived at a standoff.

Now, how might one deal with this standoff? The standard approach is to try to show how the moral principles of one's opponent lose their plausibility under analysis. It is easy to see how this is possible. On the one hand, the anti-abortionist will defend a moral principle concerning the wrongness of killing which tends to be broad in scope in order that even fetuses at an early stage of pregnancy will fall under it. The problem with broad principles is that they often embrace too much. In this particular instance, the principle "It is always prima facie wrong to take a human life" seems to entail that it is wrong to end the existence of a living human cancer-cell culture, on the grounds that the culture is both living and human. Therefore, it seems that the anti-abortionist's favored principle is too broad.

On the other hand, the pro-choicer wants to find a moral principle concerning the wrongness of killing which tends to be narrow in scope in order that fetuses will *not* fall under it. The problem with narrow principles is that they often do not embrace enough. Hence, the needed principles such as "It is prima facie seriously wrong to kill only persons" or "It is prima facie wrong to kill only rational agents" do not explain why it is wrong to kill infants or young children or the severely retarded or even perhaps the severely mentally ill. Therefore, we seem again to have a standoff. The anti-abortionist charges, not unreasonably, that pro-choice principles concerning killing are too narrow to be acceptable; the pro-choicer charges, not unreasonably, that anti-abortionist principles concerning killing are too broad to be acceptable.

Attempts by both sides to patch up the difficulties in their positions run into further difficulties. The anti-abortionist will try to remove the problem in her position by reformulating her principle concerning killing in terms of human beings. Now we end up with: "It is always prima facie seriously wrong to end the life of a human being." This principle has the advantage of avoiding the problem of the cancer-cell culture counterexample. But this advantage is purchased at a high price. For although it is clear that a fetus is both human and alive, it is not at all clear that a fetus is a human *being*. There is at least something to be said for the view that something becomes a human being only after a process of development, and that therefore first trimester fetuses and perhaps all fetuses are not yet human beings. Hence, the anti-abortionist, by this move, has merely exchanged one problem for another.[2]

The pro-choicer fares no better. She may attempt to find reasons why killing infants, young children, and the severely retarded is wrong which are independent of her major principle that is supposed to explain the wrongness of taking human life, but which will not also make abortion immoral. This is no easy task. Appeals to social utility will seem satisfactory only to those who resolve not to think of the enormous difficulties with a utilitarian account of the wrongness of killing and the significant social costs of preserving the lives of the unproductive.[3] A pro-choice strategy that extends the definition of "person" to infants or even to young children seems just as arbitrary as an anti-abortion strategy that extends the definition of "human being" to fetuses. Again, we find symmetries in the two positions and we arrive at a standoff.

There are even further problems that reflect symmetries in the two positions. In addition to counterexample problems, or the arbitrary application problems that can be exchanged for them, the standard anti-abortionist principle "It is prima facie seriously wrong to kill a human being," or one of its variants, can be objected to on the grounds of ambiguity. If "human being" is taken to be a *biological* category, then the anti-abortionist is left with the problem of explaining why a merely biological category should make a moral difference. Why, it is asked, is it any more reasonable to

---

[2]For interesting discussions of this issue, see Warren Quinn, "Abortion: Identity and Loss," *Philosophy and Public Affairs,* XIII, 1 (1984):24–54; and Lawrence C. Becker, "Human Being: The Boundaries of the Concept," *Philosophy and Public Affairs,* IV, 4 (1975):334–359.

[3]For example, see my "Ethics and the Elderly: Some Problems," in Stuart Spicker, Kathleen Woodward, and David Van Tassel, eds., *Aging and the Elderly: Humanistic Perspectives in Gerontology* (Atlantic Highlands, NJ: Humanities, 1978), pp. 341–355.

base a moral conclusion on the number of chromosomes in one's cells than on the color of one's skin?[4] If "human being," on the other hand, is taken to be a *moral* category, then the claim that a fetus is a human being cannot be taken to be a premise in the anti-abortion argument, for it is precisely what needs to be established. Hence, either the anti-abortionist's main category is a morally irrelevant, merely biological category, or it is of no use to the anti-abortionist in establishing (noncircularly, of course) that abortion is wrong.

Although this problem with the anti-abortionist position is often noticed, it is less often noticed that the pro-choice position suffers from an analogous problem. The principle "Only persons have the right to life" also suffers from an ambiguity. The term "person" is typically defined in terms of psychological characteristics, although there will certainly be disagreement concerning which characteristics are most important. Supposing that this matter can be settled, the pro-choicer is left with the problem of explaining why *psychological* characteristics should make a *moral* difference. If the pro-choicer should attempt to deal with this problem by claiming that an explanation is not necessary, that in fact we do treat such a cluster of psychological properties as having moral significance, the sharp-witted anti-abortionist should have a ready response. We do treat being both living and human as having moral significance. If it is legitimate for the pro-choicer to demand that the anti-abortionist provide an explanation of the connection between the biological character of being a human being and the wrongness of being killed (even though people accept this connection), then it is legitimate for the anti-abortionist to demand that the pro-choicer provide an explanation of the connection between psychological criteria for being a person and the wrongness of being killed (even though that connection is accepted).[5]

Feinberg has attempted to meet this objection (he calls psychological personhood "commonsense personhood"):

> The characteristics that confer commonsense personhood are not arbitrary bases for rights and duties, such as race, sex or species membership; rather they are traits that make sense out of rights and duties and without which those moral attributes would have no point or function. It is because people are conscious; have a sense of their personal identities; have plans, goals, and projects; experience emotions; are liable to pains, anxieties, and frustrations; can reason and bargain, and so on—it is because of these attributes that people have values and interests, desires and expectations of their own, including a stake in their own futures, and a personal well-being of a sort we cannot ascribe to unconscious or nonrational beings. Because of their developed capacities they can assume duties and responsibilities and can have and make claims on one another. Only because of their sense of self, their life plans, their value hierarchies, and their stakes in their own futures can they be ascribed fundamental rights. There is nothing arbitrary about these linkages. (*op. cit.,* p. 270)

The plausible aspects of this attempt should not be taken to obscure its implausible features. There is a great deal to be said for the view that being a psychological person under some description is a necessary condition for having duties. One cannot have a

---

[4]See Warren, *op. cit.,* and Tooley, "Abortion and Infanticide."

[5]This seems to be the fatal flaw in Warren's treatment of this issue.

duty unless one is capable of behaving morally, and a being's capability of behaving morally will require having a certain psychology. It is far from obvious, however, that having rights entails consciousness or rationality, as Feinberg suggests. We speak of the rights of the severely retarded or the severely mentally ill, yet some of these persons are not rational. We speak of the rights of the temporarily unconscious. The New Jersey Supreme Court based their decision in the Quinlan case on Karen Ann Quinlan's right to privacy, and she was known to be permanently unconscious at that time. Hence, Feinberg's claim that having rights entails being conscious is, on its face, obviously false.

Of course, it might not make sense to attribute rights to a being that would never in its natural history have certain psychological traits. This modest connection between psychological personhood and moral personhood will create a place for Karen Ann Quinlan and the temporarily unconscious. But then it makes a place for fetuses also. Hence, it does not serve Feinberg's pro-choice purposes. Accordingly, it seems that the pro-choicer will have as much difficulty bridging the gap between psychological personhood and personhood in the moral sense as the anti-abortionist has bridging the gap between being a biological human being and being a human being in the moral sense.

Furthermore, the pro-choicer cannot any more escape her problem by making person a purely moral category than the anti-abortionist could escape by the analogous move. For if person is a moral category, then the pro-choicer is left without the resources for establishing (noncircularly, of course) the claim that a fetus is not a person, which is an essential premise in her argument. Again, we have both a symmetry and a standoff between pro-choice and anti-abortion views.

Passions in the abortion debate run high. There are both plausibilities and difficulties with the standard positions. Accordingly, it is hardly surprising that partisans of either side embrace with fervor the moral generalizations that support the conclusions they preanalytically favor, and reject with disdain the moral generalizations of their opponents as being subject to inescapable difficulties. It is easy to believe that the counterexamples to one's own moral principles are merely temporary difficulties that will dissolve in the wake of further philosophical research, and that the counterexamples to the principles of one's opponents are as straightforward as the contradiction between A and O propositions in traditional logic. This might suggest to an impartial observer (if there are any) that the abortion issue is unresolvable.

There is a way out of this apparent dialectical quandary. The moral generalizations of both sides are not quite correct. The generalizations hold for the most part, for the usual cases. This suggests that they are all *accidental* generalizations, that the moral claims made by those on both sides of the dispute do not touch on the *essence* of the matter.

This use of the distinction between essence and accident is not meant to invoke obscure metaphysical categories. Rather, it is intended to reflect the rather atheoretical nature of the abortion discussion. If the generalization a partisan in the abortion dispute adopts were derived from the reason why ending the life of a human being is wrong, then there could not be exceptions to that generalization unless some special case obtains in which there are even more powerful countervailing reasons. Such generalizations would not be merely accidental generalizations; they would point to, or be based upon, the essence of the wrongness of killing, what it is that makes killing wrong. All this suggests that a necessary condition of resolving the abortion controversy is a more theoretical account of the wrongness of killing. After all, if we merely believe, but do not understand, why killing adult human beings such as ourselves is wrong, how could we conceivably show that abortion is either immoral or permissible?

II

In order to develop such an account, we can start from the following unproblematic assumption concerning our own case: it is wrong to kill *us*. Why is it wrong? Some answers can be easily eliminated. It might be said that what makes killing us wrong is that a killing brutalizes the one who kills. But the brutalization consists of being inured to the performance of an act that is hideously immoral; hence, the brutalization does not explain the immorality. It might be said that what makes killing us wrong is the great loss others would experience due to our absence. Although such hubris is understandable, such an explanation does not account for the wrongness of killing hermits, or those whose lives are relatively independent and whose friends find it easy to make new friends.

A more obvious answer is better. What primarily makes killing wrong is neither its effect on the murderer nor its effect on the victim's friends and relatives, but its effect on the victim. The loss of one's life is one of the greatest losses one can suffer. The loss of one's life deprives one of all the experiences, activities, projects, and enjoyments that would otherwise have constituted one's future. Therefore, killing someone is wrong, primarily because the killing inflicts (one of) the greatest possible losses on the victim. To describe this as the loss of life can be misleading, however. The change in my biological state does not by itself make killing me wrong. The effect of the loss of my biological life is the loss to me of all those activities, projects, experiences, and enjoyments which would otherwise have constituted my future personal life. These activities, projects, experiences, and enjoyments are either valuable for their own sakes or are means to something else that is valuable for its own sake. Some parts of my future are not valued by me now, but will come to be valued by me as I grow older and as my values and capacities change. When I am killed, I am deprived both of what I now value which would have been part of my future personal life, but also what I would come to value. Therefore, when I die, I am deprived of all of the value of my future. Inflicting this loss on me is ultimately what makes killing me wrong. This being the case, it would seem that what makes killing *any* adult human being prima facie seriously wrong is the loss of his or her future.[6]

How should this rudimentary theory of the wrongness of killing be evaluated? It cannot be faulted for deriving an "ought" from an "is," for it does not. The analysis assumes that killing me (or you, reader) is prima facie seriously wrong. The point of the analysis is to establish which natural property ultimately explains the wrongness of the killing, given that it is wrong. A natural property will ultimately explain the wrongness of killing, only if (1) the explanation fits with our intuitions about the matter and (2)

---

[6]I have been most influenced on this matter by Jonathan Glover, *Causing Death and Saving Lives* (New York: Penguin, 1977), ch. 3; and Robert Young, "What Is So Wrong with Killing People?" *Philosophy*, LIV, 210 (1979): 515–528.

there is no other natural property that provides the basis for a better explanation of the wrongness of killing. This analysis rests on the intuition that what makes killing a particular human or animal wrong is what it does to that particular human or animal. What makes killing wrong is some natural effect or other of the killing. Some would deny this. For instance, a divine-command theorist in ethics would deny it. Surely this denial is, however, one of those features of divine-command theory which renders it so implausible.

The claim that what makes killing wrong is the loss of the victim's future is directly supported by two considerations. In the first place, this theory explains why we regard killing as one of the worst of crimes. Killing is especially wrong, because it deprives the victim of more than perhaps any other crime. In the second place, people with AIDS or cancer who know they are dying believe, of course, that dying is a very bad thing for them. They believe that the loss of a future to them that they would otherwise have experienced is what makes their premature death a very bad thing for them. A better theory of the wrongness of killing would require a different natural property associated with killing which better fits with the attitudes of the dying. What could it be?

The view that what makes killing wrong is the loss to the victim of the value of the victim's future gains additional support when some of its implications are examined. In the first place, it is incompatible with the view that it is wrong to kill only beings who are biologically human. It is possible that there exists a different species from another planet whose members have a future like ours. Since having a future like that is what makes killing someone wrong, this theory entails that it would be wrong to kill members of such a species. Hence, this theory is opposed to the claim that only life that is biologically human has great moral worth, a claim which many anti-abortionists have seemed to adopt. This opposition, which this theory has in common with personhood theories, seems to be a merit of the theory.

In the second place, the claim that the loss of one's future is the wrong-making feature of one's being killed entails the possibility that the futures of some actual nonhuman mammals on our own planet are sufficiently like ours that it is seriously wrong to kill them also. Whether some animals do have the same right to life as human beings depends on adding to the account of the wrongness of killing some additional account of just what it is about my future or the futures of other adult human beings which makes it wrong to kill us. No such additional account will be offered in this essay. Undoubtedly, the provision of such an account would be a very difficult matter. Undoubtedly, any such account would be quite controversial. Hence, it surely should not reflect badly on this sketch of an elementary theory of the wrongness of killing that it is indeterminate with respect to some very difficult issues regarding animal rights.

In the third place, the claim that the loss of one's future is the wrong-making feature of one's being killed does not entail, as sanctity-of-human-life theories do, that active euthanasia is wrong. Persons who are severely and incurably ill, who face a future of pain and despair, and who wish to die will not have suffered a loss if they are killed. It is, strictly speaking, the value of a human's future which makes killing wrong in this theory. This being so, killing does not necessarily wrong some persons who are sick and dying. Of course, there may be other reasons for a prohibition of active euthanasia, but that is another matter. Sanctity-of-human-life theories seem to hold that active euthanasia is seriously wrong even in an individual case where there seems to be good reason for it independently of public policy considerations. This consequence is most implausible, and it is a plus for the claim that the loss of a future of value is what makes killing wrong that it does not share this consequence.

In the fourth place, the account of the wrongness of killing defended in this essay does straightforwardly entail that it is prima facie seriously wrong to kill children and infants, for we do presume that they have futures of value. Since we do believe that it is wrong to kill defenseless little babies, it is important that a theory of the wrongness of killing easily account for this. Personhood theories of the wrongness of killing, on the other hand, cannot straightforwardly account for the wrongness of killing infants and young children.[7] Hence, such theories must add special ad hoc accounts of the wrongness of killing the young. The plausibility of such ad hoc theories seems to be a function of how desperately one wants such theories to work. The claim that the primary wrong-making feature of a killing is the loss to the victim of the value of its future accounts for the wrongness of killing young children and infants directly; it makes the wrongness of such acts as obvious as we actually think it is. This is a further merit of this theory. Accordingly, it seems that this value of a future-like-ours theory of the wrongness of killing shares strengths of both sanctity-of-life and personhood accounts while avoiding weaknesses of both. In addition, it meshes with a central intuition concerning what makes killing wrong.

The claim that the primary wrong-making feature of a killing is the loss to the victim of the value of its future has obvious consequences for the ethics of abortion. The future of a standard fetus includes a set of experiences, projects, activities, and such which are identical with the futures of adult human beings and are identical with the futures of young children. Since the reason that is sufficient to explain why it is wrong to kill human beings after the time of birth is a reason that also applies to fetuses, it follows that abortion is prima facie seriously morally wrong.

This argument does not rely on the invalid inference that, since it is wrong to kill persons, it is wrong to kill potential persons also. The category that is morally central to this analysis is the category of having a valuable future like ours; it is not the category of personhood. The argument to the conclusion that abortion is prima facie seriously morally wrong proceeded independently of the notion of person or potential person or any equivalent. Someone may wish to start with this analysis in terms of the value of a human future, conclude that abortion is, except perhaps in rare circumstances, seriously morally wrong, infer that fetuses have the right to life, and then call fetuses "persons" as a result of their having the right to life. Clearly, in this case, the category of person is being used to state the *conclusion* of the analysis rather than to generate the *argument* of the analysis.

The structure of this anti-abortion argument can be both illuminated and defended by comparing it to what appears to be the best argument for the wrongness of the wanton infliction of pain on animals. This latter argument is based on the assumption that it is prima facie wrong to inflict pain on me (or you, reader). What is the natural property associated with the infliction of pain which makes such infliction wrong? The obvious answer seems to be that the infliction of pain causes suffering and that suffering is a misfortune. The suffering caused by the infliction of pain is what makes the wanton infliction of pain on me wrong. The wanton infliction of pain on other adult humans

---

[7]Feinberg, Tooley, Warren, and Engelhardt have all dealt with this problem.

causes suffering. The wanton infliction of pain on animals causes suffering. Since causing suffering is what makes the wanton infliction of pain wrong and since the wanton infliction of pain on animals causes suffering, it follows that the wanton infliction of pain on animals is wrong.

This argument for the wrongness of the wanton infliction of pain on animals shares a number of structural features with the argument for the serious prima facie wrongness of abortion. Both arguments start with an obvious assumption concerning what it is wrong to do to me (or you, reader). Both then look for the characteristic or the consequence of the wrong action which makes the action wrong. Both recognize that the wrong-making feature of these immoral actions is a property of actions sometimes directed at individuals other than postnatal human beings. If the structure of the argument for the wrongness of the wanton infliction of pain on animals is sound, then the structure of the argument for the prima facie serious wrongness of abortion is also sound, for the structure of the two arguments is the same. The structure common to both is the key to the explanation of how the wrongness of abortion can be demonstrated without recourse to the category of person. In neither argument is that category crucial.

This defense of an argument for the wrongness of abortion in terms of a structurally similar argument for the wrongness of the wanton infliction of pain on animals succeeds only if the account regarding animals is the correct account. Is it? In the first place, it seems plausible. In the second place, its major competition is Kant's account. Kant believed that we do not have direct duties to animals at all, because they are not persons. Hence, Kant had to explain and justify the wrongness of inflicting pain on animals on the grounds that "he who is hard in his dealings with animals becomes hard also in his dealing with men."[8] The problem with Kant's account is that there seems to be no reason for accepting this latter claim unless Kant's account is rejected. If the alternative to Kant's account is accepted, then it is easy to understand why someone who is indifferent to inflicting pain on animals is also indifferent to inflicting pain on humans, for one is indifferent to what makes inflicting pain wrong in both cases. But, if Kant's account is accepted, there is no intelligible reason why one who is hard in his dealings with animals (or crabgrass or stones) should also be hard in his dealings with men. After all, men are persons: animals are no more persons than crabgrass or stones. Persons are Kant's crucial moral category. Why, in short, should a Kantian accept the basic claim in Kant's argument?

Hence, Kant's argument for the wrongness of inflicting pain on animals rests on a claim that, in a world of Kantian moral agents, is demonstrably false. Therefore, the alternative analysis, being more plausible anyway, should be accepted. Since this alternative analysis has the same structure as the anti-abortion argument being defended here, we have further support for the argument for the immorality of abortion being defended in this essay.

Of course, this value of a future-like-ours argument, if sound, shows only that abortion is prima facie wrong, not that it is wrong in any and all circumstances. Since the loss of the future to a standard fetus, if killed, is, however, at least as great a loss as the loss of the future to a standard adult human being who is killed, abortion, like ordinary killing, could be justified only by the most compelling reasons. The loss of one's

---

[8]"Duties to Animals and Spirits," in *Lectures on Ethics,* Louis Infeld, trans. (New York: Harper, 1963), p. 239.

life is almost the greatest misfortune that can happen to one. Presumably abortion could be justified in some circumstances, only if the loss consequent on failing to abort would be at least as great. Accordingly, morally permissible abortions will be rare indeed unless, perhaps, they occur so early in pregnancy that a fetus is not yet definitely an individual. Hence, this argument should be taken as showing that abortion is presumptively very seriously wrong, where the presumption is very strong—as strong as the presumption that killing another adult human being is wrong.

III

How complete an account of the wrongness of killing does the value of a future-like-ours account have to be in order that the wrongness of abortion is a consequence? This account does not have to be an account of the necessary conditions for the wrongness of killing. Some persons in nursing homes may lack valuable human futures, yet it may be wrong to kill them for other reasons. Furthermore, this account does not obviously have to be the sole reason killing is wrong where the victim did have a valuable future. This analysis claims only that, for any killing where the victim did have a valuable future like ours, having that future by itself is sufficient to create the strong presumption that the killing is seriously wrong.

One way to overturn the value of a future-like-ours argument would be to find some account of the wrongness of killing which is at least as intelligible and which has different implications for the ethics of abortion. Two rival accounts possess at least some degree of plausibility. One account is based on the obvious fact that people value the experience of living and wish for that valuable experience to continue. Therefore, it might be said, what makes killing wrong is the discontinuation of that experience for the victim. Let us call this the *discontinuation account.*[9] Another rival account is based upon the obvious fact that people strongly desire to continue to live. This suggests that what makes killing us so wrong is that it interferes with the fulfillment of a strong and fundamental desire, the fulfillment of which is necessary for the fulfillment of any other desires we might have. Let us call this the *desire account.*[10]

Consider first the desire account as a rival account of the ethics of killing which would provide the basis for rejecting the anti-abortion position. Such an account will have to be stronger than the value of a future-like-ours account of the wrongness of abortion if it is to do the job expected of it. To entail the wrongness of abortion, the value of a future-like-ours account has only to provide a sufficient, but not a necessary, condition for the wrongness of killing. The desire account, on the other hand, must provide us also with a necessary condition for the wrongness of killing in order to generate a pro-choice conclusion on abortion. The reason for this is that presumably the argument from the desire account moves from the claim that what makes killing wrong is interference with a very strong desire to the claim that abortion is not wrong because

---

[9]I am indebted to Jack Bricke for raising this objection.

[10]Presumably a preference utilitarian would press such an objection. Tooley once suggested that his account has such a theoretical underpinning. See his "Abortion and Infanticide," pp. 44–45.

the fetus lacks a strong desire to live. Obviously, this inference fails if someone's having the desire to live is not a necessary condition of its being wrong to kill that individual.

One problem with the desire account is that we do regard it as seriously wrong to kill persons who have little desire to live or who have no desire to live or, indeed, have a desire not to live. We believe it is seriously wrong to kill the unconscious, the sleeping, those who are tired of life, and those who are suicidal. The value-of-a-human-future account renders standard morality intelligible in these cases; these cases appear to be incompatible with the desire account.

The desire account is subject to a deeper difficulty. We desire life, because we value the goods of this life. The goodness of life is not secondary to our desire for it. If this were not so, the pain of one's own premature death could be done away with merely by an appropriate alteration in the configuration of one's desires. This is absurd. Hence, it would seem that it is the loss of the goods of one's future, not the interference with the fulfillment of a strong desire to live, which accounts ultimately for the wrongness of killing.

It is worth noting that, if the desire account is modified so that it does not provide a necessary, but only a sufficient, condition for the wrongness of killing, the desire account is compatible with the future-like-ours account. The combined accounts will yield an anti-abortion ethic. This suggests that one can retain what is intuitively plausible about the desire account without a challenge to the basic argument of this paper.

It is also worth noting that, if future desires have moral force in a modified desire account of the wrongness of killing, one can find support for an anti-abortion ethic even in the absence of a value of a future-like-ours account. If one decides that a morally relevant property, the possession of which is sufficient to make it wrong to kill some individual, is the desire at some future time to live—one might decide to justify one's refusal to kill suicidal teenagers on these grounds, for example—then, since typical fetuses will have the desire in the future to live, it is wrong to kill typical fetuses. Accordingly, it does not seem that a desire account of the wrongness of killing can provide a justification of a pro-choice ethic of abortion which is nearly as adequate as the value of a human-future justification of an anti-abortion ethic.

The discontinuation account looks more promising as an account of the wrongness of killing. It seems just as intelligible as the value of a future-like-ours account, but it does not justify an anti-abortion position. Obviously, if it is the continuation of one's activity, experiences, and projects, the loss of which makes killing wrong, then it is not wrong to kill fetuses for that reason, for fetuses do not have experiences, activities, and projects to be continued or discontinued. Accordingly, the discontinuation account does not have the anti-abortion consequences that the value of a future-like-ours account has. Yet, it seems as intelligible as the value of a future-like-ours account, for when we think of what would be wrong with our being killed, it does seem if it is the discontinuation of what makes our lives worthwhile which makes killing us wrong.

Is the discontinuation account just as good an account as the value-of-a-future-like-ours account? The discontinuation account will not be adequate at all, if it does not refer to the *value* of the experience that may be discontinued. One does not want the discontinuation account to make it wrong to kill a patient who begs for death and who is in severe pain that cannot be relieved short of killing. (I leave open the question of whether it is wrong for other reasons.) Accordingly, the discontinuation account must be more than a bare discontinuation account. It must make some reference to the positive value of the patient's experiences. But, by the same token, the value-of-a-future-like-ours account cannot be a bare future account either. Just having a future surely does not itself rule out killing the above patient. This account must make some reference to the value of the patient's future experiences and projects also. Hence, both accounts involve the value of experiences, projects, and activities. So far we still have symmetry between the accounts.

The symmetry fades, however, when we focus on the time period of the value of the experiences, etc., which has moral consequences. Although both accounts leave open the possibility that the patient in our example may be killed, this possibility is left open only in virtue of the utterly bleak future for the patient. It makes no difference whether the patient's immediate past contains intolerable pain, or consists in being in a coma (which we can imagine is a situation of indifference), or consists in a life of value. If the patient's future is a future of value, we want our account to make it wrong to kill the patient. If the patient's future is intolerable, whatever his or her immediate past, we want our account to allow killing the patient. Obviously, then, it is the value of that patient's future which is doing the work in rendering the morality of killing the patient intelligible.

This being the case, it seems clear that whether one has immediate past experiences or not does not work in the explanation of what makes killing wrong. The addition the discontinuation account makes to the value-of-a-human-future account is otiose. Its addition to the value-of-a-future account plays no role at all in rendering intelligible the wrongness of killing. Therefore, it can be discarded with the discontinuation account of which it is a part.

IV

The analysis of the previous section suggests that alternative general accounts of the wrongness of killing are either inadequate or unsuccessful in getting around the anti-abortion consequences of the value of a future-like-ours argument. A different strategy for avoiding these anti-abortion consequences involves limiting the scope of the value-of-a-future argument. More precisely, the strategy involves arguing that fetuses lack a property that is essential for the value-of-a-future argument (or for any anti-abortion argument) to apply to them.

One move of this sort is based upon the claim that a necessary condition of one's future being valuable is that one values it. Value implies a valuer. Given this one might argue that, since fetuses cannot value their futures, their futures are not valuable to them. Hence, it does not seriously wrong them deliberately to end their lives.

This move fails, however, because of some ambiguities. Let us assume that something cannot be of value unless it is valued by someone. This does not entail that my life is of no value unless it is valued by me. I may think, in a period of despair, that my future is of no worth whatsoever, but I may be wrong because others rightly see value—even great value—in it. Furthermore, my future can be valuable to me even if I do not value it. This is the case when a young person attempts suicide, but is rescued and goes on to significant human achievements. Such young people's futures are ultimately valuable to them, even though such futures do not seem to be valuable to them at the moment of attempted suicide. A fetus's future can be valuable to it in the same way. Accordingly, this attempt to limit the anti-abortion argument fails.

Another similar attempt to reject the anti-abortion position is based on Tooley's claim that an entity cannot possess the right to life unless it has the capacity to desire its continued existence. It follows that, since fetuses lack the conceptual capacity to desire to continue to live, they lack the right to life. Accordingly, Tooley concludes that abortion cannot be seriously prima facie wrong (*op. cit.*, pp. 46–47).

What could be the evidence for Tooley's basic claim? Tooley once argued that individuals have a prima facie right to what they desire and that the lack of the capacity to desire something undercuts the basis of one's right to it (*op. cit.*, pp. 44–45). This argument plainly will not succeed in the context of the analysis of this essay, however, since the point here is to establish the fetus's right to life on other grounds. Tooley's argument assumes that the right to life cannot be established in general on some basis other than the desire for life. This position was considered and rejected in the preceding section of this paper.

One might attempt to defend Tooley's basic claim on the grounds that, because a fetus cannot apprehend continued life as a benefit, its continued life cannot be a benefit or cannot be something it has a right to or cannot be something that is in its interest. This might be defended in terms of the general proposition that, if an individual is literally incapable of caring about or taking an interest in some X, then one does not have a right to X or X is not a benefit or X is not something that is in one's interest.[11]

Each member of this family of claims seems to be open to objections. As John C. Stevens[12] has pointed out, one may have a right to be treated with a certain medical procedure (because of a health insurance policy one has purchased), even though one cannot conceive of the nature of the procedure. And, as Tooley himself has pointed out, persons who have been indoctrinated, or drugged, or rendered temporarily unconscious may be literally incapable of caring about or taking an interest in something that is in their interest or is something to which they have a right, or is something that benefits them. Hence, the Tooley claim that would restrict the scope of the value of a future-like-ours argument is undermined by counterexamples.[13]

Finally, Paul Bassen[14] has argued that, even though the prospects of an embryo might seem to be a basis for the wrongness of abortion, an embryo cannot be a victim and therefore cannot be wronged. An embryo cannot be a victim, he says, because it lacks sentience. His central argument for this seems to be that, even though plants and the permanently unconscious are alive, they clearly cannot be victims. What is the explanation of this? Bassen claims that the explanation is that their lives consist of mere

---

[11]Donald VanDeVeer seems to think this is self-evident. See his "Whither Baby Doe?" in *Matters of Life and Death*, p. 233.

[12]"Must the Bearer of a Right Have the Concept of That to Which He Has a Right?" *Ethics*, XCV, 1 (1984):68–74.

[13]See Tooley again in "Abortion and Infanticide," pp. 47–49.

[14]"Present Sakes and Future Prospects: The Status of Early Abortion," *Philosophy and Public Affairs*, XI, 4 (1982):322–326.

metabolism and mere metabolism is not enough to ground victimizability. Mentation is required.

The problem with this attempt to establish the absence of victimizability is that both plants and the permanently unconscious clearly lack what Bassen calls "prospects" or what I have called "a future life like ours." Hence, it is surely open to one to argue that the real reason we believe plants and the permanently unconscious cannot be victims is that killing them cannot deprive them of a future life like ours; the real reason is not their absence of present mentation.

Bassen recognizes that his view is subject to this difficulty, and he recognizes that the case of children seems to support this difficulty, for "much of what we do for children is based on prospects." He argues, however, that, in the case of children and in other such cases, "potentiality comes into play only where victimizability has been secured on other grounds" (*ibid.,* p. 333).

Bassen's defense of his view is patently question-begging, since what is adequate to secure victimizability is exactly what is at issue. His examples do not support his own view against the thesis of this essay. Of course, embryos can be victims: when their lives are deliberately terminated, they are deprived of their future value, their prospects. This makes them victims, for it directly wrongs them.

The seeming plausibility of Bassen's view stems from the fact that paradigmatic cases of imagining someone as a victim involve empathy, and empathy requires mentation of the victim. The victims of flood, famine, rape, or child abuse are all persons with whom we can empathize. That empathy seems to be part of seeing them as victims.[15]

In spite of the strength of these examples, the attractive intuition that a situation in which there is victimization requires the possibility of empathy is subject to counterexamples. Consider a case that Bassen himself offers: "Posthumous obliteration of an author's work constitutes a misfortune for him only if he had wished his work to endure" (*op cit.,* p. 318). The conditions Bassen wishes to impose upon the possibility of being victimized here seem far too strong. Perhaps this author, due to his unrealistic standards of excellence and his low self-esteem, regarded his work as unworthy of survival, even though it possessed genuine literary merit. Destruction of such work would surely victimize its author. In such a case, empathy with the victim concerning the loss is clearly impossible.

Of course, Bassen does not make the possibility of empathy a necessary condition of victimizability; he requires only mentation. Hence, on Bassen's actual view, this author, as I have described him, can be a victim. The problem is that the basic intuition that renders Bassen's view plausible is missing in the author's case. In order to attempt to avoid counterexamples, Bassen has made his thesis too weak to be supported by the intuitions that suggested it.

Even so, the mentation requirement of victimizability is still subject to counterexamples. Suppose a severe accident renders me totally unconscious for a month, after which I recover. Surely killing me while I am unconscious victimizes me, even though I am incapable of mentation during that time. It follows that Bassen's thesis fails. Apparently, attempts to restrict the value of a future-like-ours argument so that fetuses do not fall within its scope do not succeed.

---

[15]Note carefully the reasons he gives on the bottom of p. 316.

V

In this essay, it has been argued that the correct ethic of the wrongness of killing can be extended to fetal life and used to show that there is a strong presumption that any abortion is morally impermissible. If the ethic of killing adopted here entails, however, that contraception is also seriously immoral, then there would appear to be a difficulty with the analysis of this essay.

But this analysis does not entail that contraception is wrong. Of course, contraception prevents the actualization of a possible future of value. Hence, it follows from the claim that futures of value should be maximized that contraception is prima facie immoral. This obligation to maximize does not exist, however; furthermore, nothing in the ethics of killing in this paper entails that it does. The ethics of killing in this essay would entail that contraception is wrong only if something were denied a human future of value by contraception. Nothing at all is denied such a future by contraception, however.

Candidates for a subject of harm by contraception fall into four categories: (1) some sperm or other, (2) some ovum or other, (3) a sperm and an ovum separately, and (4) a sperm and an ovum together. Assigning the harm to some sperm is utterly arbitrary, for no reason can be given for making a sperm the subject of harm rather than an ovum. Assigning the harm to some ovum is utterly arbitrary, for no reason can be given for making an ovum the subject of harm rather than a sperm. One might attempt to avoid these problems by insisting that contraception deprives both the sperm and the ovum separately of a valuable future like ours. On this alternative, too many futures are lost. Contraception was supposed to be wrong, because it deprived us of one future of value, not two. One might attempt to avoid this problem by holding that contraception deprives the combination of sperm and ovum of a valuable future like ours. But here the definite article misleads. At the time of contraception, there are hundreds of millions of sperm, one (released) ovum and millions of possible combinations of all of these. There is no actual combination at all. Is the subject of the loss to be a merely possible combination? Which one? This alternative does not yield an actual subject of harm either. Accordingly, the immorality of contraception is not entailed by the loss of a future-like-ours argument simply because there is no nonarbitrarily identifiable subject of the loss in the case of contraception.

VI

The purpose of this essay has been to set out an argument for the serious presumptive wrongness of abortion subject to the assumption that the moral permissibility of abortion stands or falls on the moral status of the fetus. Since a fetus possesses a property, the possession of which in adult human beings is sufficient to make killing an adult human being wrong, abortion is wrong. This way of dealing with the problem of abortion seems superior to other approaches to the ethics of abortion, because it rests on an ethics of killing which is close to self-evident, because the crucial morally relevant property clearly applies to fetuses, and because the argument avoids the usual equivocations on "human life," "human being," or "person." The argument rests neither on religious claims nor on Papal dogma. It is not subject to the objection of "speciesism." Its soundness is compatible with the moral permissibility of euthanasia and contraception. It deals with our intuitions concerning young children.

Finally, this analysis can be viewed as resolving a standard problem—indeed, *the* standard problem—concerning the ethics of abortion. Clearly, it is wrong to kill adult human beings. Clearly, it is not wrong to end the life of some arbitrarily chosen single human cell. Fetuses seem to be like arbitrarily chosen single human cells in some respects and like adult humans in other respects. The problem of the ethics of abortion is the problem of determining the fetal property that settles this moral controversy. The thesis of this essay is that the problem of the ethics of abortion, so understood, is solvable.

Abortion and Infanticide[1]

Michael Tooley

This essay deals with the question of the morality of abortion and infanticide. The fundamental ethical objection traditionally advanced against these practices rests on the contention that human fetuses and infants have a right to life. It is this claim which will be the focus of attention here. The basic issue to be discussed, then, is what properties a thing must possess in order to have a serious right to life. My approach will be to set out and defend a basic moral principle specifying a condition an organism must satisfy if it is to have a serious right to life. It will be seen that this condition is not satisfied by human fetuses and infants, and thus that they do not have a right to life. So unless there are other substantial objections to abortion and infanticide, one is forced to conclude that these practices are morally acceptable ones. In contrast, it may turn out that our treatment of adult members of other species—cats, dogs, polar bears—is morally indefensible. For it is quite possible that such animals do possess properties that endow them with a right to life.

I. Abortion and Infanticide

One reason the question of the morality of infanticide is worth examining is that it seems very difficult to formulate a completely satisfactory liberal position on abortion without coming to grips with the infanticide issue. The problem the liberal encounters is essentially that of specifying a cutoff point which is not arbitrary: at what stage in the development of a human being does it cease to be morally permissible to destroy it? It is important to be clear about the difficulty here. The conservative's objection is not that since there is a continuous line of development from a zygote to a newborn baby, one must conclude that if it is seriously wrong to destroy a newborn baby it is also seriously

From Michael Tooley, "Abortion and Infanticide," *Philosophy & Public Affairs* 2 (1972): 37–65. Reprinted by permission of Princeton University Press.

[1]I am grateful to a number of people, particularly the Editors of *Philosophy & Public Affairs,* Rodelia Hapke, and Walter Kaufmann, for their helpful comments. It should not, of course, be inferred that they share the views expressed in this paper.

wrong to destroy a zygote or any intermediate stage in the development of a human being. His point is rather that if one says it is wrong to destroy a newborn baby but not a zygote or some intermediate stage in the development of a human being, one should be prepared to point to a *morally relevant* difference between a newborn baby and the earlier stage in the development of a human being.

Precisely the same difficulty can, of course, be raised for a person who holds that infanticide is morally permissible. The conservative will ask what morally relevant differences there are between an adult human being and a newborn baby. What makes it morally permissible to destroy a baby, but wrong to kill an adult? So the challenge remains. But I will argue that in this case there is an extremely plausible answer.

Reflecting on the morality of infanticide forces one to face up to this challenge. In the case of abortion a number of events—quickening or viability, for instance—might be taken as cutoff points, and it is easy to overlook the fact that none of these events involves any morally significant change in the developing human. In contrast, if one is going to defend infanticide, one has to get very clear about what makes something a person, what gives something a right to life.

One of the interesting ways in which the abortion issue differs from other moral issues is that the plausible positions on abortion appear to be extreme positions. For if a human fetus is a person, one is inclined to say that, in general, one would be justified in killing it only to save the life of the mother.[2] Such is the extreme conservative position.[3] On the other hand, if the fetus is not a person, how can it be seriously wrong to destroy it? Why would one need to point to special circumstances to justify such an action? The upshot is that there is no room for a moderate position on the issue of abortion such as one finds, for example, in the *Model Penal Code* recommendations.[4]

Aside from the light it may shed on the abortion question, the issue of infanticide is both interesting and important in its own right. The theoretical interest has been mentioned: it forces one to face up to the question of what makes something a person. The practical importance need not be labored. Most people would prefer to raise children

---

[2]Judith Jarvis Thomson, in her article "A Defense of Abortion," *Philosophy & Public Affairs* 1, no. 1 (Fall 1971): 47–66, has argued with great force and ingenuity that this conclusion is mistaken. I will comment on her argument later in this paper.

[3]While this is the position conservatives tend to hold, it is not clear that it is the position they ought to hold. For if the fetus is a person it is far from clear that it is permissible to destroy it to save the mother. Two moral principles lend support to the view that it is the fetus which should live. First, other things being equal, should not one give something to a person who has had less rather than to a person who has had more? The mother has had a chance to live, while the fetus has not. The choice is thus between giving the mother more of an opportunity to live while giving the fetus none at all and giving the fetus an opportunity to enjoy life while not giving the mother a further opportunity to do so. Surely fairness requires the latter. Secondly, since the fetus has a greater life expectancy than the mother, one is in effect distributing more goods by choosing the life of the fetus over the life of the mother.

The position I am here recommending to the conservative should not be confused with the official Catholic position. The Catholic Church holds that it is seriously wrong to kill a fetus directly even if failure to do so will result in the death of *both* the mother and the fetus. This perverse value judgment is not part of the conservative's position.

[4]Section 230.3 of the American Law Institute's *Model Penal Code* (Philadelphia, 1962). There is some interesting, though at times confused, discussion of the proposed code in *Model Penal Code—Tentative Draft No. 9* (Philadelphia, 1959), pp. 146–162.

who do not suffer from gross deformities or from severe physical, emotional, or intellectual handicaps. If it could be shown that there is no moral objection to infanticide the happiness of society could be significantly and justifiably increased.

Infanticide is also of interest because of the strong emotions it arouses. The typical reaction to infanticide is like the reaction to incest or cannibalism, or the reaction of previous generations to masturbation or oral sex. The response, rather than appealing to carefully formulated moral principles, is primarily visceral. When philosophers themselves respond this way, offering no arguments, and dismissing infanticide out of hand, it is reasonable to suspect that one is dealing with a taboo rather than with a rational prohibition.[5] I shall attempt to show that this is in fact the case.

II. Terminology: "Person" versus "Human Being"

How is the term "person" to be interpreted? I shall treat the concept of a person as a purely moral concept, free of all descriptive content. Specifically, in my usage the sentence "X is a person" will be synonymous with the sentence "X has a (serious) moral right to life."

This usage diverges slightly from what is perhaps the more common way of interpreting the term "person" when it is employed as a purely moral term, where to say that X is a person is to say that X has rights. If everything that had rights had a right to life, these interpretations would be extensionally equivalent. But I am inclined to think that it does not follow from acceptable moral principles that whatever has any rights at all has a right to life. My reason is this. Given the choice between being killed and being tortured for an hour, most adult human beings would surely choose the latter. So it seems plausible to say it is worse to kill an adult human being than it is to torture him for an hour. In contrast, it seems to me that while it is not seriously wrong to kill a newborn kitten, it is seriously wrong to torture one for an hour. This *suggests* that newborn kittens may have a right not to be tortured without having a serious right to life. For it seems to be true that an individual has a right to something whenever it is the case that, if he wants that thing, it would be wrong for others to deprive him of it. Then if it is wrong to inflict a certain sensation upon a kitten if it doesn't want to experience that sensation, it will follow that the kitten has a right not to have [that] sensation inflicted upon it.[6] I shall return to this example later. My point here is merely that it provides some reason for holding that it does follow from acceptable moral principles that if something has any rights at all, it has a serious right to life.

---

[5]A clear example of such an unwillingness to entertain seriously the possibility that moral judgments widely accepted in one's own society may nevertheless be incorrect is provided by Roger Wertheimer's superficial dismissal of infanticide on pages 69–70 of his article "Understanding the Abortion Argument," *Philosophy & Public Affairs* 1, no. 1 (Fall 1971):67–95.

[6]Compare the discussion of the concept of a right offered by Richard B. Brandt in his *Ethical Theory* (Englewood Cliffs, N.J., 1959), pp. 434–441. As Brandt points out, some philosophers have maintained that only things that can *claim* rights can have rights. I agree with Brandt's view that "inability to claim does not destroy the right" (p. 440).

There has been a tendency in recent discussions of abortion to use expressions such as "person" and "human being" interchangeably. B. A. Brody, for example, refers to the difficulty of determining "whether destroying the foetus constitutes the taking of human life," and suggests that it is very plausible that "the taking of a human life is an action that has bad consequences for him whose life is being taken."[7] When Brody refers to something as a human life he apparently construes this as entailing that the thing is a person. For if every living organism belonging to the species Homo sapiens counted as a human life, there would be no difficulty in determining whether a fetus inside a human mother was a human life.

The same tendency is found in Judith Jarvis Thomson's article, which opens with the statement: "Most opposition to abortion relies on the premise that the fetus is a human being, a person, from the moment of conception."[8] The same is true of Roger Wertheimer, who explicitly says: "First off I should note that the expressions 'a human life,' 'a human being,' 'a person,' are virtually interchangeable in this context."[9]

The tendency to use expressions like "person" and "human being" interchangeably is an unfortunate one. For one thing, it tends to lend covert support to anti-abortionist positions. Given such usage, one who holds a liberal view of abortion is put in the position of maintaining that fetuses, at least up to a certain point, are not human beings. Even philosophers are led astray by this usage. Thus Wertheimer says that "except for monstrosities, every member of our species is indubitably a person, a human being, at the very latest at birth."[10] Is it really *indubitable* that newborn babies are persons? Surely this is a wild contention. Wertheimer is falling prey to the confusion naturally engendered by the practice of using "person" and "human being" interchangeably. Another example of this is provided by Thomson: "I am inclined to think also that we shall probably have to agree that the fetus has already become a human person well before birth. Indeed, it comes as a surprise when one first learns how early in its life it begins to acquire human characteristics. By the tenth week, for example, it already has a face, arms, legs, fingers, and toes; it has internal organs, and brain activity is detectable."[11] But what do such physiological characteristics have to do with the question of whether the organism is a person? Thomson, partly, I think, because of the unfortunate use of terminology, does not even raise this question. As a result she virtually takes it for granted that there are some cases in which abortion is "positively indecent."[12]

There is a second reason why using "person" and "human being" interchangeably is unhappy philosophically. If one says that the dispute between pro- and anti-abortionists centers on whether the fetus is human, it is natural to conclude that it is essentially a disagreement about certain facts, a disagreement about what properties a fetus possesses. Thus Wertheimer says that "if one insists on using the raggy fact-value distinction, then

---

[7]B. A. Brody, "Abortion and the Law," *Journal of Philosophy,* LXVIII, no. 12 (17 June 1971): 357–369. See pp. 357–358.

[8]Thomson, "A Defense of Abortion," p. 47.

[9]Wertheimer, "Understanding the Abortion Argument," p. 69.

[10]*Ibid.*

[11]Thomson, "A Defense of Abortion," pp. 47–48.

[12]*Ibid.*, p. 65.

one ought to say that the dispute is over a matter of fact in the sense in which it is a fact that the Negro slaves were human beings."[13] I shall argue that the two cases are not parallel, and that in the case of abortion what is primarily at stake is what moral principles one should accept. If one says that the central issue between conservatives and liberals in the abortion question is whether the fetus is a person, it is clear that the dispute may be either about what properties a thing must have in order to be a person, in order to have a right to life—a moral question—or about whether a fetus at a given stage of development as a matter of fact possesses the properties in question. The temptation to suppose that the disagreement must be a factual one is removed.

It should be clear why the common practice of using expressions such as "person" and "human being" interchangeably in discussions of abortion is unfortunate. It would perhaps be best to avoid the term "human being" altogether, employing instead some expression that is more naturally interpreted as referring to a certain type of biological organism characterized in physiological terms, such as "member of the species Homo sapiens." My own approach will be use the term "human" only in contexts where it is not philosophically dangerous.

III. The Basic Issue: When Is a Member of the Species Homo sapiens a Person?

Settling the issue of the morality of abortion and infanticide will involve answering the following questions: What properties must something have to be a person, i.e., to have a serious right to life? At what point in the development of a member of the species Homo sapiens does the organism possess the properties that make it a person? The first question raises a moral issue. To answer it is to decide what basic[14] moral principles involving the ascription of a right to life one ought to accept. The second question raises a purely factual issue, since the properties in question are properties of a purely descriptive sort.

Some writers seem quite pessimistic about the possibility of resolving the question of the morality of abortion. Indeed, some have gone so far as to suggest that the question of whether the fetus is a person is in principle unanswerable: "we seem to be stuck with the indeterminateness of the fetus' humanity."[15] An understanding of some of the sources of this pessimism will, I think, help us to tackle the problem. Let us begin by considering the similarity a number of people have noted between the issue of abortion and the issue of Negro [sic] slavery. The question here is why it should be more difficult to decide whether abortion and infanticide are acceptable than it was to decide whether slavery was acceptable. The answer seems to be that in the case of slavery

---

[13]Wertheimer, "Understanding the Abortion Argument," p. 78.

[14]A moral principle accepted by a person is *basic for him* if and only if his acceptance of it is not dependent upon any of his (nonmoral) factual beliefs. That is, no change in his factual beliefs would cause him to abandon the principle in question.

[15]Wertheimer, "Understanding the Abortion Argument," p. 88.

there are moral principles of a quite uncontroversial sort that settle the issue. Thus most people would agree to some such principle as the following: No organism that has experiences, that is capable of thought and of using language, and that has harmed no one, should be made a slave. In the case of abortion, on the other hand, conditions that are generally agreed to be sufficient grounds for ascribing a right to life to something do not suffice to settle the issue. It is easy to specify other, purportedly sufficient conditions that will settle the issue, but no one has been successful in putting forward considerations that will convince others to accept those additional moral principles.

I do not share the general pessimism about the possibility of resolving the issue of abortion and infanticide because I believe it is possible to point to a very plausible moral principle dealing with the question of *necessary* conditions for something's having a right to life, where the conditions in question will provide an answer to the question of the permissibility of abortion and infanticide.

There is a second cause of pessimism that should be noted before proceeding. It is tied up with the fact that the development of an organism is one of gradual and continuous change. Given this continuity, how is one to draw a line at one point and declare it permissible to destroy a member of Homo sapiens up to, but not beyond, that point? Won't there be an arbitrariness about any point that is chosen? I will return to this worry shortly. It does not present a serious difficulty once the basic moral principles relevant to the ascription of a right to life to an individual are established.

Let us now turn to the first and most fundamental question: What properties must something have in order to be a person, i.e., to have a serious right to life? The claim I wish to defend is this: An organism possesses a serious right to life only if it possesses the concept of a self as a continuing subject of experiences and other mental states, and believes that it is itself a continuing entity.

My basic argument in support of this claim, which I will call the self-consciousness requirement, will be clearest, I think, if I first offer a simplified version of the argument, and then consider a modification that seems desirable. The simplified version of my argument is this. To ascribe a right to an individual is to assert something about the prima facie obligations of other individuals to act, or to refrain from acting, in certain ways. However, the obligations in question are conditional ones, being dependent upon the existence of certain desires of the individual to whom the right is ascribed. Thus if an individual asks one to destroy something to which he has a right, one does not violate his right to that thing if one proceeds to destroy it. This suggests the following analysis: "A has a right to X" is roughly synonymous with "If A desires X, then others are under a prima facie obligation to refrain from actions that would deprive him of it."[16]

Although this analysis is initially plausible, there are reasons for thinking it not entirely correct. I will consider these later. Even here, however, some expansion is necessary, since there are features of the concept of a right that are important in the present context, and that ought to be dealt with more explicitly. In particular, it seems to be a conceptual truth that things that lack consciousness, such as ordinary machines, cannot have rights. Does this conceptual truth follow from the above analysis of the concept of a right? The answer depends on how the term "desire" is interpreted. If one adopts a completely behavioristic interpretation of "desire," so that a machine that searches for an electrical outlet in order to get its batteries recharged is described

---

[16]Again, compare the analysis defended by Brandt in *Ethical Theory,* pp. 434–441.

as having a desire to be recharged, then it will not follow from this analysis that objects that lack consciousness cannot have rights. On the other hand, if "desire" is interpreted in such a way that desires are states necessarily standing in some sort of relationship to states of consciousness, it will follow from the analysis that a machine that is not capable of being conscious, and consequently of having desires, cannot have rights. I think those who defend analyses of the concept of a right along the lines of this one do have in mind an interpretation of the term "desire" that involves reference to something more than behavioral dispositions. However, rather than relying on this, it seems preferable to make such an interpretation explicit. The following analysis is a natural way of doing that: "A has a right to X" is roughly synonymous with "A is the sort of thing that is a subject of experiences and other mental states, A is capable of desiring X, and if A does desire X, then others are under a prima facie obligation to refrain from actions that would deprive him of it."

The next step in the argument is basically a matter of applying this analysis to the concept of a right to life. Unfortunately the expression "right to life" is not an entirely happy one, since it suggests that the right in question concerns the continued existence of a biological organism. That this is incorrect can be brought out by considering possible ways of violating an individual's right to life. Suppose, for example, that by some technology of the future the brain of an adult human were to be completely reprogrammed, so that the organism wound up with memories (or rather, apparent memories), beliefs, attitudes, and personality traits completely different from those associated with it before it was subjected to reprogramming. In such a case one would surely say that an individual has been destroyed, that an adult human's right to life had been violated, even though no biological organism had been killed. This example shows that the expression "right to life" is misleading, since what one is really concerned about is not just the continued existence of a biological organism, but the right of a subject of experiences and other mental states to continue to exist.

Given this more precise description of the right with which we are here concerned, we are now in a position to apply the analysis of the concept of a right stated above. When we do so we find that the statement "A has a right to continue as a subject of experiences and other mental states" is roughly synonymous with the statement "A is a subject of experiences and other mental states, A is capable of desiring to continue to exist as a subject of experiences and other mental states, and if A does desire to continue to exist as such an entity, then others are under a prima facie obligation not to prevent him from doing so."

The final stage in the argument is simply a matter of asking what must be the case if something is to be capable of having a desire to continue existing as a subject of experiences and other mental states. The basic point here is that the desires a thing can have are limited by the concepts it possesses. For the fundamental way of describing a given desire is as a desire that a certain proposition be true.[17] Then, since one cannot desire that a

---

[17]In everyday life one often speaks of desiring things, such as an apple or a newspaper. Such talk is elliptical, the context together with one's ordinary beliefs serving to make it clear that one wants to eat the apple and read the newspaper. To say that what one desires is that a certain proposition be true should not be construed as involving any particular ontological commitment. The point is merely that it is sentences such as "John wants it to be the case that he is eating an apple in the next few minutes" that provide a completely explicit description of a person's desires. If one fails to use such sentences one can be badly misled about what concepts are presupposed by a particular desire.

certain proposition be true unless one understands it, and since one cannot understand it without possessing the concepts involved in it, it follows that the desires one can have are limited by the concepts one possesses. Applying this to the present case results in the conclusion that an entity cannot be the sort of thing that can desire that a subject of experiences and other mental states exist unless it possesses the concept of such a subject. Moreover, an entity cannot desire that it itself *continue* existing as a subject of experiences and other mental states unless it believes that it is now such a subject. This completes the justification of the claim that it is a necessary condition of something's having a serious right to life that it possess the concept of a self as a continuing subject of experiences, and that it believe that it is itself such an entity.

Let us now consider a modification in the above argument that seems desirable. This modification concerns the crucial conceptual claim advanced about the relationship between ascription of rights and ascription of the corresponding desires. Certain situations suggest that there may be exceptions to the claim that if a person doesn't desire something, one cannot violate his right to it. There are three types of situations that call this claim into question: (i) situations in which an individual's desires reflect a state of emotional disturbance; (ii) situations in which a previously conscious individual is temporarily unconscious; (iii) situations in which an individual's desires have been distorted by conditioning or by indoctrination.

As an example of the first, consider a case in which an adult human falls into a state of depression which his psychiatrist recognizes as temporary. While in the state he tells people he wishes he were dead. His psychiatrist, accepting the view that there can be no violation of an individual's right to life unless the individual has a desire to live, decides to let his patient have his way and kills him. Or consider a related case in which one person gives another a drug that produces a state of temporary depression; the recipient expresses a wish that he were dead. The person who administered the drug then kills him. Doesn't one want to say in both these cases that the agent did something seriously wrong in killing the other person? And isn't the reason the action was seriously wrong in each case the fact that it violated the individual's right to life? If so, the right to life cannot be linked with a desire to live in the way claimed above.

The second set of situations are ones in which an individual is unconscious for some reason—that is, he is sleeping, or drugged, or in a temporary coma. Does an individual in such a state have any desires? People do sometimes say that an unconscious individual wants something, but it might be argued that if such talk is not to be simply false it must be interpreted as actually referring to the desires the individual *would* have if he were now conscious. Consequently, if the analysis of the concept of a right proposed above were correct, it would follow that one does not violate an individual's right if one takes his car, or kills him, while he is asleep.

Finally, consider situations in which an individual's desires have been distorted, either by inculcation of irrational beliefs or by direct conditioning. Thus an individual may permit someone to kill him because he has been convinced that if he allows himself to be sacrificed to the gods he will be gloriously rewarded in a life to come. Or an individual may be enslaved after first having been conditioned to desire a life of slavery. Doesn't one want to say that in the former case an individual's right to life has been violated, and in the latter his right to freedom?

Situations such as these strongly suggest that even if an individual doesn't want something, it is still possible to violate his right to it. Some modification of the earlier account of the concept of a right thus seems in order. The analysis given covers, I believe, the paradigmatic cases of violation of an individual's rights, but there are other, secondary cases where one also wants to say that someone's right has been violated which are not included.

Precisely how the revised analysis should be formulated is unclear. Here it will be sufficient merely to say that, in view of the above, an individual's right to X can be violated not only when he desires X, but also when he *would* now desire X were it not for one of the following: (i) he is in an emotionally unbalanced state; (ii) he is temporarily unconscious; (iii) he has been conditioned to desire the absence of X.

The critical point now is that, even given this extension of the conditions under which an individual's right to something can be violated, it is still true that one's right to something can be violated only when one has the conceptual capability of desiring the thing in question. For example, an individual who would now desire not to be a slave if he weren't emotionally unbalanced, or if he weren't temporarily unconscious, or if he hadn't previously been conditioned to want to be a slave, must possess the concepts involved in the desire not to be a slave. Since it is really only the conceptual capability presupposed by the desire to continue existing as a subject of experiences and other mental states, and not the desire itself, that enters into the above argument, the modification required in the account of the conditions under which an individual's rights can be violated does not undercut my defense of the self-consciousness requirement.[18]

To sum up, my argument has been that having a right to life presupposes that one is capable of desiring to continue existing as a subject of experiences and other mental states. This in turn presupposes both that one has the concept of such a continuing entity and that one believes that one is oneself such an entity. So an entity that lacks such a consciousness of itself as a continuing subject of mental states does not have a right to life.

It would be natural to ask at this point whether satisfaction of this requirement is not only necessary but also sufficient to ensure that a thing has a right to life. I am inclined to an affirmative answer. However, the issue is not urgent in the present context, since as long as the requirement is in fact a necessary one we have the basis of an adequate defense of abortion and infanticide. If an organism must satisfy some other condition before it has a serious right to life, the result will merely be that the interval during which infanticide is morally permissible may be somewhat longer. Although the point at which an organism first achieves self-consciousness and hence the capacity of desiring to continue existing as a subject of experiences and other mental states may be a theoretically incorrect cutoff point, it is at least a morally safe one: any error it involves is on the side of caution.

---

[18]There are, however, situations other than those discussed here which might seem to count against the claim that a person cannot have a right unless he is conceptually capable of having the corresponding desire. Can't a young child, for example, have a right to an estate, even though he may not be conceptually capable of wanting the estate? It is clear that such situations have to be carefully considered if one is to arrive at a satisfactory account of the concept of a right. My inclination is to say that the correct description is not that the child now has a right to the estate, but that he will come to have such a right when he is mature, and that in the meantime no one else has a right to the estate. My reason for saying that the child does not now have a right to the estate is that he cannot now do things with the estate, such as selling it or giving it away, that he will be able to do later on.

IV. Some Critical Comments
on Alternative Proposals

I now want to compare the line of demarcation I am proposing with the cutoff points traditionally advanced in discussions of abortion. My fundamental claim will be that none of these cutoff points can be defended by appeal to plausible, basic moral principles. The main suggestions as to the point past which it is seriously wrong to destroy something that will develop into an adult member of the species Homo sapiens are these: (a) conception; (b) the attainment of human form; (c) the achievement of the ability to move about spontaneously; (d) viability; (e) birth.[19] The corresponding moral principles suggested by these cutoff points are as follows: (1) It is seriously wrong to kill an organism, from a zygote on, that belongs to the species Homo sapiens. (2) It is seriously wrong to kill an organism that belongs to Homo sapiens and that has achieved human form. (3) It is seriously wrong to kill an organism that is a member of Homo sapiens and that is capable of spontaneous movement. (4) It is seriously wrong to kill an organism that belongs to Homo sapiens and that is capable of existing outside the womb. (5) It is seriously wrong to kill an organism that is a member of Homo sapiens that is no longer in the womb.

My first comment is that it would not do *simply* to omit the reference to membership in the species Homo sapiens from the above principles, with the exception of principle (2). For then the principles would be applicable to animals in general, and one would be forced to conclude that it was seriously wrong to abort a cat fetus, or that it was seriously wrong to abort a motile cat fetus, and so on.

The second and crucial comment is that none of the five principles given above can plausibly be viewed as a *basic* moral principle. To accept any of them as such would be akin to accepting as a basic moral principle the proposition that it is morally permissible to enslave black members of the species Homo sapiens but not white members. Why should it be seriously wrong to kill an unborn member of the species Homo sapiens but not seriously wrong to kill an unborn kitten? Difference in species is not per se a morally relevant difference. If one holds that it is seriously wrong to kill an unborn member of the species Homo sapiens but not an unborn kitten, one should be prepared to point to some property that is morally significant and that is possessed by unborn members of Homo sapiens but not by unborn kittens. Similarly, such a property must be identified if one believes it seriously wrong to kill unborn members of Homo sapiens that have achieved viability but not seriously wrong to kill unborn kittens that have achieved that state.

What property might account for such a difference? That is to say, what *basic* moral principles might a person who accepts one of these five principles appeal to in support of his secondary moral judgment? Why should events such as the achievement of human form, or the achievement of the ability to move about, or the achievement of viability, or birth serve to endow something with a right to life? What the liberal must do

---

[19]Another frequent suggestion as to the cutoff point not listed here is quickening. I omit it because it seems clear that if abortion after quickening is wrong, its wrongness must be tied up with the motility of the fetus, not with the mother's awareness of the fetus' ability to move about.

is to show that these events involve changes, or are associated with changes, that are morally relevant.

Let us now consider reasons why the events involved in cutoff points (b) through (e) are not morally relevant, beginning with the last two: viability and birth. The fact that an organism is not physiologically dependent upon another organism, or is capable of such physiological independence, is surely irrelevant to whether the organism has a right to life. In defense of this contention, consider a speculative case where a fetus is able to learn a language while in the womb. One would surely not say that the fetus had no right to life until it emerged from the womb, or until it was capable of existing outside the womb. A less speculative example is the case of Siamese twins who have learned to speak. One doesn't want to say that since one of the twins would die were the two to be separated, it therefore has no right to life. Consequently it seems difficult to disagree with the conservative's claim that an organism which lacks a right to life before birth or before becoming viable cannot acquire this right immediately upon birth or upon becoming viable.

This does not, however, completely rule out viability as a line of demarcation. For instead of defending viability as a cutoff point on the ground that only then does a fetus acquire a right to life, it is possible to argue rather that when one organism is physiologically dependent upon another, the former's right to life may conflict with the latter's right to use its body as it will, and moreover, that the latter's right to do what it wants with its body may often take precedence over the other organism's right to life. Thomson has defended this view: "I am arguing only that having a right to life does not guarantee having either a right to the use of or a right to be allowed continued use of another person's body—even if one needs it for life itself. So the right to life will not serve the opponents of abortion in the very simple and clear way in which they seem to have thought it would."[20] I believe that Thomson is right in contending that philosophers have been altogether too casual in assuming that if one grants the fetus a serious right to life, one must accept a conservative position on abortion.[21] I also think the only defense of viability as a cutoff point which has any hope of success at all is one based on the considerations she advances. I doubt very much, however, that this defense of abortion is ultimately tenable. I think that one can grant even stronger assumptions than those made by Thomson and still argue persuasively for a semiconservative view. What I have in mind is this. Let it be granted, for the sake of argument, that a woman's right to free her body of parasites which will inhibit her freedom of action and possibly impair her health is stronger than the parasite's right to life, and is so even if the parasite has as much right to life as an adult human. One can still argue that abortion ought not to be permitted. For if A's right is stronger than B's, and it is impossible to satisfy both, it does not follow that A's should be satisfied rather than B's. It may be possible to compensate A if his right isn't satisfied, but impossible to compensate B if his right isn't satisfied. In such a case the best thing to do may be to satisfy B's claim and to compensate A. Abortion may be a case in point. If the fetus has a right to life and the right is not satisfied, there is certainly no way the fetus can be compensated. On the other hand, if the

---

[20]Thomson, "A Defense of Abortion," p. 56.

[21]A good example of a failure to probe this issue is provided by Brody's "Abortion and Law."

woman's right to rid her body of harmful and annoying parasites is not satisfied, she can be compensated. Thus it would seem that the just thing to do would be to prohibit abortion but to compensate women for the burden of carrying a parasite to term. Then, however, we are back at a (modified) conservative position.[22] Our conclusion must be that it appears unlikely there is any satisfactory defense either of viability or of birth as cutoff points.

Let us now consider the third suggested line of demarcation, the achievement of the power to move about spontaneously. It might be argued that acquiring this power is a morally relevant event on the grounds that there is a connection between the concept of an agent and the concept of a person, and being motile is an indication that a thing is an agent.[23]

It is difficult to respond to this suggestion unless it is made more specific. Given that one's interest here is in defending a certain cutoff point, it is natural to interpret the proposal as suggesting that motility is a necessary condition of an organism's having a right to life. But this won't do, because one certainly wants to ascribe a right to life to adult humans who are completely paralyzed. Maybe the suggestion is rather that motility is a sufficient condition of something's having a right to life. However, it is clear that motility alone is not sufficient, since this would imply that all animals, and also certain machines, have a right to life. Perhaps, then, the most reasonable interpretation of the claim is that motility together with some other property is a sufficient condition of somethings having a right to life, where the other property will have to be a property possessed by unborn members of the species Homo sapiens but not by unborn members of other familiar species.

The central question, then, is what this other property is. Until one is told, it is very difficult to evaluate either the moral claim that motility together with that property is a sufficient basis for ascribing to an organism a right to life or the factual claim that a motile human fetus possesses that property while a motile fetus belonging to some other species does not. A conservative would presumably reject motility as a cutoff point by arguing that whether an organism has a right to life depends only upon its potentialities, which are of course not changed by its becoming motile. If, on the other hand, one favors a liberal view of abortion, I think that one can attack this third suggested cutoff point, in its unspecified form, only by determining what properties are necessary, or what properties sufficient, for an individual to have a right to life. Thus I would base my rejection of motility as a cutoff point on my claim, defended above, that a necessary condition of an organism's possessing a right to life is that it conceive of itself as a continuing subject of experiences and other mental states.

The second suggested cutoff point—the development of a recognizably human form—can be dismissed fairly quickly. I have already remarked that membership in a particular species is not itself a morally relevant property. For it is obvious that if we encountered other "rational animals," such as Martians, the fact that their physiological makeup was very different from our own would not be grounds for denying them a

---

[22]Admittedly the modification is a substantial one, since given a society that refused to compensate women, a woman who had an abortion would not be doing anything wrong.

[23]Compare Wertheimer's remarks, "Understanding the Abortion Argument," p. 79.

right to life.[24] Similarly, it is clear that the development of human form is not in itself a morally relevant event. Nor do there seem to be any grounds for holding that there is some other change, associated with this event, that is morally relevant. The appeal of this second cutoff point is, I think, purely emotional.

The overall conclusion seems to be that it is very difficult to defend the cutoff points traditionally advanced by those who advocate either a moderate or a liberal position on abortion. The reason is that there do not seem to be any basic moral principles one can appeal to in support of the cutoff points in question. We must now consider whether the conservative is any better off.

V. Refutation of the Conservative Position

Many have felt that the conservative's position is more defensible than the liberal's because the conservative can point to the gradual and continuous development of an organism as it changes from a zygote to an adult human being. He is then in a position to argue that it is morally arbitrary for the liberal to draw a line at some point in this continuous process and to say that abortion is permissible before, but not after, that particular point. The liberal's reply would presumably be that the emphasis upon the continuity of the process is misleading. What the conservative is really doing is simply challenging the liberal to specify the properties a thing must have in order to be a person, and to show that the developing organism does acquire the properties at the point selected by the liberal. The liberal may then reply that the difficulty he has meeting this challenge should not be taken as grounds for rejecting his position. For the conservative cannot meet this challenge either; the conservative is equally unable to say what properties something must have if it is to have a right to life.

Although this rejoinder does not dispose of the conservative's argument, it is not without bite. For defenders of the view that abortion is always wrong have failed to face up to the question of the basic moral principles on which their position rests. They have been content to assert the wrongness of killing any organism, from a zygote on, if that organism is a member of the species Homo sapiens. But they have overlooked the point that this cannot be an acceptable *basic* moral principle, since difference in species is not in itself a morally relevant difference. The conservative can reply, however, that it is possible to defend his position—but not the liberal's—*without* getting clear about the properties a thing must possess if it is to have a right to life. The conservative's defense will rest upon the following two claims: first, that there is a property, even if one is unable to specify what it is, that (i) is possessed by adult humans, and (ii) endows any organism possessing it with a serious right to life. Second, that if there are properties which satisfy (i) and (ii) above, at least one of those properties will be such that any

---

[24]This requires qualification. If their central nervous systems were radically different from ours, it might be thought that one would not be justified in ascribing to them mental states of an experiential sort. And then, since it seems to be a conceptual truth that only things having experiential states can have rights, one would be forced to conclude that one was not justified in ascribing any rights to them.

organism potentially possessing that property has a serious right to life even now, simply by virtue of that potentiality, where an organism possesses a property potentially if it will come to have that property in the normal course of its development. The second claim—which I shall refer to as the potentiality principle—is critical to the conservative's defense. Because of it he is able to defend his position without deciding what properties a thing must possess in order to have a right to life. It is enough to know that adult members of Homo sapiens do have such a right. For then one can conclude that any organism which belongs to the species Homo sapiens, from a zygote on, must also have a right to life by virtue of the potentiality principle.

The liberal, by contrast, cannot mount a comparable argument. He cannot defend his position without offering at least a partial answer to the question of what properties a thing must possess in order to have a right to life.

The importance of the potentiality principle, however, goes beyond the fact that it provides support for the conservative's position. If the principle is unacceptable, then so is his position. For if the conservative cannot defend the view that an organism's having certain potentialities is sufficient grounds for ascribing to it a right to life, his claim that a fetus which is a member of Homo sapiens has a right to life can be attacked as follows. The reason an adult member of Homo sapiens has a right to life, but an infant ape does not, is that there are certain psychological properties which the former possesses and the latter lacks. Now, even if one is unsure exactly what these psychological properties are, it is clear that an organism in the early stages of development from a zygote into an adult member of Homo sapiens does not possess these properties. One need merely compare a human fetus with an ape fetus. What mental states does the former enjoy that the latter does not? Surely it is reasonable to hold that there are no significant differences in their respective mental lives—assuming that one wishes to ascribe any mental states at all to such organisms. (Does a zygote have a mental life? Does it have experiences? Or beliefs? Or desires?) There are, of course, physiological differences, but these are not in themselves morally significant. *If* one held that potentialities were relevant to the ascription of a right to life, one could argue that the physiological differences, though not morally significant in themselves, are morally significant by virtue of their causal consequences: they will lead to later psychological differences that are morally relevant, and for this reason the physiological differences are themselves morally significant. But if the potentiality principle is not available, this line of argument cannot be used, and there will then be no differences between a human fetus and an ape fetus that the conservative can use as grounds for ascribing a serious right to life to the former but not to the latter.

It is therefore tempting to conclude that the conservative view of abortion is acceptable if and only if the potentiality principle is acceptable. But to say that the conservative position can be defended if the potentiality principle is acceptable is to assume that the argument is over once it is granted that the fetus has a right to life, and, as was noted above, Thomson has shown that there are serious grounds for questioning this assumption. In any case, the important point here is that the conservative position on abortion is acceptable *only if* the potentiality principle is sound.

One way to attack the potentiality principle is simply to argue in support of the self-consciousness requirement—the claim that only an organism that conceives of itself as a continuing subject of experiences has a right to life. For this requirement, when taken together with the claim that there is at least one property, possessed by adult humans, such that any organism possessing it has a serious right to life, entails the denial of the potentiality principle. Or at least this is so if we add the uncontroversial empirical claim that an organism that will in the normal course of events develop into an adult human does not from the very beginning of its existence possess a concept of a continuing subject of experiences together with a belief that it is itself such an entity.

I think it best, however, to scrutinize the potentiality principle itself, and not to base one's case against it simply on the self-consciousness requirement. Perhaps the first point to note is that the potentiality principle should not be confused with principles such as the following: the value of an object is related to the value of the things into which it can develop. This "valuation principle" is rather vague. There are ways of making it more precise, but we need not consider these here. Suppose now that one were to speak not of a right to life, but of the value of life. It would then be easy to make the mistake of thinking that the valuation principle was relevant to the potentiality principle—indeed, that it entailed it. But an individual's right to life is not based on the value of his life. To say that the world would be better off if it contained fewer people is not to say that it would be right to achieve such a better world by killing some of the present inhabitants. If having a right to life were a matter of a thing's value, then a thing's potentialities, being connected with its expected value, would clearly be relevant to the question of what rights it had. Conversely, once one realizes that a thing's rights are not a matter of its value, I think it becomes clear that an organism's potentialities are irrelevant to the question of whether it has a right to life.

But let us now turn to the task of finding a direct refutation of the potentiality principle. The basic issue is this. Is there any property J which satisfies the following conditions: (1) There is a property K such that any individual possessing property K has a right to life, and there is a scientific law L to the effect that any organism possessing property J will in the normal course of events come to possess property K at some later time. (2) Given the relationship between property J and property K just described, anything possessing property J has a right to life. (3) If property J were not related to property K in the way indicated, it would not be the case that anything possessing property J thereby had a right to life. In short, the question is whether there is a property J that bestows a right to life on an organism *only because* J stands in a certain causal relationship to a second property K, which is such that anything possessing that property ipso facto has a right to life.

My argument turns upon the following critical principle: Let C be a causal process that normally leads to outcome E. Let A be an action that initiates process C, and B be an action involving a minimal expenditure of energy that stops process C before outcome E occurs. Assume further that actions A and B do not have any other consequences, and that E is the only morally significant outcome of process C. Then there is no moral difference between intentionally performing action B and intentionally refraining from performing action A, assuming identical motivation in both cases. This principle, which I shall refer to as the moral symmetry principle with respect to action and inaction, would be rejected by some philosophers. They would argue that there is an important distinction to be drawn between "what we owe people in the form of aid and what we owe them in the way of non-interference,"[25] and that the latter, "negative duties," are duties that it

---

[25]Phillipa Foot, "The Problem of Abortion and the Doctrine of the Double Effect," *The Oxford Review* 5 (1967):5–15. See the discussion on pp. 11ff.

is more serious to neglect than the former, "positive" ones. This view arises from an intuitive response to examples such as the following. Even if it is wrong not to send food to starving people in other parts of the world, it is more wrong still to kill someone. And isn't the conclusion, then, that one's obligation to refrain from killing someone is a more serious obligation than one's obligation to save lives?

I want to argue that this is not the correct conclusion. I think it is tempting to draw this conclusion if one fails to consider the motivation that is likely to be associated with the respective actions. If someone performs an action he knows will kill someone else, this will usually be grounds for concluding that he wanted to kill the person in question. In contrast, failing to help someone may indicate only apathy, laziness, selfishness, or an amoral outlook: the fact that a person knowingly allows another to die will not normally be grounds for concluding that he desired that person's death. Someone who knowingly kills another is more likely to be seriously defective from a moral point of view than someone who fails to save another's life.

If we are not to be led to false conclusions by our intuitions about certain cases, we must explicitly assume identical motivations in the two situations. Compare, for example, the following: (1) Jones sees that Smith will be killed by a bomb unless he warns him. Jones's reaction is: "How lucky, it will save me the trouble of killing Smith myself." So Jones allows Smith to be killed by the bomb, even though he could easily have warned him. (2) Jones wants Smith dead, and therefore shoots him. Is one to say there is a significant difference between the wrongness of Jones's behavior in these two cases? Surely not. This shows the mistake of drawing a distinction between positive duties and negative duties and holding that the latter impose stricter obligations than the former. The difference in our intuitions about situations that involve giving aid to others and corresponding situations that involve not interfering with others is to be explained by reference to probable differences in the motivations operating in the two situations, and not by reference to a distinction between positive and negative duties. For once it is specified that the motivation is the same in the two situations, we realize that inaction is as wrong in the one case as action is in the other.

There is another point that may be relevant. Action involves effort, while inaction usually does not. It usually does not require any effort on my part to refrain from killing someone, but saving someone's life will require an expenditure of energy. One must then ask how large a sacrifice a person is morally required to make to save the life of another. If the sacrifice of time and energy is quite large it may be that one is not morally obliged to save the life of another in that situation. Superficial reflection upon such cases might easily lead us to introduce the distinction between positive and negative duties, but again it is clear that this would be a mistake. The point is not that one has a greater duty to refrain from killing others than to perform positive actions that will save them. It is rather that positive actions require effort, and this means that in deciding what to do a person has to take into account his own right to do what he wants with his life, and not only the other person's right to life. To avoid this confusion, we should confine ourselves to comparisons between situations in which the positive action involves minimal effort.

The moral symmetry principle, as formulated above, explicitly takes these two factors into account. It applies only to pairs of situations in which the motivations are identical and the positive action involves minimal effort. Without these restrictions, the principle would be open to serious objection; with them, it seems perfectly acceptable.

For the central objection to it rests on the claim that we must distinguish positive from negative duties and recognize that negative duties impose stronger obligations than positive ones. I have tried to show how this claim derives from an unsound account of our moral intuitions about certain situations.

My argument against the potentiality principle can now be stated. Suppose at some future time a chemical were to be discovered which when injected into the brain of a kitten would cause the kitten to develop into a cat possessing a brain of the sort possessed by humans, and consequently into a cat having all the psychological capabilities characteristic of adult humans. Such cats would be able to think, to use language, and so on. Now it would surely be morally indefensible in such a situation to ascribe a serious right to life to members of the species Homo sapiens without also ascribing it to cats that have undergone such a process of development: there would be no morally significant differences.

Secondly, it would not be seriously wrong to refrain from injecting a newborn kitten with the special chemical, and to kill it instead. The fact that one could initiate a causal process that would transform a kitten into an entity that would eventually possess properties such that anything possessing them ipso facto has a serious right to life does not mean that the kitten has a serious right to life even before it has been subjected to the process of injection and transformation. The possibility of transforming kittens into persons will not make it any more wrong to kill newborn kittens than it is now.

Thirdly, in view of the symmetry principle, if it is not seriously wrong to refrain from initiating such a causal process, neither is it seriously wrong to interfere with such a process. Suppose a kitten is accidentally injected with the chemical. As long as it has not yet developed those properties that in themselves endow something with a right to life, there cannot be anything wrong with interfering with the causal process and preventing the development of the properties in question. Such interference might be accomplished either by injecting the kitten with some "neutralizing" chemical or simply by killing it.

But if it is not seriously wrong to destroy an injected kitten which will naturally develop the properties that bestow a right to life, neither can it be seriously wrong to destroy a member of Homo sapiens which lacks such properties, but will naturally come to have them. The potentialities are the same in both cases. The only difference is that in the case of a human fetus the potentialities have been present from the beginning of the organism's development, while in the case of the kitten they have been present only from the time it was injected with the special chemical. This difference in the time at which the potentialities were acquired is a morally irrelevant difference.

It should be emphasized that I am not here assuming that a human fetus does not possess properties which in themselves, and irrespective of their causal relationships to other properties, provide grounds for ascribing a right to life to whatever possesses them. The point is merely that if it is seriously wrong to kill something, the reason cannot be that the thing will later acquire properties that in themselves provide something with a right to life.

Finally, it is reasonable to believe that there are properties possessed by adult members of Homo sapiens which establish their right to life, and also that any normal human fetus will come to possess those properties shared by adult humans. But it has just been shown that if it is wrong to kill a human fetus, it cannot be because of its potentialities. One is therefore forced to conclude that the conservative's potentiality principle is false.

In short, anyone who wants to defend the potentiality principle must either argue against the moral symmetry principle or hold that in a world in which kittens could be transformed into "rational animals" it would be seriously wrong to kill newborn kittens. It is hard to believe there is much to be said for the latter moral claim. Consequently one expects the conservative's rejoinder to be directed against the symmetry principle. While I have not attempted to provide a thorough defense of that principle, I have tried to show that what seems to be the most important objection to it—the one that appeals to a distinction between positive and negative duties—is based on a superficial analysis of our moral intuitions. I believe that a more thorough examination of the symmetry principle would show it to be sound. If so, we should reject the potentiality principle, and the conservative position on abortion as well.

VI. Summary and Conclusions

Let us return now to my basic claim, the self-consciousness requirement: An organism possesses a serious right to life only if it possesses the concept of a self as a continuing subject of experiences and other mental states, and believes that it is itself such a continuing entity. My defense of this claim has been twofold. I have offered a direct argument in support of it, and I have tried to show that traditional conservative and liberal views on abortion and infanticide, which involve a rejection of it, are unsound. I now want to mention one final reason why my claim should be accepted. Consider the example mentioned in section II—that of killing, as opposed to torturing, newborn kittens. I suggested there that while in the case of adult humans most people would consider it worse to kill an individual than to torture him for an hour, we do not usually view the killing of a newborn kitten as morally outrageous, although we would regard someone who tortured a newborn kitten for an hour as heinously evil. I pointed out that a possible conclusion that might be drawn from this is that newborn kittens have a right not to be tortured, but do not have a serious right to life. If this is the correct conclusion, how is one to explain it? One merit of the self-consciousness requirement is that it provides an explanation of this situation. The reason a newborn kitten does not have a right to life is explained by the fact that it does not possess the concept of a self. But how is one to explain the kitten's having a right not to be tortured? The answer is that a desire not to suffer pain can be ascribed to something without assuming that it has any concept of a continuing self. For while something that lacks the concept of a self cannot desire that a self not suffer, it can desire that a given sensation not exist. The state desired—the absence of a particular sensation, or of sensations of a certain sort—can be described in a purely phenomenalistic language, and hence without the concept of a continuing self. So long as the newborn kitten possesses the relevant phenomenal concepts, it can truly be said to desire that a certain sensation not exist. So we can ascribe to it a right not to be tortured even though, since it lacks the concept of a continuing self, we cannot ascribe to it a right to life.

This completes my discussion of the basic moral principles involved in the issue of abortion and infanticide. But I want to comment upon an important factual question, namely, at what point an organism comes to possess the concept of a self as a continuing subject of experiences and other mental states, together with the belief that it is itself such a continuing entity. This is obviously a matter for detailed psychological investigation, but everyday observation makes it perfectly clear, I believe, that a newborn baby does not possess the concept of a continuing self, any more than a newborn kitten possesses such a concept. If so, infanticide during a time interval shortly after birth must be morally acceptable.

But where is the line to be drawn? What is the cutoff point? If one maintained, as some philosophers have, that an individual possesses concepts only if he can express these concepts in language, it would be a matter of everyday observation whether or not a given organism possessed the concept of a continuing self. Infanticide would then be permissible up to the time an organism learned how to use certain expressions. However, I think the claim that acquisition of concepts is dependent on acquisition of language is mistaken. For example, one wants to ascribe mental states of a conceptual sort—such as beliefs and desires—to organisms that are incapable of learning a language. This issue of prelinguistic understanding is clearly outside the scope of this discussion. My point is simply that *if* an organism can acquire concepts without thereby acquiring a way of expressing those concepts linguistically, the question of whether a given organism possesses the concept of a self as a continuing subject of experiences and other mental states, together with the belief that it is itself such a continuing entity, may be a question that requires fairly subtle experimental techniques to answer.

If this view of the matter is roughly correct, there are two worries one is left with at the level of practical moral decisions, one of which may turn out to be deeply disturbing. The lesser worry is where the line is to be drawn in the case of infanticide. It is not troubling because there is no serious need to know the exact point at which a human infant acquires a right to life. For in the vast majority of cases in which infanticide is desirable, its desirability will be apparent within a short time after birth. Since it is virtually certain that an infant at such a stage of its development does not possess the concept of a continuing self, and thus does not possess a serious right to life, there is excellent reason to believe that infanticide is morally permissible in most cases where it is otherwise desirable. The practical moral problem can thus be satisfactorily handled by choosing some period of time, such as a week after birth, as the interval during which infanticide will be permitted. This interval could then be modified once psychologists have established the point at which a human organism comes to believe that it is a continuing subject of experiences and other mental states.

The troubling worry is whether adult animals belonging to species other than Homo sapiens may not also possess a serious right to life. For once one says that an organism can possess the concept of a continuing self, together with the belief that it is itself such an entity, without having any way of expressing that concept and that belief linguistically, one has to face up to the question of whether animals may not possess properties that bestow a serious right to life upon them. The suggestion itself is a familiar one, and one that most of us are accustomed to dismiss very casually. The line of thought advanced here suggests that this attitude may turn out to be tragically mistaken. Once one reflects upon the question of the *basic* moral principles involved in the ascription of a right to life to organisms, one may find himself driven to conclude that our everyday treatment of animals is morally indefensible, and that we are in fact murdering innocent persons.

On the Moral and Legal Status of Abortion

Mary Anne Warren

We will be concerned with both the moral status of abortion, which for our purposes we may define as the act which a woman performs in voluntarily terminating, or allowing another person to terminate, her pregnancy, and the legal status which is appropriate for this act. I will argue that, while it is not possible to produce a satisfactory defense of a woman's right to obtain an abortion without showing that a fetus is not a human being, in the morally relevant sense of that term, we ought not to conclude that the difficulties involved in determining whether or not a fetus is human make it impossible to produce any satisfactory solution to the problem of the moral status of abortion. For it is possible to show that, on the basis of intuitions which we may expect even the opponents of abortion to share, a fetus is not a person, and hence not the sort of entity to which it is proper to ascribe full moral rights.

Of course, while some philosophers would deny the possibility of any such proof,[1] others will deny that there is any need for it, since the moral permissibility of abortion appears to them to be too obvious to require proof. But the inadequacy of this attitude should be evident from the fact that both the friends and the foes of abortion consider their position to be morally self-evident. Because pro-abortionists have never adequately come to grips with the conceptual issues surrounding abortion, most, if not all, of the arguments which they advance in opposition to laws restricting access to abortion fail to refute or even weaken the traditional antiabortion argument, i.e., that a fetus is a human being, and therefore abortion is murder.

These arguments are typically of one of two sorts. Either they point to the terrible side effects of the restrictive laws, e.g., the deaths due to illegal abortions, and the fact that it is poor women who suffer the most as a result of these laws, or else they state that to deny a woman access to abortion is to deprive her of her right to control her own body. Unfortunately, however, the fact that restricting access to abortion has tragic side effects does not, in itself, show that the restrictions are unjustified, since murder is

[1]For example, Roger Wertheimer, who in "Understanding the Abortion Argument," *Philosophy and Public Affairs,* 1, no. 1 (Fall, 1971) argues that the problem of the moral status of abortion is insoluble, in that the dispute over the status of the fetus is not a question of fact at all, but only a question of how one responds to the facts.

wrong regardless of the consequences of prohibiting it; and the appeal to the right to control one's body, which is generally construed as a property right, is at best a rather feeble argument for the permissibility of abortion. Mere ownership does not give me the right to kill innocent people whom I find on my property, and indeed I am apt to be held responsible if such people injure themselves while on my property. It is equally unclear that I have any moral right to expel an innocent person from my property when I know that doing so will result in his death.

Furthermore, it is probably inappropriate to describe a woman's body as her property, since it seems natural to hold that a person is something distinct from her property, but not from her body. Even those who would object to the identification of a person with his body, or with the conjunction of his body and his mind, must admit that it would be very odd to describe, say, breaking a leg, as damaging one's property, and much more appropriate to describe it as injuring *oneself*. Thus it is probably a mistake to argue that the right to obtain an abortion is in any way derived from the right to own and regulate property.

But however we wish to construe the right to abortion, we cannot hope to convince those who consider abortion a form of murder of the existence of any such right unless we are able to produce a clear and convincing refutation of the traditional antiabortion argument, and this has not, to my knowledge, been done. With respect to the two most vital issues which that argument involves, i.e., the humanity of the fetus and its implication for the moral status of abortion, confusion has prevailed on both sides of the dispute.

Thus, both proabortionists and antiabortionists have tended to abstract the question of whether abortion is wrong to that of whether it is wrong to destroy a fetus, just as though the rights of another person were not necessarily involved. This mistaken abstraction has led to the almost universal assumption that if a fetus is a human being, with a right to life, then it follows immediately that abortion is wrong (except perhaps when necessary to save the woman's life), and that it ought to be prohibited. It has also been generally assumed that unless the question about the status of the fetus is answered, the moral status of abortion cannot possibly be determined.

Two recent papers, one by B. A. Brody,[2] and one by Judith Thomson,[3] have attempted to settle the question of whether abortion ought to be prohibited apart from the question of whether or not the fetus is human. Brody examines the possibility that the following two statements are compatible: (1) that abortion is the taking of innocent human life, and therefore wrong; and (2) that nevertheless it ought not to be prohibited by law, at least under the present circumstances.[4] Not surprisingly, Brody finds it impossible to reconcile these two statements, since, as he rightly argues, none of the unfortunate side effects of the prohibition of abortion is bad enough to justify legalizing the *wrongful* taking of human life. He is mistaken, however, in concluding that the incompatibility of (1) and (2), in itself, shows that "the legal problem about abortion cannot be resolved independently of the status of the fetus problem" [p. 369].

What Brody fails to realize is that (1) embodies the questionable assumption that if a fetus is a human being, then of course abortion is morally wrong, and that an attack on

---

[2]B. A. Brody, "Abortion and the Law," *The Journal of Philosophy,* 68, no. 12 (June 17, 1971), 357–69.

[3]Judith Thomson, "A Defense of Abortion," *Philosophy and Public Affairs,* 1, no. 1 (Fall, 1971).

[4]I have abbreviated these statements somewhat, but not in a way which affects the argument.

this assumption is more promising, as a way of reconciling the humanity of the fetus with the claim that laws prohibiting abortion are unjustified, than is an attack on the assumption that if abortion is the wrongful killing of innocent human beings then it ought to be prohibited. He thus overlooks the possibility that a fetus may have a right to life and abortion still be morally permissible, in that the right of a woman to terminate an unwanted pregnancy might override the right of the fetus to be kept alive. The immorality of abortion is no more demonstrated by the humanity of the fetus, in itself, than the immorality of killing in self-defense is demonstrated by the fact that the assailant is a human being. Neither is it demonstrated by the *innocence* of the fetus, since there may be situations in which the killing of innocent human beings is justified.

It is perhaps not surprising that Brody fails to spot this assumption, since it has been accepted with little or no argument by nearly everyone who has written on the morality of abortion. John Noonan is correct in saying that "the fundamental question in the long history of abortion is, How do you determine the humanity of a being?"[5] He summarizes his own antiabortion argument, which is a version of the official position of the Catholic Church, as follows:

> it is wrong to kill humans, however poor, weak, defenseless, and lacking in opportunity to develop their potential they may be. It is therefore morally wrong to kill Biafrans. Similarly, it is morally wrong to kill embryos.[6]

Noonan bases his claim that fetuses are human upon what he calls the theologians' criterion of humanity: that whoever is conceived of human beings is human. But although he argues at length for the appropriateness of this criterion, he never questions the assumption that if a fetus is human then abortion is wrong for exactly the same reason that murder is wrong.

Judith Thomson is, in fact, the only writer I am aware of who has seriously questioned this assumption; she has argued that, even if we grant the antiabortionist his claim that a fetus is a human being, with the same right to life as any other human being, we can still demonstrate that, in at least some and perhaps most cases, a woman is under no moral obligation to complete an unwanted pregnancy.[7] Her argument is worth examining, since if it holds up it may enable us to establish the moral permissibility of abortion without becoming involved in problems about what entitles an entity to be considered human, and accorded full moral rights. To be able to do this would be a great gain in the power and simplicity of the proabortion position, since, although I will argue that these problems can be solved at least as decisively as can any other moral problem, we should certainly be pleased to be able to avoid having to solve them as part of the justification of abortion.

On the other hand, even if Thomson's argument does not hold up, her insight, i.e., that it requires *argument* to show that if fetuses are human then abortion is properly classified as murder, is an extremely valuable one. The assumption she attacks is

---

[5]John Noonan, "Abortion and the Catholic Church: A Summary History," *Natural Law Forum,* 12 (1967), 125.

[6]John Noonan, "Deciding Who Is Human," *Natural Law Forum,* 13 (1968), 134.

[7]"A Defense of Abortion."

particularly invidious, for it amounts to the decision that it is appropriate, in deciding the moral status of abortion, to leave the rights of the pregnant woman out of consideration entirely, except possibly when her life is threatened. Obviously, this will not do; determining what moral rights, if any, a fetus possesses is only the first step in determining the moral status of abortion. Step two, which is at least equally essential, is finding a just solution to the conflict between whatever rights the fetus may have, and the rights of the woman who is unwillingly pregnant. While the historical error has been to pay far too little attention to the second step, Ms. Thomson's suggestion is that if we look at the second step first we may find that a woman has a right to obtain an abortion *regardless* of what rights the fetus has.

Our own inquiry will also have two stages. In Section I, we will consider whether or not it is possible to establish that abortion is morally permissible even on the assumption that a fetus is an entity with a full-fledged right to life. I will argue that in fact this cannot be established, at least not with the conclusiveness which is essential to our hopes of convincing those who are skeptical about the morality of abortion, and that we therefore cannot avoid dealing with the question of whether or not a fetus really does have the same right to life as a (more fully developed) human being.

In Section II, I will propose an answer to this question, namely, that a fetus cannot be considered a member of the moral community, the set of beings with full and equal moral rights, for the simple reason that it is not a person, and that it is personhood, and not genetic humanity, i.e., humanity as defined by Noonan, which is the basis for membership in this community. I will argue that a fetus, whatever its stage of development, satisfies none of the basic criteria of personhood, and is not even enough *like* a person to be accorded even some of the same rights on the basis of this resemblance. Nor, as we will see, is a fetus's *potential* personhood a threat to the morality of abortion, since, whatever the rights of potential people may be, they are invariably overridden in any conflict with the moral rights of actual people.

I

We turn now to Professor Thomson's case for the claim that even if a fetus has full moral rights, abortion is still morally permissible, at least sometimes, and for some reasons other than to save the woman's life. Her argument is based upon a clever, but I think faulty, analogy. She asks us to picture ourselves waking up one day, in bed with a famous violinist. Imagine that you have been kidnapped, and your bloodstream hooked up to that of the violinist, who happens to have an ailment which will certainly kill him unless he is permitted to share your kidneys for a period of nine months. No one else can save him, since you alone have the right type of blood. He will be unconscious all that time, and you will have to stay in bed with him, but after the nine months are over he may be unplugged, completely cured, that is provided that you have cooperated.

Now then, she continues, what are your obligations in this situation? The antiabortionist, if he is consistent, will have to say that you are obligated to stay in bed with the violinist: for all people have a right to life, and violinists are people, and therefore it would be murder for you to disconnect yourself from him and let him die. But this is outrageous, and so there must be something wrong with the same argument when it is applied to abortion. It would certainly be commendable of you to agree to save the violinist, but it is absurd to suggest that your refusal to do so would be murder. His right to life does not obligate you to do whatever is required to keep him alive; nor does it justify anyone else in forcing you to do so. A law which required you to stay in bed with the violinist would clearly be an unjust law, since it is no proper function of the law to force unwilling people to make huge sacrifices for the sake of other people toward whom they have no such prior obligation.

Thomson concludes that, if this analogy is an apt one, then we can grant the antiabortionist his claim that a fetus is a human being, and still hold that it is at least sometimes the case that a pregnant woman has the right to refuse to be a Good Samaritan towards the fetus, i.e., to obtain an abortion. For there is a great gap between the claim that x has a right to life, and the claim that y is obligated to do whatever is necessary to keep x alive, let alone that he ought to be forced to do so. It is y's duty to keep x alive only if he has somehow contracted a *special* obligation to do so; and a woman who is unwillingly pregnant, e.g., who was raped, has done nothing which obligates her to make the enormous sacrifice which is necessary to preserve the conceptus.

This argument is initially quite plausible, and in the extreme case of pregnancy due to rape it is probably conclusive. Difficulties arise, however, when we try to specify more exactly the range of cases in which abortion is clearly justifiable even on the assumption that the fetus is human. Professor Thomson considers it a virtue of her argument that it does not enable us to conclude that abortion is *always* permissible. It would, she says, be "indecent" for a woman in her seventh month to obtain an abortion just to avoid having to postpone a trip to Europe. On the other hand, her argument enables us to see that "a sick and desperately frightened schoolgirl pregnant due to rape may *of course* choose abortion, and that any law which rules this out is an insane law." So far, so good; but what are we to say about the woman who becomes pregnant not through rape but as a result of her own carelessness, or because of contraceptive failure, or who gets pregnant intentionally and then changes her mind about wanting a child? With respect to such cases, the violinist analogy is of much less use to the defender of the woman's right to obtain an abortion.

Indeed, the choice of a pregnancy due to rape, as an example of a case in which abortion is permissible even if a fetus is considered a human being, is extremely significant; for it is only in the case of pregnancy due to rape that the woman's situation is adequately analogous to the violinist case for our intuitions about the latter to transfer convincingly. The crucial difference between a pregnancy due to rape and the *normal* case of an unwanted pregnancy is that in the normal case we cannot claim that the woman is in no way responsible for her predicament; she could have remained chaste, or taken her pills more faithfully, or abstained on dangerous days, and so on. If, on the other hand, you are kidnapped by strangers, and hooked up to a strange violinist, then you are free of any shred of responsibility for the situation, on the basis of which it could be argued that you are obligated to keep the violinist alive. Only when her pregnancy is due to rape is a woman clearly just as nonresponsible.[8]

---

[8]We may safely ignore the fact that she might have avoided getting raped, e.g., by carrying a gun, since by similar means you might likewise have avoided getting kidnapped, and in neither case does the victim's failure to take all possible precautions against a highly unlikely event (as opposed to reasonable precautions against a rather likely event) mean that she is morally responsible for what happens.

On the Moral and Legal Status of Abortion

Consequently, there is room for the antiabortionist to argue that in the normal case of unwanted pregnancy a woman has, by her own actions, assumed responsibility for the fetus. For if x behaves in a way which he could have avoided, and which he knows involves, let us say, a 1 percent chance of bringing into existence a human being, with a right to life, and does so knowing that if this should happen then that human being will perish unless x does certain things to keep him alive, then it is by no means clear that when it does happen x is free of any obligation to what he knew in advance would be required to keep that human being alive.

The plausibility of such an argument is enough to show that the Thomson analogy can provide a clear and persuasive defense of a woman's right to obtain an abortion only with respect to those cases in which the woman is in no way responsible for her pregnancy, e.g., where it is due to rape. In all other cases, we would almost certainly conclude that it was necessary to look carefully at the particular circumstances in order to determine the extent of the woman's responsibility, and hence the extent of her obligation. This is an extremely unsatisfactory outcome, from the viewpoint of the opponents of restrictive abortion laws, most of whom are convinced that a woman has a right to obtain an abortion regardless of how and why she got pregnant.

Of course a supporter of the violinist analogy might point out that it is absurd to suggest that forgetting her pill one day might be sufficient to obligate a woman to complete an unwanted pregnancy. And indeed it *is* absurd to suggest this. As we will see, the moral right to obtain an abortion is not in the least dependent upon the extent to which the woman is responsible for her pregnancy. But unfortunately, once we allow the assumption that a fetus has full moral rights, we cannot avoid taking this absurd suggestion seriously. Perhaps we can make this point more clear by altering the violinist story just enough to make it more analogous to a normal unwanted pregnancy and less to a pregnancy due to rape, and then seeing whether it is still obvious that you are not obligated to stay in bed with the fellow.

Suppose, then, that violinists are peculiarly prone to the sort of illness the only cure for which is the use of someone else's bloodstream for nine months, and that because of this there has been formed a society of music lovers who agree that whenever a violinist is stricken they will draw lots and the loser will, by some means, be made the one and only person capable of saving him. Now then, would you be obligated to cooperate in curing the violinist if you had voluntarily joined this society, knowing the possible consequences, and then your name had been drawn and you had been kidnapped? Admittedly, you did not promise ahead of time that you would, but you did deliberately place yourself in a position in which it might happen that a human life would be lost if you did not. Surely this is at least a prima facie reason for supposing that you have an obligation to stay in bed with the violinist. Suppose that you had gotten your name drawn deliberately; surely *that* would be quite a strong reason for thinking that you had such an obligation.

It might be suggested that there is one important disanalogy between the modified violinist case and the case of an unwanted pregnancy, which makes the woman's responsibility significantly less, namely, the fact that the fetus *comes into existence* as the result of the result of the woman's actions. This fact might give her a right to refuse to keep it alive, whereas she would not have had this right had it existed previously, independently, and then as a result of her actions become dependent upon her for its survival.

My own intuition, however, is that x has no more right to bring into existence either deliberately or as a foreseeable result of actions he could have avoided, a being with full moral rights (y), and then refuse to do what he knew beforehand would be required to keep that being alive, than he has to enter into an agreement with an existing person, whereby he may be called upon to save that person's life, and then refuse to do so when so called upon. Thus, x's responsibility for y's existence does not seem to lessen his obligation to keep y alive, if he is also responsible for y's being in a situation in which only he can save him.

Whether or not this intuition is entirely correct, it brings us back once again to the conclusion that once we allow the assumption that a fetus has full moral rights it becomes an extremely complex and difficult question whether and when abortion is justifiable. Thus the Thomson analogy cannot help us produce a clear and persuasive proof of the moral permissibility of abortion. Nor will the opponents of the restrictive laws thank us for anything less; for their conviction (for the most part) is that abortion is obviously *not* a morally serious and extremely unfortunate, even though sometimes justified act, comparable to killing in self-defense or to letting the violinist die, but rather is closer to being a morally neutral act, like cutting one's hair.

The basis of this conviction, I believe, is the realization that a fetus is not a person, and thus does not have a full-fledged right to life. Perhaps the reason why this claim has been so inadequately defended is that it seems self-evident to those who accept it. And so it is, insofar as it follows from what I take to be perfectly obvious claims about the nature of personhood, and about the proper grounds for ascribing moral rights, claims which ought, indeed, to be obvious to both the friends and foes of abortion. Nevertheless, it is worth examining these claims and showing how they demonstrate the moral innocuousness of abortion, since this apparently has not been adequately done before.

II

The question which we must answer in order to produce a satisfactory solution to the problem of the moral status of abortion is this: How are we to define the moral community, the set of beings with full and equal moral rights, such that we can decide whether a human fetus is a member of this community or not? What sort of entity, exactly, has the inalienable rights to life, liberty, and the pursuit of happiness? Jefferson attributed these rights to all *men*, and it may or may not be fair to suggest that he intended to attribute them *only* to men. Perhaps he ought to have attributed them to all human beings. If so, then we arrive, first, at Noonan's problem of defining what makes a being human, and second, at the equally vital question which Noonan does not consider, namely, What reason is there for identifying the moral community with the set of all human beings, in whatever way we have chosen to define that term?

1. On the Definition of 'Human'

One reason why this vital second question is so frequently overlooked in the debate over the moral status of abortion is that the term 'human' has two distinct, but not often distinguished, senses. This fact results in a slide of meaning, which serves to conceal the fallaciousness of the traditional argument that since (1) it is wrong to kill innocent human beings, and (2) fetuses are innocent human beings, then (3) it is wrong to kill fetuses. For if 'human' is used in the same sense in both (1) and (2) then, whichever of the two senses is meant, one of these premises is question-begging. And if it is used in two different senses then of course the conclusion doesn't follow.

Thus, (1) is a self-evident moral truth,[9] and avoids begging the question about abortion, only if 'human being' is used to mean something like "a full-fledged member of the moral community." (It may or may not also be meant to refer exclusively to members of the species *Homo sapiens*.) We may call this the *moral* sense of 'human.' It is not to be confused with what we will call the *genetic* sense, i.e., the sense in which *any* member of the species is a human being, and no member of any other species could be. If (1) is acceptable only if the moral sense is intended, (2) is non-question-begging only if what is intended is the genetic sense.

In "Deciding Who Is Human," Noonan argues for the classification of fetuses with human beings by pointing to the presence of the full genetic code, and the potential capacity for rational thought (p. 135). It is clear that what he needs to show, for his version of the traditional argument to be valid, is that fetuses are human in the moral sense, the sense in which it is analytically true that all human beings have full moral rights. But, in the absence of any argument showing that whatever is genetically human is also morally human, and he gives none, nothing more than genetic humanity can be demonstrated by the presence of the human genetic code. And, as we will see, the *potential* capacity for rational thought can at most show that an entity has the potential for *becoming* human in the moral sense.

2. Defining the Moral Community

Can it be established that genetic humanity is sufficient for moral humanity? I think that there are very good reasons for not defining the moral community in this way. I would like to suggest an alternative way of defining the moral community, which I will argue for only to the extent of explaining why it is, or should be, self-evident. The suggestion is simply that the moral community consists of all and only *people,* rather than all and only human beings;[10] and probably the best way of demonstrating its self-evidence is by considering the concept of personhood, to see what sorts of entity are and are not persons, and what the decision that a being is or is not a person implies about its moral rights.

What characteristics entitle an entity to be considered a person? This is obviously not the place to attempt a complete analysis of the concept of personhood, but we do not need such a fully adequate analysis just to determine whether and why a fetus is or isn't a person. All we need is a rough and approximate list of the most basic criteria of

---

[9]Of course, the principle that it is (always) wrong to kill innocent human beings is in need of many other modifications, e.g., that it may be permissible to do so to save a greater number of other innocent human beings, but we may safely ignore these complications here.

[10]From here on, we will use 'human' to mean genetically human, since the moral sense seems closely connected to, and perhaps derived from, the assumption that genetic humanity is sufficient for membership in the moral community.

personhood, and some idea of which, or how many, of these an entity must satisfy in order to properly be considered a person.

In searching for such criteria, it is useful to look beyond the set of people with whom we are acquainted, and ask how we would decide whether a totally alien being was a person or not. (For we have no right to assume that genetic humanity is necessary for personhood.) Imagine a space traveler who lands on an unknown planet and encounters a race of beings utterly unlike any he has ever seen or heard of. If he wants to be sure of behaving morally toward these beings, he has to somehow decide whether they are people, and hence have full moral rights, or whether they are the sort of thing which he need not feel guilty about treating as, for example, a source of food.

How should he go about making this decision? If he has some anthropological background, he might look for such things as religion, art, and the manufacturing of tools, weapons, or shelters, since these factors have been used to distinguish our human from our prehuman ancestors, in what seems to be closer to the moral than the genetic sense of 'human.' And no doubt he would be right to consider the presence of such factors as good evidence that the alien beings were people, and morally human. It would, however, be overly anthropocentric of him to take the absence of these things as adequate evidence that they were not, since we can imagine people who have progressed beyond, or evolved without ever developing, these cultural characteristics.

I suggest that the traits which are most central to the concept of personhood, or humanity in the moral sense, are, very roughly, the following:

1. consciousness (of objects and events external and/or internal to the being), and in particular the capacity to feel pain;

2. reasoning (the *developed* capacity to solve new and relatively complex problems);

3. self-motivated activity (activity which is relatively independent of either genetic or direct external control);

4. the capacity to communicate, by whatever means, messages of an indefinite variety of types, that is, not just with an indefinite number of possible contents, but on indefinitely many possible topics;

5. the presence of self-concepts, and self-awareness, either individual or racial, or both.

Admittedly, there are apt to be a great many problems involved in formulating precise definitions of these criteria, let alone in developing universally valid behavioral criteria for deciding when they apply. But I will assume that both we and our explorer know approximately what (1)–(5) mean, and that he is also able to determine whether or not they apply. How, then, should he use his findings to decide whether or not the alien beings are people? We needn't suppose that an entity must have *all* of these attributes to be properly considered a person; (1) and (2) alone may well be sufficient for personhood, and quite probably (1)–(3) are sufficient. Neither do we need to insist that any one of these criteria is *necessary* for personhood, although once again (1) and (2) look like fairly good candidates for necessary conditions, as does (3), if 'activity' is construed so as to include the activity of reasoning.

All we need to claim, to demonstrate that a fetus is not a person, is that any being which satisfies *none* of (1)–(5) is certainly not a person. I consider this claim to be so obvious that I think anyone who denied it, and claimed that a being which satisfied none of (1)–(5) was a person all the same, would thereby demonstrate that he had no notion at all of what a person is—perhaps because he had confused the concept of a person with that of genetic humanity. If the opponents of abortion were to deny the appropriateness of these five criteria, I do not know what further arguments would convince them. We would probably have to admit that our conceptual schemes were indeed irreconcilably different, and that our dispute could not be settled objectively.

I do not expect this to happen, however, since I think that the concept of a person is one which is very nearly universal (to people), and that it is common to both proabortionists and antiabortionists, even though neither group has fully realized the relevance of this concept to the resolution of their dispute. Furthermore, I think that on reflection even antiabortionists ought to agree not only that (1)–(5) are central to the concept of personhood, but also that it is a part of this concept that all and only people have full moral rights. The concept of a person is in part a moral concept; once we have admitted that *x* is a person we have recognized, even if we have not agreed to respect, *x*'s right to be treated as a member of the moral community. It is true that the claim that *x* is a *human being* is more commonly voiced as part of an appeal to treat *x* decently than is the claim that *x* is a person, but this is either because 'human being' is here used in the sense which implies personhood, or because the genetic and moral senses of 'human' have been confused.

Now if (1)–(5) are indeed the primary criteria of personhood, then it is clear that genetic humanity is neither necessary nor sufficient for establishing that an entity is a person. Some human beings are not people, and there may well be people who are not human beings. A man or woman whose consciousness has been permanently obliterated but who remains alive is a human being which is no longer a person; defective human beings, with no appreciable mental capacity, are not and presumably never will be people; and a fetus is a human being which is not yet a person, and which therefore cannot coherently be said to have full moral rights. Citizens of the next century should be prepared to recognize highly advanced, self-aware robots or computers, should such be developed, and intelligent inhabitants of other worlds, should such be found, as people in the fullest sense, and to respect their moral rights. But to ascribe full moral rights to an entity which is not a person is as absurd as to ascribe moral obligations and responsibilities to such an entity.

3. Fetal Development and the Right to Life

Two problems arise in the application of these suggestions for the definition of the moral community to the determination of the precise moral status of a human fetus. Given that the paradigm example of a person is a normal adult human being, then (1) How like this paradigm, in particular how far advanced since conception, does a human being need to be before it begins to have a right to life by virtue, not of being fully a person as of yet, but of being *like* a person? and (2) To what extent, if any, does the fact that a fetus has the *potential* for becoming a person endow it with some of the same rights? Each of these questions requires some comment.

In answering the first question, we need not attempt a detailed consideration of the moral rights of organisms which are not developed enough, aware enough, intelligent enough, etc., to be considered people, but which resemble people in some respects. It does seem reasonable to suggest that the more like a person, in the relevant respects, a being is, the stronger is the case for regarding it as having a right to life, and indeed the stronger its right to life is. Thus we ought to take seriously the suggestion that, insofar as "the human individual develops biologically in a continuous fashion . . . the rights of a human person might develop in the same way."[11] But we must keep in mind that the attributes which are relevant in determining whether or not an entity is enough like a person to be regarded as having some of the same moral rights are no different from those which are relevant to determining whether or not it is fully a person—i.e., are no different from (1)–(5)—and that being genetically human, or having recognizably human facial and other physical features, or detectable brain activity, or the capacity to survive outside the uterus, are simply not among these relevant attributes.

Thus it is clear that even though a seven- or eight-month fetus has features which make it apt to arouse in us almost the same powerful protective instinct as is commonly aroused by a small infant, nevertheless it is not significantly more personlike than is a very small embryo. It is *somewhat* more personlike; it can apparently feel and respond to pain, and it may even have a rudimentary form of consciousness, insofar as its brain is quite active. Nevertheless, it seems safe to say that it is not fully conscious, in the way that an infant of a few months is, and that it cannot reason, or communicate messages of indefinitely many sorts, does not engage in self-motivated activity, and has no self-awareness. Thus, in the *relevant* respects, a fetus, even a fully developed one, is considerably less personlike than is the average mature mammal, indeed the average fish. And I think that a rational person must conclude that if the right to life of a fetus is to be based upon its resemblance to a person, then it cannot be said to have any more right to life than, let us say, a newborn guppy (which also seems to be capable of feeling pain), and that a right of that magnitude could never override a woman's right to obtain an abortion, at any stage of her pregnancy.

There may, of course, be other arguments in favor of placing legal limits upon the stage of pregnancy in which an abortion may be performed. Given the relative safety of the new techniques of artificially inducing labor during the third trimester, the danger to the woman's life or health is no longer such an argument. Neither is the fact that people tend to respond to the thought of abortion in the later stages of pregnancy with emotional repulsion, since mere emotional responses cannot take the place of moral reasoning in determining what ought to be permitted. Nor, finally, is the frequently heard argument that legalizing abortion, especially late in the pregnancy, may erode the level of respect for human life, leading, perhaps, to an increase in unjustified euthanasia and other crimes. For this threat, if it is a threat, can be better met by educating people to the kinds of moral distinctions which we are making here than by limiting access to abortion (which limitation may, in its disregard for the rights of women, be just as damaging to the level of respect for human rights).

Thus, since the fact that even a fully developed fetus is not personlike enough to have any significant right to life on the basis of its personlikeness shows that no legal restrictions upon the stage of pregnancy in which an abortion may be performed can be justified on the grounds that we should protect the rights of the older fetus; and since there

---

[11]Thomas L. Hayes, "A Biological View," *Commonweal,* 85 (March 17, 1967), 677–78; quoted by Daniel Callahan, in *Abortion, Law, Choice, and Morality* (London: Macmillan & Co., 1970).

is no other apparent justification for such restrictions, we may conclude that they are entirely unjustified. Whether or not it would be *indecent* (whatever that means) for a woman in her seventh month to obtain an abortion just to avoid having to postpone a trip to Europe, it would not, in itself, be *immoral,* and therefore it ought to be permitted.

4. Potential Personhood and the Right to Life

We have seen that a fetus does not resemble a person in any way which can support the claim that it has even some of the same rights. But what about its *potential,* the fact that if nurtured and allowed to develop naturally it will very probably become a person? Doesn't that alone give it at least some right to life? It is hard to deny that the fact that an entity is a potential person is a strong prima facie reason for not destroying it; but we need not conclude from this that a potential person has a right to life, by virtue of that potential. It may be that our feeling that it is better, other things being equal, not to destroy a potential person is better explained by the fact that potential people are still (felt to be) an invaluable resource, not to be lightly squandered. Surely, if every speck of dust were a potential person, we would be much less apt to conclude that every potential person has a right to become actual.

Still, we do not need to insist that a potential person has no right to life whatever. There may well be something immoral, and not just imprudent, about wantonly destroying potential people, when doing so isn't necessary to protect anyone's rights. But even if a potential person does have some prima facie right to life, such a right could not possibly outweigh the right of a woman to obtain an abortion, since the rights of any actual person invariably outweigh those of any potential person, whenever the two conflict. Since this may not be immediately obvious in the case of a human fetus, let us look at another case.

Suppose that our space explorer falls into the hands of an alien culture, whose scientists decide to create a few hundred thousand or more human beings, by breaking his body into its component cells, and using these to create fully developed human beings, with, of course, his genetic code. We may imagine that each of these newly created men will have all of the original man's abilities, skills, knowledge, and so on, and also have an individual self-concept, in short that each of them will be a bona fide (though hardly unique) person. Imagine that the whole project will take only seconds, and that its chances of success are extremely high, and that our explorer knows all of this, and also knows that these people will be treated fairly. I maintain that in such a situation he would have every right to escape if he could, and thus to deprive all of these potential people of their potential lives; for his right to life outweighs all of theirs together, in spite of the fact that they are all genetically human, all innocent, and all have a very high probability of becoming people very soon, if only he refrains from acting.

Indeed, I think he would have a right to escape even if it were not his life which the alien scientists planned to take, but only a year of his freedom, or, indeed, only a day. Nor would he be obligated to stay if he had gotten captured (thus bringing all these people-potentials into existence) because of his own carelessness, or even if he had done so deliberately, knowing the consequences. Regardless of how he got captured, he is not morally obligated to remain in captivity for *any* period of time for the sake of permitting any number of potential people to come into actuality, so great is the margin by which one actual person's right to liberty outweighs whatever right to life even a hundred thousand potential people have. And it seems reasonable to conclude that the rights of a woman will outweigh by a similar margin whatever right to life a fetus may have by virtue of its potential personhood.

Thus, neither a fetus's resemblance to a person, nor its potential for becoming a person provides any basis whatever for the claim that it has any significant right to life. Consequently, a woman's right to protect her health, happiness, freedom, and even her life,[12] by terminating an unwanted pregnancy, will always override whatever right to life it may be appropriate to ascribe to a fetus, even a fully developed one. And thus, in the absence of any overwhelming social need for every possible child, the laws which restrict the right to obtain an abortion, or limit the period of pregnancy during which an abortion may be performed, are a wholly unjustified violation of a woman's most basic moral and constitutional rights.[13]

Postscript on Infanticide, February 26, 1982

One of the most troubling objections to the argument presented in this article is that it may appear to justify not only abortion but infanticide as well. A newborn infant is not a great deal more personlike than a nine-month fetus, and thus it might seem that if late-term abortion is sometimes justified, then infanticide must also be sometimes justified. Yet most people consider that infanticide is a form of murder, and thus never justified.

While it is important to appreciate the emotional force of this objection, its logical force is far less than it may seem at first glance. There are many reasons why infanticide is much more difficult to justify than abortion, even though if my argument is correct neither constitutes the killing of a person. In this country, and in this period of history, the deliberate killing of viable newborns is virtually never justified. This is in part because neonates are so very *close* to being persons that to kill them requires a very strong moral justification—as does the killing of dolphins, whales, chimpanzees, and other highly personlike creatures. It is certainly wrong to kill such beings just for the sake of convenience, or financial profit, or "sport."

Another reason why infanticide is usually wrong, in our society, is that if the newborn's parents do not want it, or are unable to care for it, there are (in most cases) people who are able and eager to adopt it and to provide a good home for it. Many people wait years for the opportunity to adopt a

---

[12]That is, insofar as the death rate, for the woman, is higher for childbirth than for early abortion.

[13]My thanks to the following people, who were kind enough to read and criticize an earlier version of this paper: Herbert Gold, Gene Glass, Anne Lauterbach, Judith Thomson, Mary Mothersill, and Timothy Binkley.

child, and some are unable to do so even though there is every reason to believe that they would be good parents. The needless destruction of a viable infant inevitably deprives some person or persons of a source of great pleasure and satisfaction, perhaps severely impoverishing their lives. Furthermore, even if an infant is considered to be unadoptable (e.g., because of some extremely severe mental or physical handicap) it is still wrong in most cases to kill it. For most of us value the lives of infants, and would prefer to pay taxes to support orphanages and state institutions for the handicapped rather than to allow unwanted infants to be killed. So long as most people feel this way, and so long as our society can afford to provide care for infants which are unwanted or which have special needs that preclude home care, it is wrong to destroy any infant which has a chance of living a reasonably satisfactory life.

If these arguments show that infanticide is wrong, at least in this society, then why don't they also show that late-term abortion is wrong? After all, third trimester fetuses are also highly personlike, and many people value them and would much prefer that they be preserved, even at some cost to themselves. As a potential source of pleasure to some family, a viable fetus is just as valuable as a viable infant. But there is an obvious and crucial difference between the two cases: once the infant is born, its continued life cannot (except, perhaps, in very exceptional cases) pose any serious threat to the woman's life or health, since she is free to put it up for adoption, or, where this is impossible, to place it in a state-supported institution. While she might prefer that it die, rather than being raised by others, it is not clear that such a preference would constitute a right on her part. True, she may suffer greatly from the knowledge that her child will be thrown into the lottery of the adoption system, and that she will be unable to ensure its well-being, or even to know whether it is healthy, happy, doing well in school, etc.; for the law generally does not permit natural parents to remain in contact with their children, once they are adopted by another family. But there are surely better ways of dealing with these problems than by permitting infanticide in such cases. (It might help, for instance, if the natural parents of adopted children could at least receive some information about their progress, without necessarily being informed of the identity of the adopting family.)

In contrast, a pregnant woman's right to protect her own life and health clearly outweighs other people's desire that the fetus be preserved—just as, when a person's life or limb is threatened by some wild animal, and when the threat cannot be removed without killing the animal, the person's right to self-protection outweighs the desires of those who would prefer that the animal not be harmed. Thus, while the moment of birth may not mark any sharp discontinuity in the degree to which an infant possesses a right to life, it does mark the end of the mother's absolute right to determine its fate. Indeed, if and when a late-term abortion could be safely performed without killing the fetus, she would have no absolute right to insist on its death (e.g., if others wish to adopt it or to pay for its care), for the same reason that she does not have a right to insist that a viable infant be killed.

It remains true that according to my argument neither abortion nor the killing of neonates is properly considered a form of murder. Perhaps it is understandable that the law should classify infanticide as murder or homicide, since there is no other existing legal category which adequately or conveniently expresses the force of our society's disapproval of this action. But the moral distinction remains, and it has several important consequences.

In the first place, it implies that when an infant is born into a society which—unlike ours—is so impoverished that it simply cannot care for it adequately without endangering the survival of existing persons, killing it or allowing it to die is not necessarily wrong—provided that there is no *other* society which is willing and able to provide such care. Most human societies, from those at the hunting and gathering stage of economic development to the highly civilized Greeks and Romans, have permitted the practice of infanticide under such unfortunate circumstances, and I would argue that it shows a serious lack of understanding to condemn them as morally backward for this reason alone.

In the second place, the argument implies that when an infant is born with such severe physical anomalies that its life would predictably be a very short and/or very miserable one, even with the most heroic of medical treatment, and where its parents do not choose to bear the often crushing emotional, financial and other burdens attendant upon the artificial prolongation of such a tragic life, it is not morally wrong to cease or withhold treatment, thus allowing the infant a painless death. It is wrong (and sometimes a form of murder) to practice involuntary euthanasia on persons, since they have the right to decide for themselves whether or not they wish to continue to live. But terminally ill neonates cannot make this decision for themselves, and thus it is incumbent upon responsible persons to make the decision for them, as best they can. The mistaken belief that infanticide is always tantamount to murder is responsible for a great deal of unnecessary suffering, not just on the part of infants which are made to endure needlessly prolonged and painful deaths, but also on the part of parents, nurses, and other involved persons, who must watch infants suffering needlessly, helpless to end that suffering in the most humane way.

I am well aware that these conclusions, however modest and reasonable they may seem to some people, strike other people as morally monstrous, and that some people might even prefer to abandon their previous support for women's right to abortion rather than accept a theory which leads to such conclusions about infanticide. But all that these facts show is that abortion is not an isolated moral issue; to fully understand the moral status of abortion we may have to reconsider other moral issues as well, issues not just about infanticide and euthanasia, but also about the moral rights of women and of nonhuman animals. It is a philosopher's task to criticize mistaken beliefs which stand in the way of moral understanding, even when—perhaps especially when—those beliefs are popular and widespread. The belief that moral strictures against killing should apply equally to all genetically human entities, and *only* to genetically human entities, is such an error. The overcoming of this error will undoubtedly require long and often painful struggle; but it must be done.

A Defense of Abortion[1]

Judith Jarvis Thomson

Most opposition to abortion relies on the premise that the fetus is a human being, a person, from the moment of conception. The premise is argued for, but, as I think, not well. Take, for example, the most common argument. We are asked to notice that the development of a human being from conception through birth into childhood is continuous; then it is said that to draw a line, to choose a point in this development and say "before this point the thing is not a person, after this point it is a person" is to make an arbitrary choice, a choice for which in the nature of things no good reason can be given. It is concluded that the fetus is, or anyway that we had better say it is, a person from the moment of conception. But this conclusion does not follow. Similar things might be said about the development of an acorn into an oak tree, and it does not follow that acorns are oak trees, or that we had better say they are. Arguments of this form are sometimes called "slippery slope arguments"—the phrase is perhaps self-explanatory—and it is dismaying that opponents of abortion rely on them so heavily and uncritically.

I am inclined to agree, however, that the prospects for "drawing a line" in the development of the fetus look dim. I am inclined to think also that we shall probably have to agree that the fetus has already become a human person well before birth. Indeed, it comes as a surprise when one first learns how early in its life it begins to acquire human characteristics. By the tenth week, for example, it already has a face, arms and legs, fingers and toes; it has internal organs, and brain activity is detectable.[2] On the other hand, I think that the premise is false, that the fetus is not a person from the moment of conception. A newly fertilized ovum, a newly implanted clump of cells, is no more a person than an acorn is an oak tree. But I shall not discuss any of this. For it seems to me

From "A Defense of Abortion" by Judith Jarvis Thomson, *Philosophy & Public Affairs,* vol. 1, no. 1 (copyright © 1971 by Princeton University Press), pp. 47–66. Reprinted by permission of Princeton University Press.

[1] I am very much indebted to James Thomson for discussion, criticism, and many helpful suggestions.

[2] Daniel Callahan, *Abortion: Law, Choice and Morality* (New York, 1970), p. 373. This book gives a fascinating survey of the available information on abortion. The Jewish tradition is surveyed in David M. Feldman, *Birth Control in Jewish Law* (New York, 1968), Part 5; the Catholic tradition in John T. Noonan, Jr., "An Almost Absolute Value in History," in *The Morality of Abortion,* ed. John T. Noonan, Jr. (Cambridge, Mass., 1970).

to be of great interest to ask what happens if, for the sake of argument, we allow the premise. How, precisely, are we supposed to get from there to the conclusion that abortion is morally impermissible? Opponents of abortion commonly spend most of their time establishing that the fetus is a person, and hardly any time explaining the step from there to the impermissibility of abortion. Perhaps they think the step too simple and obvious to require much comment. Or perhaps instead they are simply being economical in argument. Many of those who defend abortion rely on the premise that the fetus is not a person, but only a bit of tissue that will become a person at birth; and why pay out more arguments than you have to? Whatever the explanation, I suggest that the step they take is neither easy nor obvious, that it calls for closer examination than it is commonly given, and that when we do give it this closer examination we shall feel inclined to reject it.

I propose, then, that we grant that the fetus is a person from the moment of conception. How does the argument go from here? Something like this, I take it. Every person has a right to life. So the fetus has a right to life. No doubt the mother has a right to decide what shall happen in and to her body; everyone would grant that. But surely a person's right to life is stronger and more stringent than the mother's right to decide what happens in and to her body, and so outweighs it. So the fetus may not be killed; an abortion may not be performed.

It sounds plausible. But now let me ask you to imagine this. You wake up in the morning and find yourself back to back in bed with an unconscious violinist. A famous unconscious violinist. He has been found to have a fatal kidney ailment, and the Society of Music Lovers has canvassed all the available medical records and found that you alone have the right blood type to help. They have therefore kidnapped you, and last night the violinist's circulatory system was plugged into yours, so that your kidneys can be used to extract poisons from his blood as well as your own. The director of the hospital now tells you, "Look, we're sorry the Society of Music Lovers did this to you—we would never have permitted it if we had known. But still, they did it, and the violinist now is plugged into you. To unplug you would be to kill him. But never mind, it's only for nine months. By then he will have recovered from his ailment, and can safely be unplugged from you." Is it morally incumbent on you to accede to this situation? No doubt it would be very nice of you if you did, a great kindness. But do you *have* to accede to it? What if it were not nine months, but nine years? Or longer still? What if the director of the hospital says, "Tough luck, I agree, but you've now got to stay in bed, with the violinist plugged into you, for the rest of your life. Because remember this. All persons have a right to life, and violinists are persons. Granted you have a right to decide what happens in and to your body, but a person's right to life outweighs your right to decide what happens in and to your body. So you cannot ever be unplugged from him." I imagine you would regard this as outrageous, which suggests that something really is wrong with that plausible-sounding argument I mentioned a moment ago.

In this case, of course, you were kidnapped; you didn't volunteer for the operation that plugged the violinist into your kidneys. Can those who oppose abortion on the ground I mentioned make an exception for a pregnancy due to rape? Certainly. They can say that persons have a right to life only if they didn't come into existence because of rape; or they can say that all persons have a right to life, but that some have less of a right to life than others, in particular, that those who came into existence because of rape have less. But these statements have a rather unpleasant sound. Surely the question of whether you have a right to life at all, or how much of it you have, shouldn't turn on the question of whether or not you are the product of a rape. And in fact the people who oppose abortion on the ground I mentioned do not make this distinction, and hence do not make an exception in case of rape.

Nor do they make an exception for a case in which the mother has to spend the nine months of her pregnancy in bed. They would agree that would be a great pity, and hard on the mother; but all the same, all persons have a right to life, the fetus is a person, and so on. I suspect, in fact, that they would not make an exception for a case in which, miraculously enough, the pregnancy went on for nine years, or even the rest of the mother's life.

Some won't even make an exception for a case in which continuation of the pregnancy is likely to shorten the mother's life; they regard abortion as impermissible even to save the mother's life. Such cases are nowadays very rare, and many opponents of abortion do not accept this extreme view. All the same, it is a good place to begin: a number of points of interest come out in respect to it.

1. Let us call the view that abortion is impermissible even to save the mother's life "the extreme view." I want to suggest first that it does not issue from the argument I mentioned earlier without the addition of some fairly powerful premises. Suppose a woman has become pregnant, and now learns that she has a cardiac condition such that she will die if she carries the baby to term. What may be done for her? The fetus, being a person, has a right to life, but as the mother is a person too, so has she a right to life. Presumably they have an equal right to life. How is it supposed to come out that an abortion may not be performed? If mother and child have an equal right to life, shouldn't we perhaps flip a coin? Or should we add to the mother's right to life her right to decide what happens in and to her body, which everybody seems to be ready to grant—the sum of her rights now outweighing the fetus' right to life?

The most familiar argument here is the following. We are told that performing the abortion would be directly killing[3] the child, whereas doing nothing would not be killing the mother, but only letting her die. Moreover, in killing the child, one would be killing an innocent person, for the child has committed no crime, and is not aiming at his mother's death. And then there are a variety of ways in which this might be continued. (1) But as directly killing an innocent person is always and absolutely impermissible, an abortion may not be performed. Or, (2) as directly killing an innocent person is murder, and murder is always and absolutely impermissible, an abortion may not be performed.[4] Or, (3) as one's duty to refrain from directly killing an innocent person is more stringent than one's duty to keep a person from dying, an abortion may not be performed. Or, (4) if one's only options are directly killing an innocent person or letting a

---

[3]The term "direct" in the arguments I refer to is a technical one. Roughly, what is meant by "direct killing" is either killing as an end in itself, or killing as a means of some end, for example, the end of saving someone else's life. See footnote 6 for an example of its use.

[4]Cf. *Encyclical Letter of Pope Pius XI on Christian Marriage,* St. Paul Editions (Boston, n.d.), p. 32: "however much we may pity the mother whose health and even life is gravely imperiled in the performance of the duty allotted to her by nature, nevertheless what could ever be a sufficient reason for excusing in any way the direct murder of the innocent? This is precisely what we are dealing with here." Noonan (*The Morality of Abortion,* p. 43) reads this as follows: "What cause can ever avail to excuse in any way the direct killing of the innocent? For it is a question of that."

person die, one must prefer letting the person die, and thus an abortion may not be performed.[5]

Some people seem to have thought that these are not further premises which must be added if the conclusion is to be reached, but that they follow from the very fact that an innocent person has a right to life.[6] But this seems to me to be a mistake, and perhaps the simplest way to show this is to bring out that while we must certainly grant that innocent persons have a right to life, the theses in (1) through (4) are all false. Take (2), for example. If directly killing an innocent person is murder, and thus is impermissible, then the mother's directly killing the innocent person inside her is murder, and thus is impermissible. But it cannot seriously be thought to be murder if the mother performs an abortion on herself to save her life. It cannot seriously be said that she *must* refrain, that she *must* sit passively by and wait for her death. Let us look again at the case of you and the violinist. There you are, in bed with the violinist, and the director of the hospital says to you, "It's all most distressing, and I deeply sympathize, but you see this is putting an additional strain on your kidneys, and you'll be dead within the month. But you *have* to stay where you are all the same. Because unplugging you would be directly killing an innocent violinist, and that's murder, and that's impermissible." If anything in the world is true, it is that you do not commit murder, you do not do what is impermissible, if you reach around to your back and unplug yourself from that violinist to save your life.

The main focus of attention in writings on abortion has been on what a third party may or may not do in answer to a request from a woman for an abortion. This is in a way understandable. Things being as they are, there isn't much a woman can safely do to abort herself. So the question asked is what a third party may do, and what the mother may do, if it is mentioned at all, is deduced, almost as an afterthought, from what it is concluded that third parties may do. But it seems to me that to treat the matter in this way is to refuse to grant to the mother that very status of person which is so firmly insisted on for the fetus. For we cannot simply read off what a person may do from what a third party may do. Suppose you find yourself trapped in a tiny house with a growing child. I mean a very tiny house, and a rapidly growing child—you are already up against the wall of the house and in a few minutes you'll be crushed to death. The child on the other hand won't be crushed to death; if nothing is done to stop him from growing he'll be hurt, but in the end he'll simply burst open the house and walk out a free man. Now I could well understand it if a bystander were to say, "There's nothing we can do for you. We cannot choose between your life and his, we cannot be

---

[5]The thesis in (4) is in an interesting way weaker than those in (1), (2), and (3): they rule out abortion even in cases in which both mother *and* child will die if the abortion is not performed. By contrast, one who held the view expressed in (4) could consistently say that one needn't prefer letting two persons die to killing one.

[6]Cf. the following passage from Pius XII, *Address to the Italian Catholic Society of Midwives:* "The baby in the maternal breast has the right to life immediately from God.—Hence there is no man, no human authority, no science, no medical, eugenic, social, economic or moral 'indication' which can establish or grant a valid juridical ground for a direct deliberate disposition of an innocent human life, that is a disposition which looks to its destruction either as an end or as a means to another end perhaps in itself not illicit.—The baby, still not born, is a man in the same degree and for the same reason as the mother" (quoted in Noonan, *The Morality of Abortion,* p. 45).

the ones to decide who is to live, we cannot intervene." But it cannot be concluded that you too can do nothing, that you cannot attack it to save your life. However innocent the child may be, you do not have to wait passively while it crushes you to death. Perhaps a pregnant woman is vaguely felt to have the status of house, to which we don't allow the right of self-defense. But if the woman houses the child, it should be remembered that she is a person who houses it.

I should perhaps stop to say explicitly that I am not claiming that people have a right to do anything whatever to save their lives. I think, rather, that there are drastic limits to the right of self-defense. If someone threatens you with death unless you torture someone else to death, I think you have not the right, even to save your life, to do so. But the case under consideration here is very different. In our case there are only two people involved, one whose life is threatened, and one who threatens it. Both are innocent: the one who is threatened is not threatened because of any fault, the one who threatens does not threaten because of any fault. For this reason we may feel that we bystanders cannot intervene. But the person threatened can.

In sum, a woman surely can defend her life against the threat to it posed by the unborn child, even if doing so involves its death. And this shows not merely that the theses in (1) through (4) are false; it shows also that the extreme view of abortion is false, and so we need not canvass any other possible ways of arriving at it from the argument I mentioned at the outset.

2. The extreme view could of course be weakened to say that while abortion is permissible to save the mother's life, it may not be performed by a third party, but only by the mother herself. But this cannot be right either. For what we have to keep in mind is that the mother and the unborn child are not like two tenants in a small house which has, by an unfortunate mistake, been rented to both: the mother *owns* the house. The fact that she does adds to the offensiveness of deducing that the mother can do nothing from the supposition that third parties can do nothing. But it does more than this: it casts a bright light on the supposition that third parties can do nothing. Certainly it lets us see that a third party who says "I cannot choose between you" is fooling himself if he thinks this is impartiality. If Jones has found and fastened on a certain coat, which he needs to keep him from freezing, but which Smith also needs to keep him from freezing, then it is not impartiality that says "I cannot choose between you" when Smith owns the coat. Women have said again and again "This body is *my* body!" and they have reason to feel angry, reason to feel that it has been like shouting into the wind. Smith, after all, is hardly likely to bless us if we say to him, "Of course it's your coat, anybody would grant that it is. But no one may choose between you and Jones who is to have it."

We should really ask what it is that says "no one may choose" in the face of the fact that the body that houses the child is the mother's body. It may be simply a failure to appreciate this fact. But it may be something more interesting, namely the sense that one has a right to refuse to lay hands on people, even where it would be just and fair to do so, even where justice seems to require that somebody do so. Thus justice might call for somebody to get Smith's coat back from Jones, and yet you have a right to refuse to be the one to lay hands on Jones, a right to refuse to do physical violence to him. This, I think, must be granted. But then what should be said is not "no one may choose," but only "*I* cannot choose," and indeed not even this, but "*I* will not *act*," leaving it open that somebody else can or should, and in particular that anyone in a position of authority, with the job of securing people's rights, both can and should. So this is no difficulty. I have not been arguing that any given third party must accede to the mother's request that he perform an abortion to save her life, but only that he may.

I suppose that in some views of human life the mother's body is only on loan to her, the loan not being one which gives her any prior claim to it. One who held this view might well think it impartiality to say "I cannot choose." But I shall simply ignore this possibility. My own view is that if a human being has any just, prior claim to anything at all, he has a just, prior claim to his own body. And perhaps this needn't be argued for here anyway, since, as I mentioned, the arguments against abortion we are looking at do grant that the woman has a right to decide what happens in and to her body.

But although they do grant it, I have tried to show that they do not take seriously what is done in granting it. I suggest the same thing will reappear even more clearly when we turn away from cases in which the mother's life is at stake, and attend, as I propose we now do, to the vastly more common cases in which a woman wants an abortion for some less weighty reason than preserving her own life.

3. Where the mother's life is not at stake, the argument I mentioned at the outset seems to have a much stronger pull. "Everyone has a right to life, so the unborn person has a right to life." And isn't the child's right to life weightier than anything other than the mother's own right to life, which she might put forward as ground for an abortion?

This argument treats the right to life as if it were unproblematic. It is not, and this seems to me to be precisely the source of the mistake.

For we should now, at long last, ask what it comes to, to have a right to life. In some views having a right to life includes having a right to be given at least the bare minimum one needs for continued life. But suppose that what in fact *is* the bare minimum a man needs for continued life is something he has no right at all to be given? If I am sick unto death, and the only thing that will save my life is the touch of Henry Fonda's cool hand on my fevered brow, then all the same, I have no right to be given the touch of Henry Fonda's cool hand on my fevered brow. It would be frightfully nice of him to fly in from the West Coast to provide it. It would be less nice, though no doubt well meant, if my friends flew out to the West Coast and carried Henry Fonda back with them. But I have no right at all against anybody that he should do this for me. Or again, to return to the story I told earlier, the fact that for continued life that violinist needs the continued use of your kidneys does not establish that he has a right to be given the continued use of your kidneys. He certainly has no right against you that *you* should give him continued use of your kidneys. For nobody has any right to use your kidneys unless you give him such a right; and nobody has the right against you that you shall give him this right—if you do allow him to go on using your kidneys, this is a kindness on your part, and not something he can claim from you as his due. Nor has he any right against anybody else that *they* should give him continued use of your kidneys. Certainly he had no right against the Society of Music Lovers that they should plug him into you in the first place. And if you now start to unplug yourself, having learned that you will otherwise have to spend nine years in bed with him, there is nobody in the world who must try to prevent you, in order to see to it that he is given something he has a right to be given.

Some people are rather stricter about the right to life. In their view, it does not include the right to be given anything, but amounts to, and only to, the right not to be killed by anybody. But here a related difficulty arises. If everybody is to refrain from killing that violinist, then everybody must refrain from doing a great many different sorts of things. Everybody must refrain from slitting his throat, everybody must refrain from shooting him—and everybody must refrain from unplugging you from him. But does he have a right against everybody that they shall refrain from unplugging you from him? To refrain from doing this is to allow him to continue to use your kidneys. It could be argued that he has a right against us that *we* should allow him to continue to use your kidneys. That is, while he had no right against us that we should give him the use of your kidneys, it might be argued that he anyway has a right against us that we shall not now intervene and deprive him of the use of your kidneys. I shall come back to third-party interventions later. But certainly the violinist has no right against you that *you* shall allow him to continue to use your kidneys. As I said, if you do allow him to use them, it is a kindness on your part, and not something you owe him.

The difficulty I point to here is not peculiar to the right to life. It reappears in connection with all the other natural rights; and it is something which an adequate account of rights must deal with. For present purposes it is enough just to draw attention to it. But I would stress that I am not arguing that people do not have a right to life—quite to the contrary, it seems to me that the primary control we must place on the acceptability of an account of rights is that it should turn out in that account to be a truth that all persons have a right to life. I am arguing only that having a right to life does not guarantee having either a right to be given the use of or a right to be allowed continued use of another person's body—even if one needs it for life itself. So the right to life will not serve the opponents of abortion in the very simple and clear way in which they seem to have thought it would.

4. There is another way to bring out the difficulty. In the most ordinary sort of case, to deprive someone of what he has a right to is to treat him unjustly. Suppose a boy and his small brother are jointly given a box of chocolates for Christmas. If the older boy takes the box and refuses to give his brother any of the chocolates, he is unjust to him, for the brother has been given a right to half of them. But suppose that, having learned that otherwise it means nine years in bed with that violinist, you unplug yourself from him. You surely are not being unjust to him, for you gave him no right to use your kidneys, and no one else can have given him any such right. But we have to notice that in unplugging yourself, you are killing him; and violinists, like everybody else, have a right to life, and thus in the view we were considering just now, the right not to be killed. So here you do what he supposedly has a right you shall not do, but you do not act unjustly to him in doing it.

The emendation which may be made at this point is this: the right to life consists not in the right not to be killed, but rather in the right not to be killed unjustly. This runs a risk of circularity, but never mind: it would enable us to square the fact that the violinist has a right to life with the fact that you do not act unjustly toward him in unplugging yourself, thereby killing him. For if you do not kill him unjustly, you do not violate his right to life, and so it is no wonder you do him no injustice.

But if this emendation is accepted, the gap in the argument against abortion stares us plainly in the face: it is by no means enough to show that the fetus is a person, and to remind us that all persons have a right to life—we need to be shown also that killing the fetus violates its right to life, i.e., that abortion is unjust killing. And is it?

I suppose we may take it as a datum that in a case of pregnancy due to rape the mother has not given the unborn person a right to the use of her body for food and shelter. Indeed, in what pregnancy could it be supposed that the mother has given the unborn person such a right? It is not as if there were unborn persons drifting about the world, to whom a woman who wants a child says "I invite you in."

But it might be argued that there are other ways one can have acquired a right to the use of another person's body than by having been invited to use it by that person. Suppose a woman voluntarily indulges in intercourse, knowing of the chance it will issue in pregnancy, and then she does become pregnant; is she not in part responsible for the presence, in fact the very existence, of the unborn person inside her? No doubt she did not invite it in. But doesn't her partial responsibility for its being there itself give it a right to the use of her body?[7] If so, then her aborting it would be more like the boy's taking away the chocolates, and less like your unplugging yourself from the violinist—doing so would be depriving it of what it does have a right to, and thus would be doing it an injustice.

And then, too, it might be asked whether or not she can kill it even to save her own life: If she voluntarily called it into existence, how can she now kill it, even in self-defense?

The first thing to be said about this is that it is something new. Opponents of abortion have been so concerned to make out the independence of the fetus, in order to establish that it has a right to life, just as its mother does, that they have tended to overlook the possible support they might gain from making out that the fetus is *dependent* on the mother, in order to establish that she has a special kind of responsibility for it, a responsibility that gives it rights against her which are not possessed by any independent person—such as an ailing violinist who is a stranger to her.

On the other hand, this argument would give the unborn person a right to its mother's body only if her pregnancy resulted from a voluntary act, undertaken in full knowledge of the chance a pregnancy might result from it. It would leave out entirely the unborn person whose existence is due to rape. Pending the availability of some further argument, then, we would be left with the conclusion that unborn persons whose existence is due to rape have no right to the use of their mothers' bodies, and thus that aborting them is not depriving them of anything they have a right to and hence is not unjust killing.

And we should also notice that it is not at all plain that this argument really does go even as far as it purports to. For there are cases and cases, and the details make a difference. If the room is stuffy, and I therefore open a window to air it, and a burglar climbs in, it would be absurd to say, "Ah, now he can stay, she's given him a right to the use of her house—for she is partially responsible for his presence there, having voluntarily done what enabled him to get in, in full knowledge that there are such things as burglars, and that burglars burgle." It would be still more absurd to say this if I had had bars installed outside my windows, precisely to prevent burglars from getting in, and a burglar got in only because of a defect in the bars. It remains equally absurd if we imagine it is not a burglar who climbs in, but an innocent person who blunders or falls in. Again, suppose it were like this: people-seeds drift about in the air like pollen, and if you open your windows, one may drift in and take root in your carpets or upholstery. You don't want children, so you fix up your windows with fine mesh screens, the very best you can buy. As can happen, however, and on very, very rare occasions does hap-

---

[7]The need for a discussion of this argument was brought home to me by members of the Society for Ethical and Legal Philosophy, to whom this paper was originally presented.

pen, one of the screens is defective; and a seed drifts in and takes root. Does the person-plant who now develops have a right to the use of your house? Surely not—despite the fact that you voluntarily opened your windows, you knowingly kept carpets and uphol-stered furniture, and you knew that screens were sometimes defective. Someone may argue that you are responsible for its rooting, that it does have a right to your house, be-cause after all you *could* have lived out your life with bare floors and furniture, or with sealed windows and doors. But this won't do—for by the same token anyone can avoid a pregnancy due to rape by having a hysterectomy, or anyway by never leaving home without a (reliable!) army.

It seems to me that the argument we are looking at can establish at most that there are *some* cases in which the unborn person has a right to the use of its mother's body, and therefore *some* cases in which abortion is unjust killing. There is room for much discus-sion and argument as to precisely which, if any. But I think we should sidestep this issue and leave it open, for at any rate the argument certainly does not establish that all abor-tion is unjust killing.

5. There is room for yet another argument here, however. We surely must all grant that there may be cases in which it would be morally indecent to detach a person from your body at the cost of his life. Suppose you learn that what the violinist needs is not nine years of your life, but only one hour: all you need do to save his life is to spend one hour in that bed with him. Suppose also that letting him use your kidneys for that one hour would not affect your health in the slightest. Admittedly you were kidnapped. Ad-mittedly you did not give anyone permission to plug him into you. Nevertheless it seems to me plain you *ought* to allow him to use your kidneys for that hour—it would be indecent to refuse.

Again, suppose pregnancy lasted only an hour, and constituted no threat to life or health. And suppose that a woman becomes pregnant as a result of rape. Admittedly she did not voluntarily do anything to bring about the existence of a child. Admittedly she did nothing at all which would give the unborn person a right to the use of her body. All the same it might well be said, as in the newly emended violinist story, that she *ought* to allow it to remain for that hour—that it would be indecent of her to refuse.

Now some people are inclined to use the term "right" in such a way that it follows from the fact that you ought to allow a person to use your body for the hour he needs, that he has a right to use your body for the hour he needs, even though he has not been given that right by any person or act. They may say that it follows also that if you refuse, you act unjustly toward him. This use of the term is perhaps so common that it cannot be called wrong; nevertheless it seems to me to be an unfortunate loosening of what we would do better to keep a tight rein on. Suppose that box of chocolates I men-tioned earlier has not been given to both boys jointly, but was given only to the older boy. There he sits, stolidly eating his way through the box, his small brother watching enviously. Here we are likely to say "You ought not to be so mean. You ought to give your brother some of those chocolates." My own view is that it just does not follow from the truth of this that the brother has any right to any of the chocolates. If the boy refuses to give his brother any, he is greedy, stingy, callous—but not unjust. I suppose that the people I have in mind will say it does follow that the brother has a right to some of the chocolates, and thus that the boy does act unjustly if he refuses to give his brother any. But the effect of saying this is to obscure what we should keep distinct, namely the difference between the boy's refusal in this case and the boy's refusal in the earlier case, in which the box was given to both boys jointly, and in which the small brother thus had what was from any point of view clear title to half.

A further objection to so using the term "right" that from the fact that A ought to do a thing for B, it follows that B has a right against A that A do it for him, is that it is going to make the question of whether or not a man has a right to a thing turn on how easy it is to provide him with it; and this seems not merely unfortunate, but morally unacceptable. Take the case of Henry Fonda again. I said earlier that I had no right to the touch of his cool hand on my fevered brow, even though I needed it to save my life. I said it would be frightfully nice of him to fly in from the West Coast to provide me with it, but that I had no right against him that he should do so. But suppose he isn't on the West Coast. Suppose he has only to walk across the room, place a hand briefly on my brow— and lo, my life is saved. Then surely he ought to do it, it would be indecent to refuse. Is it to be said "Ah, well, it follows that in this case she has a right to the touch of his hand on her brow, and so it would be an injustice in him to refuse"? So that I have a right to it when it is easy for him to provide it, though no right when it's hard? It's rather a shocking idea that anyone's rights should fade away and disappear as it gets harder and harder to accord them to him.

So my own view is that even though you ought to let the violinist use your kidneys for the one hour he needs, we should not conclude that he has a right to do so—we should say that if you refuse, you are, like the boy who owns all the chocolates and will give none away, self-centered and callous, indecent in fact, but not unjust. And similarly, that even supposing a case in which a woman pregnant due to rape ought to allow the unborn person to use her body for the hour he needs, we should not conclude that he has a right to do so; we should conclude that she is self-centered, callous, indecent, but not unjust, if she refuses. The complaints are no less grave; they are just different. However, there is no need to insist on this point. If anyone does wish to deduce "he has a right" from "you ought," then all the same he must surely grant that there are cases in which it is not morally required of you that you allow that violinist to use your kidneys, and in which he does not have a right to use them, and in which you do not do him an injustice if you refuse. And so also for mother and unborn child. Except in such cases as the unborn person has a right to demand it—and we were leaving open the possibility that there may be such cases—nobody is morally *required* to make large sacrifices, of health, of all other interests and concerns, of all other duties and commitments, for nine years, or even for nine months, in order to keep another person alive.

6. We have in fact to distinguish between two kinds of Samaritan: the Good Samaritan and what we might call the Minimally Decent Samaritan. The story of the Good Samaritan, you will remember, goes like this:

> A certain man went down from Jerusalem to Jericho, and fell among thieves, which stripped him of his raiment, and wounded him, and departed, leaving him half dead.
>
> And by chance there came down a certain priest that way, and when he saw him, he passed by on the other side.
>
> And likewise a Levite, when he was at the place, came and looked on him, and passed by on the other side.
>
> But a certain Samaritan, as he journeyed, came where he was; and when he saw him he had compassion on him.
>
> And went to him, and bound up his wounds, pouring in oil and wine, and set him on his own beast, and brought him to an inn, and took care of him.

> And on the morrow, when he departed, he took out two pence, and gave them to the host, and said unto him, "Take care of him; and whatsoever thou spendest more, when I come again, I will repay thee."
>
> *(Luke 10.30–35)*

The Good Samaritan went out of his way, at some cost to himself, to help one in need of it. We are not told what the options were, that is, whether or not the priest and the Levite could have helped by doing less than the Good Samaritan did, but assuming they could have, then the fact they did nothing at all shows they were not even Minimally Decent Samaritans, not because they were not Samaritans, but because they were not even minimally decent.

These things are a matter of degree, of course, but there is a difference, and it comes out perhaps most clearly in the story of Kitty Genovese, who, as you will remember, was murdered while thirty-eight people watched or listened, and did nothing at all to help her. A Good Samaritan would have rushed out to give direct assistance against the murderer. Or perhaps we had better allow that it would have been a Splendid Samaritan who did this, on the ground that it would have involved a risk of death for himself. But the thirty-eight not only did not do this, they did not even trouble to pick up a phone to call the police. Minimally Decent Samaritanism would call for doing at least that, and their not having done it was monstrous.

After telling the story of the Good Samaritan, Jesus said "Go, and do thou likewise." Perhaps he meant that we are morally required to act as the Good Samaritan did. Perhaps he was urging people to do more than is morally required of them. At all events it seems plain that it was not morally required of any of the thirty-eight that he rush out to give direct assistance at the risk of his own life, and that it is not morally required of anyone that he give long stretches of his life—nine years or nine months—to sustaining the life of a person who has no special right (we were leaving open the possibility of this) to demand it.

Indeed, with one rather striking class of exceptions; no one in any country in the world is *legally* required to do anywhere near as much as this for anyone else. The class of exceptions is obvious. My main concern here is not the state of the law in respect to abortion, but it is worth drawing attention to the fact that in no state in this country is any man compelled by law to be even a Minimally Decent Samaritan to any person; there is no law under which charges could be brought against the thirty-eight who stood by while Kitty Genovese died. By contrast, in most states in this country women are compelled by law to be not merely Minimally Decent Samaritans, but Good Samaritans to unborn persons inside them. This doesn't by itself settle anything one way or the other, because it may well be argued that there should be laws in this country—as there are in many European countries—compelling at least Minimally Decent Samaritanism.[8] But it does show that there is a gross injustice in the existing state of the law. And it shows also that the groups currently working against liberalization of abortion laws, in fact working toward having it declared unconstitutional for a state to permit abortion, had better start working for the adoption of Good Samaritan laws generally, or earn the charge that they are acting in bad faith.

---

[8]For a discussion of the difficulties involved, and a survey of the European experience with such laws, see *The Good Samaritan and the Law,* ed. James M. Ratcliffe (New York, 1966).

I should think, myself, that Minimally Decent Samaritan laws would be one thing, Good Samaritan laws quite another, and in fact highly improper. But we are not here concerned with the law. What we should ask is not whether anybody should be compelled by law to be a Good Samaritan, but whether we must accede to a situation in which somebody is being compelled—by nature, perhaps—to be a Good Samaritan. We have, in other words, to look now at third-party interventions. I have been arguing that no person is morally required to make large sacrifices to sustain the life of another who has no right to demand them, and this even where the sacrifices do not include life itself; we are not morally required to be Good Samaritans or anyway Very Good Samaritans to one another. But what if a man cannot extricate himself from such a situation? What if he appeals to us to extricate him? It seems to me plain that there are cases in which we can, cases in which a Good Samaritan would extricate him. There you are, you were kidnapped, and nine years in bed with that violinist lie ahead of you. You have your own life to lead. You are sorry, but you simply cannot see giving up so much of your life to the sustaining of his. You cannot extricate yourself, and ask us to do so. I should have thought that—in light of his having no right to the use of your body—it was obvious that we do not have to accede to your being forced to give up so much. We can do what you ask. There is no injustice to the violinist in our doing so.

7. Following the lead of the opponents of abortion, I have throughout been speaking of the fetus merely as a person, and what I have been asking is whether or not the argument we began with, which proceeds only from the fetus' being a person, really does establish its conclusion. I have argued that it does not.

But of course there are arguments and arguments, and it may be said that I have simply fastened on the wrong one. It may be said that what is important is not merely the fact that the fetus is a person, but that it is a person for whom the woman has a special kind of responsibility issuing from the fact that she is its mother. And it might be argued that all my analogies are therefore irrelevant—for you do not have that special kind of responsibility for that violinist, Henry Fonda does not have that special kind of responsibility for me. And our attention might be drawn to the fact that men and women both *are* compelled by law to provide support for their children.

I have in effect dealt (briefly) with this argument in section 4 above; but a (still briefer) recapitulation now may be in order. Surely we do not have any such "special responsibility" for a person unless we have assumed it, explicitly or implicitly. If a set of parents do not try to prevent pregnancy, do not obtain an abortion, and then at the time of birth of the child do not put it out for adoption, but rather take it home with them, then they have assumed responsibility for it, they have given it rights, and they cannot *now* withdraw support from it at the cost of its life because they now find it difficult to go on providing for it. But if they have taken all reasonable precautions against having a child, they do not simply by virtue of their biological relationship to the child who comes into existence have a special responsibility for it. They may wish to assume responsibility for it, or they may not wish to. And I am suggesting that if assuming responsibility for it would require large sacrifices, then they may refuse. A Good Samaritan would not refuse—or anyway, a Splendid Samaritan, if the sacrifices that had to be made were enormous. But then so would a Good Samaritan assume responsibility for that violinist; so would Henry Fonda, if he is a Good Samaritan, fly in from the West Coast and assume responsibility for me.

8. My argument will be found unsatisfactory on two counts by many of those who want to regard abortion as morally permissible. First, while I do argue that abortion is

not impermissible, I do not argue that it is always permissible. There may well be cases in which carrying the child to term requires only Minimally Decent Samaritanism of the mother, and this is a standard we must not fall below. I am inclined to think it a merit of my account precisely that it does *not* give a general yes or a general no. It allows for and supports our sense that, for example, a sick and desperately frightened fourteen-year-old schoolgirl, pregnant due to rape, may *of course* choose abortion, and that any law which rules this out is an insane law. And it also allows for and supports our sense that in other cases resort to abortion is even positively indecent. It would be indecent in the woman to request an abortion, and indecent in a doctor to perform it, if she is in her seventh month, and wants the abortion just to avoid the nuisance of postponing a trip abroad. The very fact that the arguments I have been drawing attention to treat all cases of abortion, or even all cases of abortion in which the mother's life is not at stake, as morally on a par ought to have made them suspect at the outset.

Secondly, while I am arguing for the permissibility of abortion in some cases, I am not arguing for the right to secure the death of the unborn child. It is easy to confuse these two things in that up to a certain point in the life of the fetus it is not able to survive outside the mother's body; hence removing it from her body guarantees its death. But they are importantly different. I have argued that you are not morally required to spend nine months in bed, sustaining the life of that violinist; but to say this is by no means to say that if, when you unplug yourself, there is a miracle and he survives, you then have a right to turn round and slit his throat. You may detach yourself even if this costs him his life; you have no right to be guaranteed his death, by some other means, if unplugging yourself does not kill him. There are some people who will feel dissatisfied by this feature of my argument. A woman may be utterly devastated by the thought of a child, a bit of herself, put out for adoption and never seen or heard of again. She may therefore want not merely that the child be detached from her, but more, that it die. Some opponents of abortion are inclined to regard this as beneath contempt—thereby showing insensitivity to what is surely a powerful source of despair. All the same, I agree that the desire for the child's death is not one which anybody may gratify, should it turn out to be possible to detach the child alive.

At this place, however, it should be remembered that we have only been pretending throughout that the fetus is a human being from the moment of conception. A very early abortion is surely not the killing of a person, and so is not dealt with by anything I have said here.

Against an Absolute Right to Abortion

Baruch Brody

1. Does a Woman Have a Right to Kill Her Fetus?

It is a common claim that a woman ought to be in control of what happens to her body to the greatest extent possible, that she ought to be able to use her body in ways that she wants to and refrain from using it in ways that she does not want to. This right is particularly pressed where certain uses of her body have deep and lasting effects upon the character of her life, personal, social, and economic. Therefore, it is argued, a woman should be free either to carry her fetus to term, thereby using her body to support it, or to abort the fetus, thereby not using her body for that purpose.

In some contexts in which this argument is advanced, it is clear that it is not addressed to the issue of the morality of abortion at all. Rather, it is made in opposition to laws against abortion on the ground that the choice to abort or not is a moral decision that should belong only to the mother. But that specific direction of the argument is irrelevant to our present purposes; I will consider it [later] when I deal with the issues raised by laws prohibiting abortions. For the moment, I am concerned solely with the use of this principle as a putative ground tending to show the permissibility of abortion, with the claim that because it is the woman's body that carries the fetus and upon which the fetus depends, she has certain rights to abort the fetus that no one else may have.

We may begin by remarking that it is obviously correct that, as carrier of the fetus, the mother has it within her power to choose whether or not to abort the fetus. And, as an autonomous and responsible agent, she must make this choice. But let us notice that this in no way entails either that whatever choice she makes is morally right or that no one else has the right to evaluate the decision that she makes.

At first glance, it would seem that this argument cannot be used by anyone who supposes, as we do for the moment, that there is a point in fetal development from

From Baruch Brody, *Abortion and the Sanctity of Human Life,* MIT Press, 1975. Reprinted by permission of the publisher and the author. And from Baruch Brody, "Fetal Humanity and Essentialism" in *Philosophy and Sex,* edited by Robert Baker and Frederick Elliston, Prometheus Books, 1975. Reprinted by permission of the author.

which time on the fetus is a human being. After all, people do not have the right to do anything whatsoever that may be necessary for them to retain control over the uses of their bodies. In particular, it would seem wrong for them kill another human being in order to do so.

In a recent article, Professor Judith Thomson has, in effect, argued that this simple view is mistaken.[1] How does Professor Thomson defend her claim that the mother has a right to abort the fetus, even if it is a human being, whether or not her life is threatened and whether or not she has consented to the act of intercourse in which the fetus is conceived? At one point, discussing just the case in which the mother's life is threatened, she makes the following suggestion:

> In [abortion], there are only two people involved, one whose life is threatened and one who threatens it. Both are innocent: the one who is threatened is not threatened because of any fault, the one who threatens does not threaten because of any fault. For this reason, we may feel that we bystanders cannot intervene. But the person threatened can.

But surely this description is equally applicable to the following case: *A* and *B* are adrift on a lifeboat, *B* has a disease that he can survive, but *A*, if he contracts it, will die, and the only way that *A* can avoid that is by killing *B* and pushing him overboard. Surely *A* has no right to do this. So there must be some special reason why the mother has, if she does, the right to abort the fetus.

There is, to be sure, an important difference between our lifeboat case and abortion, one that leads us to the heart of Professor Thomson's argument. In the case that we envisaged, both *A* and *B* have equal rights to be in the lifeboat, but the mother's body is hers and not the fetus's and she has first rights to its use. The primacy of these rights allows an abortion whether or not her life is threatened. Professor Thomson summarizes this argument in the following way:

> I am arguing only that having a right to life does not guarantee having either a right to be given the use of or a right to be allowed continued use of another person's body—even if one needs it for life itself.

One part of this claim is clearly correct. I have no duty to *X* to save *X*'s life by giving him the use of my body (or my life savings, or the only home I have, and so on), and *X* has no right, even to save his life, to any of those things. Thus, the fetus conceived in the laboratory that will perish unless it is implanted into a woman's body has in fact no right to any woman's body. But this portion of the claim is irrelevant to the abortion issue, for in abortion of the fetus that is a human being the mother must kill *X* to get back the sole use of her body, and that is an entirely different matter.

This point can also be put as follows: . . . we must distinguish the taking of *X*'s life from the saving of *X*'s life, even if we assume that one has a duty not to do the former and to do the latter. Now that latter duty, if it exists at all, is much weaker than the first duty; many circumstances may relieve us from the latter duty that will not relieve us from the former one. Thus, I am certainly relieved from my duty to save *X*'s life by the fact that fulfilling it means the loss of my life savings. It may be noble for me to save

---

[1] Editor's note: Thomson's article, "A Defense of Abortion," appears on pp. 75–87 of this volume.

X's life at the cost of everything I have, but I certainly have no duty to do that. And the same observation may be made about cases in which I can save X's life by giving him the use of my body for an extended period of time. However, I am not relieved of my duty not to take X's life by the fact that fulfilling it means the loss of everything I have and not even by the fact that fulfilling it means the loss of my life. . . .

At one point in her paper, Professor Thomson does consider this objection. She has previously imagined the following case: a famous violinist, who is dying from a kidney ailment, has been, without your consent, plugged into you for a period of time so that his body can use your kidneys:

> Some people are rather stricter about the right to life. In their view, it does not include the right to be given anything, but amounts to, and only to, the right not to be killed by anybody. But here a related difficulty arises if everybody is to refrain from killing that violinist, then everybody must refrain from doing a great many different sorts of things. . . . everybody must refrain from unplugging you from him. But does he have a right against everybody that they shall refrain from unplugging you from him? To refrain from doing this is to allow him to continue to use your kidneys. . . . certainly the violinist has no right against you that *you* shall allow him to continue to use your kidneys.

Applying this argument to the case of abortion, we can see that Professor Thomson's argument would run as follows:

1. Assume that the fetus's right to life includes the right not to be killed by the woman carrying him.

2. But to refrain from killing the fetus is to allow him the continued use of the woman's body.

3. So our first assumption entails that the fetus's right to life includes the right to the continued use of the woman's body.

4. But we all grant that the fetus does not have the right to the continued use of the woman's body.

5. Therefore, the fetus's right to life cannot include the right not to be killed by the woman in question.

And it is also now clear what is wrong with this argument. When we granted that the fetus has no right to the continued use of the woman's body, all that we meant was that he does not have this right merely because the continued use saves his life. But, of course, there may be other reasons why he has this right. One would be that the only way to take the use of the woman's body away from the fetus is by killing him, and that is something that neither she nor we have the right to do. So, I submit, the way in which Assumption 4 is true is irrelevant, and cannot be used by Professor Thomson, for Assumption 4 is true only in cases where the saving of the life of the fetus is at stake and not in cases where the taking of his life is at stake.

I conclude therefore that Professor Thomson has not established the truth of her claims about abortion, primarily because she has not sufficiently attended to the distinction between our duty to save X's life and our duty not to take it. Once one attends to that distinction, it would seem that the mother, in order to regain control over her body, has no right to abort the fetus from the point at which it becomes a human being.

It may also be useful to say a few words about the larger and less rigorous context of the argument that the woman has a right to her own body. It is surely true that one way in which women have been oppressed is by their being denied authority over their own bodies. But it seems to me that, as the struggle is carried on for meaningful amelioration of such oppression, it ought not to be carried so far that it violates the steady responsibilities all people have to one another. Parents may not desert their children, one class may not oppress another, one race or nation may not exploit another. For parents, powerful groups in society, races or nations in ascendancy there are penalties for refraining from these wrong actions, but those penalties can in no way be taken as the justification for such wrong actions. Similarly, if the fetus is a human being, the penalty of carrying it cannot, I believe, be used as the justification for destroying it. . . .

2. Abortion to Save the Mother

Let us begin by considering the case in which the continued existence of the fetus threatens the life of the mother. This would seem to be the case in which she has the strongest claim for the right to abort the fetus even if it is a human being with a right to life. . . .

Why would not it be permissible for the mother to have an abortion in order to save her life even after that point at which the fetus becomes a human being? After all, the fetus's continued existence poses a threat to the life of the mother, and why can't she void that threat by taking the life of the fetus, as an ultimate act of defense?

To be sure, it may be the physician, or other agent, who will cause the abortion, and not the mother herself, but that difference seems to be irrelevant. Our intuition is that the person whose life is threatened (call that person A) may either take the life of the person (B) who threatens his life or call upon someone else (C) to do so. And more important, it seems permissible (and perhaps even obligatory in some cases) for C to take B's life in order to save A's life. Put in traditional terms, we are really speaking of the mother's rights as the pursued, or anyone else's rights as an onlooker, to take the life of the fetus who is the pursuer.

Pope Pius XI observed, in objecting to this argument from self-defense, that in the paradigm case of killing the pursuer B is unjustly attempting to take A's life and is responsible for this attempt. It is the resulting guilt, based in part on B's intention (found in the attempt to kill A), together with the fact that A will die unless B is stopped, which permits the taking of B's life. The reader will notice that the abortion situation is quite different. Leaving aside for now—we shall return to it later on—the question as to whether the fetus can properly be described as attempting to take the mother's life, we can certainly agree that the fetus is not responsible for such an attempt (if it is occurring), that the fetus is therefore innocent, not guilty, and that the taking of fetal life cannot be compared to the paradigm case of killing the pursuer.

There is another way of putting Pope Pius' point. Consider the following case: there is, let us imagine, a medicine that A needs to stay alive, C owns some, and C will give it to A only if A kills B. Moreover, A has no other way of getting the medicine. In this case, the continued existence of B certainly poses a threat to the life of A; A can survive only if *B* does not survive. Still, it is not permissible for *A* to kill *B* in order to save *A*'s life. Why not? How does this case differ from the paradigm case of killing the pursuer? The simplest answer is that in this case, while *B*'s continued existence poses a threat to the life of *A*, *B* is not guilty of attempting to take *A*'s life because there is no attempt to be guilty about it in the first place. Now if we consider the case of a fetus whose continued existence poses a threat to the life of the mother, we see that it is like the medicine case and not like the paradigm case of killing the pursuer. The fetus does pose (in our imagined situation) a threat to the life of its mother, but it is not guilty of attempting to take its mother's life. Consequently, in an analogue to the medicine case, the mother (or her agent) could not justify destroying the fetus on the ground that it would be a permissible act of killing the pursuer.

The persuasiveness of both of the preceding arguments indicates that we have to analyze the whole issue of pursuit far more carefully before we can definitely decide whether an abortion to save the life of the mother could be viewed as a permissible act of killing the pursuer. If we look again at a paradigm case of pursuit, we see that there are three factors involved:

1.   The continued existence of *B* poses a threat to the life of *A*, a threat that can be met only by the taking of *B*'s life (we shall refer to this as the condition of *danger*).

2.   *B* is unjustly attempting to take *A*'s life (we shall refer to this as the condition of *attempt*).

3.   *B* is responsible for his attempt to take *A*'s life (we shall refer to this as the condition of *guilt*).

In the medicine case, only the danger condition was satisfied. Our intuitions that it would be wrong for *A* to take *B*'s life in that case reflects our belief that the mere fact that *B* is a danger to *A* is not sufficient to establish that killing *B* will be a justifiable act of killing a pursuer. But it would be rash to conclude, as Pope Pius did, that all three conditions must be satisfied before the killing of *B* will be a justifiable act of killing a pursuer. What would happen, for example, if the first two conditions, but not the guilt condition, were satisfied?

There are good reasons for supposing that the satisfaction of the first two conditions is sufficient justification for taking *B*'s life as an act of killing the pursuer. Consider, for example, a variation of the pursuit paradigm—one in which *B* is about to shoot *A*, and the only way by which *A* can stop him is by killing him first—but one in which *B* is a minor who is not responsible for his attempt to take *A*'s life. In this case, the only condition not satisfied is the condition of guilt. Still, despite that fact, it seems that *A* may justifiably take *B*'s life as a permissible act of killing a pursuer. The guilt of the pursuer, then, is not a requirement for legitimacy in killing the pursuer. . . .

To summarize, then, our general discussion of killing the pursuer, we can say the following: the mere satisfaction of the danger condition is not sufficient to justify the killing of the pursuer. If, in addition . . . the attempt condition . . . is satisfied, then one would be justified in killing the pursuer to save the life of the pursued. In any case, the condition of guilt, arising from full knowledge and intent, need not be satisfied. . . .

Is, then, the aborting of the fetus, when necessary to save the life of the mother, a permissible act of killing a pursuer? It is true that in such cases the fetus is a danger to his mother. But it is also clear that the condition of attempt is not satisfied. The fetus has neither the beliefs nor the intentions to which we have referred. Furthermore, there is on the part of the fetus no action that threatens the life of the mother. . . . It seems to follow, therefore, that aborting the fetus could not be a permissible act of killing a pursuer. . . .

3. Two Other Cases Considered

All of the arguments that we have looked at so far are attempts to show that there is something special about abortion that justifies its being treated differently from other cases of the taking of human life. We shall now consider claims that are confined to certain special cases of abortion: the case in which the mother has been raped . . . and the case in which having the child may cause a problem for the rest of her family (the latter case is a particular case of the societal argument). In addressing these issues, we shall see whether there is any point to the permissibility of abortions in some of the cases covered by the Model Penal Code proposals.

When the expectant mother has conceived after being raped, there are two different sorts of considerations that might support the claim that she has the right to take the life of the fetus. They are the following: (A) the woman in question has already suffered immensely from the act of rape and the physical and/or psychological aftereffects of that act. It would be particularly unjust, the argument runs, for her to have to live through an unwanted pregnancy owing to that act of rape. Therefore, even if we are at a stage at which the fetus is a human being, the mother has the right to abort it; (B) the fetus in question has no right to be in that woman. It was put there as a result of an act of aggression upon her by the rapist, and its continued presence is an act of aggression against the mother. She has a right to repel that aggression by aborting the fetus.

The first argument is very compelling. We can all agree that a terrible injustice has been committed on the woman who is raped. The question that we have to consider, however, is whether it follows that it is morally permissible for her to abort the fetus. We must make that consideration reflecting that, however unjust the act of rape, it was not the fetus who committed or commissioned it. The injustice of the act, then, should in no way impinge upon the rights of the fetus, for it is innocent. What remains is the initial misfortune of the mother (and the injustice of her having to pass through the pregnancy, and, further, to assume responsibility of at least giving the child over for adoption or assuming the burden of its care). However unfortunate that circumstance, however unjust, the misfortune and the injustice are not sufficient cause to justify the taking of the life of an innocent human being as a means of mitigation.

It is at this point that Argument B comes in, for its whole point is that the fetus, by its mere presence in the mother, is committing an act of aggression against her, one over and above the one committed by the rapist, and one that the mother has a right to repel by abortion. But . . . (1) the fetus is certainly innocent (in the sense of not responsible) for any act of aggression against the mother and (2) the mere presence of the fetus in the mother, no matter how unfortunate for her, does not constitute an act of aggression by the fetus against the mother. Argument B fails then at just that point at which Argument A needs it support, and we can therefore conclude that the fact that pregnancy is the result of rape does not give the mother the right to abort the fetus. . . .

We come finally to those cases in which the continuation of the pregnancy would cause serious problems for the rest of the family. There are a variety of cases that we have to consider here together. Perhaps the health of the mother will be affected in such a way that she cannot function effectively as a wife and mother during, or even after, the pregnancy. Or perhaps the expenses incurred as a result of the pregnancy would be utterly beyond the financial resources of the family. The important point is that the continuation of the pregnancy raises a serious problem for other innocent people involved besides the mother and the fetus, and it may be argued that the mother has the right to abort the fetus to avoid that problem.

By now, the difficulties with this argument should be apparent. We have seen earlier that the mere act that the continued existence of the fetus threatens to harm the mother does not, by itself, justify the aborting of the fetus. Why should anything be changed by the fact that the threatened harm will accrue to the other members of the family and not to the mother? Of course, it would be different if the fetus were committing an act of aggression against the other members of the family. But, once more, this is certainly not the case.

We conclude, therefore, that none of these special circumstances justifies an abortion from that point at which the fetus is a human being. . . .

4. Fetal Humanity
and Brain Function

The question which we must now consider is the question of fetal humanity. Some have argued that the fetus is a human being with a right to life (or, for convenience, just a human being) from the moment of conception. Others have argued that the fetus only becomes a human being at the moment of birth. Many positions in between these two extremes have also been suggested. How are we to decide which is correct?

The analysis which we will propose here rests upon certain metaphysical assumptions which I have defended elsewhere. These assumptions are: (a) the question is when has the fetus acquired all the properties essential (necessary) for being a human being, for when it has, it is a human being; (b) these properties are such that the loss of any one of them means that the human being in question has gone out of existence and not merely stopped being a human being; (c) human beings go out of existence when they die. It follows from these assumptions that the fetus becomes a human being when it acquires all those characteristics which are such that the loss of any one of them would result in the fetus's being dead. We must, therefore, turn to the analysis of death. . . .

We will first consider the question of what properties are essential to being human if we suppose that death and the passing out of existence occur only if there has been an irreparable cessation of brain function (keeping in mind that that condition itself, as we have noted, is a matter of medical judgment). We shall then consider the same question on the supposition that [Paul] Ramsey's more complicated theory of death (the modified traditional view) is correct.

According to what is called the brain-death theory, as long as there has not been an irreparable cessation of brain function the person in question continues to exist, no matter what else has happened to him. If so, it seems to follow that there is only one property—leaving aside those entailed by this one property—that is essential to humanity, namely, the possession of a brain that has not suffered an irreparable cessation of function.

Several consequences follow immediately from this conclusion. We can see that a variety of often advanced claims about the essence of humanity are false. For example, the claim that movement, or perhaps just the ability to move, is essential for being human is false. A human being who has stopped moving, and even one who has lost the ability to move, has not therefore stopped existing. Being able to move, and a fortiori moving, are not essential properties of human beings and therefore are not essential to being human. Similarly, the claim that being perceivable by other human beings is essential for being human is also false. A human being who has stopped being perceivable by other humans (for example, someone isolated on the other side of the moon, out of reach even of radio communication) has not stopped existing. Being perceivable by other human beings is not an essential property of human beings and is not essential to being human. And the same point can be made about the claims that viability is essential for being human, that independent existence is essential for being human, and that actual interaction with other human beings is essential for being human. The loss of any of these properties would not mean that the human being in question had gone out of existence, so none of them can be essential to that human being and none of them can be essential for being human.

Let us now look at the following argument: (1) A functioning brain (or at least, a brain that, if not functioning, is susceptible of function) is a property that every human being must have because it is essential for being human. (2) By the time an entity acquires that property, it has all the other properties that are essential for being human. Therefore, when the fetus acquires that property it becomes a human being. It is clear that the property in question is, according to the brain-death theory, one that is had essentially by all human beings. The question that we have to consider is whether the second premise is true. It might appear that its truth does follow from the brain-death theory. After all, we did see that the theory entails that only one property (together with those entailed by it) is essential for being human. Nevertheless, rather than relying solely on my earlier argument, I shall adopt an alternative approach to strengthen the conviction that this second premise is true: I shall note the important ways in which the fetus resembles and differs from an ordinary human being by the time it definitely has a functioning brain (about the end of the sixth week of development). It shall then be evident, in light of our theory of essentialism, that none of these differences involves the lack of some property in the fetus that is essential for its being human.

Structurally, there are few features of the human being that are not fully present by the end of the sixth week. Not only are the familiar external features and all the internal organs present, but the contours of the body are nicely rounded. More important, the body is functioning. Not only is the brain functioning, but the heart is beating sturdily (the fetus by this time has its own completely developed vascular system), the stomach is producing digestive juices, the liver is manufacturing blood cells, the kidney is extracting uric acid from the blood, and the nerves and muscles are operating in concert, so that reflex reactions can begin.

What are the properties that a fetus acquires after the sixth week of its development? Certain structures do appear later. These include the fingernails (which appear in the third month), the completed vocal chords (which also appear then), taste buds and salivary glands (again, in the third month), and hair and eyelashes (in the fifth month). In addition, certain functions begin later than the sixth week. The fetus begins to urinate (in the third month), to move spontaneously (in the third month), to respond to external stimuli (at least in the fifth month), and to breathe (in the sixth month). Moreover, there is a constant growth in size. And finally, at the time of birth the fetus ceases to receive its oxygen and food through the placenta and starts receiving them through the mouth and nose.

I will not examine each of these properties (structures and functions) to show that they are not essential for being human. The procedure would be essentially the one used previously to show that various essentalist claims are in error. We might, therefore, conclude, on the supposition that the brain-death theory is correct, that the fetus becomes a human being about the end of the sixth week after its development.

There is, however, one complication that should be noted here. There are, after all, progressive stages in the physical development and in the functioning of the brain. For example, the fetal brain (and nervous system) does not develop sufficiently to support spontaneous motion until some time in the third month after conception. There is, of course, no doubt that that stage of development is sufficient for the fetus to be human. No one would be likely to maintain that a spontaneously moving human being has died; and similarly, a spontaneously moving fetus would seem to have become human. One might, however, want to claim that that fetus does not become a human being until the point of spontaneous movement. So then, on the supposition that the brain-death theory is correct, one ought to conclude that the fetus becomes a human being at some time between the sixth and twelfth week after its conception.

But what if we reject the brain-death theory, and replace it with its equally plausible contender, Ramsey's theory of death? According to that theory—which we can call the brain, heart, and lung theory of death—the human being does not die, does not go out of existence, until such time as the brain, heart, and lungs have irreparably ceased functioning naturally. What are the essential features of being human according to this theory?

Actually, the adoption of Ramsey's theory requires no major modifications. According to that theory, what is essential to being human, what each human being must retain if he is to continue to exist, is the possession of a functioning (actually or potentially) heart, lung, or brain. It is only when a human being possesses none of these that he dies and goes out of existence; and the fetus comes into humanity, so to speak, when he acquires one of these.

On Ramsey's theory, the argument would now run as follows: (1) The property of having a functioning brain, heart, or lungs (or at least organs of the kind that, if not functioning, are susceptible of function) is one that every human being must have because it is essential for being human. (2) By the time that an entity acquires that property it has all the other properties that are essential for being human. Therefore, when the fetus acquires that property it becomes a human being. There remains, once more, the problem of the second premise. Since the fetal heart starts operating rather early, it is not clear that the second premise is correct. Many systems are not yet operating and many structures are not yet present. Still, following our theory of essentialism, we should conclude that the fetus becomes a human being when it acquires a functioning heart (the first of the organs to function in the fetus).

There is, however, a further complication here, and it is analogous to the one encountered if we adopt the brain-death theory: When may we properly say that the fetal heart begins to function? At two weeks, when occasional contractions of the primitive fetal heart are present? In the fourth to fifth week, when the heart, although incomplete, is beating regularly and pumping blood cells through a closed vascular system, and when the tracings obtained by an ECG exhibit the classical elements of an adult tracing? Or after the end of the seventh week, when the fetal heart is functioning complete and "normal"?

We have not reached a precise conclusion in our study of the question of when the fetus becomes a human being. We do know that it does so some time between the end of the second week and the end of the third month. But it surely is not a human being at the moment of conception and it surely is one by the end of the third month. Though we have not come to a final answer to our question, we have narrowed the range of acceptable answers considerably.

[In summary] we have argued that the fetus becomes a human being with a right to life some time between the second and twelfth week after conception. We have also argued that abortions are morally impermissible after that point except in rather unusual circumstances. What is crucial to note is that neither of these arguments appeals to any theological considerations. We conclude, therefore, that there is a human-rights basis for moral opposition to abortions. . . .

A Third Way

L. W. Sumner

T he practice of abortion confronts us with two different sets of moral questions belonging to two different decision contexts. The primary context is that in which a woman chooses whether to have an abortion and a physician chooses whether to perform it; here the focus is on the moral quality of abortion itself. Because this context is one of individual decision we will call the set of moral questions which it contains the *personal* problem of abortion. The secondary context is that in which a society chooses how, or whether, to regulate abortions; here the focus is on the merits of alternative abortion policies. Because this context is one of social decision we will call the set of moral questions which it contains the *political* problem of abortion.

Although the two kinds of problem raised by abortion are distinct, they are also connected. A complete view of the morality of abortion will therefore offer connected solutions to them. In most countries in the West, public discussion of abortion has been distorted by the dominance of two such views. The liberal view, espoused by "pro-choice" groups, holds that (voluntary) abortion is always morally innocuous and (therefore) that the only acceptable abortion policy is one which treats abortion as another variety of minor elective surgery. The conservative view, espoused by "pro-life" groups, holds that abortion is always morally serious and (therefore) that the only acceptable abortion policy is one which treats abortion as another variety of homicide.

Because they define the extremities of the continuum of possible positions, and because each is sufficiently simple and forceful to be advocated by a powerful movement, these established views constitute the familiar reference points in our abortion landscape. Yet neither has managed to command the allegiance of more than a small minority of the public. For the rest of us who are unwilling to embrace either of the extreme options the problem has been the lack of a well-defined middle ground between them. In contrast to the power of the established views more moderate alternatives may appear both indistinct and indecisive.

Public distrust of the established views is well grounded: neither stands up under critical scrutiny.[1] If their demise is not to leave us without any credible view of abortion

This is a revised version of L. W. Sumner, *Abortion and Moral Theory* (Copyright © 1981 by Princeton University Press), Chapter 4, pp. 124–160. Reprinted by permission of Princeton University Press.

[1] I will not be defending this assessment in the present paper. For the arguments see *Abortion and Moral Theory,* chs. 2 and 3.

three tasks must be successfully completed. The first is to define a third way with abortion and to distinguish it from both of the views which it will supersede. The second is to give it an intuitive defense by showing that it coheres better than either of its predecessors with our considered moral judgments both on abortion itself and on closely related issues. Then, finally, the third way must be grounded in a moral theory. The first two of these tasks will be undertaken here; the more daunting theoretical challenge is confronted elsewhere.[2]

1. Specifications

Despite their opposition, the two established views suffer from similar defects. Collating their failures will provide us with some positive guidelines to follow in building a more satisfactory alternative. The central issue in the morality of abortion is the moral status of the fetus. Let us say that a creature has *moral standing* if, for the purpose of moral decisionmaking, it must be counted for something in its own right. To count for nothing is to have no moral standing; to count for as much as possible (as much, that is, as any creature does) is to have full moral standing. We may, for the purpose of the present discussion, make this rather vague notion more precise by adopting the rights vocabulary favored by both of the established views. We will suppose that having (some) moral standing is equivalent to having (some) right to life. The central issue in the morality of abortion is then whether fetuses have moral standing in this sense.[3]

The conservative view, and also the more naive versions of the liberal view, select a precise point (conception, birth, etc.) as the threshold of moral standing, implying that the transition from no standing to full standing occurs abruptly. In doing so they rest more weight on these sudden events than they are capable of bearing. A view that avoids this defect will allow full moral standing to be acquired gradually. It will therefore attempt to locate not a threshold point, but a threshold period or stage.

Both of the established views attribute a uniform moral status to all fetuses, regardless of their dissimilarities. Each, for example, counts a newly conceived zygote for precisely as much (or as little) as a full-term fetus, despite the enormous differences between them. A view that avoids this defect will assign moral status differentially, so that the threshold stage occurs sometime during pregnancy.

A consequence of the uniform approach adopted by both of the established views is that neither can attach any significance to the development of the fetus during gestation. Yet this development is the most obvious feature of gestation. A view that avoids this defect will base the (differential) moral standing of the fetus at least in part on its level of development. It will thus assign undeveloped fetuses a moral status akin to that of ova and spermatozoa, whereas it will assign developed fetuses a moral status akin to that of infants.

---

[2]*Abortion and Moral Theory,* chs. 5 and 6.

[3]The adoption of this working definition of moral standing should not be construed as a concession that rights are the appropriate category for dealing with the moral issues posed by abortion. But since both of the established views employ the rhetoric of rights, there is some point to showing how that rhetoric is equally available to a moderate view. For a generalized notion of moral standing freed from all connection with rights, see *Abortion and Moral Theory,* Section 23.

So far, then, an adequate view of the fetus must be gradual, differential, and developmental. It must also be derived from a satisfactory criterion of moral standing. Such a criterion must be general (applicable to beings other than fetuses), it must connect moral standing with the empirical properties of such beings, and it must be morally relevant. Its moral relevance is partly testable by appeal to intuition, for arbitrary or shallow criteria will be vulnerable to counterexamples. But the final test of moral relevance is grounding in a moral theory.

An adequate view of the fetus promises a morally significant division between early abortions (before the threshold stage) and late abortions (after the threshold stage). It also promises borderline cases (during the threshold stage). Wherever that stage is located, abortions that precede it will be private matters, since the fetus will at that stage lack moral standing. Thus the provisions of the liberal view will apply to early abortions: they will be morally innocent (as long as the usual conditions of maternal consent, etc., are satisfied) and ought to be legally unregulated (except for rules equally applicable to all other medical procedures). Early abortion will have the same moral status as contraception.

Abortions that follow the threshold stage will be interpersonal matters, since the fetus will at that stage possess moral standing. Thus the provisions of the conservative view will apply to late abortions: they must be assessed on a case-by-case basis and they ought to be legally permitted only on appropriate grounds. Late abortions will have the same moral status as infanticide, except for the difference made by the physical connection between fetus and mother.

A third way with abortion is thus a moderate and differential view, combining elements of the liberal view for early abortions with elements of (a weakened version of) the conservative view for late abortions. The policy that a moderate view will support is a moderate policy, permissive in the early stages of pregnancy and more restrictive (though not as restrictive as conservatives think appropriate) in the later stages. So far as the personal question of the moral evaluation of particular abortions is concerned, there is no pressing need to resolve the borderline cases around the threshold stage. But a workable abortion policy cannot tolerate this vagueness and will need to establish a definite time limit beyond which the stipulated grounds will come into play. Although the precise location of the time limit will unavoidably be somewhat arbitrary, it will be defensible as long as it falls somewhere within the threshold stage. Abortion on request up to the time limit and only for cause thereafter: these are the elements of a satisfactory abortion policy.

A number of moderate views may be possible, each of them satisfying all of the foregoing constraints. A particular view will be defined by selecting (a) a criterion of moral standing, (b) the natural characteristics whose gradual acquisition during normal fetal development carries with it the acquisition of moral standing, and (c) a threshold stage. Of these three steps, the first is the crucial one, since it determines both of the others.

2. A Criterion of Moral Standing

We are assuming that for a creature to have moral standing is for it to have a right to life. Any such right imposes duties on moral agents; these duties may be either negative (not to deprive the creature of life) or positive (to support the creature's life). Possession of a right to life implies at least some immunity against attack by others, and possibly also some entitlement to the aid of others. As the duties may vary in strength, so may the corresponding rights. To have some moral standing is to have some right to life, whether or not it may be overridden by the rights of others. To have full moral standing is to have the strongest right to life possessed by anyone, the right to life of the paradigm person. Depending on one's moral theory, this right may or may not be inviolable and indefeasible and thus may or may not impose absolute duties on others.

To which creatures should we distribute (some degree of) moral standing? On which criterion should we base this distribution? It may be easier to answer these questions if we begin with the clear case and work outward to the unclear ones. If we can determine why we ascribe full standing to the paradigm case, we may learn what to look for in other creatures when deciding whether or not to include them in the moral sphere.

The paradigm bearer of moral standing is an adult human being with normal capacities of intellect, emotion, perception, sensation, decision, action, and the like. If we think of such a person as a complex bundle of natural properties, then in principle we could employ as a criterion any of the properties common to all normal and mature members of our species. Selecting a particular property or set of properties will define a class of creatures with moral standing, namely, all (and only) those who share that property. The extension of that class will depend on how widely the property in question is distributed. Some putative criteria will be obviously frivolous and will immediately fail the tests of generality or moral relevance. But even after excluding the silly candidates, we are left with a number of serious ones. There are four that appear to be the most serious: we might attribute full moral standing to the paradigm person on the ground that he/she is (a) intrinsically valuable, (b) alive, (c) sentient, or (d) rational. An intuitive test of the adequacy of any of these candidates will involve first enumerating the class of beings to whom it will distribute moral standing and then determining whether that class either excludes creatures that upon careful reflection we believe ought to be included or includes creatures that we believe ought to be excluded. In the former case the criterion draws the boundary of the moral sphere too narrowly and fails as a necessary condition of moral standing. In the latter case the criterion draws the boundary too broadly and fails as a sufficient condition. (A given criterion may, of course, be defective in both respects.)

Beings may depart from the paradigm along several different dimensions, each of which presents us with unclear cases that a criterion must resolve. These cases may be divided into seven categories: (1) inanimate objects (natural and artificial); (2) non-human terrestrial species of living things (animals and plants); (3) nonhuman extraterrestrial species of living things (should there be any); (4) artificial "life forms" (androids, robots, computers); (5) grossly defective human beings (the severely and permanently retarded or deranged); (6) human beings at the end of life (especially the severely and permanently senile or comatose); (7) human beings at the beginning of life (fetuses, infants, children). Since the last context is the one in which we wish to apply a criterion, it will here be set aside. This will enable us to settle on a criterion without tailoring it specially for the problem of abortion. Once a criterion has established its credentials in other domains, we will be able to trace out its implications for the case of the fetus.

The first candidate for a criterion takes a direction rather different from that of the remaining three. It is a commonplace in moral philosophy to attribute to (normal adult) human beings a special worth or value or dignity in virtue of which they possess (among other rights) a full right to life. This position implies that (some degree of) moral standing extends just as far as (some degree of) this intrinsic value, a higher degree of the latter entailing a higher degree of the former. We cannot know which things have moral standing without being told which things have intrinsic worth (and why)—without, that is, being offered a theory of intrinsic value. What is unique about this criterion, however, is that it is quite capable in principle of extending moral standing beyond the class of living beings, thus embracing such inanimate objects as rocks and lakes, entire landscapes (or indeed worlds), and artifacts. Of course, nonliving things cannot literally have a right to *life*, but it would be simple enough to generalize to a right to (continued) *existence*, where this might include both a right not to be destroyed and a right to such support as is necessary for that existence. A criterion that invokes intrinsic value is thus able to define a much more capacious moral sphere than is any of the other candidates.

Such a criterion is undeniably attractive in certain respects: how else are we to explain why it is wrong to destroy priceless icons or litter the moon even when doing so will never affect any living, sentient, or rational being? But it is clear that it cannot serve our present purpose. A criterion must connect moral standing with some property of things whose presence or absence can be confirmed by a settled, objective, and public method of investigation. The property of being intrinsically valuable is not subject to such verification. A criterion based on intrinsic value cannot be applied without a theory of intrinsic value. Such a theory will supply a criterion of intrinsic value by specifying the natural properties of things in virtue of which they possess such value. But if things have moral standing in virtue of having intrinsic value, and if they have intrinsic value in virtue of having some natural property, then it is that natural property which is serving as the real criterion of moral standing, and the middle term of intrinsic value is eliminable without loss. A theory of intrinsic value may thus entail a criterion of moral standing, but intrinsic value cannot itself serve as that criterion.

There is a further problem confronting any attempt to ground moral rights in the intrinsic worth of creatures. One must first be certain that this is not merely a verbal exercise in which attributing intrinsic value to things is just another way of attributing intrinsic moral standing to them. Assuming that the relationship between value and rights is synthetic, there are then two possibilities: the value in question is moral or it is nonmoral. If it is moral, the criterion plainly fails to break out of the circle of moral properties to connect them with the nonmoral properties of things. But if it is nonmoral, it is unclear what it has to do with moral rights. If there are realms of value, some case must be made for deriving moral duties toward things from the nonmoral value of these things.

The remaining three candidates for a criterion of moral standing (life, sentience, rationality) all satisfy the verification requirement since they all rest standing on empirical properties of things. They may be ordered in terms of the breadth of the moral spheres they define. Since rational beings are a proper subset of sentient beings, which are a proper subset of living beings, the first candidate is the weakest and will define the broadest sphere, whereas the third is the strongest and will define the narrowest sphere.[4]

---

[4]Or so we shall assume, though it is certainly possible that some (natural or artificial) entity might display signs of intelligence but no signs of either sentience or life. We might, for instance, create forms of artificial intelligence before creating forms of artificial life.

In an interesting recent discussion, Kenneth Goodpaster has urged that moral standing be accorded to all living beings, simply in virtue of the fact that they are alive.[5] Although much of his argument is negative, being directed against more restrictive criteria, he does provide a positive case for including all forms of life within the moral sphere.[6]

Let us assume that the usual signs of life—nutrition, metabolism, spontaneous growth, reproduction—enable us to draw a tolerably sharp distinction between animate and inanimate beings, so that all plant and animal species, however primitive, are collected together in the former category. All such creatures share the property of being *teleological systems:* they have functions, ends, directions, natural tendencies, and so forth. In virtue of their teleology such creatures have needs, in a nonmetaphorical sense—conditions that must be satisfied if they are to thrive or flourish. Creatures with needs can be benefited or harmed; they are benefited when their essential needs are satisfied and harmed when they are not. It also makes sense to say that such creatures have a good: the conditions that promote their life and health are good for them, whereas those that impair their normal functioning are bad for them. But it is common to construe morality as having essentially to do with benefits and harms or with the good of creatures. So doing will lead us to extend moral standing to all creatures capable of being benefited and harmed, that is, all creatures with a good. But this condition will include all organisms (and systems of organisms), and so life is the only reasonable criterion of moral standing.

This extension of moral standing to plants and to the simpler animals is of course highly counterintuitive, since most of us accord the lives of such creatures no weight whatever in our practical deliberations. How could we conduct our affairs if we were to grant protection of life to every plant and animal species? Some of the more extreme implications of this view are, however, forestalled by Goodpaster's distinction between a criterion of inclusion and a criterion of comparison.[7] The former determines which creatures have (some) moral standing and thus locates the boundary of the moral sphere; it is Goodpaster's contention that life is the proper inclusion criterion. The latter is operative entirely within the moral sphere and enables us to assign different grades of moral standing to different creatures in virtue of some natural property that they may possess in different degrees. Since all living beings are (it seems) equally

---

[5]Kenneth E. Goodpaster, "On Being Morally Considerable," *Journal of Philosophy* 75, 6 (June 1978). Goodpaster speaks of "moral considerability" where we are speaking of moral standing. The notions are identical, except for the fact that Goodpaster explicitly refrains from restricting moral considerability to possession of rights, let alone the right to life. Nothing in my assessment of Goodpaster's view will hang on this issue of rights.

[6]In the paragraph to follow I have stated that case in my own words.

[7]These are my terms; Goodpaster distinguishes between a criterion of moral considerability and a criterion of moral significance (p. 311). It is odd that when Goodpaster addresses the practical problems created by treating life as an inclusion criterion (p. 324) he does not appeal to the inclusion/comparison distinction. Instead he invokes the quite different distinction between its being reasonable to attribute standing to a creature and its being (psychologically and causally) possible to act on that attribution. One would have thought the question is not what we *can* bring ourselves to do but what we *ought* to bring ourselves to do, and that the inclusion/comparison distinction is precisely designed to help us answer this question.

alive, life cannot serve as a comparison criterion. Goodpaster does not provide such a criterion, though he recognizes its necessity. Thus his view enables him to affirm that all living creatures have (some) moral standing but to deny that all such creatures have equal standing. Though the lives of all animate beings deserve consideration, some deserve more than others. Thus, for instance, higher animals might count for more than lower ones, and all animals might count for more than plants.

In the absence of a criterion of comparison, it is difficult to ascertain just what reforms Goodpaster's view would require in our moral practice. How much weight must human beings accord to the lives of lichen or grass or bacteria or insects? When are such lives more important than some benefit for a higher form of life? How should we modify our eating habits, for example? There is a problem here that extends beyond the incompleteness and indeterminacy of Goodpaster's position. Suppose that we have settled on a comparison criterion; let it be sentience (assuming that sentience admits of degrees in some relevant respect). Then a creature's ranking in the hierarchy of moral standing will be determined by the extent of its sentience: nonsentient (living) beings will have minimal standing, whereas the most sentient beings (human beings, perhaps) will have maximal standing. But then we are faced with the obvious question: if sentience is to serve as the comparison criterion, why should it not also serve as the inclusion criterion? Conversely, if life is the inclusion criterion, does it not follow that nothing else can serve as the comparison criterion, in which case all living beings have equal standing? It is difficult to imagine an argument in favor of sentience as a comparison criterion that would not also be an argument in favor of it as an inclusion criterion.[8] Since the same will hold for any other comparison criterion, Goodpaster's view can avoid its extreme implications only at the price of inconsistency.

Goodpaster's view also faces consistency problems in its claim that life is necessary for moral standing. Beings need not be organisms in order to be teleological systems, and therefore to have needs, a good, and the capacity to be benefited and harmed. If these conditions are satisfied by a tree (as they surely are), then they are equally satisfied by a car. In order to function properly most machines need periodic maintenance; such maintenance is good for them, they are benefited by it, and they are harmed by its neglect. Why then is being alive a necessary condition of moral standing? Life is but an (imperfect) indicator of teleology and the capacity to be benefited and harmed. But Goodpaster's argument then commits him to treating these deeper characteristics as the criterion of moral standing, and thus to according standing to many (perhaps most) inanimate objects.

This inclusion of (at least some) nonliving things should incline us to reexamine Goodpaster's argument—if the inclusion of all living things has not already done so.

---

[8]Goodpaster does not defend separating the two criteria but merely says "we should not expect that the criterion for having 'moral standing' at all will be the same as the criterion for adjudicating competing claims to priority among beings that merit that standing" (p. 311). Certainly inclusion and comparison criteria can be different, as in Mill's celebrated evaluation of pleasures. For Mill every pleasure has some value simply in virtue of being a pleasure (inclusion), but its relative value is partly determined by its quality or kind (comparison). All of this is quite consistent (despite claims to the contrary by some critics) because every pleasure has some quality or other. Goodpaster's comparison criterion threatens to be narrower than his inclusion criterion; it certainly will be if degrees of standing are based on sentience, since many living things have no sentience at all. It is inconsistent to base degrees of standing on (variations) in a property and also to extend (some) standing to beings who lack that property entirely.

The connection between morality and the capacity to be benefited and harmed appears plausible, so what has gone wrong? We may form a conjecture if we again consider our paradigm bearer of moral standing. In the case of a fully normal adult human being, it does appear that moral questions are pertinent whenever the actions of another agent promise to benefit or threaten to harm such a being. Both duties and rights are intimately connected with benefits and harms. The kinds of acts that we have a (strict) duty not to do are those that typically cause harm, whereas positive duties are duties to confer benefits. Liberty-rights protect autonomy, which is usually thought of as one of the chief goods for human beings, and the connection between welfare-rights and benefits is obvious. But if we ask what counts as a benefit or a harm for a human being, the usual answers take one or both of the following directions:

(1)   *The desire model.* Human beings are benefited to the extent that their desires (or perhaps their considered and informed desires) are satisfied; they are harmed to the extent that these desires are frustrated.

(2)   *The experience model.* Human beings (are) benefited to the extent that they are brought to have experiences that they like or find agreeable; they are harmed to the extent that they are brought to have experiences that they dislike or find disagreeable.

We need not worry at this stage whether one of these models is more satisfactory than the other. On both models benefits and harms for particular persons are interpreted in terms of the psychological states of those persons, in terms, that is, of their interests or welfare. Such states are possible only for beings who are conscious or sentient. Thus, if morality has to do with the promotion and protection of interests or welfare, morality can concern itself only with beings who are conscious or sentient.[9] No other beings can be beneficiaries or victims *in the morally relevant way.* Goodpaster is not mistaken in suggesting that nonsentient beings can be benefited and harmed. But he is mistaken in suggesting that morality has to do with benefits and harms as such, rather than with a particular category of them. And that can be seen the more clearly when we realize that the broadest capacity to be benefited and harmed extends not only out to but beyond the frontier of life. Leaving my lawn mower out in the rain is bad for the mower, pulling weeds is bad for the weeds, and swatting mosquitoes is bad for the mosquitoes; but there are no moral dimensions to any of these acts unless the interests or welfare of some sentient creature is at stake. Morality requires the existence of sentience in order to obtain a purchase on our actions.

The failure of Goodpaster's view has thus given us some reason to look to sentience as a criterion of moral standing. Before considering this possibility directly, it will be helpful to turn to the much narrower criterion of rationality. The rational/nonrational boundary is more difficult to locate with certainty than the animate/inanimate boundary,

---

[9]Goodpaster does not shrink from attributing interests to nonsentient organisms since he assumes that if a being has needs, a good, and a capacity to be benefited and harmed, then that being has interests. There is much support for this assumption in the dictionary definitions of both "interest" and "welfare," though talk of protecting the interests or welfare of plants seems contrived and strained. But philosophers and economists have evolved technical definitions of "interest" and "welfare" that clearly tie these notions to the psychological states of sentient beings. It is the existence of beings with interests or welfare *in this sense* that is a necessary condition of the existence of moral issues.

since rationality (or intelligence) embraces a number of distinct but related capacities for thought, memory, foresight, language, self-consciousness, objectivity, planning, reasoning, judgment, deliberation, and the like.[10] It is perhaps possible for a being to possess some of these capacities and entirely lack others, but for simplicity we will assume that the higher-order cognitive processes are typically owned as a bundle.[11] The bundle is possessed to one extent or another by normal adult human beings, by adolescents and older children, by persons suffering from the milder cognitive disorders, and by some other animal species (some primates and cetaceans for example). It is not possessed to any appreciable extent by fetuses and infants, by the severely retarded or disordered, by the irreversibly comatose, and by most other animal species. To base moral standing on rationality is thus to deny it alike to most nonhuman beings and to many human beings. Since the implications for fetuses and infants have already been examined, they will be ignored in the present discussion. Instead we will focus on why one might settle on rationality as a criterion in the first place.

That rationality is sufficient for moral standing is not controversial (though there are some interesting questions to be explored here about forms of artificial intelligence). As a necessary condition, however, rationality will exclude a good many sentient beings— just how many, and which ones, to be determined by the kind and the stringency of the standards employed. Many will find objectionable this constriction of the sphere of moral concern. Because moral standing has been defined in terms of the right to life, to lack moral standing is not necessarily to lack all rights. Thus one could hold that, although we have no duty to (nonrational) animals to respect their lives, we do have a duty to them not to cause them suffering. For the right not to suffer, one might choose a different (and broader) criterion—sentience, for example. (However, if this is the criterion appropriate for that right, why is it not also the criterion appropriate for the right to life?) But even if we focus strictly on the (painless) killing of animals, the implications of the criterion are harsh. Certainly we regularly kill nonhuman animals to satisfy our own needs or desires. But the justification usually offered for these practices is either that the satisfaction of those needs and desires outweighs the costs to the animals (livestock farming, hunting, fishing, trapping, experimentation) or that no decent life would have been available for them anyway (the killing of stray dogs and cats). Although some of these arguments doubtless are rationalizations, their common theme is that the lives of animals do have some weight (however slight) in the moral scales, which is why the practice of killing animals is one that requires moral justification (raises moral issues). If rationality is the criterion of moral standing, and if (most) nonhuman animals are nonrational, killing such creatures could be morally questionable only when it im-

---

[10]Possession of a capacity at a given time does not entail that the capacity is being manifested or displayed at that time. A person does not lose the capacity to use language, for instance, in virtue of remaining silent or being asleep. The capacity remains as long as the appropriate performance could be elicited by the appropriate stimuli. It is lost only when this performance can no longer be evoked (as when the person has become catatonic or comatose). Basing moral standing on the possession of some capacity or set of capacities does not therefore entail silly results, such as that persons lose their rights when they fall asleep. This applies, of course, not only to rationality but also to other capacities, such as sentience.

[11]The practical impact of basing moral standing on rationality will, however, depend on which particular capacities are treated as central. Practical rationality (the ability to adjust means to ends, and vice versa) is, for instance, much more widely distributed through the animal kingdom than is the use of language.

pinges on the interests of rational beings (as where animals are items of property). In no case could killing an animal be a wrong against it. However callous and chauvinistic the common run of our treatment of animals may be, still the view that killing a dog or a horse is morally no more serious (ceteris paribus) than weeding a garden can be the considered judgment of only a small minority.

The standard that we apply to other species we must in consistency apply to our own. The greater the number of animals who are excluded by that standard, the greater the number of human beings who will also be excluded. In the absence of a determinate criterion it is unclear just where the moral line will be drawn on the normal/abnormal spectrum: will a right to life be withheld from mongoloids, psychotics, the autistic, the senile, the profoundly retarded? If so, killing such persons will again be no wrong *to them*. Needless to say, most such persons (in company with many animals) are sentient and capable to some extent of enjoyable and satisfying lives. To kill them is to deprive them of lives that are of value to them. If such creatures are denied standing, this loss will be entirely discounted in our moral reasoning. Their lack of rationality may ensure that their lives are less full and rich than ours, that they consist of simpler pleasures and more basic enjoyments. But what could be the justification for treating their deaths as though they cost them nothing at all?

There is a tradition, extending back at least to Kant, that attempts just such a justification. One of its modern spokesmen is A. I. Melden, who treats the capacity for moral agency as the criterion of moral standing.[12] This capacity is manifested by participation in a moral community—a set of beings sharing allegiance to moral rules and recognition of one another's integrity. Rights can be attributed only to beings with whom we can have such moral intercourse, thus only to beings who have interests similar to ours, who show concern for the well-being of others, who are capable of uniting in cooperative endeavors, who regulate their activities by a sense of right and wrong, and who display the characteristically moral emotions of indignation, remorse, and guilt.[13] Rationality is a necessary condition (though not a sufficient one) for possessing this bundle of capacities. Melden believes that of all living creatures known to us only human beings are capable of moral agency.[14] Natural rights, including the right to life, are thus human rights.

We may pass over the obvious difficulty of extending moral standing to all human beings on this basis (including the immature and abnormal) and focus on the question of why the capacity for moral agency should be thought necessary for possession of a right to life. The notion of a moral community to which Melden appeals contains a crucial ambiguity. On the one hand it can be thought of as a community of moral agents—

---

[12]A. I. Melden, *Rights and Persons* (Oxford: Basil Blackwell, 1977).

[13]Melden rejects rationality as a criterion of standing (p. 187), but only on the ground that a being's rationality does not ensure its possessing a sense of morality. Clearly rationality is a necessary condition of moral agency. Thus a criterion of moral agency will not extend standing beyond the class of rational beings.

[14]Whether or not this is so will depend on how strong the conditions of moral agency are. Certainly many nonhuman species display altruism, if we mean by this a concern for the well-being of conspecifics and a willingness to accept personal sacrifices for their good. On p. 199 Melden enumerates a number of features of our lives that are to serve as the basis of our possession of rights; virtually all mammals display all of these features.

the bearers of moral duties. Clearly to be a member of such a community one must be capable of moral agency. On the other hand a moral community can be thought of as embracing all beings to whom moral agents owe duties—the bearers of moral rights. It cannot simply be assumed that the class of moral agents (duty-bearers) is coextensive with the class of moral patients (right-bearers). It is quite conceivable that some beings (infants, nonhuman animals) might have rights though they lack duties (because incapable of moral agency). The capacity for moral agency is (trivially) a condition of having moral duties. It is not obviously also a condition of having moral rights. The claim that the criterion for rights is the same as the criterion for duties is substantive and controversial. The necessity of defending this claim is merely concealed by equivocating on the notion of a moral community.

Beings who acknowledge one another as moral agents can also acknowledge that (some) creatures who are not themselves capable of moral agency nonetheless merit (some) protection of life. The more we reflect on the function of rights, the stronger becomes the inclination to extend them to such creatures. Rights are securities for beings who are sufficiently autonomous to conduct their own lives but who are also vulnerable to the aggression of others and dependent upon these others for some of the necessaries of life. Rights protect the goods of their owners and shield them from evils. We ascribe rights to one another because we all alike satisfy these minimal conditions of autonomy, vulnerability, and dependence. In order to satisfy these conditions a creature need not itself be capable of morality: it need only possess interests that can be protected by rights. A higher standard thus seems appropriate for possession of moral duties than for possession of moral rights. Rationality appears to be the right sort of criterion for the former, but something less demanding (such as sentience) is better suited to the latter.

A criterion of life (or teleology) is too weak, admitting classes of beings (animate and inanimate) who are not suitable loci for moral rights; being alive is necessary for having standing, but it is not sufficient. A criterion of rationality (or moral agency) is too strong, excluding classes of beings (human and nonhuman) who are suitable loci for rights; being rational is sufficient for having standing, but it is not necessary. A criterion of sentience (or consciousness) is a promising middle path between these extremes. Sentience is the capacity for feeling or affect. In its most primitive form it is the ability to experience sensations of pleasure and pain, and thus the ability to enjoy and suffer. Its more developed forms include wants, aims, and desires (and thus the ability to be satisfied and frustrated); attitudes, tastes, and values; and moods, emotions, sentiments, and passions. Consciousness is a necessary condition of sentience, for feelings are states of mind of which their owner is aware. But it is not sufficient; it is at least possible in principle for beings to be conscious (percipient, for instance, or even rational) while utterly lacking feelings. If rationality embraces a set of cognitive capacities, then sentience is rooted in a being's affective and conative life. It is in virtue of being sentient that creatures have interests, which are compounded either out of their desires or out of the experiences they find agreeable (or both). If morality has to do with the protection and promotion of interests, it is a plausible conjecture that we owe moral duties to all those beings capable of having interests. But this will include all sentient creatures.

Like rationality, and unlike life, it makes sense to think of sentience as admitting of degrees. Within any given mode, such as the perception of pain, one creature may be more or less sensitive than another. But there is a further sense in which more developed (more rational) creatures possess a higher degree of sentience. The expansion of consciousness and of intelligence opens up new ways of experiencing the world, and therefore new ways of being affected by the world. More rational beings are capable of finding either fulfillment or frustration in activities and states of affairs to which less developed creatures are, both cognitively and affectively, blind. It is in this sense of a broader and deeper sensibility that a higher being is capable of a richer, fuller, and more varied existence. The fact that sentience admits of degrees (whether of sensitivity or sensibility) enables us to employ it both as an inclusion criterion and as a comparison criterion of moral standing. The animal kingdom presents us with a hierarchy of sentience. Nonsentient beings have no moral standing; among sentient beings the more developed have greater standing than the less developed, the upper limit being occupied by the paradigm of a normal adult human being. Although sentience is the criterion of moral standing, it is also possible to explain the relevance of rationality. The evolutionary order is one of ascending intelligence. Since rationality expands a creature's interests, it is a reliable indicator of the degree of moral standing which that creature possesses. Creatures less rational than human beings do not altogether lack standing, but they do lack full standing.

An analysis of degrees of standing would require a graded right to life, in which the strength of the right varied inversely with the range of considerations capable of overriding it. The details of any such analysis will be complex and need not be worked out here. However, it seems that we are committed to extending (some) moral standing at least to all vertebrate animals, and also to counting higher animals for more than lower.[15] Thus we should expect the higher vertebrates (mammals) to merit greater protection of life than the lower (fish, reptiles, amphibia, birds) and we should also expect the higher mammals (primates, cetaceans) to merit greater protection of life than the lower (canines, felines, etc.). Crude as this division may be, it seems to accord reasonably well with most people's intuitions that in our moral reasoning paramecia and horseflies count for nothing, dogs and cats count for something, chimpanzees and dolphins count for more, and human beings count for most of all.

A criterion of sentience can thus allow for the gradual emergence of moral standing in the order of nature. It can explain why no moral issues arise (directly) in our dealings with inanimate objects, plants, and the simpler forms of animal life. It can also function as a moral guideline in our encounters with novel life forms on other planets. If the creatures we meet have interests and are capable of enjoyment and suffering, we must grant them some moral standing. We thereby constrain ourselves not to exploit them ruthlessly for our own advantage. The kind of standing that they deserve may be determined by the range and depth of their sensibility, and in ordinary circumstances this will vary with their intelligence. We should therefore recognize as equals beings who are as rational and sensitive as ourselves. The criterion also implies that if we encounter creatures who are rational but nonsentient—who utterly lack affect and desire—nothing we can do will adversely affect such creatures (in morally relevant ways). We would be entitled, for instance, to treat them as a species of organic computer. The same obviously holds for forms of artificial intelligence; in deciding whether to extend moral standing to sophisticated machines, the question (as Bentham put it) is not whether they can reason but whether they can suffer.

---

[15]It is unclear at present whether invertebrates are capable of feeling pain, though the discovery of endorphins (opiates manufactured by the body) even in very simple organisms suggests that they may be. If so, then we are committed to extending (some) moral standing to invertebrates as well.

A criterion of sentience also requires gentle usage of the severely abnormal. Cognitive disabilities and disorders may impair a person's range of sensibility, but they do not generally reduce that person to the level of a nonsentient being. Even the grossly retarded or deranged will still be capable of some forms of enjoyment and suffering and thus will still possess (some) moral standing in their own right. This standing diminishes to the vanishing point only when sentience is entirely lost or never gained in the first place. If all affect and responsivity are absent, and if they cannot be engendered, then (but only then) are we no longer dealing with a sentient creature. This verdict accords well with the contemporary trend toward defining death in terms of the permanent loss of cerebral functioning. Although such patients are in one obvious sense still alive (their blood circulates and is oxygenated), in the morally relevant sense they are now beyond our reach, for we can cause them neither good nor ill. A criterion of life would require us to continue treating them as beings with (full?) moral standing, whereas a criterion of rationality would withdraw that standing when reason was lost even though sensibility should remain. Again a criterion of sentience enables us to find a middle way.

Fastening upon sentience as the criterion for possession of a right to life thus opens up the possibility of a reasonable and moderate treatment of moral problems other than abortion, problems pertaining to the treatment of nonhuman animals, extraterrestrial life, artificial intelligence, "defective" human beings, and persons at the end of life. We need now to trace out its implications for the fetus.

3. The Morality of Abortion

The adoption of sentience as a criterion determines the location of a threshold of moral standing. Since sentience admits of degrees, we can in principle construct a continuum ranging from fully sentient creatures at one extreme to completely nonsentient creatures at the other. The threshold of moral standing is that area of the continuum through which sentience fades into nonsentience. In phylogenesis the continuum extends from homo sapiens to the simple animals and plants, and the threshold area is the boundary between vertebrates and invertebrates. In pathology the continuum extends from the fully normal to the totally incapacitated, and the threshold area is the transition from consciousness to unconsciousness. Human ontogenesis also presents us with a continuum from adult to zygote. The threshold area will be the stage at which sentience first emerges, but where is that to be located?

A mental life is built upon a physical base. The capacity for sentience is present only when the necessary physiological structures are present. Physiology, and in particular neurophysiology, is our principal guide in locating a threshold in the phylogenetic continuum. Like a stereo system, the brain of our paradigm sentient being is a set of connected components. These components may be roughly sorted into three groups: forebrain (cerebral hemispheres, thalamus, hypothalamus, amygdala), midbrain (cerebellum), and brainstem (upper part of the spinal cord, pineal and pituitary glands). The brainstem and midbrain play no direct role in the individual's conscious life; their various parts regulate homeostasis (temperature, respiration, heartbeat, etc.), secrete hormones, make reflex connections, route nerves, coordinate motor activities, and so on.

All of these functions can be carried on in the total absence of consciousness. Cognitive, perceptual, and voluntary motor functions are all localized in the forebrain, more particularly in the cerebral cortex. Sensation (pleasure/pain), emotion, and basic drives (hunger, thirst, sex, etc.) are controlled by subcortical areas in the forebrain. Although the nerves that transmit pleasure/pain impulses are routed through the cortex, their ultimate destination is the limbic system (amygdala, hypothalamus). The most primitive forms of sentience are thus possible in the absence of cortical activity.

Possession of particular neural structures cannot serve as a criterion of moral standing, for we cannot rule out encounters with sentient beings whose structures are quite different from ours. But in all of the species with which we are familiar, the components of the forebrain (or some analogues) are the minimal conditions of sentience. Thus the evolution of the forebrain serves as an indicator of the kind and degree of sentience possessed by a particular animal species. When we turn to human ontogenesis we may rely on the same indicator.

The normal gestation period for our species is 280 days from the onset of the last menstrual period to birth. This duration is usually divided into three equal trimesters of approximately thirteen weeks each. A zygote has no central nervous system of any sort. The spinal cord makes its first appearance early in the embryonic period (third week), and the major divisions between forebrain, midbrain, and brainstem are evident by the end of the eighth week. At the conclusion of the first trimester virtually all of the major neural components can be clearly differentiated and EEG activity is detectable. The months to follow are marked chiefly by the growth and elaboration of the cerebral hemispheres, especially the cortex. The brain of a seven-month fetus is indistinguishable, at least in its gross anatomy, from that of a newborn infant. Furthermore, by the seventh month most of the neurons that the individual's brain will contain during its entire lifetime are already in existence. In the newborn the brain is closer than any other organ to its mature level of development.

There is no doubt that a newborn infant is sentient—that it feels hunger, thirst, physical pain, the pleasure of sucking, and other agreeable and disagreeable sensations. There is also no doubt that a zygote, and also an embryo, are presentient. It is difficult to locate with accuracy the stage during which feeling first emerges in fetal development. The structure of the fetal brain, including the cortex, is well laid down by the end of the second trimester. But there is reason to expect the more primitive and ancient parts of that brain to function before the rest. The needs of the fetus dictate the order of appearance of neural functions. Thus the brainstem is established and functioning first, since it is required for the regulation of heartbeat and other metabolic processes. Since the mammalian fetus develops in an enclosed and protected environment, cognition and perception are not essential for survival and their advent is delayed. It is therefore not surprising that the cortex, the most complex part of the brain and the least important to the fetus, is the last to develop to an operational level.

Simple pleasure/pain sensations would seem to occupy a medial position in this priority ranking. They are localized in a part of the brain that is more primitive than the cortex, but they could have little practical role for a being that is by and large unable either to seek pleasurable stimuli or to avoid painful ones. Behavioral evidence is by its very nature ambiguous. Before the end of the first trimester, the fetus will react to unpleasant stimuli by flinching and withdrawing. However, this reaction is probably a reflex that is entirely automatic. How are we to tell when mere reflex has crossed over into consciousness? The information we now possess does not enable us to date with accuracy the emergence of fetal sentience. Of some judgments, however, we can be reasonably confident. First-trimester fetuses are clearly not yet sentient. Third-trimester fetuses probably possess some degree of sentience, however minimal. The threshold of sentience thus appears to fall in the second trimester. More ancient and primitive than cognition, the ability to discriminate simple sensations of pleasure and pain is probably the first form of consciousness to appear in the ontogenetic order. Further, when sentience emerges it does not do so suddenly. The best we can hope for is to locate a threshold stage or period in the second trimester. It is at present unclear just how far into that trimester this stage occurs.

The phylogenetic and pathological continua yield us clear cases at the extremes and unclear cases in the middle. The ontogenetic continuum does the same. Because there is no quantum leap into consciousness during fetal development, there is no clean and sharp boundary between sentient and nonsentient fetuses. There is therefore no precise point at which a fetus acquires moral standing. More and better information may enable us to locate the threshold stage ever more accurately, but it will never collapse that stage into a point. We are therefore inevitably confronted with a class of fetuses around the threshold stage whose sentience, and therefore whose moral status, is indeterminate.

A criterion based on sentience enables us to explain the status of other putative thresholds. Neither conception nor birth marks the transition from a presentient to a sentient being. A zygote has not one whit more consciousness than the gametes out of which it is formed. Likewise, although a neonate has more opportunity to employ its powers, it also has no greater capacity for sensation than a full-term fetus. Of thresholds located during gestation, quickening is the perception of fetal movement that is probably reflex and therefore preconscious. Only viability has some relevance, though at one remove. A fetus is viable when it is equipped to survive in the outside world. A being that is aware of, and can respond to, its own inner states is able to communicate its needs to others. This ability is of no use in utero but may aid survival in an extrauterine environment. A fetus is therefore probably sentient by the conventional stage of viability (around the end of the second trimester). Viability can therefore serve as a (rough) indicator of moral standing.

Our common moral consciousness locates contraception and infanticide in quite different moral categories. This fact suggests implicit recognition of a basic asymmetry between choosing not to create a new life in the first place and choosing to destroy a new life once it has been created. The boundary between the two kinds of act is the threshold at which that life gains moral protection. Since gametes lack moral standing, contraception (however it is carried out) merely prevents the creation of a new person. Since an infant has moral standing, infanticide (however it is carried out) destroys a new person. A second-trimester threshold of moral standing introduces this asymmetry into the moral assessment of abortion. We may define an early abortion as one performed sometime during the first trimester or early in the second, and a late abortion as one performed sometime late in the second trimester or during the third. An early abortion belongs in the same moral category as contraception: it prevents the emergence of a new being with moral standing. A late abortion belongs in the same moral category as infanticide: it terminates the life of a new being with moral standing. The threshold of sentience thus extends the morality of contraception forward to cover early abortion and extends the morality of infanticide backward to cover late abortion. One of the sentiments voiced by many people who contemplate the problem of abortion is that early abortions are importantly different from late ones. The abortion techniques of the first trimester (the IUD, menstrual extraction, vacuum aspiration) are not to be treated as cases of homicide. Those employed later in pregnancy (saline induction, hysterotomy) may, however, have a moral quality approaching that of infanticide. For most people, qualms about abortion are qualms about late abortion. It is a virtue of the sentience criterion that it explains and supports this differential approach.

The moral issues raised by early abortion are precisely those raised by contraception. It is for early abortions that the liberal view is appropriate. Since the fetus at this stage has no right to life, early abortion (like contraception) cannot violate its rights. But if it violates no one's rights, early abortion (like contraception) is a private act. There are of course significant differences between contraception and early abortion, since the former is generally less hazardous, less arduous, and less expensive. A woman has, therefore, good prudential reasons for relying on contraception as her primary means of birth control. But if she elects an early abortion, then, whatever the circumstances and whatever her reasons, she does nothing immoral.[16]

The moral issues raised by late abortion are similar to those raised by infanticide. It is for late abortions that (a weakened form of) the conservative view is appropriate. Since the fetus at this stage has a right to life, late abortion (like infanticide) may violate its rights. But if it may violate the fetus' rights, then late abortion (like infanticide) is a public act. There is, however, a morally significant difference between late abortion and infanticide. A fetus is parasitic upon a unique individual in a manner in which a newborn infant is not. That parasitic relation will justify late abortion more liberally than infanticide, for they do not occur under the same circumstances.

Since we have already explored the morality of abortion for those cases in which the fetus has moral standing, the general approach to late abortions is clear enough. Unlike the simple and uniform treatment of early abortion, only a case-by-case analysis will here suffice. We should expect a serious threat to the woman's life or health (physical or mental) to justify abortion, especially if that threat becomes apparent only late in pregnancy. We should also expect a risk of serious fetal deformity to justify abortion, again especially if that risk becomes apparent (as it usually does) only late in pregnancy. On the other hand, it should not be necessary to justify abortion on the ground that pregnancy was not consented to, since a woman will have ample opportunity to seek an abortion before the threshold stage. If a woman freely elects to continue a pregnancy past that stage, she will thereafter need a serious reason to end it.

A differential view of abortion is therefore liberal concerning early abortion and conservative (in an extended sense) concerning late abortion. The status of the borderline cases in the middle weeks of the second trimester is simply indeterminate. We cannot say of them with certainty either that the fetus has a right to life or that it does not. Therefore we also cannot say either that a liberal approach to these abortions is suitable or that a conservative treatment of them is required. What we can say is that, from the moral point of view, the earlier an abortion is performed the better. There are thus good moral reasons, as well as good prudential ones, for women not to delay their abortions.

A liberal view of early abortion in effect extends a woman's deadline for deciding whether to have a child. If all abortion is immoral, her sovereignty over that decision

---

[16]Unless there are circumstances (such as extreme underpopulation) in which contraception would also be immoral.

ends at conception. Given the vicissitudes of contraception, a deadline drawn that early is an enormous practical burden. A deadline in the second trimester allows a woman enough time to discover that she is pregnant and to decide whether to continue the pregnancy. If she chooses not to continue it, her decision violates neither her duties nor any other being's rights. From the point of view of the fetus, the upshot of this treatment of early abortion is that its life is for a period merely probationary; only when it has passed the threshold will that life be accorded protection. If an abortion is elected before the threshold, it is as though from the moral point of view that individual had never existed.

Settling on sentience as a criterion of moral standing thus leads us to a view of the moral status of the fetus, and of the morality of abortion, which satisfies the constraints set out in Section 1. It is gradual, since it locates a threshold stage rather than a point and allows moral standing to be acquired incrementally. It is differential, since it locates the threshold stage during gestation and thus distinguishes the moral status of newly conceived and full-term fetuses. It is developmental, since it grounds the acquisition of moral standing in one aspect of the normal development of the fetus. And it is moderate, since it distinguishes the moral status of early and late abortions and applies each of the established views to that range of cases for which it is appropriate.

4. An Abortion Policy

A differential view of the morality of abortion leads to a differential abortion policy—one that draws a legal distinction between early and late abortions. If we work within the framework of a liberal social theory, then it is understood that the state has no right to interfere in the private activities of individuals. An early abortion is a private act—or, rather, a private transaction between a woman and her physician. No regulation of this transaction will be legitimate unless it is also legitimate for other contractual arrangements between patients and physicians. It might be quite in place for the state to require that abortions be performed by qualified (perhaps licensed) personnel in properly equipped (perhaps licensed) facilities: whether or not this is so will depend on whether the state is in general competent to regulate trade in medical skills. Both the decision to abort and the decision to use contraceptives are private ones on which a woman ought to seek medical advice and medical assistance. There is no justification in either case for restricting access to that advice or that assistance.

An abortion policy must therefore be permissive for early abortions. There is at this stage no question of inquiring into a woman's reason for seeking an abortion. Her autonomy here is absolute; the simple desire not to have a child (or not to have one now) is sufficient. Grounds for abortion become pertinent only when we turn to late abortions. Since virtually all such abortions will result in the death of a being that has a right to life (though not all will violate that right), the state has a legitimate role to play in governing trade in abortion at this stage. Legal grounds for late abortion are a special case of conditions for justifiable homicide. As much as possible (allowing for the unique relation between mother and fetus) these grounds should authorize abortion when killing would also be justified in relevantly similar cases not involving fetuses. Two general conditions for justifiable homicide will be applicable to abortions: self-defense and euthanasia.

The usual legal grounds for abortion provided by moderate policies may be divided into four categories: (a) therapeutic (threat to maternal life or health); (b) eugenic (risk of fetal abnormality); (c) humanitarian (pregnancy due to the commission of a crime, such as rape or incest); (d) socioeconomic (poverty, family size, etc.). If a moderate treatment of late abortion is coupled (as it should be) with a permissive treatment of early ones, only the first two categories are necessary. Therapeutic grounds for abortion follow from a woman's right of self-defense. The threat, however, must be serious in two different respects: the injury in prospect must be more than trivial and the probability of its occurrence must be greater than normal. The risks generally associated with pregnancy will not here suffice. Further, there must be good medical reason not to delay until the fetus has a better chance of survival, and every effort must be made to save the fetus' life if this is possible. Thus late abortion for therapeutic reasons ought to be reserved for genuine medical emergencies in which no other course of action would qualify as proper care of the mother. In many putatively moderate policies therapeutic grounds for abortion (especially mental health clauses) are interpreted so liberally as to cover large numbers of cases that are not by any stretch of the imagination medical emergencies. This is the standard device whereby a policy moderate in principle becomes permissive in practice. Since the policy here advanced is permissive in principle (for early abortions), a strict interpretation of the therapeutic grounds for late abortions will be mandatory.

The same strictures will apply to eugenic grounds. Where there is a substantial risk of some severe anomaly (rubella, spina bifida, Tay-Sachs disease, etc.), abortion may be the best course of action for the fetus. This is not obviously the case for less severe defects (Down's syndrome, dwarfism, etc.). Again there will be no justification for an interpretation of eugenic grounds so elastic that it permits abortion whenever the child is unwanted (because, say, it is the "wrong" sex). A rough rule of thumb is that late abortion for reasons of fetal abnormality is permissible only in those cases in which euthanasia for defective newborns would also be permissible. Probability will play a different role in the two kinds of case, since prenatal diagnosis of these conditions is often less certain than postnatal. But against this reason for delay we must balance the anguish of a woman carrying a fetus who may turn out at birth to be grossly deformed. Since diagnostic techniques such as ultrasound and amniocentesis cannot be employed until the second trimester, a permissive treatment of early abortions will not eliminate the need for late abortions on eugenic grounds.

Both therapeutic and eugenic grounds can be alleged for a wide range of abortions. Some of these cases will be clearly justified, others will be just as clearly unjustified, and the remainder will just be hard cases. There is no formula that can be applied mechanically to decide the hard cases. We should look to a statute for only the most perfunctory statement of justifying grounds for abortion. Particular decisions (the analogue of case law) are best undertaken by persons with the relevant medical expertise. This might be a hospital or clinic committee established especially to monitor late abortions or an "ethics committee" with broader responsibilities. In either case, establishing the right sort of screening mechanism is the best means of ensuring that the justifying grounds are given a reasonable application.

There is no need for any special notice of humanitarian grounds. It is doubtful indeed whether incest ought to be a crime, except in those cases in which someone is being exploited. In any case, any woman who has become pregnant due to incestuous intercourse will have ready access to an early abortion. If she declines this opportunity and if there is no evidence of genetic abnormality, she may not simply change her mind later. The same obviously applies to pregnancy due to rape, including statutory rape. The practical problems should be approached by providing suitable counseling.

A permissive policy for early abortions will also render socioeconomic grounds redundant. Since social constraints do not normally create an emergency for which abortion is the only solution, and since women will be able to terminate pregnancies at will in the early stages, there is no need for separate recognition of social or economic justifications for abortion.

An adequate abortion policy is thus a conjunction of a permissive policy for early abortions and a moderate policy for late abortions. The obvious remaining question is where to draw the boundary between the two classes of cases. When we are dealing with the morality of abortion, borderline fuzziness is both inevitable and tolerable. Many moral problems turn on factors that are matters of degree. Where such factors are present, we cannot avoid borderline cases whose status is unclear or indeterminate. It is a defect in a moral theory to draw sharp lines where there are none, or to treat hard cases as though they were easy. But what makes for good morals may also make for bad law. An abortion policy must be enforceable and so must divide cases as clearly as possible. A threshold stage separating early from late abortions must here give way to a cutoff point.

Since there is no threshold point in fetal development, any precise upper limit on the application of a permissive policy will be to some extent arbitrary. Clearly it must be located within the threshold period, thus sometime in the second trimester. Beyond this constraint the choice of a time limit may be made on pragmatic grounds. If a permissive policy for early abortions is to promote their autonomy, women must have time to discover that they are pregnant and to decide on a course of action. This factor will tend to push the cutoff point toward the end of the second trimester. On the other hand, earlier abortions are substantially safer and more economical of scarce medical resources than later ones. This factor will tend to pull the cutoff point toward the beginning of the second trimester. Balancing these considerations would incline one toward a time limit located sometime around the midpoint of pregnancy. But it should not be pretended that there is a unique solution to this policy problem. Differential policies may legitimately vary (within constraints) in their choice of a boundary between permissiveness and moderation.

Since abortion is a controversial matter, a society's abortion policy ought to include a "conscience clause" that allows medical personnel with conscientious objections to avoid involvement in abortions. It is in general preferable not to require doctors and nurses to perform tasks that deeply offend their moral principles, at least as long as others are willing to meet patients' needs. But it should be stated plainly that dissenting scruples are here being honored, not because they are correct (for they are not), but because a pluralistic society thrives when it promotes as much mutual respect of values as is compatible with the common good. The position of hospitals may be quite different. Any institution that is publicly funded is obliged to provide a suitably wide range of public services. Individual persons may opt out of performing abortions without thereby rendering abortions unavailable, but if entire hospitals do so, substantial numbers of women may have no meaningful access to this service. Whether abortions ought to be subsidized by government medical insurance plans is a question of social justice that cannot be answered without investigating the moral basis of compulsory social welfare programs in general. However, once a society has installed such a plan, there is no justification for omitting abortions from the list of services covered by it.[17]

The abortion policy here proposed is not novel: a differential policy with a time limit in the second trimester is already in operation in a number of countries.[18] But these policies seem usually to have been settled on as compromises between the opposed demands of liberals and conservatives rather than as matters of principle. Such compromises are attractive to politicians, who do not seek any deeper justification for the policies they devise. But there is a deeper justification for this policy. Although it does define a middle ground between the established views, it has not been defended here as the outcome of a bargaining procedure. Instead it has been advanced as the only policy congruent with an adequate criterion of moral standing and proper recognition of both a woman's right to autonomy and a fetus' right to life. A differential policy does not mediate between alternatives both of which are rationally defensible; instead it supersedes alternatives both of which have been discredited.

There is, therefore, a third way with the abortion issue. Its superiority over the established views lies largely in its sensitivity to a factor which both of them are committed to ignoring: the manifest differences between a fetus at the beginning and at the end of its prenatal existence. Views which deny the relevance of this factor deserve to command no more than minority support. Those who, for this reason, can embrace neither of the established views need feel no diffidence about seeking a middle ground between them. A moderate and differential view of abortion is capable of drawing the common-sense distinction between early and late abortions, and of showing that such a distinction is neither shallow nor arbitrary. The view from the middle lacks of course the simplicity which has made it so easy to market its more extreme counterparts. But then why should we think that the moral problems raised by abortion are simple?

---

[17]If abortion should be omitted on the ground that most pregnancies can be easily avoided then treatment for lung cancer must also be omitted since most cases of lung cancer can be even more easily avoided. There is no justification for restricting a woman's access to abortion by requiring the consent of the father. Until men learn to become pregnant, if a man wishes to father a child he must find a woman willing to carry and bear it. Parental consent is a slightly more complicated issue, since it raises questions about the competence of minors. In most cases a girl who is mature enough to be sexually active is also mature enough to decide on an abortion; in any case no parental consent regulation is justified for abortion that is not also justified for all comparable forms of minor surgery.

[18]Notably the United States, Great Britain, France, Italy, Sweden, the Soviet Union, China, India, Japan, and most of the countries of Eastern Europe. The cutoff points in these jurisdictions vary from the beginning to the end of the second trimester.

Viability

Heather J. Gert

I

Most people believe that while any abortion is regrettable, an abortion in the late stages of pregnancy is more so than one in the earlier stages. Many who are not seriously troubled by the thought of an abortion performed during the first weeks of pregnancy are very uncomfortable with the idea of an abortion performed in the last week. Nevertheless, it is difficult to feel wholly comfortable with any of the suggestions that have been made as to how far into a pregnancy a line should be drawn between when an abortion is easily justifiable, and when strong reasons are necessary to justify it.

For the purpose of this discussion, I will define an abortion as a procedure which intentionally brings about the premature termination of a pregnancy, except when that termination is intended to protect the health of the fetus. In keeping with the way in which the term 'abort' is used in other contexts (i.e. an aborted project, or mission), I will say that what is aborted is the pregnancy; thus, 'abortion' as used in this paper is short for 'abortion of a pregnancy.'

Perhaps the most often cited criterion for drawing the line between permissible and impermissible abortions is the viability of the fetus. However, many of us are uncomfortable with this criterion for the permissibility of abortion. Two main objections are usually given against using viability as such a criterion. First, it is far from clear why one's moral status should change as one develops the ability to survive on one's own— or, more accurately, as one develops the ability to survive independent of any *particular* person. It is objected that one's ability to survive on one's own has nothing to do with one's right to life; this appears to be a morally irrelevant factor. The second main objection is that the developmental stage at which a fetus becomes viable depends on the current state of medical technology, and it is unintuitive to claim that the current state of medical technology can have a bearing on the moral status of a being. How can it be that today a six-month-old fetus has a right to life, while a fetus of the same age

From Heather J. Gert, "Viability," *International Journal of Philosophical Studies* 3 (1995): 133–142. Reprinted by permission of Routledge.

and developmental stage did not have this right twenty years ago? Surely a being's moral status should not depend on outside factors in this way.

Nevertheless, a careful consideration of the real moral significance of viability can be used to shed new light on the abortion discussion. In this paper I will present a new objection to using viability as a criterion for determining the permissibility of abortion. One of its advantages over the above-mentioned objections is that, whereas they bring us nowhere nearer to solving the problem that viability was proposed to solve, the objection that I will present does just that. There are, however, many other ethical and philosophical problems associated with abortion that this paper will not touch upon.

Before we go on, let us consider in more detail the two commonly cited objections to viability mentioned above. In pressing the first objection—that viability is not a morally relevant factor—it is common to cite cases in which fully developed persons are not viable, in the sense of being able to survive on their own, but in which we would not allow them to be killed. Thus, for instance, no one who has undergone major surgery is viable, in this sense, for a considerable time after the operation, nor are persons with many sorts of serious handicaps. But we are not prepared to say that such persons may be killed. On the contrary, we may well feel that we have a special obligation to protect and assist them. To take a specific example: Who would say that a brilliant researcher should be killed because she has become a quadriplegic as the result of an accident? (In fact, given the way we have all been spoiled by life in modern society, most of us may not be viable!)

Unfortunately, this objection appears to rest on an illegitimate interpretation of 'viability.' 'Viability,' at least as it is used in respect to fetuses, is not correctly understood as the ability to survive on one's own. If this is how the term were intended there would be absolutely no sense at all in talking about a fetus achieving viability; but, of course, there is. A fetus is viable when it has reached a stage in its development such that it can survive without its gestational mother; *as a fetus* it never reaches a stage at which it can survive without anyone to care for it.[1]

Nevertheless, while the recognition that this is what is meant by 'viable' shows us that examples such as the ones used above are illegitimate, one might still argue that being viable, even in this more restricted sense of being able to survive without the assistance of another particular individual, does not add to one's moral worth. Surely, a being is no more or less worthy of a right to life in virtue of being viable in this narrower sense either.

The second objection—that the stage at which the fetus reaches viability changes with advances in medical technology—is related to the first in the following way: If viability itself were morally relevant, it would make no difference that the age at which viability is achieved changes. So for instance, if we believe that the ability to feel pain is a morally relevant feature, then if we discovered that fetuses were developing this

---

[1]Joel Feinberg has point out to me that there is a whole spectrum of senses in which the term 'viable' is used. These range from the definition that is used in the argument just discussed, unable to survive without assistance; to the definition according to which a fetus is said to be viable when it can survive outside its gestational mother's womb. Two intermediate senses are: (a) a fetus is viable when it can survive outside any natural womb, and (b) a fetus is viable when it can survive outside any natural or artificial womb. I believe that in discussions of abortion a fetus is generally considered to be viable as soon as it can survive outside its gestational mother's womb.

ability earlier and earlier, the age at which they developed the ability would not be an issue, we would simply be concerned to know when today's fetuses are able to feel pain.

What this objection adds to the first, however, is a clearer appeal to our intuition that the moral status of a being should not be determined by factors outside of itself. When we use viability as a criterion for determining when abortions are permissible we are using a fact about the current state of medical technology to pick out a fetus at a certain stage of development. We might have thought that this criterion *happened* to pick out fetuses which had reached a special morally significant stage in their own development, but because technology picks out fetuses at different stages as it advances, it cannot be doing this. Thus, this second objection can be used to strengthen the first: viability does not affect the moral status of the fetus, nor does it direct us to a morally relevant stage in its development.[2]

Despite these objections, however, there is something to the idea that the viability of the fetus is relevant to a woman's decision to abort her pregnancy. After having considered the following objection we will be able to see what, after all, is right about caring about viability.

II

As we saw in the previous section, there is a spectrum of senses in which the term 'viable' is used. As it is most often used in discussions of abortion, a fetus is said to be viable if it is able to survive outside its gestational mother's womb. More precisely, the term 'viable' is often used as shorthand for 'at the age of viability': the age of viability being *the earliest* age at which any fetus has been known to survive outside its gestational mother's womb. Needless to say, a fetus which has just reached the age of viability (and thus is viable in this shorthand sense) will not usually be viable in the sense of being able to survive outside its mother. In what follows I will depart somewhat from this usual practice and will take the age of viability to be the age at which a fetus is reasonably likely to be able to survive outside its mother.

How likely must it be that a fetus will survive outside its mother before we can say that it is *reasonably* likely to survive? This is a question that will have to be answered in much the same way that we answer other questions about the likelihood of death resulting from other policies and procedures. Governments create policies about speed limits, hazardous waste disposal, workplace safety, aid to poor families, and so on, knowing that these policies will result in a certain percentage of deaths. Presumably there will be a similar way to determine a standard in the case of viability.

---

[2]It might be argued that our responsibilities are determined, in part, by our abilities, and thus that our responsibilities to fetuses increase as our technology develops. Notice, however, that it is an impossibly circuitous route from here to the claim that viability is the proper cutoff point for abortions. *If* abortion is impermissible as long as we have the ability to preserve the life of the fetus, then *all* abortions will be impermissible since, by hypothesis, the fetus will survive as long as we simply refrain from performing the abortion. In this case, our level of technology is irrelevant.

It will no doubt be objected that it is not simply a matter of whether or not the fetus will survive the removal from its mother's womb. There is also the question of how severely the surviving fetus may be handicapped—physically, mentally, or both—by that removal. Again, governments legislate as to the "acceptable risk" of disability resulting from all types of hazards. This last objection suggests that we should further refine our definition. Finally, therefore, let us say that a fetus is viable when it is reasonably likely that it will survive outside its mother's womb without suffering a serious handicap as a result of its removal.

Now let us consider what we are really saying when we say that having an abortion after the fetus becomes viable is a more serious matter than having an abortion before it has reached viability. We seem to be saying that a woman is free to withdraw support from a fetus as long as this fetus is wholly dependent on her, but that as soon as it gains the ability to survive on its own (more accurately, as soon as it gains the ability to survive without her), she is no longer permitted to withdraw that support. Isn't it odd to give as a justification for requiring a pregnant woman to support a fetus the fact that it could be supported by others?[3]

Looking at the idea that the permissibility of aborting a pregnancy depends on the viability of the fetus in this way allows us to see that the suggestion seems almost backwards. (As long as it needs you, you are not responsible to it; when it doesn't need you any more, you are.) Does this mean that I intend to suggest that abortions should be more restricted in the early stages, and less restricted in the later? Should a woman be required to carry the fetus until it achieves viability, and then be permitted to have an abortion?

Before I explain my answer, let us step back for a moment and consider the moral distinction between abortion and infanticide. While some who argue for the permissibility of abortion find that regrettably, but for the sake of consistency, they must be willing to permit infanticide,[4] most of those who argue for the importance of allowing a woman the freedom to have an abortion are not willing to allow infanticide. Those who argue for the permissibility of abortion while denying the permissibility of infanticide point out that once the child is born, and is therefore physically separated from the woman, the woman is able to avoid its needs and demands without killing it. This, they say, is the explanation for the fact that she is not permitted to kill the newborn child. In fact, even those who feel that they must allow infanticide often seem to find solace in the knowledge that most women would be content to give the child away rather than kill it.

Here, then, is my response to the earlier questions. A pregnant woman, just as any other woman, has the right to control her own body.[5] *Prima facie,* that a woman has the

---

[3]Francis Kamm makes a very similar point in her book *Creation and Abortion* (New York: Oxford University Press, 1992).

[4]For example: Michael Tooley, "A Defense of Abortion and Infanticide," in Joel Feinberg (ed.), *The Problem of Abortion* (Belmont, CA: Wadsworth Publishing Co., 1973), pp. 51–91, and Mary Anne Warren, "On the Moral and Legal Status of Abortion," including postscript, in Richard Wasserstrom (ed.), *Today's Moral Problems*, 2nd ed., (New York: Macmillan, 1979), pp. 35–51.

[5]Just as with any other woman, it may sometimes be the case that a pregnant woman's right to control her own body comes into conflict with the rights of others. I will leave it open whether or not the fetus has rights that might come into conflict with its mother's.

right to control her own body means that she has the right to have a fetus taken from her body. In the early stages of pregnancy this necessarily means that the fetus will die, and so *if* the fetus has rights against the woman, it *may* be that her right is overridden and she cannot remove it. I have nothing philosophically interesting to say about this one way or the other. But, in the later stages of pregnancy, where the fetus is viable in the sense explained above, the woman has the right to have the fetus removed. That is, if there is no possibility that the fetus's possible right to life conflicts with the woman's rights she should be free to exercise those rights and abort her pregnancy.

Thus, whether or not abortions ought to be permitted before viability, a woman should be permitted to abort her pregnancy once the fetus is viable. On the other hand, barring a significantly increased risk to her own welfare, in the latter stages of pregnancy a woman seeking to have her pregnancy aborted should consent to allowing the fetus to be removed in such a way as to preserve its life. By saying that a woman should *consent* to allowing the fetus to live I am not committing myself to the claim that once viability is achieved the fetus must be kept alive; that is a further question, the answer to which will depend on what is said about the justification of abortions in general.[6] All I am saying here is that others should be permitted to care for the fetus, if they choose to do so. For instance, a biological father might choose to raise his child, or society might decide to allocate resources to caring for these children. Once a fetus has been removed from the body of a woman, her rights and responsibilities in regards to that fetus are no different from the rights and responsibilities of the biological father.[7] Nor, it seems to me, do these rights extend to demanding the death of the fetus.

Let us look at how this policy would apply to one of the most imaginative examples that has been presented in an article of abortion: Judith Jarvis Thomson's example of the famous violinist.[8] Briefly: Thomson tells a story in which we are encouraged to imagine ourselves to have been kidnapped and hooked up to an ailing but famous violinist, in such a way that if we detach ourselves he will die. According to Thomson, our intuitions tell us that while it may be admirable to consent to remain hooked up to the violinist until he is well and able to survive on his own, we are not obligated to do so.

So far, my intuitions agree with Thomson's. But let us make a change in her story. Let us say that there is one procedure to unhook ourselves from the violinist that will kill him, and another procedure that will allow him to live if someone else can be found to take care of him. Clearly, if one procedure is as easy as the other we have an obligation to choose the procedure that will allow him to live. (Notice that I have not claimed that we must remain hooked up to the violinist unless someone else will take care of him. I have only claimed that *if* there are others who are willing to care for him we should allow them to do so.)

---

[6] If, for instance, abortions are justified on the grounds that fetuses do not have a conscious desire for a future, then the fetus's removal is permissible even if it is certain that this removal will result in its death. On the other hand, if abortions are unjustified on the grounds that a fetus has a future like ours, then the permissibility of removing a fetus may be contingent on seeing to it that other means are provided for ensuring its survival.

[7] This is true in the normal case, but not in every one. For instance, men who donate sperm to a sperm bank do not have the responsibilities that the typical biological father does. Also, one might well argue that a woman who becomes pregnant as the result of rape has fewer responsibilities towards her child than does its father.

[8] Judith Jarvis Thomson, "A Defense of Abortion," *Philosophy and Public Affairs*, 1(1) (1971), pp. 47–66.

What if the procedure that would allow him to remain alive is more difficult or painful than the other? It seems to me that unless there is a significant difference in the amounts of difficulty and/or pain involved and provided that someone else is willing to be hooked up to him we have an obligation to choose that procedure which allows the violinist to survive. Thus I find that my intuitions in this case support the above suggestion.

III

With our discussion of viability in mind let us look at the reasoning used by the United States Supreme Court in arriving at its decision in *Roe v. Wade*:

In arriving at its decision, the Court asserts that the State has certain interests in restricting a woman's access to abortion. The first interest cited is that of the physical welfare of the woman. However, as the Court acknowledges, as medical technology has advanced having an abortion has become less and less risky:

> Consequently, an interest of the State in protecting the woman from an inherently hazardous procedure except when it would be equally dangerous for her to forgo it, has largely disappeared.[9]

Thus, while the State's interest in the health of the woman means that it retains an interest in ensuring that abortions are performed by qualified physicians using adequate facilities, it does not mean that the State can prohibit a woman from having an abortion on the grounds that the procedure places her at risk.

The second State interest cited is that of protecting the life of the fetus, insofar as it is a potential person (and citizen). On this issue the Court's opinion is that the State has an interest in preserving the life of the fetus, and that this interest becomes compelling when the fetus achieves viability:

> With respect to the State's important and legitimate interest in potential life, the "compelling" point is at viability. This is so because the fetus then presumably has the capability of meaningful life outside the mother's womb.[10]

But if the Court's argument for allowing restrictions on abortion rests on *the State's* interest in protecting the potential person, this can only mean that the State may use its power to protect the fetus. It need not follow from this that the State may impose responsibility for a fetus on any particular person. (Notice that the Court does *not* claim that *the woman* has a special obligation to the fetus or even that the fetus itself has a right to life; the conflict is between the rights of the woman and those of the State.) Thus, according to the Court's reasoning, it does not follow that the State can prohibit a woman from having a fetus removed from her body after that fetus has achieved

---

[9]United States Supreme Court, 410 U.S. 151.

[10]*Ibid.*, 163.

viability and the State can pursue its interest in other ways. To grant the State the right to protect a viable fetus is not the same as granting the State the right to require a pregnant woman to carry or subsequently care for that fetus. It never follows from the fact that the State has a certain interest that there are no restrictions on the ways in which it may protect that interest.[11]

While the decision in *Roe v. Wade* talks about the State's *interest* in the life of the fetus, those who oppose abortion often talk in terms of the State's *duty* to protect this life. Unfortunately there is at least one passage in the decision that encourages the impression that talk of interests is translatable into talk of duties.[12] This is an erroneous impression. There has never been any question that the Court's decision *allows* the State to place restrictions on abortions; it does not require such restrictions. From this it is clear that the Court does *not* hold that the State (or the woman) has a duty to protect the life of the fetus; legally, the fetus does not have any rights at all.[13] On the other hand, the State presumably does have a duty to protect a woman's constitutional rights. Thus, it seems most consistent with the U.S. Supreme Court's reasoning to conclude that while the State may require a woman to allow it to take care of her fetus, it cannot prohibit her from aborting her pregnancy once the fetus has achieved viability.

It might be argued that whether or not the State has, in fact, claimed that a woman has a responsibility to the fetus that she carries, she does, and that, moreover, it is a unique responsibility. But even if we grant that a woman has some sort of responsibility to a fetus, it would be extremely difficult to argue that her responsibility is unique. Even if it were argued that by engaging in sexual intercourse a woman knowingly risks becoming pregnant, and that in choosing to take this risk she must be responsible for the life she creates, this very argument shows that the man with whom she has had sexual intercourse is in precisely the same position. Thus, such a claim may provide the basis for an argument to the effect that the couple is jointly responsible for protecting that life, and so, perhaps, that they must pay for the facilities to keep the fetus alive if the woman is unwilling to carry it; it will not provide a basis for claiming that the woman must carry the child to term.

In fact, however, even if a couple is thought to have a special responsibility for a fetus, this responsibility cannot be so strong as to preclude the possibility of transferring that responsibility to other agents. Hardly anyone, as far as I know, has advocated the position that if a woman becomes pregnant she must not only bring the child to term, but must also keep the child after it has been born. Once the child is born, and is no longer essentially dependent on its mother, a prohibition on giving the child up for

---

[11]Sometimes this may even mean, in effect, that the State cannot pursue an acknowledged interest. For instance, the financial cost of pursuing that interest may be prohibitive. Thus, even if the State does not have the resources to support unwanted fetuses, it will not necessarily follow that it can require a pregnant woman to carry her child to term.

[12]"The third reason is the State's interest—*some phrase it in terms of duty*—in protecting prenatal life. . . . The States interest and *general obligation* to protect life then extends, it is argued, to prenatal life" (*ibid.*, 151, my emphasis).

[13]"All this, together with our observation, *supra*, that throughout the major portion of the 19th century prevailing legal abortion practices were far freer than they are today, persuades us that the word 'person,' as used in the Fourteenth Amendment, does not include the unborn" (*ibid.*, 159).

adoption is clearly undesirable. (Isn't the main alternative to abortion, suggested by right-to-life groups, giving the child up for adoption?) On what grounds, then, can it be argued that a viable fetus is the non-transferable responsibility of its biological parents?

In saying that the parents do not have a non-transferable responsibility, I have not ruled out the possibility that they have a transferable one. Certainly, parents have a transferable responsibility for their children. This responsibility is temporarily transferred when they hire a babysitter, or permanently transferred if they give their children up for adoption.[14] In either case the parents are responsible for seeing to it that their responsibility is properly transferred. If this is the correct analogy, then it would seem that a couple must make certain that the fetus which the woman plans to have removed will be cared for.[15] But another analogy can be made with our attitudes about one's moral responsibility towards unwanted kittens. While hardly anyone would consider it morally permissible to drown a kitten someone else has volunteered to care for, many consider it morally permissible to drown kittens when no one can be found to take responsibility for them. Which, if either of these, provides a proper analogy for our moral responsibilities towards viable fetuses can only be answered once we've taken a stand on what does, or does not, justify abortion in general. As noted above, I have not done this.

IV

Here is the final position advocated by this paper: Perhaps abortions should be permitted up until the fetus achieves viability. We have not touched on this. After that point a woman is definitely free to choose to abort her pregnancy when others are willing to care for the fetus which will be removed. It may also be that it is permissible for a woman to abort her pregnancy even if no one will care for the removed fetus. Whether or not this is permissible depends on the ultimate justification for permitting or forbidding pre-viability abortions. Again, pre-viability abortions have not been the topic of this paper.

Surprisingly, we have arrived at a conclusion that can give both those who hold the pro-choice position and those who hold the pro-life position more of what each claimed to want. It's interesting to note that each side defines itself in positive terms, in terms of what it values, and that neither claims to *want* the opposite of what the other wants. That is, the pro-choice side insists on the right of a woman to control her own body, and usually admits regretting that this will sometimes mean that the fetus is killed; while the pro-life side insists on the fetus's right to life, but regrets that upholding this right infringes on some of the woman's rights. Thus, each side thinks of itself as insisting on the upholding of a value (or right) that is, *unfortunately,* in conflict with the value or right insisted upon by the other side. But what we have just seen is that this need not be true; at least, it need not be true once viability is achieved.

---

[14]I owe this example to an anonymous referee.

[15]Note that there is at least a legal disanalogy here. The Court recognizes that children have rights, and has assigned responsibilities to parents in regards to their children. On the other hand, as noted above, it does not recognize any rights of a fetus.

Moreover, we can now see medical technology as part of the solution, rather than as adding to the problem, at least theoretically.[16] In the past, advances in medical technology have often widened the gulf between those who declared themselves to be pro-choice, and those who declared themselves to be pro-life. When abortion was a dangerous option it was not a choice to be actively sought, and in making abortions safer the medical community has seemed to some to have created a demand for something that should not be demanded. On the other hand, those with a moderate view on abortion, those who felt that abortion should be permissible until the fetus became viable, have been pushed closer to the pro-life position, as medical technology has brought viability closer to conception. On the position I have been suggesting, advocates of both positions should welcome all of these medical advances. When (and if) it becomes possible to safely remove a fetus any time after conception there will be no argument against allowing a woman the freedom to do this.

---

[16]While I would like to be able to say that the prospects look good for continuing advances in reducing the age of viability, many in the medical profession doubt that technology will advance so as to allow fetuses to become viable at an earlier age than they now are.

Abortion and the Sanctity of Life

Ronald Dworkin

The public argument over abortion has failed to recognize an absolutely crucial distinction. One side insists that human life begins at conception, that a fetus is a person from that moment, that abortion is murder or homicide or an assault on the sanctity of human life. But each of these phrases can be used to describe two very different ideas.

First, they can be used to make the claim that fetuses are creatures with interests of their own right from the start, including, preeminently, an interest in remaining alive, and that therefore they have the rights that all human beings have to protect these basic interests, including a right not to be killed. Abortion is wrong in principle, according to this claim, because abortion violates someone's right not to be killed, just as killing an adult is normally wrong because it violates the adult's right not to be killed. I shall call this the *derivative* objection to abortion because it presupposes and is derived from rights and interests that it assumes all human beings, including fetuses, have. Someone who accepts this objection, and who believes that government should prohibit or regulate abortion for this reason, believes that government has a derivative responsibility to protect a fetus.

The second claim that the familiar rhetoric can be used to make is very different: that human life has an intrinsic, innate value; that human life is sacred just in itself; and that the sacred nature of a human life begins when its biological life begins, even before the creature whose life it is has movement or sensation or interests or rights of its own. According to this second claim, abortion is wrong in principle because it disregards and insults the intrinsic value, the sacred character, of any stage or form of human life. I shall call this the *detached* objection, because it does not depend on or presuppose any particular rights or interests. Someone who accepts *this* objection, and argues that abortion should be prohibited or regulated by law for *this* reason, believes that government has a detached responsibility for protecting the intrinsic value of life. . . .

. . . [T]he idea that abortion is sinful or wicked because human life is sacred is very different from the claim that it is sinful or wicked because a fetus has a right to live. The former offers an argument against abortion that does not in any way presume that a fetus is a person with rights or interests of its own. For just as someone can think it wrong to remove life support from a permanently vegetative patient or to assist a dying cancer patient to kill himself, whether or not death is in the patient's interests, so one can think it wrong to destroy a fetus whether or not a fetus has any interests to protect. The belief that human life in any form has intrinsic, sacred value can therefore provide a reason for people to object violently to abortion, to regard it as wicked in all circumstances, without in any way believing that a tiny collection of cells just implanted in the womb, with as yet no organs or brain or nervous system, is already something with interests and rights. Someone who does not regard a fetus as a person with rights and interests may thus object to abortion just as strenuously as someone who insists it is. But he will object for a different reason and, as I shall try to show, with very different implications for the political question of whether and when the state ought to prohibit or permit abortion.

The confusion that I believe has poisoned the public controversy about abortion, and made it more confrontational and less open to argument and accommodation than it should be, is the confusion between these two kinds of reasons for believing that abortion is often, perhaps always, morally wrong. The scalding rhetoric of the "pro-life" movement seems to presuppose the derivative claim that a fetus is from the moment of its conception a full moral person with rights and interests equal in importance to those of any other member of the moral community. But very few people—even those who belong to the most vehemently anti-abortion groups—actually believe that, whatever they say. The disagreement that actually divides people is a markedly less polar disagreement about how best to respect a fundamental idea we almost all share in some form: that individual human life is sacred. Almost everyone who opposes abortion really objects to it, as they might realize after reflection, on the detached rather than the derivative ground. They believe that a fetus is a living, growing human creature and that it is intrinsically a bad thing, a kind of cosmic shame, when human life at any stage is deliberately extinguished. . . .

. . . [I]t is very hard to make any sense of the idea that an early fetus has interests of its own, in particular an interest in not being destroyed, from the moment of its conception.

Not everything that can be destroyed has an interest in not being destroyed, of course. A beautiful sculpture can be smashed, and that would be a terrible insult to the intrinsic value that great works of art embody and also very much against the interests of people who take pleasure in seeing or studying them. But a sculpture has no interests of its own; a savage act of vandalism is not unfair to *it*. Nor is it enough, for something to have interests, that it be alive and in the process of developing into something more mature—it is not against the interests of a baby carrot that it be picked early and brought to the table as a delicacy—nor even that it be something that will naturally develop into something different or more marvelous: a butterfly is much more beautiful than a caterpillar, but it is not better for the *caterpillar* to become one. Nor is it enough, for something to have interests, that it might, if treated in the right way, grow or develop into a human being. Imagine that (as some scientists apparently think conceivable) doctors were able to produce a child from an unfertilized ovum, by parthenogenesis. Menstruation would still not be against an ovum's interests; a woman who used contraception would not be violating some creature's fundamental right every month.

Nor is it even enough, for something to have interests, that it be actually en route to becoming a full human being. Imagine that, just as Dr. Frankenstein reached for the lever that would bring life to the assemblage of body parts on his laboratory table, someone appalled at the experiment smashed the apparatus. That act, whatever we think of it, would not have been harmful or unfair to the assemblage, or against its interests. It might be objected that a newly conceived fetus, unlike an unfertilized ovum or a collection of spare body parts, is growing into a full human being on its own, with no outside help needed. But that isn't true—external help, either from a pregnant woman or from scientific ingenuity, is essential. In any case, the difference is irrelevant to the present question; the collection of body parts wouldn't have interests—stopping the experiment before it came to life wouldn't be harmful to it—even if Dr. Frankenstein had designed the procedure to work automatically unless interrupted, and that automatic procedure had already begun. It makes no sense to suppose that something has interests of *its own*—as distinct from its being important what happens to it—unless it has, or has had, some form of consciousness: some mental as well as physical life.

Creatures that can feel pain have an interest in avoiding it, of course. It is very much against the interests of animals to subject them to pain, in trapping them or experimenting on them, for example. It is also very much against the interests of a fetus with a nervous system sufficiently developed to feel pain to inflict pain on it. But a fetus cannot be aware of pain until late in its mother's pregnancy, because its brain is not sufficiently developed before then. True, electrical brain activity arises in a fetus's brain stem, and it is capable of reflex movement, by approximately the seventh week after conception.[1] But there is no ground for supposing that pain is possible before a connection is made between the fetus's thalamus, into which peripheral nerve receptors flow, and its developing neocortex; and though the timing of that connection is still uncertain, it almost certainly takes place after mid-gestation. (One recent study concluded that "thalamic fibers pass into the human neocortex at about 22–23 weeks' gestation.")[2] These thalamic fibers do not begin to form synapses with cortical neurons until some later time, moreover, which has been estimated to be at about twenty-five weeks. According to a leading embryologist, "This process of vastly enhanced connectivity among cortical neurons presages a change in the electrical patterns observed in the brain via electroencephalograms. The patterns tend to become more regular and to show resemblance to adult patterns associated with sleeping and waking states. Such criteria lead some investigators to suggest that an adequate neural substrate for experienced pain does not exist until about the seventh month of pregnancy (thirty weeks), well into the period when prematurely born fetuses are viable with intensive life support. . . . To provide a safe margin against intrusion into possible primitive sentience," that expert continued, "the cortical maturation beginning at about thirty weeks is a reasonable landmark until more precise information becomes available. Therefore, since we should use extreme caution in respecting and protecting possible sentience, a provisional boundary at about twenty-six weeks should provide safety against reasonable concerns. This time is coincident with the present definition of viability."[3]

---

[1] See Michael Flower, "Neuromaturation of the Human Fetus," *Journal of Medicine and Philosophy* 10(1985): 237–251. According to F. Cunningham, P. MacDonald, and N. Grant, *Williams Obstetrics, 103* (18th ed., 1989), "local stimuli may evoke squinting, opening the mouth, incomplete finger closure, and plantar flexion of the toes" at eight weeks after conception.

[2] Flower, "Neuromaturation of the Human Fetus," 245.

[3] See Clifford Grobstein, *Science and the Unborn* (New York: Basic Books, 1988), 55, 130.

Of course, many acts that cause people no physical pain are against their interests. Someone acts against my interests when he chooses someone else for a job I want, or sues me, or smashes into my car, or writes a bad review of my book, or brings out a better mousetrap and prices it lower than mine, even when these actions cause me no physical pain and, indeed, even when I am unaware that they have happened. My interests are in play in these circumstances not because of my capacity to feel pain but because of a different and more complex set of capacities: to enjoy or fail to enjoy, to form affections and emotions, to hope and expect, to suffer disappointment and frustration. Since a creature can be killed painlessly, even after it has the capacity to feel pain, it is these more complex capacities, not the capacity to feel pain, that ground a creature's interests in continuing to live. It is not known when these more complex capacities begin to develop, in primitive or trace or shadowy form, in human beings. But it seems very unlikely that they develop in a human fetus before the point of cortical maturation, at around thirty weeks of gestational age, at which cortical electrical activity becomes more complex and periods of wakefulness can be distinguished by electroencephalogram from periods of sleep.[4] . . .

[The] important point—that an immature fetus cannot have interests and therefore cannot have an interest in surviving—is often overlooked because people are mistakenly drawn to an argument to the contrary something like this: It is very much in my interests that I am alive now and was not killed at any moment in the past. So when I was a just-conceived fetus, it must have been in my interests not to be aborted. Therefore any fetus has interests from the moment of its conception, and abortion is against those interests. This argument is fallacious, but we will have to take care to see why.

Once creatures with interests exist, then it makes sense to say, in retrospect, that certain events would have been against those interests if they had happened in the past. But it doesn't follow that if these events had happened they would have been against anyone's interests when they did. It is in the interests of every human being now alive, we might assume, that the earth did not explode in a collision with a gigantic meteor millions of years ago. But it does not follow that it would have been against any human being's interests if the earth had exploded then, because there would then never have been any human beings against whose interests that *could* have been. It is in my interests that my father didn't go on a long business trip the day before I was conceived. But it would not have been against anyone's interests, in that way, if he had done so because, once again, there would never have been anyone whose interests it could have harmed.

Of course, when a fetus is aborted, there is a creature for whom someone might think this bad; there is at least a candidate for that role. But the fetus's existence before it is aborted makes no difference to the logical point. If Frankenstein's monster were actually brought to life, and felt and acted like a real person, then it would have interests like any other such person, and it would plainly have been against those interests, in retrospect, if Frankenstein's apparatus had been smashed before the monster was created. But it doesn't follow that the collection of body parts on the laboratory table had interests before the switch was thrown, even though those body parts did exist, as just body parts, at that time. Whether abortion is against the interests of a fetus must depend on whether the fetus itself has interests at the time the abortion is performed, not whether interests will develop if no abortion takes place.

---

[4]Flower, "Neuromaturation of the Human Fetus," 246.

That distinction may help explain what some observers have found puzzling. Many people who believe that abortion is morally permissible nevertheless think it wrong for a pregnant woman to smoke or otherwise behave in ways injurious to the child she intends to bear. Critics find that contradictory; they say that because killing something is worse than injuring it, it cannot be wrong to smoke and yet not wrong to abort. The mistake in this criticism is just the mistake we have been analyzing. If a woman smokes during her pregnancy, a human being may later exist whose interests will have been seriously damaged by her behavior; but if she aborts, no one will exist whose interests her behavior will have damaged. This does not mean, of course, that there is nothing wrong with abortion, nor even that abortion is not morally worse than risking the health of a child who will be born. But it does mean that if early abortion is wrong, it is not for this reason; it is not because abortion is against the interests of the fetus whose life it terminates.

So my suggestion that most people who oppose abortion do so on the "detached" grounds I described has important advantages. It makes that opposition more self-consistent than the "derivative" interpretation can, and ties it to an important tradition of religious toleration with substantial roots in all genuine modern democracies. It avoids attributing to people the scarcely comprehensible idea that an organism that has never had a mental life can still have interests. But you may nevertheless find my suggestion arrogant, because it seems to claim to understand people's views about abortion better than they do themselves. After all, many people do say, and many of them carry banners declaring, that abortion is murder and that unborn people have a right to live. These phrases do seem to claim that fetuses have interests and rights. . . .

. . . We must be careful not to be misled by emotionally charged descriptions about human life and persons and murder that reveal strong emotions but are not a clear guide to the beliefs that people are emotional about. We must be especially careful about the highly ambiguous claims that human life begins at conception and that a fetus is a person from that moment. When someone makes one or the other of these claims, we cannot tell whether he means to make the derivative claim—that a fetus already has interests and rights of its own from the instant of conception, and that abortion is wrong for that reason—or the detached claim—that from the moment of conception a fetus embodies a form of human life which is sacred, a claim that does not imply that a fetus has interests of its own.

The familiar questions about when life begins and whether a fetus is a person are not simply but multiply ambiguous, and because these questions have become such familiar parts of the abortion debate, it is important that we understand the multiple ambiguities. Consider the question of whether human life begins at conception. Scientists disagree about exactly when the biological life of any animal begins, but it seems undeniable that a human embryo is an identifiable living organism at least by the time it is implanted in a womb, which is approximately fourteen days after its conception. It is also undeniable that the cells that compose an implanted embryo already contain biological codes that will govern its later physical development. When an opponent of abortion insists that a fetus is a human being, he may mean only to report these undeniable biological facts.

But it does not follow from those facts that a fetus also has rights or interests of the kind that government might have a derivative responsibility to protect. That is plainly a further question, and it is in large part a moral rather than a biological one. Nor does it follow that a fetus already embodies an intrinsic value that government might claim a detached responsibility to guard. That is also a different question, and also a moral rather than a biological one. The question of whether a fetus is a human being, either at conception or at some later point in pregnancy, is simply too ambiguous to be useful. The crucial questions are the two moral ones I have just described, and we should consider these directly and unambiguously. When does a human creature acquire interests and rights? When does the life of a human creature begin to embody intrinsic value, and with what consequences? We do not have to decide whether a fetus is a full human being at conception, or at what point it becomes one, or whether that process is gradual or abrupt, in order to answer those crucial questions.

Is a fetus a person? That is an even more treacherous question, because the term "person" has a great many uses and senses that can easily be confused. Suppose it is discovered that pigs are much more intelligent and emotionally complex than zoologists now think they are, and someone then asks whether a pig should therefore be considered a person. We might treat that as a philosophical question, asking us to refine our conception of what a person really is to see whether pigs, on the basis of our new information, qualify for that title. Or we might treat the question as a practical one, asking whether we should now treat pigs as we treat creatures we regard as people, acknowledging that pigs have a right to life so that it is wrong to kill them for food and a right not to be enslaved so that it is wrong to imprison them in pens. Of course, we might think that the two questions are connected: that if pigs are persons in the philosophical sense, they should be treated as others persons are, and that if they are not, they should not. But that does not necessarily follow, in either direction. We might believe philosophically that pigs are persons but that human beings have no reason to treat them as we treat one another; or, on the contrary, we might decide that pigs are not persons according to our best understanding of that complex concept but that nevertheless their capacities entitle them to the treatment persons give one another.

Once again it would be wise, therefore, to set aside the question of whether a fetus is a person, not because that question is unanswerable or metaphysical, as many judges and commentators have declared, but because it is too ambiguous to be helpful. Once again, we must ask, instead, the key moral questions I distinguished. Does a fetus have interests that should be protected by rights, including a right to life? Should we treat the life of a fetus as sacred, whether a fetus has interests or not? Once again, we do not need to decide whether a fetus is a person in order to answer these questions, and these are the questions that count. . . .

. . . Most people assume that the great, divisive abortion argument is at bottom an argument about a moral and metaphysical issue: whether even a just-fertilized embryo is already a human creature with rights and interests of its own, . . . an unborn child, helpless against the abortionist's slaughtering knife. The political rhetoric is explicit that this is the issue in controversy. . . .

I have suggested some preliminary reasons for thinking that this account of the abortion debate, in spite of its great popularity, is fatally misleading. We cannot understand most people's actual moral and political convictions about when abortion is permissible, and what government should do about abortion, in this way. The detailed structure of most conservative opinion about abortion is actually inconsistent with the assumption that a fetus has rights from the moment of conception, and the detailed structure of most liberal opinion cannot be explained only on the supposition that it does not. . . .

. . . [A] great many people who are morally very conservative about abortion—who believe that it is never, or almost never, morally permissible, and who would be appalled if any relative or close friend chose to have one—nevertheless think that the law should leave women free to make decisions about abortion for themselves, that it is wrong for the majority or for the government to impose its view upon them. . . .

Some conservatives who take that position base it . . . on the principle that church and state should be separate: they believe that freedom of decision about abortion is part of the freedom people have to make their own religious decisions. Others base their tolerance on a more general notion of privacy and freedom: they believe that the government should not dictate to individuals on any matter of personal morality. But people who really consider a fetus a person with a right to live could not maintain either version. Protecting people from murderous assault—particularly people too weak to protect themselves—is one of government's most central and inescapable duties.

Of course, a great many people who are very conservative about abortion do not take this tolerant view: they believe that governments should ban abortion, and some of them have devoted their lives to achieving that end. But even those conservatives who believe that the law should prohibit abortion recognize some exceptions. It is a very common view, for example, that abortion should be permitted when necessary to save the mother's life. Yet this exception is also inconsistent with any belief that a fetus is a person with a right to live. Some people say that in this case a mother is justified in aborting a fetus as a matter of self-defense; but any safe abortion is carried out by someone else—a doctor—and very few people believe that it is morally justifiable for a third party, even a doctor, to kill one innocent person to save another.

Abortion conservatives often allow further exceptions. Some of them believe that abortion is morally permissible not only to save the mother's life but also when pregnancy is the result of rape or incest. The more such exceptions are allowed, the clearer it becomes that conservative opposition to abortion does not presume that a fetus is a person with a right to live. It would be contradictory to insist that a fetus has a right to live that is strong enough to justify prohibiting abortion even when childbirth would ruin a mother's or a family's life but that ceases to exist when the pregnancy is the result of a sexual crime of which the fetus is, of course, wholly innocent.

On the other side, a parallel story emerges. Liberal views about abortion do not follow simply from denying that a fetus is a person with a right to live; they presuppose some other important value at stake. I exempt here the views of people who think that abortion is never even morally problematic . . . and that women who have scruples about abortion, or regret or remorse, are silly. Most people who regard themselves as liberal about abortion hold a more moderate, more complex view. I will construct an example of such a view, though I do not mean to suggest that all moderate liberals accept all parts of it.

A paradigm liberal position on abortion has four parts. First, it rejects the extreme opinion that abortion is morally unproblematic, and insists, on the contrary, that abortion is always a grave moral decision, at least from the moment at which the genetic individuality of the fetus is fixed and it has successfully implanted in the womb, normally after about fourteen days. From that point on, abortion means the extinction of a human life that has already begun, and for that reason alone involves a serious moral cost.

Abortion and the Sanctity of Life

Abortion is never permissible for a trivial or frivolous reason; it is never justifiable except to prevent serious damage of some kind. It would be wrong for a woman to abort her pregnancy because she would otherwise have to forfeit a long-awaited European trip, or because she would find it more comfortable to be pregnant at a different time of year, or because she has discovered that her child would be a girl and she wanted a boy.

Second, abortion is nevertheless morally justified for a variety of serious reasons. It is justified not only to save the life of the mother and in cases of rape or incest but also in cases in which a severe fetal abnormality has been diagnosed—the abnormalities of thalidomide babies, for example, or of Tay-Sachs disease—that makes it likely that the child, if carried to full term, will have only a brief, painful, and frustrating life. Indeed, in some cases, when the abnormality is very severe and the potential life inevitably a cruelly crippled and short one, the paradigm liberal view holds that abortion is not only morally permitted but may be morally required, that it would be wrong knowingly to bring such a child into the world.

Third, a woman's concern for her own interests is considered an adequate justification for abortion if the consequences of childbirth would be permanent and grave for her or her family's life. Depending on the circumstances, it may be permissible for her to abort her pregnancy if she would otherwise have to leave school or give up a chance for a career or a satisfying and independent life. For many women, these are the most difficult cases, and people who take the paradigm liberal view would assume that this expectant mother would suffer some regret if she decided to abort. But they would not condemn the decision as selfish; on the contrary, they might well suppose that the contrary decision would be a serious moral mistake.

The fourth component in the liberal view is the political opinion that I said moral conservatives about abortion sometimes share: that at least until late in pregnancy, when a fetus is sufficiently developed to have interests of its own, the state has no business intervening even to prevent morally impermissible abortions, because the question of whether an abortion is justifiable is, ultimately, for the woman who carries the fetus to decide. Others—mate, family, friends, the public—may disapprove, and they might be right, morally, to do so. The law might, in some circumstances, oblige her to discuss her decision with others. But the state in the end must let her decide for herself; it must not impose other people's moral convictions upon her.

I believe that these four components in the paradigm liberal view represent the moral convictions of many people—at least a very substantial minority in the United States and other Western countries. The liberal view they compose is obviously inconsistent with any assumption that an early-stage fetus is a person with rights and interests of its own. That assumption would, of course, justify the view that abortion is always morally problematic, but it would plainly be incompatible with the fourth component of the package, that the state has no right to protect a fetus's interests through the criminal law, and even more plainly with the third component: if a fetus does have a right to live, a mother's interests in having a fulfilling life could hardly be thought more important than that right. Even the second component, which insists that abortion may be morally permissible when a fetus is seriously deformed, is hard to justify if one assumes that a fetus has a right to remain alive. In cases when a child's physical deformities are so painful or otherwise crippling that we believe it would be in the best interests of the child to die, we might say that abortion, too, would have been in the child's best interests. But that is not so in every case in which the paradigm liberal view allows abortion; even children with quite terrible deformities may form attachments, give and receive love, struggle, and to some degree conquer their handicaps. If their lives are worth a great deal, then, how could it have been better for *them* to have been killed in the womb?

But though the presumption that a fetus has no rights or interests of its own is *necessary* to explain the paradigm liberal view, it is not sufficient because it cannot, alone, explain why abortion is ever morally wrong. Why should abortion raise any moral issue at all if there is no one whom it harms? Why is abortion then *not* like a tonsillectomy? Why should a woman feel any regret after an abortion? Why should she feel more regret than she does after sex with contraception? The truth is that liberal opinion, like the conservative view, presupposes that human life itself has intrinsic moral significance, so that it is in principle wrong to terminate a life even when no one's interests are at stake. Once we see this clearly, then we can explain why liberal and conservative opinions differ in the ways they do. . . .

The Idea of the Sacred

What does it mean to say that human life is intrinsically important? Something is *instrumentally* important if its value depends on its usefulness, its capacity to help people get something else they want. Money and medicine, for example, are only instrumentally valuable: no one thinks that money has value beyond its power to purchase things that people want or need, or that medicine has value beyond its ability to cure. Something is *subjectively* valuable only to people who happen to desire it. Scotch whiskey, watching football games, and lying in the sun are valuable only for people, like me, who happen to enjoy them. I do not think that others who detest them are making any kind of a mistake or failing to show proper respect for what is truly valuable. They just happen not to like or want what I do.

Something is intrinsically valuable, on the contrary, if its value is *independent* of what people happen to enjoy or want or need or what is good for them. Most of us treat at least some objects or events as intrinsically valuable in that way: we think we should admire and protect them because they are important in themselves, and not just if or because we or others want or enjoy them. Many people think that great paintings, for example, are intrinsically valuable. They are valuable, and must be respected and protected, because of their inherent quality as art, and not because people happen to enjoy looking at them or find instruction or some pleasurable aesthetic experience standing before them. We say that we want to look at one of Rembrandt's self-portraits because it is wonderful, not that it is wonderful because we want to look at it. . . .

Is human life subjectively or instrumentally or intrinsically valuable? Most of us think it is all three. We treat the value of someone's life as instrumental when we measure it in terms of how much his being alive serves the interests of others: of how much what he produces makes other people's lives better, for example. When we say that Mozart's or Pasteur's life had great value because the music and medicine they created served the interests of others, we are treating their lives as instrumentally valuable. We treat a person's life as subjectively valuable when we measure its value to him, that is, in terms of how much *he* wants to be alive or how much being alive is good for him. So if we say that life has lost its value to someone who is miserable or in great pain, we are treating that life in a subjective way.

Let us call the subjective value a life has for the person whose life it is its *personal* value. It is personal value we have in mind when we say that normally a person's life is the most important thing he or she has. It is personal value that a government aims to protect, as fundamentally important, when it recognizes and enforces people's right to life. So it is understandable that the debate about abortion should include the question of whether a fetus has rights and interests of its own. If it does, then it has a personal interest in continuing to live, an interest that should be protected by recognizing and enforcing a right to life. I have argued that an early fetus has no interests and rights, and that almost no one thinks it does; if personal value were the only pertinent kind of value at stake in abortion, then abortion would be morally unproblematic.

If we think, however, that the life of any human organism, including a fetus, has intrinsic value whether or not it also has instrumental or personal value—if we treat any form of human life as something we should respect and honor and protect as marvelous in itself—then abortion remains morally problematic. If it is a horrible desecration to destroy a painting, for example, even though a painting is not a person, why should it not be a much greater desecration to destroy something whose intrinsic value may be vastly greater?

We must notice a further and crucial distinction: between what we value incrementally—what we want more of, no matter how much we already have—and what we value only once it already exists. Some things are not only intrinsically but incrementally valuable. We tend to treat knowledge that way, for example. Our culture wants to know about archaeology and cosmology and galaxies many millions of light-years away—even though little of that knowledge is likely to be of any practical benefit— and we want to know as much of all that as we can. But we do not value human life that way. Instead, we treat human life as sacred or inviolable. . . . The hallmark of the sacred as distinct from the incrementally valuable is that the sacred is intrinsically valuable because—and therefore only once—it exists. It is inviolable because of what it represents or embodies. It is not important that there be more people. But once a human life has begun, it is very important that it flourish and not be wasted. . . .

Something is sacred or inviolable when its deliberate destruction would dishonor what ought to be honored. What makes something sacred in that way? We can distinguish between two processes through which something becomes sacred for a given culture or person. The first is by association or designation. In ancient Egypt, for example, certain animals were held sacred to certain gods; because cats were associated with a certain goddess, and for no other reason, it was sacrilegious to injure them. In many cultures, people take that attitude toward national symbols, including flags. Many Americans consider the flag sacred because of its conventional association with the life of the nation; the respect they believe they owe their country is transferred to the flag. . . .

The second way something may become sacred is through its history, how it came to be. In the case of art, for example, inviolability is not associational but genetic: it is not what a painting symbolizes or is associated with but how it came to be that makes it valuable. We protect even a painting we do not much like, just as we try to preserve cultures we do not especially admire, because they embody processes of human creation we consider important and admirable.

We take a parallel attitude, we must now notice, toward aspects of the natural world: in our culture, we tend to treat distinct animal species (though not individual animals) as sacred. We think it very important, and worth considerable economic expense, to

protect endangered species from destruction at human hands or by a human enterprise—a market in rhinoceros tusks, valued for the supposed aphrodisiac power; dams
that threaten the only habitat of a certain species of fish; or timbering practices that will
destroy the last horned owls. We are upset—it would be terrible if the rhinoceros ceased
to exist—as we are indignant: surely it is wrong to allow such a catastrophe just so that
human beings can make more money or increase their power. . . .

. . . We consider it a kind of cosmic shame when a species that nature has developed
ceases, through human actions, to exist.

I put the point that way—about not destroying what nature has created—to emphasize the similarity I claim between our reverence for art and our concern for the survival
of species. Both art and species are examples of things inviolable to us not by association but in virtue of their history, of how they came to exist. We see the evolutionary
process through which species were developed as itself contributing, in some way, to
the shame of what we do when we cause their extinction now. Indeed, people who are
concerned to protect threatened species often stress the connection between art and nature themselves by describing the evolution of species as a process of creation.

For most Americans, and for many people in other countries, the evolutionary process is quite literally creative, for they believe that God is the author of nature. On that
assumption, causing a species to disappear, wholly to be lost, is destroying a creative
design of the most exalted artist of all. But even people who do not take that view, but
who instead accept the Darwinian thesis that the evolution of species is a matter of accidental mutation rather than divine design, nevertheless often use artistic metaphors of
creation. They describe discrete animal species as not just accidents but as achievements of adaptation, as something that nature has not just produced but wrought. . . .

Our concern for the preservation of animal species reaches its most dramatic and intense form, of course, in the case of one particular species: our own. It is an inarticulate, unchallenged, almost unnoticed, but nevertheless absolute premise of our political
and economic planning that the human race must survive and prosper. This unspoken
assumption unites the two different examples of sanctity we have so far identified. Our
special concern for art and culture reflects the respect in which we hold artistic creation, and our special concern for the survival of animal species reflects a parallel respect for what nature, understood either as divine or as secular, has produced. These
twin bases of the sacred come together in the case of the survival of our own species,
because we treat it as crucially important that we survive not only biologically but culturally, that our species not only lives but thrives. That is the premise of a good part of
our concern about conservation and about the survival and health of cultural and artistic traditions. We are concerned not only about ourselves and others now alive, but
about untold generations of people in centuries to come. . . .

. . . Our concern for future generations is not a matter of justice . . . but of our instinctive sense that human flourishing as well as human survival is of sacred importance. . . .

The Sanctity of Each Human Life

An obscure nineteenth-century Austrian philosopher, Joseph Popper-Lynkeus, said that
the death of any human being, except of a murderer or a suicide, was "a far more important happening than any political or religious or national occurrence, or the sum total of

the scientific and artistic and technological advances made throughout the ages by all the peoples of the world."[5] He added that anyone tempted to regard this extraordinary claim as an exaggeration should "imagine the individual concerned to be himself or his best beloved." His addition confuses the intrinsic value of human life with what I called its personal value. My life may be personally more important to me than anything else, but it does not follow that it is intrinsically more important, and once that distinction is made, it is ludicrous to suppose that even a premature and tragic death, let alone a natural death after a long life, is intrinsically a worse event than the destruction of all human art and knowledge would be. But Popper-Lynkeus's claim does capture, in hyperbolic form, a conviction that must now be our main concern: that in some circumstances the deliberate ending of a single human life is intrinsically bad—objectively a shame—in the same way as the destruction of great art or the loss of important knowledge would be.

We are now in a better position to appreciate that conviction. I said that we treat the preservation and prosperity of our own species as of capital importance because we believe that we are the highest achievements of God's creation, if we are conventionally religious, or of evolution, if we are not, and also because we know that all knowledge and art and culture would disappear if humanity did. That combination of nature and art—two traditions of the sacred—supports the further and more dramatic claim that each individual human life, on its own, is also inviolable, because each individual life, on its own, can be understood as the product of both creative traditions. The first of these traditions—the idea that nature is creative—has had a prominent role as a basis for that claim. The dominant Western religious traditions insist that God made humankind "in His own image," that each individual human being is a representation and not merely a product of a divine creator, and people who accept that article of faith will understandably think that each human being, not just the species as a whole, is a creative masterpiece. A secular form of the same idea, which assigns the masterpiece to nature rather than God, is also a staple of our culture—the image of a human being as the highest product of natural creation is one of Shakespeare's most powerful, for example "What a piece of work is a man!" says Hamlet. . . . In these and other ways, the idea that human beings are special among natural creations is offered to explain why it is horrible that even a single human individual life should be extinguished.

The role of the other tradition of the sacred in supporting the sanctity of life is less evident but equally crucial: each developed human being is the product not just of natural creation, but also of the kind of deliberative human creative force that we honor in honoring art. A mature woman, for example, is in her personality, training, capacity, interests, ambitions, and emotions, something like a work of art because in those respects she is the product of human creative intelligence, partly that of her parents and other people, partly that of her culture, and also, through the choices she has made, her *own* creation. . . .

The idea that each individual human life is inviolable is therefore rooted, like our concern for the survival of our species as a whole, in two combined and intersecting bases of the sacred: natural *and* human creation. Any human creature, including the most immature embryo, is a triumph of divine or evolutionary creation, which produces a complex, reasoning being from, as it were, nothing, and also of what we often call the

---

[5]See Paul Edwards, ed., *The Encyclopedia of Philosophy* 6 (New York: Macmillan, 1967; New York: The Free Press, 1972), 403.

"miracle" of human reproduction, which makes each new human being both different from and yet a continuation of the human beings who created it. . . .

. . . The second form of sacred creation, the human as distinct from the natural investment, is also immediate when pregnancy is planned, because a deliberate decision of parents to have and bear a child is of course a creative one. Any surviving child is shaped in character and capacity by the decisions of parents and by the cultural background of community. As that child matures, in all but pathological cases, his own creative choices progressively determine his thoughts, personality, ambitions, emotions, connections, and achievements. He creates his life just as much as an artist creates a painting or a poem. I am not suggesting, as some nineteenth-century Romantic writers did, that a human life is literally a work of art. That is a dangerous idea, because it suggests that we should value a person in the same way that we value a painting or a poem, valuing him for beauty or style or originality rather than personal or moral or intellectual qualities. But we can—and do—treat leading a life as itself a kind of creative activity, which we have at least as much reason to honor as artistic creation.

The life of a single human organism commands respect and protection, then, no matter in what form or shape, because of the complex creative investment it represents and because of our wonder at the divine or evolutionary processes that produce new lives from old ones, at the processes of nation and community and language through which a human being will come to absorb and continue hundreds of generations of cultures and forms of life and value, and, finally, when mental life has begun and flourishes, at the process of internal personal creation and judgment by which a person will make and remake himself, a mysterious, inescapable process in which we each participate, and which is therefore the most powerful and inevitable source of empathy and communion we have with every other creature who faces the same frightening challenge. The horror we feel in the willful destruction of a human life reflects our shared inarticulate sense of the intrinsic importance of each of these dimensions of investment.

The Metric of Disrespect

I must now try to show how this understanding of the sacredness of human life allows us better to explain the two opposing attitudes toward abortion than does the traditional account, which supposes that these attitudes are based on different views about whether and when a fetus is a person with a right to life. I shall assume that conservatives and liberals all accept that in principle human life is inviolable in the sense I have defined, that any abortion involves a waste of human life and is therefore, in itself, a bad thing to happen, a shame. And I shall try to show how that assumption explains why the two sides both agree and disagree in the ways that they do.

I begin with their agreement. Conservatives and liberals both suppose, as I said, that though abortion is always morally problematic and often morally wrong, it is worse on some occasions than on others. They suppose, in other words, that there are degrees of badness in the waste of human life. What measure are they assuming in those judgments? Let us put that question in a more general form. We all assume that some cases of premature death are greater tragedies than others, not only when we are puzzling about abortion, but in the context of many other events as well. Most of us would think it worse when a young woman dies in a plane crash than when an elderly man does, for example, or a boy than a middle-aged man. What measure of tragedy are we assuming when we think this? What measure should we assume? . . .

. . . How should we measure and compare the waste of life, and therefore the insult to the sanctity of life, on different occasions?

We should consider, first, a simple and perhaps natural answer to that question. Life is wasted, on this simple view, when life is lost, so that the question of how much has been wasted by a premature death is answered by estimating how long the life cut short would probably otherwise have lasted. This simple answer seems to fit many of our intuitive convictions. It seems to explain the opinion I just mentioned, for example: that the death of a young woman in an airplane crash is worse than the death of an old man would be. The young woman would probably otherwise have had many more years left to live.

The simple answer is incomplete, because we can measure life—and therefore loss of life—in different ways. Should we take into account only the duration of life lost with no regard to its quality? Or should we take quality into account as well? Should we say that the loss of the young woman who died in the crash would be greater if she had been looking forward to a life full of promise and pleasure than if she was physically or psychologically handicapped in some permanent and grave way? Should we also take into account the loss her death would cause to the lives of others? Is the death of a parent of young children, or of a brilliant employer of large number of people, or of a musical genius, a worse waste of life than the death at the same age of someone whose life was equally satisfying to himself but less valuable to others?

We should not puzzle over these alternatives, however, because this simple answer, which measures waste of life only in terms of life lost, is unacceptable whether we define that loss only as duration of life or include quality of life or benefits to others. It is unacceptable, in any of these forms, for two compelling reasons.

First, though the simple answer seems to fit some of our convictions, it contradicts other important and deeply held ones. If the waste of life were to be measured only in chronological terms, for example, then an early-stage abortion would be a worse insult to the sanctity of life, a worse instance of life being wasted, than a late-stage abortion. But almost everyone holds the contrary assumption that the later the abortion—the more like a child the aborted fetus has already become—the worse it is. We take a similar view about the death of young children. It is terrible when an infant dies but worse, most people think, when a three-year-old child dies and worse still when an adolescent does. Almost no one thinks that the tragedy of premature death decreases in a linear way as age increases. Most people's sense of that tragedy, if it were rendered as a graph relating the degree of tragedy to the age at which death occurs, would slope upward from birth to some point in late childhood or early adolescence, then follow a flat line until at least very early middle age, and then slope down again toward extreme old age. . . .

Nor does the simple interpretation of how death wastes life fit our feelings better in the more elaborate forms I mentioned. Our common view that it is worse when a late-stage fetus is aborted or miscarried than an early-stage one, and worse when a ten-year-old child dies than an infant, makes no assumptions about the quality of the lives lost or their value for others.

The simple view of wasted life fails for a second, equally important reason. It wholly fails to explain the important truth . . . that though we treat human life as sacred, we do not treat it as incrementally good; we do not believe abstractly that the more human lives that are lived the better. The simple claim that a premature death is tragic only because life is lost—only because some period of life that might have been lived by someone will not be—gives us no more reason to grieve over an abortion or any premature death than we have to grieve over contraception or any other form of birth control. In both cases, less human life is lived than might otherwise be.

The "simple loss" view we have been considering is inadequate because it focuses only on future possibilities, on what will or will not happen in the future. It ignores the crucial truth that waste of life is often greater and more tragic because of what has already happened in the past. The death of an adolescent girl is worse than the death of an infant girl because the adolescent's death frustrates the investments she and others have already made in her life—the ambitions and expectations she constructed, the plans and projects she made, the love and interest and emotional involvement she formed for and with others, and they for and with her.

I shall use "frustration" (though the word has other associations) to describe this more complex measure of the waste of life because I can think of no better word to suggest the combination of past and future considerations that figure in our assessment of a tragic death. Most of us hold to something like the following set of instinctive assumptions about death and tragedy. We believe, as I said, that a successful human life has a certain natural course. It starts in mere biological development—conception, fetal development, and infancy—but it then extends into childhood, adolescence, and adult life in ways that are determined not just by biological formation but by social and individual training and choice, and that culminate in satisfying relationships and achievements of different kinds. It ends, after a normal life span, in a natural death. It is a waste of the natural and human creative investments that make up the story of a normal life when this normal progression is frustrated by premature death or in other ways. But how bad this is—how great the frustration—depends on the stage of life in which it occurs, because the frustration is greater if it takes place after rather than before the person has made a significant personal investment in his own life, and less it if occurs after any investment has been substantially fulfilled, or as substantially fulfilled as is anyway likely.

This more complex structure fits our convictions about tragedy better than the simple loss-of-life measure does. It explains why the death of an adolescent seems to us worse in most circumstances than the death of an infant. It also explains how we can consistently maintain that it is sometimes undesirable to create new human lives while still insisting that it is bad when any human life, once begun, ends prematurely. No frustration of life is involved when fewer rather than more human beings are born, because there is no creative investment in lives that never exist. But once a human life starts, a process has begun, and interrupting that process frustrates an adventure already under way.

. . . Both conservatives and liberals assume that in some circumstances abortion is more serious and more likely to be unjustifiable than in others. Notably, both agree that a late-term abortion is graver than an early-term one. We cannot explain this shared conviction simply on the ground that fetuses more closely resemble infants as

pregnancy continues. People believe that abortion is not just emotionally more difficult but morally worse the later in pregnancy it occurs, and increasing resemblance
alone has no moral significance. Nor can we explain the shared conviction by noticing
that at some point in pregnancy a fetus becomes sentient. Most people think that abortion is morally worse early in the second trimester—well before sentience is possible—than early in the first one (several European nations, which permit abortion in
the first but not the second trimester, have made that distinction part of their criminal
law). And though that widely shared belief cannot be explained by the simple lost-life
theory, the frustration thesis gives us a natural and compelling justification of it. Fetal
development is a continuing creative process, a process that has barely begun at the instant of conception. Indeed, since genetic individuation is not yet complete at that
point, we might say that the development of a unique human being has not started until approximately fourteen days later, at implantation. But after implantation, as fetal
growth continues, the natural investment that would be wasted in an abortion grows
steadily larger and more significant.

Human and Divine

So our sense that frustration rather than just loss compromises the inviolability of human life does seem helpful in explaining what unites most people about abortion. The
more difficult question is whether it also helps in explaining what divides them. Let us
begin our answer by posing another question. I just described a natural course of human
life—beginning in conception, extending through birth and childhood, culminating in
successful and engaged adulthood in which the natural biological investment and the
personal human investment in that life are realized, and finally ending in natural death
after a normal span of years. Life so understood can be frustrated in two main ways. It
can be frustrated by premature death, which leaves any previous natural and personal
investment unrealized. Or it can be frustrated by other forms of failure: by handicaps or
poverty or misconceived projects or irredeemable mistakes or lack of training or even
brute bad luck; any one of these may in different ways frustrate a person's opportunity
to redeem his ambitions or otherwise to lead a full and flourishing life. Is premature
death always, inevitably, a more serious frustration of life than any of these other forms
of failure?

Decisions about abortion often raise this question. Suppose parents discover, early in
the mother's pregnancy, that the fetus is genetically so deformed that the life it would
lead after birth will inevitably be both short and sharply limited. They must decide
whether it is a worse frustration of life if the gravely deformed fetus were to die at
once—wasting the miracle of its creation and its development so far—or if it were to
continue to grow in utero, to be born, and to live only a short and crippled life. We
know that people divide about that question, and we now have a way to describe the division. On one view, immediate death of the fetus, even in a case like this one, is a more
terrible frustration of the miracle of life than even a sharply diminished and brief infant
life would be, for the latter would at least redeem some small part, however limited, of
the natural investment. On the rival view, it would be a worse frustration of life to allow

this fetal life to continue because that would add, to the sad waste of a deformed human's biological creation, the further, heartbreaking waste of personal emotional investments made in that life by others but principally by the child himself before his inevitable early death.

We should therefore consider this hypothesis: though almost everyone accepts the abstract principle that it is intrinsically bad when human life, once begun, is frustrated, people disagree about the best answer to the question of whether avoidable premature death is always or invariably the most serious possible frustration of life. Very conservative opinion, on this hypothesis, is grounded in the conviction that immediate death is inevitably a more serious frustration than any option that postpones death, even at the cost of greater frustration in other respects. Liberal opinion, on the same hypothesis, is grounded in the opposite conviction: that in some cases, at least, a choice for premature death minimizes the frustration of life and is therefore not a compromise of the principle that human life is sacred but, on the contrary, best respects that principle.

What reasons do people have for embracing one rather than the other of these positions? It seems plain that whatever they are, they are deep reasons, drawn consciously or unconsciously from a great network of other convictions about the point of life and the moral significance of death. If the hypothesis I just described holds—if conservatives and liberals disagree on whether premature death is always the worst frustration of life—then the disagreement must be in virtue of a more general contrast between religious and philosophical orientations.

So I offer another hypothesis. Almost everyone recognizes, as I have suggested, that a normal, successful human life is the product of two morally significant modes of creative investment in that life, the natural and the human. But people disagree about the relative importance of these modes, not just when abortion is in question but on many other mortal occasions as well. If you believe that the natural investment in a human life is transcendently important, that the gift of life itself is infinitely more significant than anything the person whose life it is may do for himself, important though that may be, you will also believe that a deliberate, premature death is the greatest frustration of life possible, no matter how limited or cramped or unsuccessful the continued life would be.[6] On the other hand, if you assign much greater relative importance to the human contribution to life's creative value, then you will consider the frustration of that contribution to be a more serious evil, and will accordingly see more point in deciding that life should end before further significant human investment is doomed to frustration.

We can best understand some of our serious disagreements about abortion, in other words, as reflecting deep differences about the relative moral importance of the natural and human contributions to the inviolability of individual human lives. In fact, we can make a bolder version of that claim: we can best understand the full range of opinion

---

[6]Many people who hold that view will make exceptions: for capital punishment, for example, and for killing the enemy in war. I cannot consider, [here], the large and important question of how far these exceptions contradict the principle. But people who believe that the natural contribution to life is paramount for a particular reason—that God has created all life—will obviously not count these as contradictions if they also believe that executing murderers or killing enemy soldiers in a just war is also God's will.

about abortion, from the most conservative to the most liberal, by ranking each opinion about the relative gravity of the two forms of frustration along a range extending from one extreme position to the other—from treating any frustration of the biological investment as worse than any possible frustration of human investment, through more moderate and complex balances, to the opinion that frustrating mere biological investment in human life barely matters and that frustrating a human investment is always worse.

If we look at the controversy this way, it is hardly surprising that many people who hold views on the natural or biological end of that spectrum are fundamentalist or Roman Catholic or strongly religious in some other orthodox religious faith—people who believe that God is the author of everything natural and that each human fetus is a distinct instance of his most sublime achievement. Our hypothesis explains how orthodox religion can play a crucial role in forming people's opinions about abortion even if they do not believe that a fetus is a person with its own right to life. . . .

This is not to suggest, however, that only conventionally religious people who believe in a creator God are conservatives about abortion. Many other people stand in awe of human reproduction as a natural miracle. Some of them, as I said, embrace the mysterious but apparently powerful idea that the natural order is in itself purposive and commands respect as sacred. . . . They may well think that any frustration of the natural investment in human life is so grave a matter that it is rarely if ever justified. . . . They might therefore be just as firmly opposed to aborting a seriously deformed fetus as any religiously orthodox conservative would be.

Nor does it follow, on the other hand, that everyone who is religious in an orthodox way or everyone who reveres nature is therefore conservative about abortion. As we have seen, many such people, who agree that unnecessary death is a great evil, are also sensitive to and emphatic about the intrinsic badness of the waste of human investment in life. They believe that the frustration of that contribution—for example, in the birth of a grievously deformed fetus whose investment in its own life is doomed to be frustrated—may in some circumstances be the worse of two evils, and they believe that their religious conviction or reverence for nature is not only consistent with but actually requires that position. Some of them take the same view about what many believe to be an even more problematic case: they say that their religious convictions entail that a woman should choose abortion rather than bear a child when that would jeopardize her investment in her *own* life.

I described extreme positions at two ends of the spectrum: that only natural investment counts in deciding whether abortion wastes human life, and that only human investment counts. In fact, very few people take either of these extreme positions. For most people, the balance is more complex and involves compromise and accommodation rather than giving absolute priority to avoiding frustration of either the natural or the human investment. People's opinions become progressively less conservative and more liberal as the balance they strike gives more weight to the importance of not frustrating the human investment in life; more liberal views emphasize, in various degrees, that a human life is created not just by divine or natural forces but also, in a different but still central way, by personal choice, training, commitment, and decision. The shift in emphasis leads liberals to see the crucial creative investment in life, the investment that must not be frustrated if at all possible, as extending far beyond conception and biological growth and well into a human being's adult life. On that liberal opinion, as I have already suggested, it may be more frustrating of life's miracle when an adult's ambitions, talents, training, and expectations are wasted because of an unforeseen and unwanted pregnancy than when a fetus dies before any significant investment of that kind has been made. . . .

Conservative Exceptions: Reconsidering the Natural

I am defending the view that the debate over abortion should be understood as essentially about the following philosophical issue: is the frustration of a biological life, which wastes human life, nevertheless sometimes justified in order to avoid frustrating a human contribution to that life or to other people's lives, which would be a different kind of waste? If so, when and why? People who are very conservative about abortion answer the first of these questions No.

There is an even more extreme position, which holds that abortion is never justified, even when necessary to save the life of the mother. Though that is the official view of the Catholic church and of some other religious groups, only a small minority even of devout Catholics accept it, and even Justice Rehnquist, who dissented in *Roe v. Wade*, said that he had little doubt that it would be unconstitutional for states to prohibit abortion when a mother's life was at stake. So I have defined "very conservative" opinion to permit abortion in this circumstance. This exceedingly popular exception would be unacceptable to all conservatives, as I have said, if they really thought that a fetus is a person with protected rights and interests. It is morally and legally impermissible for any third party, such as a doctor, to murder one innocent person even to save the life of another one. But the exception is easily explicable if we understand conservative opinion as based on a view of the sanctity of life that gives strict priority to the divine or natural investment in life. If either the mother or the fetus must die, then the tragedy of avoidable death and the loss of nature's investment in life is inevitable. But a choice in favor of the mother may well seem justified to very conservative people on the ground that a choice against her would in addition frustrate the personal and social investments in her life; even they want only to minimize the overall frustration of human life, and that requires saving the mother's life in this terrible situation.

The important debate is therefore between people who believe that abortion is permissible *only* when it is necessary to save the mother's life and people who believe that abortion may be morally permissible in other circumstances as well. I shall consider the further exceptions the latter group of people claim, beginning with those that are accepted even by people who regard themselves as moderately conservative about abortion and continuing to those associated with a distinctly liberal position.

Moderate conservatives believe that abortion is morally permissible to end a pregnancy that began in rape. . . . On the a-fetus-is-a-person view, an exception for rape is even harder to justify than an exception to protect the life of the mother. Why should a fetus be made to forfeit its right to live, and pay with its life, for the wrongdoing of someone else? But once again, the exception is much easier to understand when we shift from the claim of fetal personhood to a concern for protecting the divine or natural investment in human life. Very conservative people, who believe that the divine contribution to a human life is everything and the human contribution almost nothing beside it, believe that abortion is automatically and in every case the worst possible compromise of life's inviolability, and they do not recognize an exception for rape. But moderately conservative people, who believe that the natural contribution normally *outweighs* the human contribution, will find two features of rape that argue for an exception.

First, according to every prominent religion, rape is itself a brutal violation of God's law and will, and abortion may well seem less insulting to God's creative power when the life it ends itself began in such an insult. Though rape would not justify violating the rights of an innocent person, it could well diminish the horror conservatives feel at an abortion's deliberate frustration of God's investment in life. . . .

Second, rape is a terrible desecration of its victim's investment in her own life, and even those who count a human investment in life as less important than God's or nature's may nevertheless recoil from so violent a frustration of that human investment. Rape is sickeningly, comprehensively contemptuous because it reduces a woman to a physical convenience, a creature whose importance is exhausted by her genital use, someone whose love and sense of self—aspects of personality particularly at stake in sex—have no significance whatsoever except as vehicles for sadistic degradation.

Requiring a woman to bear a child conceived in such an assault is especially destructive to her self-realization because it frustrates her creative choice not only in sex but in reproduction as well. In the ideal case, reproduction is a joint decision rooted in love and in a desire to continue one's life mixed with the life of another person. In Catholic tradition, and in the imagination of many people who are not Catholics, it is itself an offense against the sanctity of life to make love without that desire: that is the basis of many people's moral opposition to contraception. But we can dispute that sex is valuable only for reproduction, or creative only in that way—as most people do—while yet believing that sex is maximally creative when reproduction is contemplated and desired, and that reproduction frustrates creative power when it is neither. Of course, people in love often conceive by accident, and people not in love sometimes conceive deliberately, perhaps out of a misguided hope of finding love through children. Rape is not just the absence of contemplation and desire, however. For the victim, rape is the direct opposite of these, and if a child is conceived, it will be not only without the victim's desire to reproduce but in circumstances made especially horrible because of that possibility.

Moderate conservatives therefore find it difficult to insist that abortion is impermissible in cases of rape. It is sometimes said that conservatives who allow the rape exception but not, for example, an exception for unmarried teenagers whose lives would be ruined by childbirth must be motivated by a desire to punish unmarried women who have sex voluntarily. Though some conservatives may indeed believe that pregnancy is a fit punishment for sexual immorality, our hypothesis shows why conservatives who make only the rape exception do not necessarily hold that appalling view. The grounds on which I said conservatives might make an exception for rape do not extend so forcefully to pregnancies that follow voluntary intercourse. Though many religious people do think that unmarried sex also violates God's will, few consider it as grave as rape, and the argument that an unwanted pregnancy grotesquely frustrates a woman's creative role in framing her own life is weaker when the pregnancy follows voluntary sex. Of course, the difference would not be pertinent at all, as I said, if a fetus were a person with rights and interests of its own, because that person would be completely innocent whatever the nature or level of its mother's guilt.

Liberal Exceptions: Protecting Life in Earnest

Other, more permissive exceptions to the principle that abortion is wrong are associated with a generally liberal attitude toward abortion, and we should therefore expect, on the basis of the hypothesis we are testing, that they will reflect a greater respect for the human contribution to life and a correspondingly diminished concern with the natural. But we must not forget that people's attitudes about abortion range over a gradually changing spectrum from one extreme to the other, and that any sharp distinction between conservative and liberal camps is just an expository convenience.

Liberals think that abortion is permissible when the birth of a fetus would have a very bad effect on the quality of lives. The exceptions liberals recognize on that ground fall into two main groups: those that seek to avoid frustration of the life of the child, and those that seek to prevent frustration of the life of the mother and other family members.

Liberals believe that abortion is justified when it seems inevitable that the fetus, if born, will have a seriously frustrated life. That kind of justification is strongest, according to most liberals, when the frustration is caused by a very grave physical deformity that would make any life deprived, painful, frustrating for both child and parent, and, in any case, short. But many liberals also believe that abortion is justified when the family circumstances are so economically barren, or otherwise so unpromising, that any new life would be seriously stunted for that reason. It is important to understand that these exceptions are not based, as they might seem to be, on concern for the rights or interests of the fetus. It is a mistake to suppose that an early fetus has interests of its own; it especially makes no sense to argue that it might have an interest in being aborted. Perhaps we could understand that latter argument to mean that if the fetus does develop into a child, that child would be better off dead. But many liberals find abortion justified even when this is not so. I do not mean to deny that sometimes people would be better off dead—when they are in great and terminal pain, for example, or because their lives are otherwise irremediably frustrated. . . . But this is rarely true of children born into even very great poverty. Nor is it necessarily true even of children born with terrible, crippling handicaps who are doomed shortly to die; sometimes such children establish relationships and manage achievements that give content and meaning to their lives, and it becomes plain that it is in their interests, and in the interests of those who love and care for them, that they continue living as long as possible. The liberal judgment that abortion is justified when the prospects for life are especially bleak is based on a more impersonal judgment: that the child's existence would be intrinsically a bad thing, that it is regrettable that such a deprived and difficult life must be lived.

Sometimes this liberal judgment is wrongly taken to imply contempt for the lives of handicapped children or adults, or even as a suggestion, associated with loathsome Nazi eugenics, that society would be improved by the death of such people. That is a mistake twice over. First, . . . the general question of the relative intrinsic tragedy of different events is very different from any question about the *rights* of people now living or about how they should be treated. The former is a question about the intrinsic goodness or evil of events, the latter about rights and fairness. Second, in any case, the liberal opinion about abortion of deformed fetuses in no way implies that it should be better if even grievously handicapped people were now to die. On the contrary, the very concern the liberal judgment embodies—respect for the human contribution to life and anxiety that it not be frustrated—normally sponsors exactly the opposite conclusion. The investment a seriously handicapped person makes in his own life, in his struggle to overcome his handicap as best he can, is intense, and the investment his family and others make is likely to be intense as well. The liberal position insists that these investments in life should be realized as fully as possible, for as long and as successfully as the handicapped person and his community together can manage; and liberals are even more likely than conservatives to support social legislation that promotes that end. One may think that in the worst of such cases it would have been better had the life in question never begun, that the investment we are so eager to redeem should never have been necessary. But that judgment does not detract from concern for handicapped people; on the contrary, it is rooted in the same fundamental respect for human investment in human life, the same horror at the investment being wasted.

The second distinctly liberal group of exceptions, which take into account the effects of pregnancy and childbirth on the lives of mothers and other family members, are even harder to justify on any presumption that includes the idea that a fetus is a person with rights and interests. But the popularity of these exceptions is immediately explicable once we recognize that they are based on respect for the intrinsic value of human life. Liberals are especially concerned about the waste of the human contribution to that value, and they believe that the waste of life, measured in frustration rather than mere loss, is very much greater when a teenage single mother's life is wrecked than when an early-stage fetus, in whose life human investment has thus far been negligible, ceases to live. That judgment does not, of course, depend on comparing the quality of the mother's life, if her fetus is aborted, with that of the child, had it been allowed to live. Recognizing the sanctity of life does not mean attempting to engineer fate so that the best possible lives are lived overall; it means, rather, not frustrating investments in life that have already been made. For that reason, liberal opinion cares more about the lives that people are now leading, lives in earnest, than about the possibility of other lives to come.

The prospects of a child and of its mother for a fulfilling life obviously each depend very much on the prospects of the other. A child whose birth frustrates the chances of its mother to redeem her own life or jeopardizes her ability to care for the rest of her family is likely, just for that reason, to have a more frustrating life itself. And though many people have become superb parents to disabled or disadvantaged children, and some extraordinary ones have found a special vocation in that responsibility, it will sometimes be a devastating blow to a parent's prospects to have a crippled child rather than a normal one, or a child whose bearing and care will seriously strain family resources.

This is only another instance of the difficulty any theoretical analysis of an intricate personal and social problem, like abortion, must face. Analysis can proceed only by abstraction, but abstraction, which ignores the complexity and interdependencies of real life, obscures much of the content on which each actual, concrete decision is made. So we have no formulas for actual decision but only, at best, a schema for understanding the arguments and decisions that we and other people make in real life. I have argued that we do badly, in understanding and evaluating these decisions and arguments, if we try to match them to procrustean assumptions about fetal personhood or rights. We do better to see them as reflecting more nuanced and individual judgments about how and why human life is sacred, and about which decision of life and death, in all the concrete circumstances, most respects what is really important about life.

There will be disagreement in these judgments, not only between large parties of opinion, like those I have been calling conservative and liberal, but within these parties as well. Indeed, very few people, even those who share the same religion and social and intellectual background, will agree in every case. Nor is it possible for anyone to compose a general theory of abortion, some careful weighing of different kinds or modes of life's frustration from which particular decisions could be generated to fit every concrete case. On the contrary, we discover what we think about these grave matters not in advance of having to decide on particular occasions, but in the course of and by making them. . . .

Virtue Theory and Abortion

Rosalind Hursthouse

L et us consider what a skeletal virtue theory looks like. It begins with a specification of right action:

> P.1. An action is right iff it is what a virtuous agent would do in the circumstances.[1]

This . . . is a purely formal principle, giving one no guidance as to what to do, that forges the conceptual link between *right action* and *virtuous agent*. . . . [I]t must, of course, go on to specify what the latter is. The first step toward this may appear quite trivial, but is needed to correct a prevailing tendency among many critics to define the virtuous agent as one who is disposed to act in accordance with a deontologist's moral rules.

> P.1a. A virtuous agent is one who acts virtuously, that is, one who has and exercises the virtues.

This subsidiary premise lays bare the fact that virtue theory aims to provide a nontrivial specification of the virtuous agent *via* a nontrivial specification of the virtues, which is given in its second premise:

> P.2. A virtue is a character trait a human being needs to flourish or live well.

From Rosalind Hursthouse, "Virtue Theory and Abortion," *Philosophy & Public Affairs* 20 (1991): 223–246. Reprinted by permission of Princeton University Press.

[1]It should be noted that this premise intentionally allows for the possibility that two virtuous agents, faced with the same choice in the same circumstances, may act differently. For example, one might opt for taking her father off the life-support machine and the other for leaving her father on it. The theory requires that neither agent thinks that what the other does is wrong . . ., but it explicitly allows that no action is uniquely right in such a case—both are right. It also intentionally allows for the possibility that in some circumstances—those into which no virtuous agent could have got herself—no action is right. I explore this premise at greater length in "Applying Virtue Ethics," in a *festschrift* for Philippa Foot [Rosalind Hursthouse, Gavin Lawrence, and Warren Quinn, eds., *Virtues and Reasons, Philippa Foot and Moral Theory* (Oxford: Oxford University Press, 1996)].

This premise forges a conceptual link between *virtue* and *flourishing* (or *living well* or *eudaimonia*). And, just as deontology, in theory, then goes on to argue that each favored rule meets its specification, so virtue ethics, in theory, goes on to argue that each favored character trait meets its.

These are the bare bones of virtue theory. . . .

Abortion

As everyone knows, the morality of abortion is commonly discussed in relation to just two considerations: first, and predominantly, the status of the fetus and whether or not it is the sort of thing that may or may not be innocuously or justifiably killed; and second, and less predominantly (when, that is, the discussion concerns the *morality* of abortion rather than the question of permissible legislation in a just society), women's rights. If one thinks within this familiar framework, one may well be puzzled about what virtue theory, as such, could contribute. Some people assume the discussion will be conducted solely in terms of what the virtuous agent would or would not do. . . . Others assume that only justice, or at most justice and charity, will be applied to the issue, generating a discussion very similar to Judith Jarvis Thomson's.[2]

Now if this is the way the virtue theorist's discussion of abortion is imagined to be, no wonder people think little of it. It seems obvious in advance that in any such discussion there must be either a great deal of extremely tendentious application of the virtue terms *just, charitable,* and so on or a lot of rhetorical appeal to "this is what only the virtuous agent knows." But these are caricatures; they fail to appreciate the way in which virtue theory quite transforms the discussion of abortion by dismissing the two familiar dominating considerations as, in a way, fundamentally irrelevant. In what way or ways, I hope to make both clear and plausible.

Let us first consider women's rights. Let me emphasize again that we are discussing the *morality* of abortion, not the rights and wrongs of laws prohibiting or permitting it. If we suppose that women do have a moral right to do as they choose with their own bodies, or, more particularly, to terminate their pregnancies, then it may well follow that a *law* forbidding abortion would be unjust. Indeed, even if they have no such right, such a law might be, as things stand at the moment, unjust, or impractical, or inhumane: on this issue I have nothing to say in this article. But, putting all questions about the justice or injustice of laws to one side, and supposing only that women have such a moral right, *nothing* follows from this supposition about the morality of abortion, according to virtue theory, once it is noted (quite generally, not with particular reference to abortion) that in exercising a moral right I can do something cruel, or callous, or selfish, light-minded, self-righteous, stupid, inconsiderate disloyal, dishonest—that is, act viciously.[3]

---

[2]Judith Jarvis Thomson, "A Defense of Abortion," *Philosophy & Public Affairs* 1, no. 1 (Fall 1971): 47–66. One could indeed regard this article as proto-virtue theory (no doubt to the surprise of the author) if the concepts of callousness and kindness were allowed more weight.

[3]One possible qualification: if one ties the concept of justice very closely to rights, then if women do have a moral right to terminate their pregnancies it *may* follow that in doing so they do not act unjustly. (Cf. Thomson, "A Defense of Abortion.") But it is debatable whether even that much follows.

Love and friendship do not survive their parties' constantly insisting on their rights, nor do people live well when they think that getting what they have a right to is of preeminent importance; they harm others, and they harm themselves. So whether women have a moral right to terminate their pregnancies is irrelevant within virtue theory, for it is irrelevant to the question "In having an abortion in these circumstances, would the agent be acting virtuously or viciously or neither?"

What about the consideration of the status of the fetus—what can virtue theory say about that? One might say that this issue is not in the province of *any* moral theory; it is a metaphysical question, and an extremely difficult one at that. Must virtue theory then wait upon metaphysics to come up with the answer?

At first sight it might seem so. For virtue is said to involve knowledge, and part of this knowledge consists in having the *right* attitude to things. "Right" here does not just mean "morally right" or "proper" or "nice" in the modern sense; it means "accurate, true." One cannot have the right or correct attitude to something if the attitude is based on or involves false beliefs. And this suggests that if the status of the fetus is relevant to the rightness or wrongness of abortion, its status must be known, as a truth, to the fully wise and virtuous person.

But the sort of wisdom that the fully virtuous person has is not supposed to be recondite; it does not call for fancy philosophical sophistication, and it does not depend upon, let alone wait upon, the discoveries of academic philosophers.[4] And this entails the following, rather startling conclusion: that the status of the fetus—that issue over which so much ink has been spilt—is, according to virtue theory, simply not relevant to the rightness or wrongness of abortion (within, that is, a secular morality).

Or rather, since that is clearly too radical a conclusion, it is in a sense relevant, but only in the sense that the familiar biological facts are relevant. By "the familiar biological facts" I mean the facts that most human societies are and have been familiar with—that, standardly (but not invariably), pregnancy occurs as the result of sexual intercourse, that it lasts about nine months, during which time the fetus grows and develops, that standardly it terminates in the birth of a living baby, and that this is how we all come to be.

It might be thought that this distinction—between the familiar biological facts and the status of the fetus—is a distinction without a difference. But this is not so. To attach relevance to the status of the fetus, in the sense in which virtue theory claims it is not relevant, is to be gripped by the conviction that we must go beyond the familiar biological facts, deriving some sort of conclusion from them, such as that the fetus has rights, or is not a person, or something similar. It is also to believe that this exhausts the relevance of the familiar biological facts, that all they are relevant to is the status of the fetus and whether or not it is the sort of thing that may or may not be killed.

These convictions, I suspect, are rooted in the desire to solve the problem of abortion by getting it to fall under some general rule such as "you ought not to kill anything with

---

[4]This is an assumption of virtue theory, and I do not attempt to defend it here. An adequate discussion of it would require a separate article, since, although most moral philosophers would be chary of claiming that intellectual sophistication is a necessary condition of moral wisdom of virtue, most of us, from Plato onward, tend to write as if this were so. Sorting out which claims about moral knowledge are committed to this kind of elitism and which can, albeit with difficulty, be reconciled with the idea that moral knowledge can be acquired by anyone who really wants it would be a major task.

the right to life but may kill anything else." But they have resulted in what should surely strike any nonphilosopher as a most bizarre aspect of nearly all the current philosophical literature on abortion, namely, that, far from treating abortion as a unique moral problem, markedly unlike any other, nearly everything written on the status of the fetus and its bearing on the abortion issue would be consistent with the human reproductive facts' (to say nothing of family life) being totally different from what they are. Imagine that you are an alien extraterrestrial anthropologist who does not know that the human race is roughly 50 percent female and 50 percent male, or that our only (natural) form of reproduction involves heterosexual intercourse, viviparous birth, and the female's (and only the female's) being pregnant for nine months, or that females are capable of childbearing from late childhood to late middle age, or that childbearing is painful, dangerous, and emotionally charged—do you think you would pick up these facts from the hundreds of articles written on the status of the fetus? I am quite sure you would not. And that, I think, shows that the current philosophical literature on abortion has got badly out of touch with reality.

Now if we are using virtue theory, our first question is not "What do the familiar biological facts show—what can be derived from them about the status of the fetus?" but "How do these facts figure in the practical reasoning, action and passions, thoughts and reactions, of the virtuous and the nonvirtuous? What is the mark of having the right attitude to these facts and what manifests having the wrong attitude to them?" This immediately makes essentially relevant not only all the facts about human reproduction I mentioned above, but a whole range of facts about our emotions in relation to them as well. I mean such facts as that human parents, both male and female, tend to care passionately about their offspring, and that family relationships are among the deepest and strongest in our lives—and, significantly, among the longest-lasting.

These facts make it obvious that pregnancy is not just one among many other physical conditions, and hence that anyone who genuinely believes that an abortion is comparable to a haircut or an appendectomy is mistaken.[5] The fact that the premature termination of a pregnancy is, in some sense, the cutting off of a new human life, and thereby, like the procreation of a new human life, connects with all our thoughts about human life and death, parenthood, and family relationships, must make it a serious matter. To disregard this fact about it, to think of abortion as nothing but the killing of something that does not matter, or as nothing but the exercise of some right or rights one has, or as the incidental means to some desirable state of affairs, is to do something callous and light-minded, the sort of thing that no virtuous and wise person would do.

---

[5]Mary Anne Warren, in "On the Moral and Legal Status of Abortion," *Monist* 57 (1973) sec. 1, says of the opponents of restrictive laws governing abortion that "their conviction (for the most part) is that abortion is not a *morally* serious and extremely unfortunate, even though sometimes justified, act, comparable to killing in self-defense or to letting the violinist die, but rather is closer to being a *morally neutral* act, like cutting one's hair" (italics mine). I would like to think that no one *genuinely* believes this. But certainly in discussion, particularly when arguing against restrictive laws or the suggestion that remorse over abortion might be appropriate, I have found that some people say they believe it (and often cite Warren's article, albeit inaccurately, despite its age). Those who allow that it is morally serious, and far from morally neutral, have to argue against restrictive laws, or the appropriateness of remorse, on a very different ground from that laid down by the premise. "The fetus is just part of the woman's body (and she has a right to determine what happens to her body and should not feel guilt about anything she does to it)."

It is to have the wrong attitude not only to fetuses, but more generally to human life and death, parenthood and family relationships.

Although I say that the facts make this obvious, I know that this is one of my tendentious points. In partial support of it I note that even the most dedicated proponents of the view that deliberate abortion is just like an appendectomy or haircut rarely hold the same view of spontaneous abortion, that is, miscarriage. It is not so tendentious of me to claim that to react to people's grief over miscarriage by saying, or even thinking, "What a fuss about nothing?" would be callous and light-minded, whereas to try to laugh someone out of grief over an appendectomy scar or a botched haircut would not be. It is hard to give this point due prominence within act-centered theories, for the inconsistency is an inconsistency in attitude about the seriousness of loss of life, not in beliefs about which acts are right or wrong. Moreover, an act-centered theorist may say, "Well, there is nothing wrong with *thinking* 'What a fuss about nothing!' as long as you do not say it and hurt the person who is grieving. And besides, we cannot be held responsible for our thoughts, only for the intentional actions they give rise to." But the character traits that virtue theory emphasizes are not simply dispositions to intentional actions, but a seamless disposition to certain actions and passions, thoughts and reactions.

To say that the cutting off of a human life is always a matter of some seriousness, at any stage is not to deny the relevance of gradual fetal development. Notwithstanding the well-worn point that clear boundary lines cannot be drawn, our emotions and attitudes regarding the fetus do change as it develops, and again when it is born, and indeed further as the baby grows. Abortion for shallow reasons in the later stages is much more shocking than abortion for the same reasons in the early stages in a way that matches the fact that deep grief over miscarriage in the later stages is more appropriate than it is over miscarriage in the earlier stages (when, that is, the grief is solely about the loss of *this* child, not about, as might be the case, the loss of one's only hope of having a child or of having one's husband's child). Imagine (or recall) a woman who already has children; she had not intended to have more, but finds herself unexpectedly pregnant. Though contrary to her plans, the pregnancy, once established as a fact, is welcomed—and then she loses the embryo almost immediately. If this were bemoaned as a tragedy, it would, I think, be a misapplication of the concept of what is tragic. But it may still properly be mourned as a loss. The grief is expressed in such terms as "I shall always wonder how she or he would have turned out" or "When I look at the others, I shall think," 'How different their lives would have been if this other one had been part of them.'" It would, I take it, be callous and light-minded to say, or think, "Well, she has already *got* four children; what's the problem?"; it would be neither, nor arrogantly intrusive in the case of a close friend, to try to correct prolonged mourning by saying, "I know it's sad, but it's not a tragedy; rejoice in the ones you have." The application of *tragic* becomes more appropriate as the fetus grows, for the mere fact that one has lived with it for longer, conscious of its existence, makes a difference. To shrug off an early abortion is understandable just because it is very hard to be fully conscious of the fetus's existence in the early stages and hence hard to appreciate that an early abortion is the destruction of life. It is particularly hard for the young and inexperienced to appreciate this, because appreciation of it usually comes only with experience.

I do not mean "with the experience of having an abortion" (though that may be part of it) but, quite generally, "with the experience of life." Many women who have borne children contrast their later pregnancies with their first successful one, saying that in the later ones they were conscious of a new life growing in them from very early on. And, more generally, as one reaches the age at which the next generation is coming up close behind one, the counterfactuals "If I, or she, had had an abortion, Alice, or Bob, would not have been born" acquire a significant application, which casts a new light on the conditionals "If I or Alice have an abortion then some Caroline or Bill will not be born."

The fact that pregnancy is not just one among many physical conditions does not mean that one can never regard it in that light without manifesting a vice. When women are in very poor physical health, or worn out from childbearing, or forced to do very physically demanding jobs, then they cannot be described as self-indulgent, callous, irresponsible, or light-minded if they seek abortions mainly with a view to avoiding pregnancy as the physical condition that it is. To go through with a pregnancy when one is utterly exhausted, or when one's job consists of crawling along tunnels hauling coal, as many women in the nineteenth century were obliged to do, is perhaps heroic, but people who do not achieve heroism are not necessarily vicious. That they can view the pregnancy only as eight months of misery, followed by hours if not days of agony and exhaustion, and abortion only as the blessed escape from this prospect, is entirely understandable and does not manifest any lack of serious respect for human life or a shallow attitude to motherhood. What it does show is that something is terribly amiss in the conditions of their lives, which make it so hard to recognize pregnancy and childbearing as the good that they can be.

In relation to this last point I should draw attention to the way in which virtue theory has a sort of built-in indexicality. Philosophers arguing against anything remotely resembling a belief in the sanctity of life (which the above claims clearly embody) frequently appeal to the existence of other communities in which abortion and infanticide are practiced. We should not automatically assume that it is impossible that some other communities could be morally inferior to our own; maybe some are, or have been, precisely insofar as their members are, typically, callous or light-minded or unjust. But in communities in which life is a great deal tougher for everyone than it is in ours, having the right attitude to human life and death, parenthood, and family relationships might well manifest itself in ways that are unlike ours. When it is essential to survival that most members of the community fend for themselves at a very young age or work during most of their waking hours, selective abortion or infanticide might be practiced either as a form of genuine euthanasia or for the sake of the community and not, I think, be thought callous or light-minded. But this does not make everything all right; as before, it shows that there is something amiss with the conditions of their lives, which are making it impossible for them to live really well.

The foregoing discussion, insofar as it emphasizes the right attitude to human life and death, parallels to a certain extent those standard discussions of abortion that concentrate on it solely as an issue of killing. But it does not, as those discussions do, gloss over the fact, emphasized by those who discuss the morality of abortion in terms of women's rights, that abortion, wildly unlike any other form of killing, is the termination of a pregnancy, which is a condition of a woman's body and results in *her* having a child if it is not aborted. This fact is given due recognition not by appeal to women's rights but by emphasizing the relevance of the familiar biological and psychological facts and their connection with having the right attitude to parenthood and family relationships. But it may well be thought that failing to bring in women's rights still leaves some important aspects of the problem of abortion untouched.

Speaking in terms of women's rights, people sometimes say things like, "Well, it's her life you're talking about too, you know; she's got a right to her own life, her own happiness." And the discussion stops there. But in the context of virtue theory, given that we are particularly concerned with what constitutes a good human life, with what true happiness or *eudaimonia* is, that is no place to stop. We go on to ask, "And is this life of hers a good one? Is she living well?"

If we are to go on to talk about good human lives, in the context of abortion, we have to bring in our thoughts about the value of love and family life, and our proper emotional development through a natural life cycle. The familiar facts support the view that parenthood in general, and motherhood and childbearing in particular, are intrinsically worthwhile, are among the things that can be correctly thought to be partially constitutive of a flourishing human life.[6] If this is right, then a woman who opts for not being a mother (at all, or again, or now) by opting for abortion may thereby be manifesting a flawed grasp of what her life should be, and be about—a grasp that is childish, or grossly materialistic or shortsighted, or shallow.

I said "*may* thereby": this *need* not be so. Consider, for instance, a woman who has already had several children and fears that to have another will seriously affect her capacity to be a good mother to the ones she has—she does not show a lack of appreciation of the intrinsic value of being a parent by opting for abortion. Nor does a woman who has been a good mother and is approaching the age at which she may be looking forward to being a good grandmother. Nor does a woman who discovers that her pregnancy may well kill her, and opts for abortion and adoption. Nor, necessarily, does a woman who had decided to lead a life centered around some other worthwhile activity or activities with which motherhood would compete.

People who are childless by choice are sometimes described as "irresponsible," or "selfish," or "refusing to grow up," or "not knowing what life is about." But one can hold that having children is intrinsically worthwhile without endorsing this, for we are, after all, in the happy position of there being more worthwhile things to do that can be fitted into one lifetime. Parenthood, and motherhood in particular, even if granted to be intrinsically worthwhile, undoubtedly take up a lot of one's adult life, leaving no room for some other worthwhile pursuits. But some women who choose abortion rather than have their first child, and some men who encourage their partners to choose abortion, are not avoiding parenthood for the sake of other worthwhile pursuits, but for the worthless one of "having a good time," or for the pursuit of some false vision of the ideals of freedom or self-realization. And some others who say "I am not ready for parenthood yet" are making some sort of mistake about the extent to which one can manipulate the circumstances of one's life so as to make it fulfill some dream that one has. Perhaps one's dream is to have two perfect children, a girl and a boy, within a perfect marriage, in financially secure circumstances, with an interesting job of one's own. But to care too much about that dream, to demand of life that it give it to one and act accordingly, may be both greedy and foolish, and is to run the risk of missing out on happiness entirely. Not only may fate make the dream impossible, or destroy it, but one's own at-

---

[6]I take this as a premise here, but argue for it in some detail in my *Beginning Lives* (Oxford: Basil Blackwell, 1987). In this connection I also discuss adoption and the sense in which it may be regarded as "second best," and the difficult question of whether the good of parenthood may properly be sought, or indeed bought, by surrogacy.

tachment to it may make it impossible. Good marriages, and the most promising children, can be destroyed by just one adult's excessive demand for perfection.

Once again, this is not to deny that girls may quite properly say "I am not ready for motherhood yet," especially in our society, and, far from manifesting irresponsibility or light-mindedness, show an appropriate modesty or humility, or a fearfulness that does not amount to cowardice. However, even when the decision to have an abortion is the right decision—one that does not itself fall under a vice-related term and thereby one that the perfectly virtuous could recommend—it does not follow that there is no sense in which having the abortion is wrong, or guilt inappropriate. For, by virtue of the fact that a human life has been cut short, some evil has probably been brought about,[7] and that circumstances make the decision to bring about some evil the right decision will be a ground for guilt if getting into those circumstances in the first place itself manifested a flaw in character.

What "gets one into those circumstances" in the case of abortion is, except in the case of rape, one's sexual activity and one's choices, or the lack of them, about one's sexual partner and about contraception. The virtuous woman (which here of course does not mean simply "chaste woman" but "woman with the virtues") has such character traits as strength, independence, resoluteness, decisiveness, self-confidence, responsibility, serious-mindedness, and self-determination—and no one, I think, could deny that many women become pregnant in circumstances in which they cannot welcome or cannot face the thought of having *this* child precisely because they lack one or some of these character traits. So even in the cases where the decision to have an abortion is the right one, it can still be the reflection of a moral failing—not because the decision itself is weak or cowardly or irresolute or irresponsible or light-minded, but because the lack of the requisite opposite of these failings landed one in the circumstances in the first place. Hence the common universalized claim that guilt and remorse are never appropriate emotions about an abortion is denied. They may be appropriate, and appropriately inculcated, even when the decision was the right one.

Another motivation for bringing women's rights into the discussion may be to attempt to correct the implication, carried by the killing-centered approach, that insofar as abortion is wrong, it is a wrong that only women do, or at least (given the preponderance of male doctors) that only women instigate. I do not myself believe that we can thus escape the fact that nature bears harder on women than it does on men,[8] but virtue theory can certainly correct many of the injustices that the emphasis on women's rights is rightly concerned about. With very little amendment, everything that has been said above applies to boys and men too. Although the abortion decision is, in a natural sense, the woman's decision, proper to her, boys and men are often party to it, for well or ill, and even when they are not, they are bound to have been party to the circumstances that brought it up. No less than girls and women, boys and men can in their actions, manifest self-centeredness, callousness, and light-mindedness about life and parenthood in

---

[7]I say "some evil has probably been brought about" on the ground that (human) life is (usually) a good and hence (human) death usually an evil. The exceptions would be (a) where death is actually a good or a benefit, because the baby that would come to be if the life were not cut short would be better off dead than alive, and (b) where death, though not a good, is not an evil either, because the life that would be led (e.g., in a state of permanent coma) would not be a good.

[8]I discuss this point at greater length in *Beginning Lives*.

relation to abortion. They can be self-centered or courageous about the possibility of disability in their offspring; they need to reflect on their sexual activity and their choices, or the lack of them, about their sexual partner and contraception; they need to grow up and take responsibility for their own actions and life in relation to fatherhood. If it is true, as I maintain, that insofar as motherhood is intrinsically worthwhile, being a mother is an important purpose in women's lives, being a father (rather than a mere generator) is an important purpose in men's lives as well, and it is adolescent of men to turn a blind eye to this and pretend that they have many more important things to do.

Conclusion

Much more might be said, but I shall end the actual discussion of the problem of abortion here, and conclude by highlighting what I take to be its significant features. . . .

The discussion does not proceed simply by our trying to answer the question "Would the perfectly virtuous agent ever have an abortion and, if so, when?"; virtue theory is not limited to considering "Would Socrates have had an abortion if he were a raped fifteen-year-old [girl]?" nor automatically stumped when we are considering circumstances into which no virtuous agent would have got herself. Instead, much of the discussion proceeds in the virtue- and vice-related terms whose applications, in several cases, yields practical conclusions. . . . These terms are difficult to apply correctly, and anyone might challenge my application of any one of them. So, for example, I have claimed that some abortions, done for certain reasons, would be callous or light-minded; that others might indicate an appropriate modesty or humility; that others would reflect a greedy and foolish attitude to what one could expect out of life. Any of these examples may be disputed; but what is at issue is, should these difficult terms be there, or should the discussion be couched in terms that all clever adolescents can apply correctly? . . .

Proceeding as it does in virtue- and vice-related terms, the discussion thereby, inevitably, also contains claims about what is worthwhile, serious and important, good and evil, in our lives. So, for example, I claimed that parenthood is intrinsically worthwhile, and that having a good time was a worthless end (in life, not on individual occasions); that losing a fetus is always a serious matter (albeit not a tragedy in itself in the first trimester) whereas acquiring an appendectomy scar is a trivial one; that (human) death is an evil. Once again, these are difficult matters, and anyone might challenge any one of my claims. But what is at issue is, as before, should these difficult claims be there, or can one reach practical conclusions about real moral issues that are in no way determined by premises about such matters? . . .

The discussion also thereby, inevitably, contains claims about what life is like (e.g., my claim that love and friendship do not survive their parties' constantly insisting on their rights; or the claim that to demand perfection of life is to run the risk of missing out on happiness entirely). What is at issue is, should those disputable claims be there, or is our knowledge (or are our false opinions) about what life is like irrelevant to our understanding of real moral issues? . . .

Naturally, my own view is that all these concepts should be there in any discussion of real moral issues and that virtue theory, which uses all of them, is the right theory to apply to them. I do not pretend to have shown this. I realize that proponents of rival theories may say that, now that they have understood how virtue theory uses the range of concepts it draws on, they are more convinced than ever that such concepts should not figure in an adequate normative theory, because they are sectarian, or vague, or too particular, or improperly anthropocentric. . . . Or, finding many of the details of the discussion appropriate, they may agree that many, perhaps even all, of the concepts should figure, but argue that virtue theory gives an inaccurate account of the way the concepts fit together (and indeed of the concepts themselves) and that another theory provides a better account; that would be interesting to see. . . .

Abortion and the "Feminine Voice"

Celia Wolf-Devine

A growing number of feminists now seek to articulate the "feminine voice," to draw attention to women's special strengths, and to correct the systematic devaluation of these by our male-dominated society. Carol Gilligan's book, *In a Different Voice,* was especially important to the emergence of this strain of feminist thought. It was her intention to help women identify more positively with their own distinctive style of reasoning about ethics, instead of feeling that there is something wrong with them because they do not think like men (as Kohlberg's and Freud's theories would imply). Inspired by her work, feminists such as Nel Noddings, Annette Baier, and the contributors to *Women and Moral Theory,*[1] have tried to articulate further the feminine voice in moral reasoning. Others such as Carol McMillan, Adrienne Rich, Sara Ruddick, and Nancy Hartsock agree that women have distinct virtues, and argue that these need not be self-victimizing.[2] When properly transformed by a feminist consciousness, women's different characteristics can, they suggest, be productive of new social visions.

Similar work is also being done by feminists who try to correct for masculine bias in other areas such as our conception of human nature, the way we view the relationship between people and nature, and the kinds of paradigms we employ in thinking about society.[3]

From Celia Wolf-Devine, "Abortion and the 'Feminine' Voice," *Public Affairs Quarterly* 3 (1989): 81–97. Reprinted by permission.

[1]See Nel Noddings, *Caring: A Feminine Approach to Ethics* (Berkeley: University of California Press, 1984), Annette Baier, "What Do Women Want in a Moral Theory?" *Nous,* vol. 19 (March, 1985), and "Hume, the Women's Moral Theorist?" in *Women and Moral Theory,* Kittay and Meyers (eds.) (Totowa, N.J.: Rowman & Littlefield, 1987).

[2]Carol McMillan, *Women, Reason and Nature* (Princeton: Princeton University Press, 1982), Adrienne Rich, *Of Woman Born* (N.Y.: Norton, 1976), Sara Ruddick, "Remarks on the Sexual Politics of Reason" in *Women and Moral Theory,* "Maternal Thinking" and "Preservative Love and Military Destruction: Some Reflections on Mothering and Peace" in Joyce Treblicot (ed.), *Mothering: Essays in Feminist Theory* (Totowa, N.J.: Rowman & Allanheld, 1983), and Nancy Hartsock "The Feminist Standpoint" in *Discovering Reality,* Harding (ed.) (Boston: D. Reidel, 1983).

[3]Among them are such writers as Rosemary Radford Reuther, Susan Griffin, Elizabeth Dodson Gray, Brian Easla, Sally Miller Gearhart, Carolyn Merchant, Genevieve Lloyd, the pacifist feminists, and a number of feminists involved in the ecology movement.

Some of those engaged in this enterprise hold that women *by nature* possess certain valuable traits that men do not, but more frequently, they espouse the weaker position that, on the whole, the traits they label "feminine" are more common among women (for reasons which are at least partly cultural), but that they also can be found in men, and that they should be encouraged as good traits for a human being to have, regardless of sex.[4]

Virtually all of those feminists who are trying to reassert the value of the feminine voice, also express the sort of unqualified support for free access to abortion which has come to be regarded as a central tenet of feminist "orthodoxy." What I wish to argue in this paper is that: (1) abortion is, by their own accounts, clearly a masculine response to the problems posed by an unwanted pregnancy, and is thus highly problematic for those who seek to articulate and defend the "feminine voice" as the proper mode of moral response, and that (2) on the contrary the "feminine voice" as it has been articulated generates a strong presumption against abortion as a way of responding to an unwanted pregnancy.[5]

These conclusions, I believe, can be argued without relying on a precise determination of the moral status of the fetus. A case at least can be made that the fetus is a person since it is biologically a member of the human species and will, in time, develop normal human abilities. Whether the burden of proof rests on those who defend the personhood of the fetus, or on those who deny it, is a matter of moral methodology, and for that reason will depend in part on whether one adopts a masculine or feminine approach to moral issues.

I. Masculine Voice/Feminine Voice

A. Moral Reasoning

According to Gilligan, girls, being brought up by mothers, identify with them, while males must define themselves through separation from their mothers. As a result, girls have "a basis for empathy built into their primary definition of self in a way that boys do not."[6] Thus while masculinity is defined by separation and threatened by intimacy, femininity is defined through attachment and threatened by separation; girls come to understand themselves as imbedded within a network of personal relationships.

A second difference concerns attitudes toward general rules and principles. Boys tend to play in larger groups than girls, and become "increasingly fascinated with the legal elaboration of rules, and the development of fair procedures for adjudicating conflicts."[7] We thus find men conceiving of morality largely in terms of adjudicating fairly between the conflicting rights of self-assertive individuals.

---

[4]In this paper I shall use the terms "masculine" and "feminine" only in this weaker sense, which is agnostic about the existence of biologically based differences.

[5]A strong presumption against abortion is not, of course, the same thing as an absolute ban on all abortions. I do not attempt here to resolve the really hard cases; it is not clear that the feminine voice (at least as it has been articulated so far) is sufficiently fine-grained to tell us exactly where to draw the line in such cases.

[6]See Carol Gilligan, *In a Different Voice* (Cambridge, MA: Harvard University Press, 1982), p. 8.

[7]*Ibid.*, p. 10.

Girls play in smaller groups, and accord a greater importance to relationships than to following rules. They are especially sensitive to the needs of the particular other, instead of emphasizing impartiality, which is more characteristic of the masculine perspective. They think of morality more in terms of having responsibilities for taking care of others, and place a high priority upon preserving the network of relationships which makes this possible. While the masculine justice perspective requires detachment, the feminine care perspective sees detachment and separation as themselves the moral problem.[8]

Inspired by Gilligan, many feminist philosophers have discovered a masculine bias in traditional ethical theories. Nel Noddings has written a book called *Caring: A Feminine Approach to Ethics*. Annette Baier has praised Hume for his emphasis on the role of the affections in ethics[9] and proposed that trust be taken as the central notion for ethical theory.[10] Christina Hoff Sommers has argued for giving a central role to special relationships in ethics."[11] And Virginia Held has suggested that the mother-child relationship be seen as paradigmatic of human relationships, instead of the economic relationship of buyer/seller (which she sees to be the ruling paradigm now).[12]

The feminine voice in ethics attends to the particular other, thinks in terms of responsibilities to care for others, is sensitive to our interconnectedness, and strives to preserve relationships. It contrasts with the masculine voice, which speaks in terms of justice and rights, stresses consistency and principles, and emphasizes the autonomy of the individual and impartiality in one's dealings with others.

B. Human Nature: Mind and Body

Feminist writers have also discovered a masculine bias in the way we think of mind and body and the relationship between them. A large number of feminists, for example, regard radical mind/body dualism as a masculine way of understanding human nature. Alison Jaggar, for example, criticizes what she calls "normative dualism" for being "male biased,"[13] and defines "normative dualism" as "the belief that what is especially valuable about human beings is a particular 'mental' capacity, the capacity for rationality."[14]

Another critic of dualism is Rosemary Radford Reuther, a theologian. Her book *New Woman, New Earth* is an extended attack upon what she calls transcendent hierarchical dualism, which she regards as a "male ideology."[15] By "transcendent dualism" she means the view that consciousness is "transcendent to visible nature"[16] and that there is

---

[8]See Gilligan, "Moral Orientation and Moral Development" in *Women and Moral Theory*, p. 31.

[9]Annette Baier, "Hume, the Woman's Moral Theorist?" in *Women and Moral Theory*, pp. 37–39.

[10]Annette Baier, "What Do Women Want in a Moral Theory?" *Nous*, vol. 19 (March, 1985), p. 53.

[11]Christina Hoff Sommers, "Filial Morality" in *Women and Moral Theory*, pp. 69–84.

[12]Virginia Held, "Feminism and Moral Theory," in *Women and Moral Theory*, pp. 111–128.

[13]Alison Jaggar, *Feminist Politics and Human Nature* (Totowa, N.J.: Rowman & Allanheld, 1983), p. 46.

[14]*Ibid.*, p. 28.

[15]Rosemary Radford Reuther, *New Woman, New Earth* (New York: The Seabury Press, 1975), p. 195.

[16]*Ibid.*, p. 188.

a sharp split between spirit and nature. In the attempt to deny our own mortality, our essential humanity is then identified with a "transcendent divine sphere beyond the matrix of coming to be and passing away."[17] In using the term "hierarchical," she means that the mental or spiritual component is taken to be superior to the physical. Thus "the relation of spirit and body is one of repression, subjugation and mastery."[18]

Dodson Gray, whose views resemble Reuther's, poetically contrasts the feminine attitude with the masculine one as follows:

> I see that life is not a line but a circle. Why do men imagine for themselves the illusory freedom of a soaring mind, so that the body of nature becomes a cage? 'Tis not true. To be human is to be circled in the cycles of nature, rooted in the processes that nurture us in life, breathing in and breathing out human life just as plants breathe in and out their photosynthesis.[19]

Feminists critical of traditional masculine ways of thinking about human nature also examine critically the conception of "reason" which has become engrained in our Western cultural heritage from the Greeks on. Genevieve Lloyd, for example, in *The Man of Reason: Male and Female in Western Philosophy*,[20] suggests that the very notion of reason itself has been defined in part by the exclusion of the feminine. And if the thing which makes us distinctively human—namely our reason—is thought of as male, women and the things usually associated with them such as the body, emotion and nature, will be placed in an inferior position.

C. Our Relationship with Nature

Many feminists hold that mind-body dualism which sees mind as transcendent to and superior to the body, leads to the devaluation of both women and nature. For the transcendent mind is conceived as masculine, and women, the body and nature assigned an inferior and subservient status.[21] As Rosemary Radford Reuther puts it:

> The woman, the body and the world are the lower half of a dualism that must be declared posterior to, created by, subject to, and ultimately alien to the nature of (male) consciousness in whose image man made his God.[22]

Women are to be subject to men, and nature may be used by man in any way he chooses. Thus the male ideology of transcendent dualism sanctions unlimited technological manipulation of nature; nature is an alien object to be conquered.

---

[17]*Ibid.*, p. 195.

[18]*Ibid.*, p. 189.

[19]Elizabeth Dodson Gray, *Why the Green Nigger* (Wellesley, MA: Roundtable Press, 1979), p. 54.

[20]Genevieve Lloyd, *The Man of Reason: Male and Female in Western Philosophy* (Minneapolis: University of Minnesota Press, 1984).

[21]See, e.g., Rosemary Radford Reuther, *New Woman, New Earth,* Elizabeth Dodson Gray, *Why the Green Nigger,* and Brian Easla, *Science and Sexual Oppression* (London: Weidenfeld and Nicolson, 1981).

[22]Reuther, *op. cit.,* p. 195.

Carolyn Merchant, in her book *The Death of Nature: Women, Ecology and the Scientific Revolution*,[23] focuses on the Cartesian version of dualism as particularly disastrous to our relationship with nature, and finds the roots of our present ecological crisis to lie in the 17th Century scientific revolution—itself based on Cartesian dualism and the mechanization of nature. According to Merchant, both feminism and the ecology movement are egalitarian movements which have a vision of our interconnectedness with each other and with nature.

Feminists who stress the deep affinities between feminism and the ecology movement are often called "ecofeminists." Stephanie Leland, radical feminist and co-editor of a recent collection of ecofeminist writings, has explained that:

> Ecology is universally defined as the study of the balance and interrelationship of all life on earth. The motivating force behind feminism is the expression of the feminine principle. As the essential impulse of the feminine principle is the striving towards balance and interrelationship, it follows that feminism and ecology are inextricably connected.[24]

The masculine urge is, she says, to "separate, discriminate and control," while the feminine impulse is "towards belonging, relationship and letting be."[25] The urge to discriminate leads, she thinks, to the need to dominate "in order to feel secure in the choice of a particular set of differences."[26] The feminine attitude springs from a more holistic view of the human person and sees us as imbedded in nature rather than standing over and above it. It entails a more egalitarian attitude, regarding the needs of other creatures as important and deserving of consideration. It seeks to "let be" rather than to control, and maintains a pervasive awareness of the interconnectedness of all things and the need to preserve this if all are to flourish.

Interconnectedness, which we found to be an important theme in feminist ethics, thus reappears in the writings of the ecofeminists as one of the central aspects of the feminine attitude toward nature.

D. Paradigms of Social Life

Feminists' descriptions of characteristically masculine and feminine paradigms of social life center around two different focuses. Those influenced by Gilligan tend to stress the contrast between individualism (which they take to be characteristic of the masculine "justice tradition") and the view of society as "a web of relationships sus-

---

[23]Carolyn Merchant, *The Death of Nature: Women, Ecology and the Scientific Revolution* (San Francisco: Harper & Row, 1980).

[24]Stephanie Leland and Leonie Caldecott, (eds.), *Reclaim the Earth: Women Speak out for Life on Earth* (London: The Women's Press, 1983), p. 72. For an overview of ecofeminist thought which focuses on the role of mind/body dualism, see Val Plumwood, "Ecofeminism: An Overview," *Australasian Journal of Philosophy,* Supplement to Vol. 64 (June, 1986), pp. 120–138.

[25]Leland and Caldecott, *op. cit.*, p. 71.

[26]*Ibid.*, p. 69.

tained by a process of communication"[27] (which they take to characterize the feminine "care perspective"). According to them, the masculine paradigm sees society as a collection of self-assertive individuals seeking rules which will allow them to pursue their own goals without interfering with each other. The whole contractarian tradition from Locke and Hobbes through Rawls is thus seen as a masculine paradigm of social life; we are only connected to others and responsible to them through our own choice to relinquish part of our autonomy in favor of the state. The feminine care perspective guides us to think about societal problems in a different way. We are already imbedded in a network of relationships, and must never exploit or hurt the other. We must strive to preserve those relationships as much as possible without sacrificing the integrity of the self.

The ecofeminists, pacifist feminists, and those whose starting point is a rejection of dualism, tend to focus more on the contrast between viewing social relationships in terms of hierarchy, power, and domination (the masculine paradigm) and viewing them in a more egalitarian and nonviolent manner (the feminine one). Feminists taking this position range from the moderate ones who believe that masculine social thought tends to be more hierarchical than feminine thought, to the extreme radicals who believe males are irredeemably aggressive and dominating, and prone to violence in order to preserve their domination.

The more moderate characterization of masculine social thought would claim that men tend to prefer a clear structure of authority; they want to know who is in control and have a clear set of procedures or rules for resolving difficult cases. The more extreme view, common among ecofeminists and a large number of radical feminists, is that males seek to establish and maintain patriarchy (systematic domination by males) and use violence to maintain their control. These feminists thus see an affinity between feminism (which combats male violence against women) and the pacifist movement (which does so on a more global scale). Mary Daly, for example, holds that "the rulers of patriarchy—males with power—wage an unceasing war against life itself. . . . female energy is essentially biophilic."[28] Another radical feminist, Sally Miller Gearhart, says that men possess the qualities of objectification, violence, and competitiveness, while women possess empathy, nurturance, and cooperation.[29] Thus the feminine virtues must prevail if we are to survive at all, and the entire hierarchical power structure must be replaced by "horizontal patterns of relationship."[30]

Women are thus viewed by the pacifist feminists as attuned in some special way to the values and attitudes underlying a pacifist commitment. Sara Ruddick, for example, believes that maternal practice, because it involves "preservative love" and nurtures growth, involves the kinds of virtues which, when put to work in the public domain, lead us in the direction of pacifism.[31]

---

[27]Introduction to *Women and Moral Theory*, by Kittay and Meyers, p. 7.

[28]Cited by Barbara Zanotti, "Patriarchy: A State of War," in *Reweaving the Web of Life*, Pam McAllister, (ed.), (Philadelphia: New Society Publishers, 1982), p. 17.

[29]See, e.g., Sally Miller Gearhart, "The Future—If There Is One—Is Female" in *Reweaving the Web of Life*, p. 266.

[30]*Ibid.*, p. 272.

[31]See Sara Ruddick, "Remarks on the Sexual Politics of Reason."

II. Abortion

A person who had characteristically masculine traits, attitudes and values as defined above would very naturally choose abortion, and justify it ethically in the same way in which most feminists do. Conversely, a person manifesting feminine traits, attitudes and values would not make such a choice, or justify it in that way.

According to the ecofeminists, the masculine principle is insensitive to the interconnectedness of all life; it strives to discriminate, separate and control. It does not respect the natural cycles of nature, but objectifies it, and imposes its will upon it through unrestrained technological manipulation. Such a way of thinking would naturally lead to abortion. If the woman does not *want* to be pregnant, she has recourse to an operation involving highly sophisticated technology in order to defend her control of her body. This fits the characterization of the masculine principle perfectly.

Abortion is a separation—a severing of a life-preserving connection between the woman and the fetus. It thus fails to respect the interconnectedness of all life. Nor does it respect the natural cycles of nature. The mother and the developing child together form a delicately balanced ecosystem with the woman's entire hormonal system geared towards sustaining the pregnancy.[32] The abortionist forces the cervical muscles (which have become thick and hard in order to hold in the developing fetus) open and disrupts her hormonal system by removing it.

Abortion has something further in common with [what] the behavior ecofeminists and pacifist feminists take to be characteristically masculine; it shows a willingness to use violence in order to maintain control. The fetus is destroyed by being pulled apart by suction, cut in pieces, or poisoned. It is not merely killed inadvertently as fish might be by toxic wastes, but it is deliberately targeted for destruction. Clearly this is not the expression of a "biophilic" attitude. This point was recently brought home to me by a Quaker woman who had reached the conclusion that the abortion she had had was contrary to her pacifist principles. She said, "we must seek peaceableness both within and without."

In terms of social thought, again, it is the masculine models which are most frequently employed in thinking about abortion. If masculine thought is naturally hierarchical and oriented toward power and control, then the interests of the fetus (who has no power) would naturally be suppressed in favor of the interests of the mother. But to the extent that feminist social thought is egalitarian, the question must be raised of why the mother's interests should prevail over the child's.

Feminist thought about abortion has, in addition, been deeply pervaded by the individualism which they so ardently criticize. The woman is supposed to have the sole authority to decide the outcome of the pregnancy. But what of her interconnectedness with the child and with others? Both she and the unborn child already exist within a network of relationships ranging from the closest ones—the father, grandparents, siblings, uncles and aunts, and so on—to ones with the broader society—including the mother's friends, employer, employees, potential adoptive parents, taxpayers who may be asked to fund the abortion or subsidize the child, and all the numerous other people affected by her choice. To dismiss this already existing network of relationships as irrelevant to

---

[32]I owe the idea of regarding mother and child as an ecosystem to a conversation with Leonie Caldecott, co-editor of *Reclaim the Earth.*

the mother's decision is to manifest the sort of social atomism which feminist thinkers condemn as characteristically masculine.

Those feminists who are seeking to articulate the feminine voice in ethics also face a *prima facie* inconsistency between an ethics of care and abortion. Quite simply, abortion is a failure to care for one living being who exists in a particularly intimate relationship to oneself. If empathy, nurturance, and taking responsibility for caring for others are characteristic of the feminine voice, then abortion does not appear to be a feminine response to an unwanted pregnancy. If, as Gilligan says, "an ethic of care rests on the premise of non-violence—that no one should be hurt,"[33] then surely the feminine response to an unwanted pregnancy would be to try to find a solution which does not involve injury to anyone, including the unborn.

"Rights" have been invoked in the abortion controversy in a bewildering variety of ways, ranging from the "right to life" to the "right to control one's body." But clearly those who defend unrestricted access to abortion in terms of such things as the woman's right to privacy or her right to control her body are speaking the language of an ethics of justice rather than an ethics of care. For example, Judith Jarvis Thomson's widely read article "A Defense of Abortion"[34] treats the moral issue involved in abortion as a conflict between the rights of the fetus and the mother's rights over her own body. Mary Anne Warren also sees the issue in terms of a conflict of rights, but since the fetus does not meet her criteria for being a person, she weighs the woman's rights to "freedom, happiness and self-determination" against the rights of other people in the society who would like to see the fetus preserved for whatever reason.[35] And, insofar as she appeals to consciousness, reasoning, self-motivated activity, the capacity to communicate, and the presence of self-concepts and self-awareness as criteria of personhood, she relies on the kind of opposition between mind and nature criticized by many feminists as masculine. In particular, she is committed to what Jaggar calls "normative dualism"—the view that what is especially valuable about humans is their mental capacity for rational thought.

It is rather striking that feminists defending abortion lapse so quickly into speaking in the masculine voice. Is it because they feel they must do so in order to be heard in our male dominated society, or is it because no persuasive defense of abortion can be constructed from within the ethics of care tradition? We now consider several possible "feminine voice" defenses of abortion.

III. Possible Responses and Replies

Among the feminists seeking to articulate and defend the value of the feminine voice, very few have made any serious attempt to grapple with abortion. The writings of the ecofeminists and the pacifist feminists abound with impassioned defenses of such values as non-violence, a democratic attitude towards the needs of all living things, letting

---

[33]Gilligan, *op. cit.*, p. 174.

[34]Judith Jarvis Thomson, "A Defense of Abortion," *Philosophy and Public Affairs,* vol. 1 (1971), pp. 47–66.

[35]Mary Anne Warren, "On the Moral and Legal Status of Abortion," *The Monist,* vol. 57 (January, 1973), reprinted in Wasserstrom, *Today's Moral Problems* (New York: Macmillan, 1985), p. 448.

others be and nurturing them, and so on, existing side by side with impassioned defenses of "reproductive rights." They see denying women access to abortion as just another aspect of male domination and violence against women.

This will not do for several reasons. First, it is not true that males are the chief opponents of abortion. Many women are strongly opposed to it. The pro-life movement at every level is largely composed of women. For example, as of May 1988, 38 of the state delegates to the National Right to Life Board of Directors were women, and only 13 were men. Indeed as Jean Bethke Elshtain has observed,[36] the pro-life movement has mobilized into political action an enormous number of women who were never politically active before. And a Gallup poll in 1981 found that 51% of women surveyed believed a person is present at conception, compared with only 33% of the men. The pro-life movement, thus, cannot be dismissed as representing male concerns and desires only. Granted, a pro-choice feminist could argue that women involved in the pro-life movement suffer from "colonized minds," but this sort of argument clearly can be made to cut both directions. After all, many of the strongest supporters of "reproductive rights" have been men—ranging from the Supreme Court in *Roe v. Wade* to the Playboy Philosopher.

Secondly, terms like violence and domination are used far too loosely by those who condemn anti-abortion laws. If there are laws against wife abuse, does this mean that abusive husbands are being subjected to domination and violence? One does not exercise violence against someone merely by crossing his or her will, or even by crossing his or her will and backing this up by threats of legal retribution.

Finally, those who see violence and domination in laws against abortion, but not in abortion itself, generally fail to look at the nature of the act itself, and thus fail to judge that act in light of their professed values and principles. This is not surprising; abortion is a bloody and distressing thing to contemplate. But one cannot talk about it intelligently without being willing to look concretely at the act itself.

One line of thought is suggested by Gilligan, who holds that at the highest level of moral development, we must balance our responsibility to care for others against our need to care for ourselves. Perhaps we could, then, see the woman who has an abortion as still being caring and nurturing in that she is acting out of a legitimate care for herself. This is an implausible view of the actual feelings of women who undergo abortions. They may believe they're "doing something for themselves" in the sense of doing what they must do to safeguard their legitimate interests. But the operation is more naturally regarded as a violation of oneself than as a nurturing of oneself. This has been noted, even by feminists who support permissive abortion laws. For example, Carolyn Whitbeck speaks of "the unappealing prospect of having someone scraping away at one's core,"[37] and Adrienne Rich says that "Abortion is violence: a deep, desperate violence inflicted by a woman upon, first of all, herself."[38]

We here come up against the problem that a directive to care, to nurture, to take responsibility for others, and so on, provides a moral orientation, but leaves unanswered

[36]Jean Bethke Elshtain, *Public Man, Private Woman* (Princeton, N.J.: Princeton University Press, 1981), p. 312.

[37]Carolyn Whitbeck, "Women as People: Pregnancy and Personhood," in *Abortion and the Status of the Fetus,* W. B. Bondeson, et al. (eds.) (Boston: D. Reidel Publishing Co., 1983), p. 252.

[38]Rich, *op. cit.*, p. 269.

many important questions and hence provides little guidance in problem situations. What do we do when caring for one person involves being uncaring toward another? How widely must we extend our circle of care? Are some kinds of not caring worse than others? Is it caring to give someone what they want even though it may be bad for them?

Thinking in terms of preserving relationships suggests another possible "feminine" defense of abortion—namely that the woman is striving to preserve her interconnectedness with her family, husband, or boyfriend. Or perhaps she is concerned to strengthen her relationship with her other children by having enough time and resources to devote to their care. To simply tell a woman to preserve *all* her existing relationships is not the answer. Besides the fact that it may not be possible (women *do* sometimes have to sever relationships), it is not clear that it would be desirable even if it were possible. Attempting to preserve our existing relationships has conservative tendencies in several unfortunate ways. It fails to invite us to reflect critically on whether those relationships are good, healthy or worthy of preservation.[39] It also puts the unborn at a particular disadvantage, since the mother's relationship with him or her is just beginning, while her relationships with others have had time to develop. And not only the unborn, but any needy stranger who shows up at our door can be excluded on the grounds that caring for them would disrupt our existing pattern of relationships. Thus the care perspective could degenerate into a rationalization for a purely tribal morality; I take care of myself and my friends.

But how are decisions about severing relationships to be made? One possibility is suggested by Gilligan in a recent article. She looks at the network of connections within which the woman who is considering abortion finds herself entangled, and says "to ask what actions constitute care or are more caring directs attention to the parameters of connection and the *costs of detachment* . . . (emphasis added)."[40] Thus, the woman considering abortion, should reflect upon the comparative costs of severing various relationships. This method of decision, however, makes her vulnerable to emotional and psychological pressure from others, by encouraging her to sever whichever connection is easiest to break (the squeaky wheel principle).[41]

But perhaps we can lay out some guidelines (or, at least, rules of thumb) for making these difficult decisions. One way we might reason, from the point of view of the feminine voice, is that since preserving interconnectedness is good, we should prefer a short term estrangement to an irremediable severing of relationship. And we should choose an action which *may* cause an irremediable break in relationship over one which is certain to cause such a break. By either of these criteria, abortion is clearly to be avoided.[42]

---

[39]Joan Tronto makes this point in "Beyond Gender Differences to a Theory of Care," *Signs*, vol. 22 (Summer, 1987), p. 666.

[40]Carol Gilligan, "Moral Orientation and Moral Development" in *Women and Moral Theory*, p. 24.

[41]This was evident in the reasoning of the women in Gilligan's case studies, many of whom had abortions in order to please or placate other significant persons in their lives.

[42]Some post-abortion counselors find the sense of irremediable break in relationship to be one of the most painful aspects of the post-abortion experience, and try to urge the woman to imaginatively re-create a relationship with the baby in order to be better able to complete the necessary grieving process. Conversation with Teresa Patterson, post-abortion counselor at Crisis Pregnancy Center in Walnut Creek, California.

Another consideration suggested by Gilligan's work is that since avoiding hurt to others (or non-violence) is integral to an ethics of care, severing a relationship where the other person will be only slightly hurt would be preferable to severing one where deep or lasting injury will be inflicted by our action. But on this criterion, again, it would seem she should avoid abortion, since loss of life is clearly a graver harm than emotional distress.

Two other possible criteria which would also tell against abortion are: (1) that it is permissible to cut ties with someone who behaves unjustly and oppressively toward one, but not with someone who is innocent of any wrong against one, or (2) we have special obligations to our own offspring, and thus should not sever relationship with them.

Criteria can, perhaps, be found which would dictate severing relationship with the fetus rather than others, but it is hard to specify one which clearly reflects the feminine voice. Certainly the right to control one's body will not do. The claim that the unborn is not a person and therefore does not deserve moral consideration can be faulted on several grounds. First, if the feminine voice is one which accepts the interconnectedness of all life and strives to avoid harm to nature and to other species, then the non-personhood of the fetus (supposing it could be proved) would not imply that its needs can be discounted. And secondly, the entire debate over personhood has standardly been carried on very much in the masculine voice.[43] One feminist, Janice Raymond,[44] has suggested that the question of when life begins is a masculine one, and if this is a masculine question, it would seem that personhood, with its juridical connotations, would be also. It is not clear that the care perspective has the resources to resolve this issue. If it cannot, then, one cannot rely on the non-personhood of the fetus in constructing a "feminine voice" defense of abortion. A care perspective would at least seem to place the burden of proof on those who would restrict the scope of care, in this case to those that have been born.

It seems that the only way open to the person who seeks to defend abortion from the point of view of the feminine voice is to deny that a relationship (or at least any morally significant relationship) exists between the embryo/fetus and the mother. The question of how to tell when a relationship (or a morally significant relationship) exists is a deep and important one, which has, as yet, received insufficient attention from those who are trying to articulate the feminine voice in moral reasoning. The whole ecofeminist position relies on the assumption that our relationship with nature and with other species is a real and morally significant one. They, thus, have no basis at all for excluding the unborn from moral consideration.

There are those, however, who wish to define morally significant relationships more narrowly—thus effectively limiting our obligation to extend care. While many philosophers within the "justice tradition" (for example, Kant) have seen moral significance only where there is some impact upon rational beings, Nel Noddings, coming from the "care perspective" tries to limit our obligation to extend care in terms of the possibility

---

[43]For an excellent "masculine voice" discussion of the personhood issues, see, e.g., Philip E. Devine, *The Ethics of Homicide* (Ithaca, NY: Cornell University Press, 1978).

[44]Janice Raymond, *The Transsexual Empire* (Boston: Beacon Press, 1979), p. 114.

of "completion" or "reciprocity" in a caring relationship.[45] Since she takes the mother-child relationship to be paradigmatic of caring, it comes as something of a surprise that she regards abortion as a permissible response to an unwanted pregnancy.[46]

There are, on Noddings' view, two different ways in which we may be bound, as caring persons, to extend our care to one for whom we do not already have the sort of feelings of love and affection which would lead us to do the caring action naturally. One is by virtue of being connected with our "inner circle" of caring (which is formed by natural relations of love and friendship) through "chains" of "personal or formal relations."[47] As an example of a person appropriately linked to the inner circle, she cites her daughter's fiancé. It would certainly *seem* that the embryo in one's womb would belong to one's "inner circle" (via natural caring), or at least be connected to it by a "formal relation" (that is, that of parenthood). But Noddings does not concede this. Who is part of my inner circle, and who is connected to it in such a way that I am obligated to extend care to him or her seems to be, for Noddings, largely a matter of my feelings toward the person and/or my choice to include him or her. Thus the mother *may* "confer sacredness" upon the "information speck"[48] in her womb, but need not if, for example, her relationship with the father is not a stable and loving one. During pregnancy "many women recognize the relation as established when the fetus begins to move about. It is not a question of when life begins, but of when relation begins."

But making the existence of a relation between the unborn and the mother a matter of her choice or feelings, seems to run contrary to one of the most central insights of the feminine perspective in moral reasoning—namely that we already *are* interconnected with others, and thus have responsibilities to them. The view that we are connected with others only when we choose to be or when we *feel* we are, presupposes the kind of individualism and social atomism which Noddings and other feminists criticize as masculine.

Noddings also claims that we sometimes are obligated to care for "the proximate stranger." She says:

> We cannot refuse obligation in human affairs by merely refusing to enter relation; we are, by virtue of our mutual humanity, already and perpetually in potential relation.[49]

---

[45]It would seem that in using the term "obligation," Noddings is blurring the distinction between the masculine and feminine voice, since obligations imply rights. When she speaks of obligations to extend care, however, these are not absolute, but relative to the individual's choice of being a caring person as an ethical ideal. They are binding on us only as a result of our own prior choice, and our care is not something the other can claim as a matter of justice.

[46]Nodding's discussion of abortion occurs on pp. 87–90 of *Caring: A Feminine Approach to Ethics, op. cit.,* and all quotes are from these pages unless otherwise noted.

[47]*Ibid.*, p. 47.

[48]It is inaccurate to call even the newly implanted zygote an "information speck." Unlike a blueprint or pattern of information, it is alive and growing.

[49]I realize that Noddings would not be happy with the extent to which I lean on her use of the term "criteria," since she prefers to argue by autobiographical example. However, since moral intuitions about abortion vary so widely, this sort of argument is not effective here.

Why, then, are we not obligated to extend care to the unborn? She gives two criteria for when we have an obligation to extend care: there must be "the existence of or potential for present relation" and the "dynamic potential for growth in relation, including the potential for increased reciprocity. . . ." Animals are, she believes, excluded by this second criterion since their response is nearly static (unlike a human infant).

She regards the embryo/fetus as not having the potential for present relationships of caring and reciprocity, and thus as having no claim upon our care. As the fetus matures, he or she develops increasing potential for caring relationships, and thus our obligation increases also. There are problems with her position, however.

First of all, the only relationships which can be relevant to *my* obligation to extend care, for Noddings, must be relationships with *me*. Whatever the criteria for having a relationship are, it must be that at a given time, an entity either has a relationship with me or it does not. If it does not, it may either have no potential for a morally significant relationship with me (for example, my word processor), or it may have such potential in several ways: (1) The relationship may become actual at the will of one or both parties (for example, the stranger sitting next to me on the bus). (2) The relationship may become actual only after a change in relative spatial locations which will take time, and thus can occur only in the future (for example, walking several blocks to meet a new neighbor, or traveling to Tibet to meet a specific Tibetan). Or (3) The relationship may become actual only after some internal change occurs within the other (for example by waiting for a sleeping drug to wear off, for a deep but reversible coma to pass, or for the embryo to mature more fully) and thus can also happen only in the future.

In all three of these cases there is present now in the other the potential for relations of a caring and reciprocal sort. In cases (1) and (2) this is uncontroversial, but (3) requires some defense in the case of the unborn. The human embryo differs now from a rabbit embryo in that it possesses potential for these kinds of relationships although neither of them is presently able to enter into relationships of any sort.[50] That potential becomes actualized only over time, but it can become actualized only because it is there to be actualized (as it is not in the rabbit embryo).[51] Noddings fails to give any reason why the necessity for some internal change to occur in the other before relation can become actual has such moral importance that we are entitled to kill the other in case (3), but not in the others, especially since my refraining from killing it is a sufficient condition for the actualization of the embryo's potential for caring relationships. Her criterion as it stands would also seem to imply that we may kill persons in deep but predictably reversible comas.

Whichever strand of Noddings' thought we choose, then, it is hard to see how the unborn can be excluded from being ones for whom we ought to care. If we focus on the narrow, tribal morality of "inner circles" and "chains," then an objective connection exists tying the unborn to the mother and other relatives. If we are to be open to the needy stranger because of the real potential for relationship and reciprocity, then we should be open to the unborn because he or she also has the real and present potential for a relationship of reciprocity and mutuality which comes with species membership.

Many feminists will object to my argument so far on the grounds that they do not, after all, consider abortion to be a *good* thing. They aren't pro-abortion in the sense that

---

[50]I omit here consideration of such difficult cases as severe genetic retardation.

[51]The notion of potentiality I am relying on here is roughly an Aristotelian one.

they encourage women to have abortions. They merely regard it as something which must be available as a kind of "grim option"—something a woman would choose only when the other alternatives are all immeasurably worse.[52]

First of all, the grim options view sounds very much like the "masculine voice"—we must grit our teeth, and do the distasteful but necessary deed (the more so where the deed involves killing).[53] Furthermore, it is in danger of collapsing into total subjectivism unless one is willing to specify some criteria for when an option is a genuinely grim one, beyond the agent's feeling that it is. What if she chooses to abort in order not to have to postpone her trip to Europe, or because she prefers sons to daughters? Surely these are not grim options no matter what she may say. Granted, the complicated circumstances surrounding her decision are best known to the woman herself. But this does not imply that no one is *ever* in a position to make judgments about whether her option is sufficiently grim to justify abortion. We do not generally concede that only the agent is in a position to judge the morality of his or her action.

Feminists standardly hold that absolutely no restrictions may be placed on a woman's right to choose abortion.[54] This position cannot be supported by the grim options argument. One who believes something is a grim option will be inclined to try to avoid or prevent it, and thus be willing, at least in principle, to place some restrictions on what counts as a grim option. Granted, practical problems exist about how such decisions are to be made and by whom. But someone who refuses in principle to allow any restrictions on women's right to abort, cannot in good faith claim that they regard abortion only as a grim option.

Some feminists will say: yes, feminine virtues are a good thing for any person to have, and yes, abortion is a characteristically masculine way of dealing with an unwanted pregnancy, but in the current state of things we live in a male dominated society, and we must be willing to use now weapons which, ideally, in a good, matriarchal society, we would not use.[55] But there are no indications that an ideal utopian society is just around the corner; thus we are condemned to a constant violation of our own

---

[52]Carolyn Whitbeck articulates a view of this sort in "Women as People: Pregnancy and Personhood," *op. cit.*

[53]Granted, this sort of judgment is, at least in part, an impressionistic one. It is supported, however, by Gilligan's findings about the difference between boys and girls in their response to the "Heinz dilemma" (where the man is faced with a choice between allowing his wife to die or stealing an expensive drug from the druggist to save her). Although the females she studies do not all respond to the dilemma in the same way (e.g. Betty at first sounds more like Hobbes than like what has been characterized as the feminine voice—pp. 75–76), some recurring patterns which she singles out as representative of the feminine voice are: resisting being forced to accept either horn of the dilemma, seeing all those involved as in relationship with each other, viewing the dilemma in terms of conflicting responsibilities rather than rights, and seeking to avoid or minimize harm to anyone (see, e.g., Sarah p. 95). Since the abortion decision involves killing and not merely letting die, it would seem that the impetus to find a way through the horns of the dilemma would be, if anything, greater than in the Heinz dilemma.

[54]For example, one feminist, Roberta Steinbach, argues that we must not restrict a woman's rights to abort for reasons of sex selection *against females* because it might endanger our hard won "reproductive rights"! (See "Sex Selection: From Here to Fraternity" in Carol Gould (ed.), *Beyond Domination* (Totowa, NJ: Rowman & Allanheld, 1984), p. 280.)

[55]For example, Annette Baier regards trust as the central concept in a feminine ethics, but speaks of "the principled betrayal of the exploiter's trust" (Baier, "What Do Women Want in a Moral Theory?" p. 62).

deepest commitments. If the traits, values and attitudes characteristic of the "feminine voice" are asserted to be good ones, we ought to act according to them. And such values and attitudes simply do not lend support to either the choice of abortion as a way of dealing with an unwanted pregnancy in individual cases, or to the political demand for unrestricted[56] access to abortion which has become so entrenched in the feminist movement. Quite the contrary.[57]

[56]Restrictions can take many forms, including laws against abortion, mandatory counseling which includes information about the facts of fetal development and encourages the woman to choose other options, obligatory waiting periods, legal requirements to notify (and/or obtain the consent of) the father, or in the case of a minor the girl's parents, etc. To defend the appropriateness of any particular sort of restrictions goes beyond the scope of this paper.

[57]I wish to thank the following for reading and commenting on an earlier draft of this paper: Edith Black, Tony Celano, Phil Devine, James Nelson, Alan Soble, and Michael Wreen.

Abortion and Embodiment[1]

Catriona Mackenzie

1. Introduction

Feminist perspectives on abortion focus on a fact the moral implications of which are either overlooked or considered unimportant by most other disputants in the debate. This is the fact that a foetus is not a free-floating entity about whom questions of potentiality and personhood arise as though in a vacuum. Rather a foetus is a being whose existence and welfare are biologically and morally inseparable from the woman in whose body it develops. From a feminist perspective the central moral subjects of the abortion question are thus not only, or not primarily, foetuses but women.

Within an influential strand of the feminist philosophical literature it has been usual to understand the moral dilemmas arising from this unique relationship between a foetus and a woman in terms of a conflict of rights and to defend a woman's right to abortion via the notion of bodily autonomy. In its crudest form, the alleged conflict is between a) the "right to life" of the foetus, a right based on the presumption that it is a being deserving of some moral consideration, and b) the right of the woman to bodily autonomy, that is, her right to decide what happens in and to her body. In attempting to resolve this conflict in women's favour feminist defenders of abortion have taken two main lines of argument.

The first, articulated best by Mary Anne Warren, argues that in abortion decisions the woman's right to bodily autonomy must always prevail over any rights which may be

From Catriona Mackenzie, "Abortion and Embodiment," *Australasian Journal of Philosophy* 70 (1992): 136–155. Reprinted by permission of the author and the publisher.

[1]I am grateful to the editorial panel and to anonymous referees for their comments on earlier versions of this article. Earlier versions were also read to the Philosophy Department at Monash University, the Philosophy Society at Princeton University, and a seminar on "Legal and Conceptual Aspects of Abortion" at the University of New South Wales. I would like to thank participants in those discussions for their comments. I would also like to thank the following people for their helpful discussions and/or comments: John Bigelow, John Burgess, Genevieve Lloyd, Michaelis Michael, Robert Pargetter, Peter Singer, Michael Smith, C. L. Ten.

claimed on behalf of the foetus.[2] This is because the only beings with full moral standing are persons. Not only are foetuses not persons, they are not even personlike enough to warrant our regarding them as if they were persons. Indeed, Warren claims that an eight-month foetus is no more personlike than the average fish. On this view then, the "right to life" of the foetus, to the extent that it has such a right, cannot possibly outweigh the right of a person to one of the fundamental rights of persons—the right to bodily autonomy. In fact, Warren claims that having an abortion is morally equivalent to cutting one's hair.

The second line of argument is best represented by Judith Jarvis Thomson and, following her, Christine Overall.[3] Their claim involves a sophisticated reinterpretation of the claim that even if a foetus does have a right to life, the woman's right to bodily autonomy overrides that right. By trying to show that even if the foetus is a being with moral standing it has no automatic right to occupancy of a woman's womb, their argument seeks to undermine the basic premise of the conservative position on abortion—namely the premise that if foetuses are persons, that is, beings with full moral rights, then abortion is necessarily wrong.

My aim in this article is to defend a feminist perspective on abortion by showing that questions of women's autonomy lie at the heart of the abortion issue. I shall argue, however, that the conflict-of-rights framework and rights-based models of bodily autonomy are liable seriously to misrepresent both the nature of abortion decisions and the reasons why the availability of abortion is essential to women's autonomy. My dissatisfaction with this kind of approach centers on four related concerns. Firstly, a conflict-of-rights approach fails adequately to address the issue of responsibility in pregnancy and abortion. Hence it mischaracterises both the nature of the moral relationship between woman and foetus and the kind of autonomy that is exercised in pregnancy and abortion. Secondly, it tends to oversimplify our conception of the status of the foetus. Thirdly, it leads to a misconstrual of the notion of bodily autonomy because it is inattentive to the kind of reflective bodily perspective that arises from a phenomenological account of pregnant embodiment. Finally, defending abortion solely on the grounds of women's right to bodily autonomy logically requires that the right to abortion cannot entail a right to secure the death of the foetus but only a right to foetal evacuation.

I shall argue that a strong feminist case for abortion needs to construe a woman's right to obtain an abortion as the right of an autonomous moral agent to be able to make a decision about whether she wishes to take responsibility for the future well-being of a being dependent upon her. In choosing an abortion in other words, a woman is not merely choosing not to allow the foetus occupancy of her uterus. Nor is she merely choosing not to undertake responsibility for a particular future child. Rather, as Steven Ross has pointed out, she is choosing that there be *no being at all* in relation to whom she is in a

---

[2]My argument in this part of the article refers to Mary Anne Warren's paper "On the Moral and Legal Status of Abortion" in R. Wasserstrom (ed.) *Today's Moral Problems* (London: Macmillan, 1975). In a very recent paper, to which I refer in more detail later, Warren's characterization of the foetus is markedly different although her basic position on a woman's right to bodily autonomy remains unaltered. See "The Moral Significance of Birth," *Hypatia* 4(1989) pp. 46–65. This paper is a modified version of an earlier paper with the same title which appeared in *Bioethics News*. Publication of the Centre for Human Bioethics, Monash University, vol. 7, no. 2, January 1988.

[3]Judith Jarvis Thomson, "A Defense of Abortion," *Philosophy and Public Affairs*, 1(1971) pp. 47–66; Christine Overall, *Ethics and Human Reproduction* (Boston: Allen & Unwin, 1987) chs. 3, 4.

situation of such responsibility.[4] To require that a woman has no right to secure the death of the foetus, at least in the early stages of pregnancy, thus violates her autonomy.

Now against this claim it could be argued that here the woman is not only making decisions about her own life but about that of another. What entitles her to make such a decision? The next three sections of the article attempt to answer this question. In the second section I make some suggestions as to how we should understand the notions of responsibility and autonomy in pregnancy, while the third section assesses the moral status of the foetus both from the point of view of its intrinsic moral properties and from the point of view of its relationship with the woman in whose body it develops. Building on the previous two sections, the final section draws on a phenomenological account of pregnancy in order to explain the connection between autonomy, bodily autonomy and pregnant embodiment. My criticisms of the rights-based accounts of bodily autonomy emerge from this discussion.

II. Responsibility and Autonomy

Appeals to responsibility in the context of the abortion debate usually trade on the asymmetry between the situation of men and women with regard to pregnancy. The asymmetry is that while it is always possible for men to evade or even remain blissfully unaware of the consequences of their actions where those actions result in pregnancy, the same is not true for women. Further it is women alone who are physically able to sustain the foetus. Thus women come to be held "responsible" for what was after all a joint action. Given this context it is hardly surprising that feminist defenses of abortion often attempt to shift discussions of the abortion issue away from the question of responsibility. Thorny as it may be however, one of my central claims is that the issue of responsibility is crucial for an understanding of women's moral autonomy with respect to pregnancy and abortion. In this section I attempt to outline an adequate feminist approach to the question of responsibility in pregnancy and abortion.

A number of different aspects of responsibility are often conflated in the abortion debate. To disentangle these I want firstly to distinguish *causal responsibility* from *moral responsibility*. By causal responsibility I mean simply responsibility for the direct causal consequences of one's actions in cases where those consequences can be said to be reasonably foreseeable and where a person's actions were freely chosen. In this sense a woman can be said to be responsible for the existence of the foetus in much the same way as she can be said to be responsible for getting drunk, in that it is her actions, in this case along with those of another, which have brought about this outcome.[5] Although conservatives do not usually make an explicit distinction between causal and

---

[4]Steven Ross, "Abortion and the Death of the Foetus," *Philosophy and Public Affairs* 11 (1982) pp. 232–245.

[5]I discuss the question of men's responsibility below. Given this account of causal responsibility, a woman is, of course, not causally responsible in the case of rape. In cases where a woman cannot and cannot reasonably be expected to foresee the consequences of her actions (e.g., if she is a minor or mentally disabled), or if her actions were performed under duress (the distinction between rape and consent is not as hard and fast as many would think), or if she cannot be said to be acting autonomously (e.g. in

moral responsibility, the conservative claim seems to be that in the case of pregnancy, because the outcome here is to have brought into existence a being with full moral standing, then a woman's *causal responsibility* necessarily entails a moral responsibility towards maintaining the existence of the foetus.[6]

Feminists and liberals have responded to this claim in a number of ways. The approach of Warren and Tooley, for example, is to attempt to shift the focus of the abortion debate away from questions of moral responsibility and towards a consideration of the actual present status of the foetus with respect to personhood. Their argument is that because foetuses are not persons and therefore do not have rights, abortion is morally permissible.[7] A second approach aims to show that one does not necessarily have automatic moral responsibility to maintain the existence of a being dependent upon oneself—even if that being does have full moral standing and hence a right to life. This is Thomson's approach in the examples of the violinist and Henry Fonda.[8] As Warren and Feinberg have shown, however, this strategy fails because the examples chosen are disanalogous to the case of the foetus in one relevant respect, namely with respect to causal responsibility.[9] The strategy thus begs the question. Yet another tactic is to claim that the attribution of causal responsibility is a lot less straightforward than it might appear and thus to argue that causal responsibility for the existence of a being does not necessarily mean that one is required to assume moral responsibility for maintaining its existence. For to what extent is a person still morally responsible for the consequences of an action if she has taken reasonable precautions against those consequences occurring? Thomson's example of the house-owner covering her windows in wire mesh to prevent the entry of "people-seeds" seeks to undermine in this way any necessary connection between causal and moral responsibility.[10]

While these responses have been partially successful in exposing some of the assumptions at work behind the seeming self-evidence of the conservative argument, they nevertheless fail adequately to come to terms with the question of moral responsibility

---

a case of drug addiction or alcoholism or some other dependency), I would argue that, although a woman may have some causal responsibility for the outcome of her actions, she cannot be considered to be morally responsible for this outcome.

[6]Somewhat surprisingly, some feminists have argued for a similar view. See Hilde and James Lindeman Nelson, "Cutting Motherhood in Two: Some Suspicions Concerning Surrogacy," *Hypatia* 4 (1989) pp. 85–94.

[7]Warren, "On the Moral and Legal Status of Abortion," *op. cit*; Michael Tooley, "Abortion and Infanticide," *Philosophy and Public Affairs* 2 (1972) pp. 37–65.

[8]The violinist example seeks to show that a person has no moral obligation to sustain the life of a famous violinist who has been attached to her without her consent, and whose survival is dependent on being connected to her circulatory system for nine months. The Henry Fonda example involves the case of a person who is dying but would be revived by the touch of Henry Fonda's hand on her brow. The example seeks to show that a person does not necessarily have a right to whatever is required to ensure her survival. See Thomson, "A Defense of Abortion," *op. cit.* I discuss the problem with such examples in the final section of this article.

[9]Warren, "On the Moral and Legal Status of Abortion," *op. cit.*; Joel Feinberg. "Abortion," in Tom Regan (ed.), *Matters of Life and Death* (Random House, 1980).

[10]In this example "people-seeds" are seeds which blow in through house windows like dust, take root in carpets, and then grow into people who demand food and shelter!

in pregnancy because they concede too much at the outset to the conservative notion of moral responsibility. This is particularly true of the last approach which forces Thomson, after a series of increasingly bizarre examples, to attempt to dissolve the question of responsibility by an appeal to decency.[11] What needs to be pointed out is that the conservative account of moral responsibility is premised on a set of assumptions which are fundamentally oppressive to women. For it is significant that in this whole debate about responsibility there seem to be only two possible ways for women to get pregnant. Either they are raped, in which case they have no causal responsibility for the existence of the foetus—although according to some conservatives they nevertheless have a moral responsibility towards it. Or else they are not raped, in which case they are held to be fully responsible, in both a causal and moral sense. In neither case however is men's moral responsibility ever seriously discussed, despite their obvious causal involvement in the pregnancy. The consequence of this blindness is that moral responsibility in pregnancy gets construed extremely narrowly, as just responsibility towards the foetus, and in a way that seems to commit women to maternity.

The challenge then seems to be to envision a notion of moral responsibility in pregnancy that acknowledges the moral complexities of the situation, and of the decision facing a woman who is weighing up the choices of abortion or maternity, but that does not imply that the only possible morally responsible course of action is to choose maternity. My starting point here is to accept, without argument at this stage, both that the foetus does have some moral significance and that this is in part why causal responsibility does entail some kind of moral responsibility. Having conceded that much to the conservatives I want to disentangle two aspects of moral responsibility which are confused in conservative arguments.

The first aspect, which I call *decision responsibility*, emerges as a strong theme in Carol Gilligan's interviews with women making the abortion decision.[12] Gilligan's women reveal that in their thinking about abortion, acceptance of causal responsibility means assuming a moral responsibility to make a decision or a series of decisions about your future relationship with the being whose existence you have directly brought about. The decision process is focused on questions such as whether you are in a position adequately to care for it both now when it is in the foetal stage and, more importantly, when it is an independent being; how and whether it can be integrated into your life and the lives of others, for example, other children, whose lives will also be significantly affected by your decision; whether you feel yourself able or prepared, to provide the physical and emotional care and nurture needed in order for both foetus and child to flourish. What emerges from these discussions of responsibility is that the assumption

---

[11]I have in mind here Thomson's discussion of the woman who at seven months requests an abortion in order to avoid having to postpone an overseas trip. Thomson realizes that her argument does not allow her to claim that such a request would be immoral, so she resorts to the claim that it would be indecent. This issue aside, Thomson's example is somewhat offensive in its presentation of women's moral attitude towards abortion. Those women seeking abortions at this stage of pregnancy are usually those whose health is in some way gravely threatened by continuation of the pregnancy, or those who, due to drug addiction, mental disability or some other such reason, cannot be said ever to have made a moral decision with regard to their pregnancies.

[12]Carol Gilligan, *In a Different Voice* (Cambridge, MA: Harvard University Press, 1982). It should be noted here that the kinds of moral reflection in which these women engage is in part made possible by the fact that these women do have reproductive choice.

of moral responsibility in pregnancy cannot be construed just in terms of responsibility towards the foetus but has a wider focus—on the self, on relations with significant others, on a person's other commitments and projects. When responsibility is construed in such a way it is clear that exercising moral responsibility in no way entails a commitment to maternity and that the choice of abortion is in many cases the morally responsible decision.

The second aspect of moral responsibility in pregnancy, which I call *parental responsibility*, is the one which a person assumes when a commitment has been made to maternity.[13] What this kind of assumption of responsibility involves is a responsibility not just to maintaining the existence of the foetus, nor even just a commitment to providing the care and nurture needed for it to flourish, but a commitment to bringing into existence a future child. Often, though not necessarily, it also involves a commitment to long-term care and nurture of that future child. My claim is that the decision to abort is a decision, for whatever reason, that one is not prepared to bring such a child into existence.

It should be pointed out here that with respect to all aspects of responsibility the situation of men and women—in pregnancy at least—is asymmetrical. The asymmetry is that while men and women are equally responsible for pregnancy in the causal sense, causal responsibility and decision responsibility are in effect completely separable for men, but inseparable for women. This is because a woman's bodily connection with the foetus makes causal responsibility and hence decision responsibility inescapable for her.[14] On the other hand men's bodily alienation from the consequences of their actions and from the physical, psychic and emotional experience of pregnancy means that they may be in a position where they are either unaware of their causal responsibility for the existence of the foetus or *choose* not to acknowledge their causal responsibility or assume decision responsibility.

A sensitivity to this difference illuminates two important points. Firstly, if causal and decision responsibility are inseparable for women, then pregnancy cannot be thought of simply as a merely "natural" event which just *happens* to women and in relation to which they are passive. Although pregnancy certainly involves biological processes which are beyond the woman's control, these processes are always mediated by the cultural meanings of pregnancy, by the woman's personal and social context, and by the way she constitutes herself in response to these factors through the decisions she makes. In other words, pregnancy is never simply a biological process, it is always an active process of shaping for oneself a bodily and a moral perspective.[15] For this reason, the

---

[13]As I have indicated, decision responsibility is a process, not a single decision. Thus a woman may change her mind a number of times before finally assuming parental responsibility. She may also change her mind after having assumed it. For reasons which I explain below I think there is a significant *moral* difference between such a change of mind in the first trimester or early in the second trimester and a change of mind during the latter half of pregnancy—except of course where such a change is made for medical reasons or because of foetal deformity discoverable only by amniocentesis during the second trimester. It does not follow from this however that women should be *legally* prevented from obtaining abortions for other reasons later in pregnancy. I discuss the distinction between moral and legal responsibility below.

[14]I discuss the nature of this bodily connection in detail in section IV below.

[15]I develop this point in more detail in section IV below.

moral issues associated with pregnancy and abortion cannot be viewed in abstraction from the first-person perspective of the woman concerned.[16]

Secondly, because of the particularity of the woman's situation in pregnancy, in cases of conflict over abortion ultimately it should be up to the woman to decide whether or not she will choose abortion.[17] To say this does not imply, however, that in situations where men are aware of and do acknowledge causal responsibility, they should have no say in an abortion decision. In such circumstances, because the decision made will obviously affect their autonomy, they should also be party to, and involved in, both decision responsibility and, where appropriate, parental responsibility. Indeed after birth, they may assume most, or even all, parental responsibility. Nevertheless prior to birth the impact upon their autonomy of any decision is very different from its impact on the autonomy of the woman. This is why in cases of conflict the woman's decision should prevail.

Two objections are likely to be raised at this point. The first is that a woman may also choose to relinquish moral responsibility, for example to others through adoption. Further it is often argued that abortion is just a relinquishing of moral responsibility for the foetus. From the preceding discussion it should be clear that this objection conflates the two senses of moral responsibility distinguished above. Deciding against assuming parental responsibility does not mean that one has relinquished moral responsibility, not even for the foetus. For no matter what a woman decides—maternity, abortion, adoption—she is still responsible to herself, to others, to the child if there is one, for the decision she has made. Further, as I have already pointed out, the decision to abort is often the most morally responsible course of action.

The second objection is that I have placed a great deal of moral weight on a decision process which in some cases just never occurs. For some women's lives are so chaotic and so little under their control that they cannot be said to be making any autonomous decisions about their own welfare, let alone about the welfare of any foetus that may be developing inside their body. My response to this objection, as I have already indicated, is to say that I would not attribute moral responsibility to a woman in such a situation. However given the difficulty of actually deciding in any given case, whether or not a woman does have any moral responsibility for a pregnancy, what the objection forces us to recognize is that a distinction needs to be made between our moral assessment of a situation and the matter of legal sanctions. Although I have argued that the decision to continue with a pregnancy entails some kind of parental responsibility, this is quite different from claiming that a woman should be legally liable for the foetus' welfare. Arguments to this effect must be vigorously resisted for they wrongly presume that foetuses are the moral and legal equivalents of women. In fact, as Mary Anne Warren has argued, "There is room for only one person with full and equal legal rights inside a single human skin."[18]

---

[16]I would like to thank one of the Journal's anonymous referees for helping me clarify this point.

[17]I have in mind here recent cases in the UK and Australia where men have attempted to obtain court orders, on the grounds of paternal right, to prevent women from obtaining an abortion. My analysis of the asymmetry in the positions of men and women with respect to responsibility in pregnancy should make it clear why feminists have been so outraged by the men's presumption in these cases that they should be able to overrule the decisions of the women concerned.

[18]My insert, Warren, "The Moral Significance of Birth," op cit., p. 63.

While this analysis of responsibility still leaves unanswered questions about the intrinsic moral status of the foetus it does tend to suggest that at least in part, its moral status is dependent on the relational properties it has with others and that the abortion issue cannot adequately be broached if we focus on intrinsic properties alone.[19] This relational aspect of the foetus' moral standing is best captured through the notion of moral guardianship. I want to suggest that although a foetus cannot be a bearer of full moral rights because, as I shall argue in the next section, it lacks the requisite intrinsic properties (namely personhood), nevertheless in a context in which some one or more members of the moral community have decided to take parental responsibility for its future well-being, it has moral significance by virtue of its relations with her or them. We might say that in such a case it has *de facto* significance through her or them until such a point when it can be considered a full moral being in its own right. This significance does not guarantee the foetus a "right to life" which overrides all other possible competing claims, but rather provides some grounds for the foetus' claims to nurture and care, that is, guardianship, from the woman who bears it and protection from harm from others.

In this context it should be noted that once again the situation of men and women with regard to moral guardianship is inescapably asymmetrical in pregnancy. A man, no matter how well-intentioned, cannot act as the primary guardian of an *in utero* foetus. The reason for this asymmetry is not hard to discern, namely the physical inseparability of the foetus from the woman, but its moral implications are often overlooked. The main implications are firstly that, as I argued earlier, in cases of conflict it should be the woman who has the right to decide the fate of the foetus. Secondly, this asymmetry makes it clear that, as Warren has argued, the event of birth is morally significant.[20] Its significance lies in the fact that at birth the infant becomes a member of the human moral community in its own right because its relationship with its mother and other human beings changes significantly. Not only is its body now separate from that of its mother, but it no longer needs to stand in a relation of moral and physical dependence on her in particular. Any responsible human adult will now be able to provide it with the care nurture and moral protection required for it to flourish.

Having assessed the relational moral status of the foetus I want now to justify my earlier claim that causal responsibility for the existence of the foetus entails decision responsibility because the foetus is a morally significant being. A useful starting point for this discussion is Warren's account of foetal status.

III. Foetal Status and Potentiality

If, following Warren, we distinguish between "human beings" and "persons" and argue that only persons can be members of the moral community, then it seems clear that the foetus is not a bearer of moral rights in the same sense that a person is and so does not

---

[19]Warren also criticizes what she calls "the intrinsic-properties assumption" on the grounds that it cannot account for the moral significance of birth. *Ibid.,* pp. 47–56.

[20]Warren, *ibid.,* p. 56.

have the same "right to life" as a person.[21] Nevertheless, as Warren herself argues with respect to infants, it does not follow from the fact that, because anyone who is a person is entitled to strong moral protections, that it is wrong to extend moral protections to beings that are not persons.[22] The more personlike the being, the more it should be treated as a person. The question arises therefore of how far advanced since conception a human being needs to be before it begins to have a right to life by virtue of being like a person, that is, at what stage should we start treating a foetus as if it were a person? On this point Warren in her earlier paper claims that the foetus of seven or eight months is no more personlike, or even less personlike, than the average fish and thus should not be treated as a person. For although, like the fish, the late term foetus is sentient, sentience is not sufficient for personhood. *Contra* Thomson, she thus concludes that "whether or not it would be indecent (whatever that means) for a woman in her seventh month to obtain an abortion just to avoid having to postpone a trip to Europe, it would not, in itself, be immoral, and therefore it ought to be permitted."[23]

Warren's comparison between foetuses and fish occurs in the context of a discussion of the nature of personhood. The intention of the comparison is to show that, while the foetus is indeed a member of the human species, as far as personhood and hence claims to rights are concerned the foetus is morally on a par with a fish. With respect to driving home the distinction between human beings and persons I do not dispute the effectiveness of Warren's comparison. However I want to suggest that the metaphor is problematic for two reasons. Firstly, it invites us to ignore the fact that, contingent though it may be, personhood is constituted by a complex of properties which supervene on a specific physical constitution.[24] Yet despite its contingency, or perhaps because of it, I believe that this fact is morally significant. Secondly, although the foetus/fish metaphor should not be read as providing a model of the relationship between a woman and a foetus, it has the serious, if unintended, effect of downplaying the moral significance and particularity of this relationship. In particular, it has the effect of de-emphasizing both the

---

[21]Warren, "On the Moral and Legal Status of Abortion," *op. cit.* Warren supports this distinction by outlining five criteria for personhood, specifying that a person need not satisfy all these criteria but that a being which satisfied none of them could not be considered a person. The five criteria are:

1. Consciousness (of objects and events external and/or internal to the being), and in particular the capacity to feel pain.

2. Reasoning (the *developed* capacity to solve new and relatively complex problems);

3. Self-motivated activity (activity which is relatively independent of either genetic or direct external control);

4. The capacity to communicate, by whatever means, messages of an indefinite variety of types, that is, not just with an indefinite number of possible contents, but on indefinitely many possible topics;

5. The presence of self-concepts, and self-awareness, either individual or racial, or both.

[22]Warren, "The Moral Significance of Birth," *op. cit.* I follow Warren here in using the term "person" because I think that in the context of abortion the distinction between "human beings" and "persons" is an important distinction to maintain. However I am not happy with the legalistic and individualist connotations of the term which tend to downplay the intersubjective processes of development by means of which infants become self-conscious subjects.

[23]Warren, "On the Moral and Legal Status of Abortion," *op. cit.*, p. 133.

[24]In stressing the connection between the development of subjectivity and physical development I am not denying the significance of the social relationships in the context of which these developments must occur.

woman's role as moral guardian and her parental responsibility for the present and future well-being of the foetus. The force of the feminist defense of abortion must lie in its highlighting of the moral particularity of the relationship between a woman and a foetus.

On the question of foetal status and potentiality my claim is that foetuses are morally significant beings by virtue of the fact that they are potential persons. This makes them morally different in kind from fish. However, I think it is plausible to suggest that the moral value of the foetus' potential personhood is not static, but changes during the course of a normal pregnancy. This is because potential for personhood is not the only thing that bestows moral status on the being with that potentiality. Rather, the moral value of a being's potential personhood is related to the physical or biological basis of the potentiality, in particular it is grounded in the degree of complexity and development of this physical basis. Thus the more physically complex and developed the being is, the more value we attribute to its potential for personhood. There are two ways in which this claim could be developed. One way would accept an on/off view of potentiality and argue that potential for personhood remains constant although its moral significance changes. On this view conceptus and late term foetus both have the same potentiality but the moral value of those beings is different because the physical basis of the potentiality is different. In the one case we have a clump of undifferentiated cells, in the other a highly complex organism. Thus in the one case we have a being very far from being able to actualise its potentialities because it lacks the very physical basis to do so, in the other we have a being fairly close to being able to actualise its potentialities to the extent that the physical basis of those potentialities is highly developed.[25] Another way would be to question the on/off view of potentiality and to argue that potential for personhood itself changes as the foetus develops physically.[26]

For my purposes here nothing hinges on the differences between these positions. But what is appealing about the general suggestion is that it enables us to agree with Warren's criteria of personhood while nevertheless resisting the counter intuitive implications of these criteria, *viz.,* that a being has no intrinsic moral significance unless it is a person and that there is no important moral difference between a conceptus and a late term foetus. For now it can be argued that the intrinsic moral status of the foetus changes in direct relation to its changing physical basis. Thus, at least in terms of its intrinsic properties, an early stage foetus does not have great value. With respect to a highly developed foetus, although it is not a being with full moral rights, its gradually increasing moral significance warrants our treating it, in most circumstances at least, as if it were such a being.

Combining this view with the guardianship view outlined earlier we get the idea that the moral position of the foetus changes over the course of pregnancy. At the early stages its moral standing is defined in relational terms, because it is a being with moral significance for the woman in whose body it develops and who acts as its moral guardian. As the foetus develops physically however its intrinsic moral significance

---

[25]This argument is a simplified version of an argument of John Bigelow and Robert Pargetter. See "Morality, Potential Persons and Abortion," *American Philosophical Quarterly* 25 (1988) pp. 173–181.

[26]An argument for this view is presented by Michaelis Michael in "The Moral Significance of Potential for Personhood" (unpublished paper, Monash University, 1986). His view is that the potential for personhood of a being can be expressed as a function, from situations the being is (normally) in, to the probabilities of its giving rise to a person from those situations. We have greater potential when we have one function dominating another.

increases. Its moral standing is less and less dependent on its relational properties with the woman in whose body it develops and more and more tied to its own intrinsic value. This does not mean, however, that the foetus is ever the moral equivalent of the woman. Hence in cases where the foetus' continued existence severely threatens the woman's physical or mental survival, her interests should always prevail up until the moment of birth. It does however suggest that late term abortion is morally different from early abortion and that they cannot be justified on the same grounds.

On the question of guardianship, I suggested above that the rationale behind Warren's defense of abortion (namely that the foetus is not a person), particularly in the context of the foetus/fish comparison, has the effect of downplaying the moral significance of the woman's parental responsibility for the present and future well-being of the foetus. This effect is reinforced by Warren's claim, which she justifies on the grounds of a woman's right to bodily autonomy, that a decision to abort is morally permissible up until the moment of birth. For now it looks as though the foetus is a potential threat to the woman's bodily autonomy up until the moment of birth, rather than a being in relation to whom the woman has a unique bodily and moral connection. In the next section I shall argue that this view is based on a flawed conception of bodily autonomy. Here I simply want to point out that in pregnancy the assumption of parental responsibility necessarily involves a certain commitment of one's body. In other words, the decision to continue a pregnancy (and presumably by seven months some prior decision has been made) is a decision to assume responsibility (even if only for nine months) for the well-being of the foetus and this entails providing bodily nurture for it, perhaps even at some bodily risk to yourself. Now obviously there are limits to this risk. I am not suggesting that women have responsibility to the foetus whatever the risk. As I have already indicated, I am also not suggesting that parties other than the woman, for example the medical establishment, or the state-legal apparatus, have a right to determine the limits of that risk. Like many other feminists, including Warren, I am alarmed by the recent movements advocating both so-called "foetal rights" and the introduction of charges of "foetal abuse" against women who do not do what is required to nurture the foetus in the uterus. Further the whole question of what is "required" for adequate nurture is open to much interpretation against women's autonomy as persons. Nevertheless, I think that my accounts of potentiality, guardianship and responsibility explain why there is a genuine moral requirement upon a woman to protect and nurture a foetus once she has assumed parental responsibility for its future well-being, without that requirement involving any infringement of her autonomy. In this context it should be noted that Warren's downplaying of the question of responsibility also fails to stress men's obligations with respect to a pregnancy.

IV. Pregnant Embodiment
and Bodily Autonomy

I have argued so far that, at least in the early stages of its development, the moral standing of a foetus is dependent upon its relationship with the woman who bears it and who acts as its moral guardian. In terms of its own intrinsic properties its moral standing is not particularly significant. This is a necessary condition for the permissibility of abortion, but it is not sufficient. For it fails to explain why the availability of abortion is necessary for the moral autonomy of women and hence why a restriction on its accessibility violates their autonomy. In this section I attempt to explain and justify this claim. From my discussion it will also become clear why, in order to secure women's autonomy, abortion must be understood as foetal death rather than foetal evacuation.

What has emerged so far is that in order to understand the kind of autonomy that is exercised by women in pregnancy and abortion we must be attentive to the moral particularity of pregnancy. As we have seen there are a number of different factors which make pregnancy morally unique. To begin with, pregnancy is not simply a biological event with respect to which women are passive. Rather it is an active process and a social process which places women in a situation of moral responsibility—which I earlier called decision responsibility. This responsibility is due in part to the foetus' potential moral significance, but it is also due to the fact that the decision to commit or not to commit oneself to the existence of such a future person has far-reaching implications for the woman's own life as well as, possibly, for the lives of others—for example, the "father" of the possible future child, other children, relatives, friends and so on. But pregnancy is also morally unique because the physical connection between the woman and the foetus, and the physical processes which occur during pregnancy, give rise to a unique bodily perspective.

In what follows I shall draw on a phenomenological account of pregnant embodiment in order to give an account of the kind of reflective bodily perspective that emerges out of the experience of pregnancy. I shall also suggest that the experience of moral responsibility in pregnancy which I have detailed above, is mediated by this reflective bodily perspective, which both structures and points to the moral particularity of the relationship between woman and foetus—especially to the fact that this relationship and the responsibilities it entails cannot be conceived of as extrinsic to the woman's subjectivity. I want to make it clear that this phenomenological description is not a description of the subjective feelings of individual women, but is rather a normative and reflective apprehension of the way in which conscious experience is structured by our (bodily) situations, perspectives and modes of perception. The phenomenological experience I describe is therefore not meant to be an empirical description of the way in which all women experience or feel about their pregnancies, since women's individual bodily perspectives, feelings and experiences depend upon a wide range of factors, including the cultural, social and historical context in which they live their lives.[27]

My suggestion is that although in some ways (for example, biologically) it makes sense to speak of the foetus as a separate being from the woman, in other ways (for example in terms of talking of a conflict of rights), it makes no sense at all—especially in the early stages of pregnancy.[28] Phenomenologically, the experience of pregnancy, particularly in the early stages, is unique in the sense that it defies a sharp opposition between self and other, between the inside and the outside of the body. From the perspec-

---

[27]My account here builds on psychoanalytic insights into the mother-child relation, on some of the descriptions of pregnancy and maternity in the work of Julia Kristeva, on Iris Young's phenomenology of pregnant embodiment, and on my own *a posteriori* reconstructions. See Julia Kristeva, "Motherhood According to Giovanni Bellini" in *Desire in Language* (Oxford: Blackwell, 1980) and "Stabat Mater" in T. Moi (ed.), *The Kristeva Reader* (Oxford: Blackwell, 1986); Iris Marion Young, "Pregnant Embodiment: Subjectivity and Alienation," *The Journal of Medicine and Philosophy* 9 (1984) pp. 45–62.

[28]The rights-based model has also been criticized on different but related grounds by other feminists. See Janet Farrell Smith, "Rights-conflict, Pregnancy and Abortion" in Carol Gould (ed.), *Beyond Domination* (Totowa, NJ: Rowman & Allanheld, 1984) pp. 265–273.

tive of the woman, there *is* no clear-cut boundary between herself and the foetus, between her body boundaries and the body boundaries of the foetus. The foetus, to the extent that it is experienced as part of the woman's body, is also experienced as part of her self, but as a part that is also other than herself. On the one hand it is another being, but it is another being growing inside her body, a being whose separateness is not fully realised as such by her. This is the case even with an unwanted pregnancy. The uniqueness and intimacy of this kind of relationship, one where the distinction between self and other is blurred, suggests that the welfare of the foetus, at least early on, is not easily separable from that of the woman. The foetus is not simply an entity extrinsic to her which happens to be developing inside her body and which she desires either to remove or to allow to develop. It is a being, both inseparable and yet separate from her, both part of and yet soon to be independent from her, whose existence calls into question her own present and future identity.

The changing phenomenology of pregnancy also concurs with the account I have given of foetal status. For it seems to me that one of the main reasons for the experience I have described is that in early pregnancy, although the woman's body is undergoing massive changes, the foetus itself is not very physically developed. The foetus' separateness is thus neither physically well established nor is it felt as such by the woman. What happens as pregnancy continues is that, as the foetus develops physically, a triple process occurs. Firstly, from the perspective of the woman, the foetus becomes more and more physically differentiated from her as her own body boundaries alter. Secondly, this gradual physical differentiation (which becomes very pronounced as soon as the foetus starts moving around—perhaps explaining why "quickening" used to be considered morally significant) is paralleled by and gives rise to a gradual psychic differentiation, in the experience of the woman, between herself and the foetus. In other words, as the foetus' body develops it seems to become less and less a part of the woman and of her body although, as psychoanalysis reminds us, the psychic experiences of unity and differentiation continue to resonate for both mother and child right through infancy and early childhood. Thirdly, physical and psychic differentiation are usually accompanied by an increasing emotional attachment of the woman to the foetus, an attachment which is based both in her physical connection with the foetus and in an anticipation of her future relationship with a separate being who is also intimately related to her.

From the reflective perspective of the woman the foetus thus has a double and ambivalent status. On the one hand, it is experienced as interior to her own subjectivity, and this sense of interiority is grounded in the bodily connection between the woman and the foetus. On the other hand, this experience of interiority and connection is interrupted by an awareness that, if the pregnancy continues, this being which is now a part of her will become a separate being for whose welfare she is morally responsible. But this awareness itself arises in part from the woman's bodily experiences—for example, from the changes to her body shape and from feelings of the strangeness of her body to her—which remind her of the other being which is growing within her. I think it is this double character of the foetus' bodily and moral relationship to the woman that explains both why questions of responsibility are central to the experience of pregnancy and why the right of determination over the fate of the foetus is essential for a woman's autonomy.[29]

---

[29]At this point I would like to respond to an objection which is often made against the view I have proposed here. It could be argued that the woman's experience of the foetus as part of herself and as interior to her subjectivity is simply mistaken. So why should any moral weight be given to this

I think this reflective perspective also explains why it is a mistake to construe bodily autonomy in pregnancy and abortion simply as a matter preserving the integrity of one's body boundaries. It is this kind of understanding of bodily autonomy which seems to inform the views of Thomson and Warren, at least in her [Warren's] early paper, who construe the right to bodily integrity along the lines of a property-right. The idea seems to be that a woman has a right to preserve the integrity of her body boundaries, and to control what happens in and to her body, in the same way as she has a right to dispose of her property as she sees fit, and that the denial to women of access to abortion might be said to be akin to a system of coverture. I think this idea is quite explicit in such feminist slogans as "Keep *your* filthy laws off *my* body" and in some of Thomson's metaphors—for example, the metaphor of the body as a house. Now it seems to me that underlying this view of the body is the mistaken idea that I am the owner of my body and my body parts and that, as their owner, I can dispose of them, use them, or contract them out for use as I see fit. This view of the body often underlies defenses of surrogacy but I think it is also evident in Thomson's assumptions about pregnancy. In her argument pregnancy emerges as a kind of contract between the woman and the foetus such that she contracts with it for it to use her body for the required period until it is able to survive without her. Thus in Thomson's violinist example the idea seems to be that the unwanted foetus is attempting to use a woman's body without her having contracted with it to do so and it is this which makes abortion permissible. A similar kind of presumption seems to be operating in Warren's view that the foetus represents a potential threat to the woman's bodily autonomy up to the moment of birth.

For the remainder of this article I shall argue that this conception of bodily autonomy, and the rights-based model which provides the framework for it, are seriously

---

experience? How is it different, for example, from the experience of a slave-owner who regards his/her slaves as a part of him/herself and thinks that because of this he/she has a right to determine their fate? My response to this suggestion is that these cases are completely disanalogous, and for two reasons. Firstly, I have argued that a necessary condition for the permissibility of abortion is that the foetus, especially in the early stages of pregnancy, has little moral value in and of itself, although it may have a great deal of value for the woman in whose body it develops. This is not a merely arbitrary claim, like the claim of the slave-owner who may think that his/her slaves have little moral value in and of themselves. Rather it is justified by the fact that the foetus simply does not yet have the capacities which ground the moral worth of persons, and by the fact that the foetus' possible potential for personhood has little significance until those capacities are close to being actualised.

But, secondly, this objection ignores what I have been insisting on throughout this article, namely that the relationship of the woman to the foetus is morally unique. It is not a relationship of domination and subordination and inhuman ownership, as in the case of the slave-owner. Rather, it is a relationship in which one human being grows and develops inside the body of another, and in which the moral significance of the foetus is in part bound up with its significance for the woman. The moral particularity of this situation, in other words, is grounded in the nature of the bodily connection between woman and foetus. The woman's sense of the foetus as a part of herself is thus not arbitrary. It arises, as I have tried to show, from her own reflective bodily perspective and from the kind of moral reflection to which pregnancy gives rise.

Certainly it is possible to think up all kinds of examples in which the relationship between the woman and the foetus might have been different—as in Thomson's examples. But my point is that these examples cannot give us an adequate understanding of the moral complexities of the issues raised by pregnancy and abortion precisely because they overlook the context out of which these complexities arise, namely the bodily and moral connection between the woman and the foetus.

flawed. My first set of objections to this way of defending abortion is that it misrepresents both the nature of pregnancy and the woman-foetus relationship. As a result, it is unable to come to terms with the question of moral responsibility in pregnancy. The second and connected objection is that it justifies the demand for abortion in terms of a right to an evacuated uterus, rather than a right to autonomy with respect to one's own life. This misrepresents the nature of the abortion decision. These two objections are explained in the next two subsections.

A. Bodily Autonomy, Subjectivity and Responsibility

It seems that underlying the property-contract model of bodily autonomy is a very inert view of pregnancy in which pregnancy is represented as a purely biological process with respect to which women are passive. It is as though, having agreed to the terms of the contract, the woman then simply allows her body to be used by the foetus. But this view of pregnancy blinds us to the fact that the relationship between the woman and the foetus is a special relationship of a very particular nature. The foetus is not a stranger contracting with the woman for use of her body but another, not yet separate, being growing within her body, a being implicated in her own sense of self and whose very existence places her in a situation of moral responsibility.

However, if we take seriously both the issue of responsibility in pregnancy and the kind of reflective bodily perspective that I have argued emerges from the process of pregnancy, then pregnancy seems to defy the making of a sharp distinction between a passive, unconscious, biological process and an active, conscious, rational process. To a large extent the biological processes occurring in a woman's body *are* beyond her control. Nevertheless, as I have already argued, these processes are always mediated by the cultural meanings of pregnancy, by the woman's personal and social context, and by the way she constitutes herself in response to these factors through the decisions she makes. Thus coming to terms with pregnancy and its implications, taking responsibility of whatever kind for the future of the foetus, are the activities of an autonomous moral agent. Bodily autonomy in pregnancy and abortion thus cannot be construed simply as the right to bodily integrity. Rather it is a question of being able to shape for oneself an integrated bodily perspective, a perspective by means of which a woman can respond to the bodily processes which she experiences in a way with which she identifies, and which is consistent with the decision she makes concerning her future moral relationship with the foetus.

To think that the question of autonomy in abortion is just a question about preserving the integrity of one's body boundaries, and to see the foetus merely as an occupant of the woman's uterus, is thus to divorce women's bodies from their subjectivities. Ironically it comes close to regarding women's bodies simply as foetal containers—the very charge which many feminists have levelled against the "foetal rights" movement. If, however, we see our subjectivities as constituted through the constitution of our bodily perspectives so that, following Merleau-Ponty, we see the body as our point of view upon the world, then my body is no more my property than I myself am my own property.[30] Rather my body is my mode of being-in-the-world. Consequently changes to my

---

[30]I am drawing here on Maurice Merleau-Ponty's discussion of the body in *The Phenomenology of Perception* (1945), translated by Colin Smith (London: Routledge, 1962).

body or to my perceptions of my body-image must affect my relation to the world. The experience of pregnant embodiment, that is, the gradual differentiation and development from within her own body of another being which is now a part of herself, thus affects a woman's mode of being-in-the-world both physically and morally and, as a consequence, re-shapes her sense of self. She is now no longer just herself but herself and another, but this other is not yet separate from herself. It is because of this psychic and bodily connectedness between the woman and the foetus that in pregnancy questions about the fate of the foetus cannot be separated out from the issue of a woman's right to self-determination.

B. Evacuation and Abortion

If, as I have argued, the early stage foetus is both morally insignificant (in terms of its own intrinsic properties), and its identity and very existence are as yet indistinguishable from that of the woman, it becomes nonsensical to speak of a conflict of rights between them because we cannot talk about the needs and rights of the foetus in abstraction from those of the woman.[31] The idea of such a conflict only makes any sense later in pregnancy where the foetus is physically well developed and differentiated from the woman and where this physical basis now grounds a definite and significant moral value. Combining my earlier discussion of the moral insignificance of the early stage foetus with my claim that the early stage foetus is phenomenologically and psychically experienced by the woman as both part and not part of herself, thus grounds the moral permissibility of securing its death. At present the foetus is in itself a morally insignificant part of herself but it is a part of herself which, if the pregnancy continues, will become a separate, independent and significant being, for whose future existence she will be required to take parental responsibility and to whom she will become increasingly emotionally attached. What the abortion decision involves is a decision that this part of herself should not *become* a being in relation to whom such questions of parental responsibility and emotional attachment arise. In other words abortion is not a matter of wanting to kill *this particular being,* which is, after all, as yet indistinguishable from oneself. It is rather a matter of not wanting there to *be* a future child, so intimately related to oneself, for which one either has to take responsibility or give up to another.

Because property-contract models of bodily autonomy are inattentive to the phenomenological experience of pregnancy and ignore questions of moral responsibility they misrepresent the nature of this decision. For if the demand for abortion is just the demand to control one's own body and use its parts as one sees fit, then abortion cannot involve the right to choose whether or not to bring a child into existence but only the right to evacuate a foetus from one's body. While Thomson and Warren explicitly acknowledge this as an implication of their account of bodily autonomy, they do not defend the position to which they are committed. In her discussion of abortion in *Ethics and Human Reproduction* Christine Overall does, however, attempt to defend this position even though she is explicitly critical of a property-contract view of women's bodies. My argument is that such a position is inconsistent with a concern for women's

---

[31]This does not, of course, mean that we cannot talk of what is physically harmful or beneficial to the development of the foetus.

autonomy.[32] In what follows I shall develop this argument via a critical analysis of Overall's discussion.

Overall argues that abortion consists of two conceptually and morally distinct events which, though inseparable in current gynecological practice may yet, with the advancing state of technology, become separable. These are: (1) the evacuation of the foetus from the uterus, and (2) the destruction of the foetus. Overall's argument is that while (1) is morally permissible, (2) is not. In other words, if the foetus could be kept alive in some kind of incubator or if some form of foetal transplant and adoption were possible—that is, the evacuation of the foetus from one woman's uterus and its implantation in the uterus of another—then such procedures would be morally required.

Overall's argument, which is very similar to a double-effect argument, involves a reconstrual of the alleged rights conflict in abortion. Where the original formulation is a conflict between (a) the foetus' right to life, and (b) a woman's right to bodily autonomy, she reconstrues this, in terms of an absence of rights, as a conflict between (c) the pregnant woman (or anyone else, e.g. a physician) who has no right to kill the embryo/foetus, and (d) the embryo/foetus which has no right to occupancy of its mother's (or anyone else's) uterus. Overall's claim is that the right to bodily autonomy reconstrued as (d) does not entail (2). (d) involves a simple taking-over of Thomson's formulation without further argumentation. Overall's main argument in defense of (c) is an appeal to the foetus' potential personhood, but "appeal" is all it is because Overall does not discuss the criteria for personhood, nor explain how we should understand the claim that foetuses are potential persons. In addition she simply assumes that foetuses at all stages of development have the same moral significance.[33]

---

[32]Anne Donchin has expressed similar worries about the implications of Overall's position. See her review essay "The Growing Feminist Debate Over the New Reproductive Technologies," *Hypatia* 4 (1989) pp. 136–149.

[33]Overall offers three supposedly analogous cases which are supposed to back up this appeal and to show why the right to bodily autonomy, reconstrued as (d), does not entail a woman's right to demand (2), that is, the destruction of the foetus. The problem with these cases however is that Overall fails to make any moral discriminations between different stages of foetal development. The cases are as follows:

(A) If an aborted foetus lives we have no right to kill it, although we are not morally obliged to keep it alive. Here Overall seems to be appealing to the acts and omissions doctrine which in this context I would reject on compassionate grounds. If the foetus is likely to die and will presumably suffer more if simply allowed to die (which is pretty certain if we are talking about an abortion prior to twenty weeks), it seems morally preferable that we kill it.

(B) We have no right to kill premature babies in a case, for example, where the mother might have wanted an abortion but was prevented from obtaining one. But if there is no moral difference between a twenty six week premature baby and a twenty six week *in utero* foetus, it should be just as morally wrong to kill the foetus as the baby. Overall's argument here appeals to the claim that all foetuses, as whatever stage of development, are morally indistinguishable. I have already argued against this claim and have agreed that the killing of a late term foetus is morally different from killing an early foetus, although I have also indicated that I would not rule it out *a priori*, for example, in cases where it is unlikely it would ever acquire the complex physical basis required for personhood. I would agree though with Overall that were it possible to abort a late term foetus alive, in most cases where the foetus was likely to survive and become a healthy infant the mother would not have the right to kill it. Having said that I would nevertheless take issue with Overall's claim that there is no moral difference between a

Overall is aware that her position gives rise to many difficult questions: ought we to save all aborted foetuses?; should we try to adopt them out were that possible?; what if foetal adoption caused more suffering for women or for foetuses? She attempts to avoid some of these and to resolve the conflict between conflicting rights (c) and (d) by arguing that they apply to different periods of pregnancy. Hence right (d) may be regarded as overriding in early pregnancy (with abortion then resulting in the foreseeable but unintended death of the foetus), whereas right (c) may be regarded as overriding in late pregnancy.

While I agree with Overall that, in most cases, it is morally indefensible to demand the death of a late term foetus, the problem with her argument is that she offers no reasons as to why this should be the case, nor does she offer an explanation as to why, if, as she thinks, there is no significant difference in moral standing between a conceptus and a late term foetus, the foreseeable consequence of the foetus' death should be any more allowable early in pregnancy than later on. As I have shown, however, there are a number of reasons why there is a morally significant difference between a conceptus and a late term foetus and it is this difference which makes foetal death in early abortions morally permissible. I conclude then that Overall's defense of abortion as foetal evacuation fails.

More importantly however, Overall's failure to make any significant moral discriminations between different stages of foetal development renders her "solution" to the conflict between (c) and (d) arbitrary and far too contingent upon what is technologically feasible. For were it to become possible to evacuate an early stage foetus from the uterus of one woman and implant it into the uterus of another or to rear it in an incubator, Overall would be committed to the moral desirability of this procedure. Not only that, she would be committed to arguing that such a procedure, rather than abortion, is morally required. For the reasons outlined in this article, it seems to me disturbing that this outcome should seem to follow from a feminist defense of abortion. Apart from oversimplifying the complex issue of foetal status, this position ignores the fact that much more is at stake in the demand for abortion than the misconceived demand to dispose of or use one's own body parts as one sees fit. What is at issue is women's moral autonomy, an autonomy which, because of the specificity of women's embodiment, must include autonomy with respect to the fate of any foetus developing within her body. Because of the connection between the foetus, which is both part and not part of herself, and the woman's moral and bodily subjecthood, to allow the fate of the foetus to be settled by what is or is not technologically feasible once again removes from women what the availability of abortion helps make possible—the right to autonomous moral agency with respect to one's own life.

---

twenty six week premature baby and a twenty six week *in utero* foetus. Her claim assumes that birth has no moral significance. This is an assumption which I have already contested.

(C) At the other end of the process, Overall claims that neither foetus nor embryo is the property of the parents. Thus, she argues, just as parents involved in *in vitro* fertilization programmes should not have the right to demand the destruction of embryos, neither do women have the right to secure the death of the foetus. While I would agree with Overall that neither conceptus nor foetus is the property of its parents, I disagree that it is only on such grounds that we might regard it as their right to determine its fate. I don't want here to tackle the issue of the "disposal" of *in vitro* fertilization embryos and/or foetal tissue. Suffice it to say that Overall's argument once again trades on the unargued claim that foetuses at all stages of development have intrinsic moral worth as "potential" persons.

V. Conclusion: Metaphors, Experience and Moral Thinking

I shall conclude this discussion with some brief reflections on the methodological implications of the analysis I have given. A survey of the philosophical literature on abortion, including some of the feminist philosophical literature, shows that philosophical thinking on this topic has been dominated by bizarre metaphors and fantastic examples (Warren's fish, Tooley's kittens, Thomson's violinists, people-seeds, houses and so on) and has given rise to abstruse metaphysical speculations about the nature of personal identity (Parfit). These examples and speculations have undoubtedly served to question certain common unreflective prejudices and to highlight the philosophical ramifications and complexities of some of the questions raised by abortion. Unfortunately they have also contributed to the representation of pregnancy as a mere *event* which simply takes over women's lives and with respect to which women are passive. In addition, they have focused philosophical and moral reflection away from the contexts in which deliberations about abortion are usually made and away from the concerns and experiences which motivate those involved in the processes of deliberation. The result is that philosophical analyses of abortion often seem beside the point, if not completely irrelevant, to the lives of the countless women who daily not only have to make moral decisions about abortion but, more importantly, who often face serious risks to their lives in contexts where abortion is not a safe and readily accessible procedure. While I do not pretend to have addressed the social, religious, political and legal obstacles which give rise to this abhorrent situation, I do hope to have explained why the morality of abortion is not simply or even primarily about questions concerning personhood and foetal status but more fundamentally is about women's self-determination.

Abortion and Feminism

Sally Markowitz

I n the past few decades, the issue of abortion, long of concern to women, has gained a prominent place in the platforms of politicians and a respectable, if marginal, one in the writings of moral philosophers. It is natural to speculate that the rise of and reactions to the women's liberation movement explain the feverish pitch of the recent debate, and no doubt there is much to this speculation. And yet, philosophical analyses of abortion have had surprisingly little to say directly about either women or feminism. Instead, their primary concern has been to decide whether or not the fetus is a person, with a right to life like yours or mine. That this question deserves philosophical attention becomes especially clear when we consider the frightening (if fanciful) ways it is asked and answered by those in power. Nevertheless, as many feminists and some philosophers have recognized, the way we respond to the problem of personhood will not necessarily settle the dispute over abortion once and for all. On some views, a full account must deal with the rights of pregnant women as well.

In fact, one popular defense of abortion is based on the woman's right to autonomy and avoids the personhood issue altogether. The central claim of the autonomy defense is that anti-abortion policies simply interfere in an impermissible way with the pregnant woman's autonomy. In what has become the classic philosophical statement of this view, Judith Jarvis Thomson ingeniously argues that even if the fetus has a right to life, it need not also have the right to use its mother's body to stay alive. The woman's body is her own property, to dispose of as she wishes.[1] But autonomy theorists need not rest their case on the vaguely disturbing notion of the pregnant woman's property rights to her own body. For example, Jane English, in another version of the view, argues that a woman is justified in aborting if pregnancy and childbearing will prevent her from pursuing the life she wants to live, the expression of her own autonomy.[2]

Philosophers have come to call this strategy the "feminist" or "woman's liberation" approach, and indeed some version of it seems to be favored by many feminists.[3] This

From Sally Markowitz, "Abortion and Feminism," *Social Theory and Practice* 16 (1990): 1–17. Reprinted by permission.

[1]Judith Jarvis Thomson, "A Defense of Abortion," *Philosophy and Public Affairs* 1 (1971): 47–66.

[2]Jane English, "Abortion and the Concept of a Person," in *Today's Moral Problems*, ed. by Richard A. Wasserstrom (New York: Macmillan, 1985), pp. 448–57.

[3]Peter Singer, *Practical Ethics* (Cambridge: Cambridge University Press, 1979), p. 113.

is no surprise since such a view may seem to be quite an improvement over accounts that regard personhood as the only essential issue. At least it recognizes women as bearers of rights as well as of babies. In what follows, however, I shall suggest that this defense may fall short of the feminist mark. Then I shall offer another defense, one derived not from the right to autonomy, but from an awareness of women's oppression and a commitment to a more egalitarian society.

I will assume throughout that the fetus has a serious right to life. I do so not because I believe this to be true, but rather because a feminist defense of abortion rights should be independent of the status of the fetus. For if, as many feminists believe, the move towards a sexually egalitarian society requires women's control of their reproductive lives, and if the permissibility of this control depends ultimately upon the status of the fetus, then the future of feminism rests upon how we resolve the personhood issue. This is not acceptable to most feminists. No doubt many feminists are comforted by arguments against the fetus's personhood. But regardless of the fetus's status, more must be said.

1

What, then, from a feminist point of view, is wrong with an autonomy defense? Feminists should be wary on three counts. First, most feminists believe not only that women in our society are oppressed, but also that our failure to face the scope and depth of this oppression does much to maintain it. This makes feminists suspicious of perspectives, often called humanist or liberal ones, that focus only on the individual and re-emphasize the issue of gender by either refusing to acknowledge that women have less power than men or denying that this inequity is worth much attention. While liberals and humanists may try to discuss social issues, including abortion, with as little mention as possible of gender, feminists tend to search for the hidden, unexpected, and perhaps unwelcome ways in which gender is relevant. From this perspective, defenses of abortion which focus only on the personhood of the fetus are not essentially or even especially feminist ones since they completely avoid any mention of gender. Autonomy arguments, though, are not much of an improvement. They may take into account the well-being of individual women, but they manage to skirt the issue of women's status, as a group, in a sexist society.

Secondly, the autonomy defense incorporates a (supposedly) gender-neutral right, one that belongs to every citizen; there's nothing special about being a woman—except, of course, for the inescapable fact that only women find themselves pregnant against their wills. Some feminists have become disillusioned with this gender-neutral approach. They reject it both on principle, because it shifts attention away from gender inequality, and for practical reasons, because it often works against women in the courts.[4] Instead, feminists have come to realize that sometimes gender should be relevant in claiming rights. Some of these rights, like adequate gynecological care, may be based on women's special physiology; others may stem from the special needs experienced by female casualties of a sexist society: the impoverished, divorced, or unwed mother, the rape victim, the anorexic teen, the coed who has been convinced that she lacks (or had

---

[4]Catharine A. MacKinnon, *Feminism Unmodified: Discourses on Life and Law* (Cambridge: Harvard University Press, 1987), pp. 35–36.

better lack) mathematical aptitude. A thoroughly feminist analysis, then will not hesitate, when appropriate, to claim a right on the basis of gender, rather than in spite of it.[5] And to do otherwise in the case of abortion may be not only to deny the obvious, but also to obscure the relation of reproductive practices to women's oppression.

The third problem feminists might have with an autonomy defense involves the content of the human ideal on which the right to autonomy rests. Some feminists, influenced by Marxist and socialist traditions, may reject an ideal that seems to be so intimately connected with the individualistic ideology of capitalism. Others may suspect that this ideology is not just capitalist but male-biased. And if feminists hesitate to justify abortion by appeal to a gender-neutral right derived from a gender-neutral ideal, they are even more suspicious of an ideal that seems to be gender-neutral when really it's not. Increasingly, feminists reject the ideals of older feminists, like Simone de Beauvoir, who, in promoting for women what appeared to be an androgynous human ideal, unwittingly adopted one what was androcentric, or male-centered. Instead, feminists seek to free themselves from the misogynist perspective that sees women as incomplete men and ignores, devalues, or denies the existence of particularly female psychologies, values and experiences. On this view, to fashion a feminist human ideal we must look to women's values and experiences—or, at least, we must not look only to men's.[6]

This reevaluation has important implications for the abortion issue, since many feminists consider an overriding right to autonomy to be a characteristically male ideal, while nurturance and responsibility for others (the paradigmatic case of which, of course, is motherhood) to be characteristically female ones. Indeed, in the name of such women's values, some women who call themselves feminists have actually joined the anti-abortionist camp.[7] Most feminists, of course, don't go this far. But, paradoxically, many seem to find the ideal of autonomy less acceptable than the right to abortion it is supposed to justify. Clearly, something is awry. (I shall have more to say in section 4 about how autonomy is important to feminists.)

Feminists, therefore, need another argument. Instead of resting on an ideal many feminists reject, a feminist defense of abortion should somehow reflect an awareness of women's oppression and a commitment to ending it.

2

Of all the philosophers, feminists and otherwise, who have discussed abortion, Alison Jaggar seems to be the only one to address the problem from this perspective. Jaggar argues that in societies where mothers bear the responsibility for pregnancy, birth and

[5]See, for example, Alison Jaggar, *Feminism Politics and Human Nature* (Totowa, New Jersey: Rowman & Allanheld, 1983), especially Parts One and Two; and Catharine A. MacKinnon, *Feminism Unmodified: Discourses on Life and Law.*

[6]See Sara Ruddick, "Maternal Thinking," *Feminist Studies* 6 (1980): 345–46; Nancy Chodorow, *The Reproduction of Mothering: Psychoanalysis and the Sociology of Gender* (Berkeley and Los Angeles: University of California Press, 1978); Carol Gilligan, *In a Different Voice: Psychological Theory and Women's Development* (Cambridge: Harvard University Press, 1982).

[7]Sidney Callahan, "A Pro-Life Feminist Makes Her Case," *Commonweal* (April 25, 1986), quoted in the *Utne Reader* 20 (1987): 104–108.

child-rearing, women should control abortion decisions. Women who live in other, more cooperative social communities (wherever they are), where members of both sexes share such responsibilities, cannot claim a right of the same force. The strength of a woman's say about whether or not to abort, then should be relative to the amount of support (financial, emotional, physical, medical, and otherwise) she can expect from those around her.[8]

It is disheartening that the philosophical community has not paid Jaggar's paper the attention it merits in the decade and a half since its publication, but this lapse is hardly surprising. The notion of the individual's right to autonomy is so firmly entrenched that we have difficulty even entertaining other approaches. We find ourselves invoking such rights perhaps without realizing it even when we neither want nor need to. And, indeed, Jaggar is no exception; despite the promising intuition with which she starts, Jaggar finally offers us another, albeit more sophisticated, version of the autonomy argument. Quite simply, her argument implies that if abortion ought to be permissible in some societies but not in others, this is only because pregnancy and motherhood create obstacles to personal autonomy in some societies but not in others.

Jaggar bases her argument for abortion rights in our society on two principles. The first, or Right to Life principle, holds that

> the right to life, when it is claimed for a human being, means the right to a full human life and to whatever means are necessary to achieve this. . . .To be born, then, is only one of the necessary conditions for a full human life. The others presumably include nutritious food, breathable air, warm human companionship, and so on. If anyone has a right to life, she or he must be entitled to all of these.[9]

According to the second, or Personal Control Principle, "Decisions should be made by those, and only by those, who are importantly affect by them"[10] In our society, then, the state cannot legitimately set itself up as the protector of the fetus's right to life (as Jaggar has characterized it) because the mother and not the state will be expected to provide for this right, both during pregnancy and afterwards. But since, by the Personal Control Principle, only those whose lives will be importantly affected have the right to make a decision, in our society the pregnant woman should determine whether to continue her pregnancy.

Jaggar's argument incorporates both liberal and feminist perspectives, and there is a tension between them. Her argument is feminist rather than merely liberal because it does not rest exclusively on a universal right to autonomy. Instead, it takes seriously the contingent and socially variable features of reproduction and parenting, their relationship to women's position in a society, and the effect of anti-abortion policy on this position. But her argument is also a liberal one. Consider, for example, the Personal Control Principle. While Jaggar doesn't explicitly spell out its motivation, she does state that the principle "provides the fundamental justification for democracy and is accepted

---

[8]Alison Jaggar, "Abortion and a Woman's Right to Decide," In *Philosophy and Sex*, ed. Robert Baker and Frederick Elliston (Buffalo: Prometheus Press, 1975), pp. 324–37.

[9]"Abortion and a Woman's Right to Decide," p. 328.

[10]"Abortion and a Woman's Right to Decide," p. 328.

Abortion and Feminism

by most shades of political opinion."[11] Surely this wide acceptance has something to do with the belief, equally widely held, that citizens should be able to decide for themselves what courses their lives should take, especially when some courses involve sacrifices or burdens. This becomes clear when Jaggar explains that an individual or organization has no moral claim as a protector of the right to life "that would justify its insistence on just one of the many conditions necessary to a full human life, in circumstances where this would place the burden of fulfilling all the other conditions squarely on the shoulders of some other individual or organization."[12] Once again we have an appeal to a universal right to personal autonomy, indeed a right based on an ideal which not only might be unacceptable to many feminists, but may cast the net too widely even for some liberals. For example, one might claim that taxation policies designed to finance social programs interfere with personal choices about how to spend earnings, a matter that will have important consequences for one's life. Such a view also permits a range of private actions which some liberals may believe are immoral: for example, an adult grandchild may decide to stop caring for a burdensome and senile grandparent if such care places a heavy burden on the grandchild.

I shall not attempt to pass judgment here on the desirability of either redistributing income through taxation or passing laws requiring us to be Good Samaritans in our private lives. Nor do I want to beg the question, which I shall discuss later, of whether reproductive autonomy is, in all circumstances, overridingly important in a way other sorts of autonomy may not be. I can leave these matters open because a feminist defense of abortion need not depend on how we settle them. For there is a significant difference between the sacrifices required by restrictive abortion policies and those required by enforcing other sorts of Good Samaritanism: taxes and laws against letting the aged or handicapped starve to death apply to everyone; those prohibiting abortion apply only to women. While anyone might end up with a helpless, cantankerous grandparent and most of us end up paying taxes, only women end up pregnant. So anti-abortion laws require sacrifices not of everyone, but only of women.

3

This brings us to what I regard as the crucial question: When, if ever, can people be required to sacrifice for the sake of others? And how can feminists answer this question in a way that rests not on the individual right to personal autonomy, but on a view of social reality that takes seriously power relations between genders? I suggest the following principle, which I shall call the Impermissible Sacrifice Principle: *When one social group in a society is systematically oppressed by another, it is impermissible to require the oppressed group to make sacrifices that will exacerbate or perpetuate this oppression.* (Note that this principle does not exempt the members of oppressed groups

---

[11]"Abortion and a Woman's Right to Decide," p. 329.

[12]For classic discussions of sexism in the civil rights movement, see Susan Brownmiller, *Against Our Will: Men, Women, and Rape* (New York: Simon and Schuster, 1975), especially pp. 210–55; ;and Michelle Wallace, *Black Macho and the Myth of the Superwoman* (New York: Dial Press, 1978).

from *all* sorts of sacrifices just because they are oppressed; they may be as morally responsible as anyone for rendering aid in some circumstances. Only sacrifices that will clearly perpetuate their oppression are ruled out.)

The Impermissible Sacrifice Principle focuses on power relationships between groups rather than on the rights of individuals. This approach will suit not only feminists but all who recognize and deplore other sorts of systematic social oppression as well. Indeed, if we take our opposition to oppression seriously, this approach may be necessary. Otherwise, when policy decisions are made, competing goals and commitments may distract us from the conditions we claim to deplore and encourage decisions that allow such conditions to remain. Even worse, these other goals and commitments can be used as excuses for perpetuating oppression. Testing policies against the Impermissible Sacrifices Principle keeps this from happening.

Feminists should welcome the applicability of the Impermissible Sacrifice Principle to groups other than women. Radical feminists are sometimes accused of being blind to any sort of oppression but their own. The Impermissible Sacrifice Principle, however, enables feminists to demonstrate solidarity with other oppressed groups by resting the case for abortion on the same principle that might, for example, block a policy requiring the poor rather than the rich to bear the tax burden, or workers rather than management to take a pay cut. On the other hand, feminists may worry that the Impermissible Sacrifice Principle, taken by itself, may not yield the verdict on abortion feminists seek. For if some radical feminists err by recognizing only women's oppression, some men err by not recognizing it at all. So the Impermissible Sacrifice Principle must be supplemented by what I shall call the Feminist Proviso: *Women are, as a group, sexually oppressed by men; and this oppression can neither be completely understood in terms of, nor otherwise reduced to, oppressions of other sorts.*

Feminists often understand this oppression to involve men's treating women as breeding machines, sexual or aesthetic objects, nurturers who need no nurturance. Women become alienated from their bodies, their sexuality, their work, their intellect, their emotions, their moral agency. Of course, feminists disagree about exactly how to formulate this analysis, especially since women experience oppression differently depending on their class, race, and ethnicity. But however we decide to understand women's oppression, we can be sure an anti-abortion policy will make it worse.

Adding the Feminist Proviso, then, keeps (or makes) sexism visible, ensuring that women are one of the oppressed groups to which the Principle applies. This should hardly need saying. Yet by focusing on other sorts of oppression the Principle might cover, men often trivialize or ignore feminists' demands and women's pain. For example, someone (perhaps a white male) who is more sympathetic to the claims of racial minorities or workers than to those of women might try to trivialize or deny the sexual oppression of a white, affluent woman (perhaps his wife) by reminding her that she's richer than an unemployed black male and so should not complain. The Feminist Proviso also prevents an affluent white woman who rejects the unwelcome sexual advances of a minority or working class male from being dismissed (or dismissing herself) as a racist or classist. She may well be both. But she also lives in a world where, all things being equal, she is fair sexual game, in one way or another, for any male. Finally, the Impermissible Sacrifice Principle in conjunction with the Feminist Proviso might be used to block the view that a black or Third World woman's first obligation is to bear children to swell the ranks of the revolution, regardless of the consequences of maternity within her culture. Having children for this reason may be a legitimate choice; but she also may have independent grounds to refuse.

I have added the Feminist Proviso so that the Impermissible Sacrifice Principle cannot be used to frustrate a feminist analysis. But I must also emphasize that the point is not to pit one oppressed group against another, but to make sure that the men in otherwise progressive social movements do not ignore women's oppression or, worse, find "politically correct" justifications for it. Women refuse to wait until "after the revolution" not just because they are impatient, but also because they have learned that not all revolutions are feminist ones.

The Impermissible Sacrifice Principle and the Feminist Proviso together, then, justify abortion on demand for women *because they live in a sexist society.* This approach not only gives a more explicitly feminist justification of abortion than the autonomy defense; it also gives a stronger one. For autonomy defenses are open to objections and qualifications that a feminist one avoids. Consider the ways the feminist approach handles these four challenges to the autonomy defense.

First, some philosophers have dismissed autonomy defenses by suggesting blithely that we simply compensate the pregnant woman.[13] Of what, though, will such compensation consist? Maternity leave? Tax breaks? Prenatal healthcare? Twenty points added to her civil-service exam score? Such benefits lighten one's load, no doubt. But what women suffer by being forced to continue unwanted pregnancies is not merely a matter of finances or missed opportunities; in a sexist society, there is reason to expect that an anti-abortion policy will reinforce a specifically *sexual* oppression, whatever sorts of compensation are offered. Indeed, even talk of compensation may be misguided, since it implies a prior state when things were as they should be; compensation seeks to restore the balance after a temporary upset. But in a sexist society, there is no original balance; women's oppression is the status quo. Even if individual women are compensated by money, services, or opportunities, sexual oppression may remain.

Second, an autonomy defense may seem appropriate only in cases where a woman engages in "responsible" sex: it is one thing to be a victim of rape or even contraceptive failure, one might argue; it is quite another voluntarily to have unprotected intercourse. A feminist defense suggests another approach. First, we might question the double standard that requires that women pay for "irresponsible" sex while men don't have to, even though women are oppressed by men. More importantly, if we focus on the *way* women are oppressed, we may understand many unwanted pregnancies to result from fear and paralysis rather than irresponsibility. For in a sexist society, many women simply do not believe they can control the conditions under which they have sex. And, sad to say, often they may be right.[14]

Third, what about poor women's access to abortion? The sort of right the autonomy theorists invoke, after all, seems to be a right to noninterference by the state. But this negative right seems to be in tension with a demand for state-funded abortions, especially since not everyone supports abortion. At any rate, we will need another argument to justify the funding of abortion for poor women. The defense I suggest, however, is clearly committed to providing all women with access to abortion, since to allow abor-

---

[13]Michael Tooley, "Abortion and Infanticide," in Joel Feinberg, ed. *The Problem of Abortion* (Belmont, California: Wadsworth, 1983).

[14]MacKinnon, *Feminism Unmodified,* p. 95.

tions only for those who can afford them forces poor women, who are doubly oppressed, to make special sacrifices. An egalitarian society must liberate all women, not just the rich ones.

Finally, autonomy defenses allow, indeed invite, the charge that the choice to abort is selfish. Even Thomson finds abortion, while not unjust, often to be "selfish" or "indecent." Although she has deprived nothing of its rights, the woman who aborts has chosen self-interested autonomy over altruism in the same way one might choose to watch while a child starves. Of course, one is tempted to point out that the (largely male) world of commerce and politics thrives on such "morally indecent" but legal actions. But then feminists are reduced to claiming a right to be as selfish as men are. Moreover, once the specter of selfishness is raised, this defense does not allow feminists to make enough of male anti-abortionists' motives. On an autonomy defense, these motives are simply not relevant, let alone damning, and feminists who dwell on them seem to be resorting to *ad hominems*. From a feminist perspective, however, abortion is a political issue, one which essentially concerns the interests of and power relations between men and women. Thus, what women and men can expect to gain or lose from an abortion policy becomes the point rather than the subject of *ad hominem* arguments.[15]

The approach I propose does well on each of these important counts. But its real test comes when we weigh the demands of the Impermissible Sacrifice Principle against fetal rights; for we have required that a feminist analysis be independent of the status of the fetus. Indeed, we may even be tempted to regard fetuses as constituting just the sort of oppressed group to whom the principle applies, and surely a fetus about to be aborted is in worse shape than the woman who carries it.

However, it may not make sense to count fetuses as a oppressed group. A disadvantaged one, perhaps. But the Impermissible Sacrifice Principle does not prescribe that more disadvantaged groups have a right to aid from less disadvantaged ones; it focuses only on the particular disadvantage of social oppression. That the fetus has a serious right to life does not imply that it's the sort of being that can be oppressed, if it cannot yet enter into the sorts of social relationships that constitute oppression. I cannot argue for this here; in any case, I suspect my best argument will not convince everyone. But feminists have another, more pointed response.

Whether or not we can weigh the disadvantage of fetuses against the oppression of women, we must realize what insisting on such a comparison does to the debate. It narrows our focus, turning it back to the conflict between the rights of fetuses and of women (even if now this conflict is between the rights of groups rather than of individuals). This is certainly not to deny that fetal rights should be relevant to an abortion policy. But feminists must insist that the oppression of women should be relevant too. And it is also relevant that unless our society changes in deep and global ways, anti-abortion policies, intentionally or not, will perpetuate women's oppression by men. This, then, is where feminists must stand firm.

Does this mean that instead of overriding the fetus's right to life by women's right to autonomy, I am proposing that feminists override the fetus's right by the right of

---

[15]This approach also allows us to understand the deep divisions between women on this issue. For many women in traditional roles fear the immediate effects on their lives of women's liberation generally and a permissive abortion policy in particular. On this, see Kristen Luker, *Abortion and the Politics of Motherhood* (Berkeley: University of California Press, 1984), especially pp. 158–215.

women to live in a sexually egalitarian society? This is a difficult position for feminists but not an impossible one, especially for feminists with utilitarian leanings. Many feminists, for example, see sexism as responsible for a culture of death: war, violence, child abuse, ecological disaster. Eradicate sexism, it might be argued, and we will save more lives than we will lose. Some feminists even claim that an oppressed woman's fate can be worse than that of an aborted fetus. Although I will not argue for such claims, they may be less implausible than they seem. But feminists need not rest their case on them. Instead, they may simply insist that society must change so that women are no longer oppressed. Such changes, of course, may require of men sacrifices unwelcome beyond their wildest dreams. But that, according to a feminist analysis, is the point.

So we should not see the choice as between liberating women and saving fetuses, but between two ways of respecting the fetus's right to life. The first requires women to sacrifice while men benefit. The second requires deep social changes that will ensure that men no longer gain and women lose through our practices of sexuality, reproduction, and parenthood. To point out how men gain from women's compulsory pregnancy is to steal the misplaced moral thunder from those male authorities—fathers, husbands, judges, congressmen, priests, philosophers—who, exhorting women to do their duty, present themselves as the benevolent, disinterested protectors of fetuses against women's selfishness. Let feminists insist that the condition for refraining from having abortions is a sexually egalitarian society. If men do not respond, and quickly, they will have indicated that fetal life isn't so important to them after all, or at least not important enough to give up the privileges of being male in a sexist society. If this makes feminists look bad, it makes men look worse still.

A Short Legal History of Abortion in the United States and Canada

The problem of abortion is as much a public policy issue as it is a moral issue. Naturally, what one thinks about the moral permissibility of abortion will affect how one thinks about what the state can or should do by way of regulating abortion. For example, if you think that abortion is murder, then you will be strongly inclined to argue that the state should prohibit all abortions: how could a state allow citizens to take innocent lives? On the other hand, if you think that abortion is morally innocuous—an activity akin to cutting one's hair—then you will be strongly inclined to argue that the state has no business interfering with pregnant women who seek abortions or with physicians who provide them. The formulation of public policy would be a relatively simple matter if either of these extreme positions about the moral permissibility of abortion were widely held. But most people's views about abortion are much more complicated.

Many people who identify with the pro-life position believe that a woman who is pregnant as the result of rape or incest or whose life is endangered by her pregnancy should be permitted to have an abortion. Also, few people who identify with the pro-choice position claim that abortion is never a matter of moral consequence. However, even the belief that abortion inevitably raises serious moral questions is not determinative of any particular public policy on abortion. One might hold that the morally weighty decision whether or not to continue a pregnancy can be made only by the individual woman concerned, and that any governmental interference with this decision constitutes an unjust infringement on women's autonomy. Still others, who share the intuition that there is a morally significant difference between early-term and late-term abortions believe that, although the state may not regulate abortion during the first trimester of pregnancy, it may restrict or even prohibit abortions in the second and third trimesters.

In both the United States and Canada, any law regarding abortion must pass constitutional scrutiny; that is, the restrictions on abortion embodied in the legislation must not illegitimately infringe women's rights. Again, matters would be somewhat more straightforward if the right to abortion were enumerated in either the U.S. Bill of Rights or in the Canadian Charter of Rights and Freedoms, but it is not. When confronted with the problem of abortion, the Supreme Court in each country has had to grapple with complex jurisprudential questions. The two sections that follow provide a brief overview of judicial discussion about abortion in the United States and in Canada.

At the beginning of the nineteenth century, no state in the Union had a statute governing abortion; yet by 1900, every state in the Union had enacted a law prohibiting the use of drugs or instruments designed to procure an abortion, except where this was required to save the woman's life. Throughout the first half of the twentieth century, abortion law became more liberal. In 1962, the American Law Institute recommended that abortions be legal for a number of reasons in addition to saving a pregnant woman's life, for example, in cases in which the pregnancy is the result of rape, or when the fetus is severely deformed. By 1970, fourteen states had enacted some or all of these recommendations. No doubt some of this legislative action also reflected changes in public views about sex and women's social status.

In addition to these legislative and social factors, in 1965, the U.S. Supreme Court struck down a Connecticut law that prohibited the use of contraceptives, on the grounds that the law violated the right of privacy (*Griswold v. Connecticut*). A right of privacy is nowhere articulated in the Bill of Rights, but in *Griswold*, Justice Douglas argued that many of the rights explicitly guaranteed in that document "create zones of privacy," in the sense that their purpose is to restrict governmental interference in certain aspects of citizens' lives.[1] An underlying idea is that although the state may regulate activity in the public domain—consider, for example, the Food and Drug Administration—there are areas of human life that are none of the state's business. Central to classical liberal thought, this public/private distinction is thought to be justified in terms of individual autonomy. Roughly, a person's autonomy refers to her capacity to make decisions for herself regarding how best to live her life, and exercising this capacity is thought to be necessary for the maintenance of dignity and self-respect. A state that unduly interferes with its citizens in the exercise of their autonomy fails to accord them respect. Arguably, among the most important personal decisions a person can make about her life is how she will manage her sexual relations, and so, in *Griswold*, the Court ruled that the state could not prohibit the use of contraceptives. *Griswold*, together with the factors mentioned above, formed the backdrop for the landmark abortion case of *Roe v. Wade*, which was decided in 1973.

At issue in *Roe* was a Texas statute, dating from 1857, that made abortion a crime unless it was performed to save the life of the pregnant woman. Drawing on the line of cases in which the Court had articulated the right of privacy, Justice Blackmun claimed: "The right of privacy . . . is broad enough to encompass a woman's decision whether or not to terminate her pregnancy"(153). But while the Court declared that a woman has a fundamental constitutional right to choose abortion, it also argued that that right is not absolute. States have legitimate interests in preserving and protecting both maternal

---

[1] *Griswold* was not the only case in which the notion of privacy was central. The Court has variously found the right of privacy implied in the First, Fourth, Fifth, Ninth, and Fourteenth Amendments, and (prior to *Roe*) it had argued that the right of privacy extends to activities relating to marriage, procreation, family relationships, childrearing, and education, as well as to contraception. See *Roe v. Wade*, 410 U.S. 113, 152. It is also important to note that the idea of implied rights is a controversial one among Supreme Court justices and others; see, for example, Robert Bork, *The Tempting of America* (New York: The Free Press, 1990).

health and potential human life; when these interests are compelling, the Court said, states may regulate abortion. Thus, the Court needed to say at what point these interests become compelling.

Blackmun's approach was to employ the so-called trimester framework. The majority in *Roe* held that the state cannot interfere with a woman's right to choose abortion during the first trimester of her pregnancy (that is, during the first twelve weeks) but that the state's interest in protecting maternal health becomes compelling during the second trimester, so some restrictions on second-trimester abortion are permissible. The state's interest in protecting potential human life was said to become compelling during the third trimester, so the Court held that the state can prohibit abortion in the final twelve weeks of pregnancy. It is important to note that the Court did not address the question of when human life begins. However, it did argue that the fetus is not a person in the sense of *person* relevant to the Fourteenth Amendment, which specifies in part that no "State [shall] deprive any person of life, liberty, or property, without due process of law."

The immediate effect of *Roe* was to overturn forty-six of the fifty states' laws governing abortion. Public, political, and academic reaction was swift. Pro-life forces began to organize against liberal abortion laws. Only eight days after the announcement of the *Roe* decision, Maryland Republican representative Lawrence J. Hogan introduced the first of several suggested constitutional amendments, proposing that the fetus be declared a Fourteenth Amendment person from the moment of conception. The debate engendered by *Roe* has not subsided. Throughout the 1980s, vigorous lobbying began to restrict the use of public funds to support abortion services and counseling. In addition, a candidate's stand on abortion has been, for better or worse, a central factor in recent presidential campaigns and in the ratification of Supreme Court and surgeon-general nominees.

For a variety of reasons, *Roe* is a controversial decision. It has been criticized from the political Right and the political Left, by feminists and nonfeminists. Two lines of criticism are worth focusing on. First is the complaint that the Court overstepped its authority to engage in judicial *review*; some argue that the Court's decision in *Roe* amounted to judicial law*making*. The second criticism is motivated by concerns about the implications of the fact that *Roe* grounds a woman's right to choose an abortion in the right of privacy. Let us look at each in turn.

Abortion has always been a divisive issue. And some critics of *Roe* have argued that, when no explicit guidance is offered by the Constitution, the resolution of such issues should be left to individual legislatures. By effectively invalidating the vast majority of existing state legislation on abortion, the Court appeared to foreclose the opportunity for individual states to decide the matter for themselves. In his dissent in *Roe*, Justice White declared,

> I find nothing in the language or history of the Constitution to support the Court's judgment. The Court simply fashions and announces a new constitutional right for pregnant mothers and, with scarcely any reason or authority for its action, invests that right with sufficient substance to override most existing state abortion statutes. The upshot is that the people and the legislatures of the 50 States are constitutionally disentitled to weigh the relative importance of the continued existence and development of the fetus, on the one hand, against a spectrum of possible impacts on the mother, on the other hand. (222)

Legal History of Abortion in the United States and Canada   **205**

More recently, Mary Ann Glendon and Ruth Bader Ginsburg, both of whom favor women's access to abortion, have argued that such access would have been better secured had the Court not decided *Roe* the way it did but, rather, left the abortion question to individual states.[2]

The second line of criticism that bears mention here concerns the idea that abortion is an issue of privacy. The criticism actually takes two different forms, depending on whether it is advanced as part of a pragmatic argument or as part of a constitutional argument. Quite aside from the question of whether there is a constitutional right of privacy, feminist critics of *Roe* have argued that framing women's right to choose abortion in terms of privacy seriously distorts the meaning of an unwanted pregnancy in women's lives and, moreover, has negative consequences for women's access to abortion. Some worry that the language of privacy and personal choice is easily appropriated by those opposed to abortion, and others have argued that casting abortion as a privacy issue isolates abortion from other issues of reproductive health.[3] Rosalind Petchesky argues that interpreting abortion as a matter of privacy renders the right to abortion a "mere legality . . . [and one that] is perfectly compatible with a wide range of constraints on abortion *access*. . . . Legality assures women neither material means nor moral support and political legitimation in their abortion decisions."[4] Petchesky's complaint is arguably borne out by the Supreme Court's subsequent decisions upholding the prohibition of federal funding for abortion services and counseling.[5] The Court has argued that the denial of public funding for abortion does not infringe the right guaranteed by *Roe*. In *Harris v. McRae*, for example, Justice Powell writes: "Although the government may not place obstacles in the path of a woman's exercise of her freedom of choice, it need not remove those not of its own creation. Indigency falls in the latter category" (316).

Other pro-choice critics of *Roe* have argued that privacy was the wrong *constitutional* strategy for assessing abortion legislation. Rather, they claim, the question should be addressed in terms of sex equality. Matters here are complex, because it is very difficult to say when the law may take sex-based differences into account and when it may not. Moreover, when sex-based differences have been enshrined in law, the effect has generally been detrimental for women's equality. Nonetheless, women

---

[2]See Mary Ann Glendon, *Abortion and Divorce in Western Law: American Failures, European Challenges* (Cambridge, Mass.: Harvard University Press, 1987); Ruth Bader Ginsburg, "Some Thoughts on Autonomy and Equality in Relation to *Roe v. Wade*," *North Carolina Law Review* 63 (1985): 357–386. For an excellent discussion of the plausibility of the claim that access to abortion would have been better without *Roe*, see Archon Fung, "Making Rights Real: *Roe*'s Impact on Abortion Access," *Politics and Society* 21 (1993): 465–504.

[3]See, for example, Christine Overall, *Human Reproduction: Principles, Practices, Policies* (Toronto: Oxford University Press, 1993).

[4]Rosalind Petchesky, *Abortion and Woman's Choice*, rev. ed. (Boston: Northeastern University Press, 1990), xxiv.

[5]These cases include *Beal v. Doe* (1977); *Maher v. Roe* (1977); and *Harris v. McRae* (1980). See also *Webster v. Reproductive Health Services* (1989), in which the Court argued that the prohibition on the use of state hospitals for abortions does not impair a woman's ability to choose abortion. See the Annotated Chronology of U.S. and Canadian Supreme Court cases for details. For an argument explicitly linking privacy to the funding decisions, see Catharine A. MacKinnon, "Privacy v. Equality: Beyond *Roe v. Wade*," in *Feminism Unmodified* (Cambridge, Mass.: Harvard University Press, 1987).

and men do differ in terms of their respective reproductive capacities; only women become pregnant. Because pregnancy carries a significant set of burdens and risks, this biological difference between women and men arguably implicates equality concerns. For example, when a law prohibits women from choosing abortion, it imposes a burden on women that they need not, as a matter of course, bear. In other words, when women alone are denied the ability to control their reproductive lives, they fail to enjoy the equal protection of the law.

Sylvia Law has suggested the following equality approach to law governing aspects of reproductive biology. For any particular piece of legislation, we should "consider whether the state can meet the burden of showing that [such a law] . . . either (1) has no significant impact in perpetuating the oppression of women or culturally imposed sex role constraints on individual freedom or (2) is the best means for meeting a compelling state interest."[6] Applied to abortion, then, the relevant test of a law restricting abortion would require that, in the first instance, the Court examine whether the restrictions in question serve to perpetuate women's oppression. Any legislation that bans abortion outright would fail this test, because in denying pregnant women's ability to make independent moral decisions and by impairing women's capacity for self-determination, such a law would serve to perpetuate women's oppression. Certain restrictions embodied in a more liberal abortion law would also fail Law's test—for example, spousal consent and notification provisions—but others, like record-keeping provisions, might pass.

The equality approach sketched here appears to be consistent with the Supreme Court's recognition in *Roe* and subsequent decisions that the state has a legitimate interest in protecting fetal life, at least postviability, for it is arguable that a restriction on third-trimester abortion, except when it is necessary to save the life of the pregnant woman, would be the best means for the state to meet its compelling interest in protecting fetal life. But while an equality approach to the legal problem of abortion might deliver results similar to those of the privacy approach adopted by the Court, advocates of the former stress the superiority of their account on the grounds that it best mirrors the reality surrounding decisions about reproduction.[7]

While the reasoning in *Roe* has been criticized by academics, women's access to abortion, which many thought had been secured by *Roe*, has been under attack socially and politically. The Hyde Amendment, passed by Congress in 1976, forbade the use of Medicaid funds for abortion; in 1980, President Ronald Reagan promised to appoint justices to the Supreme Court who would overrule *Roe*; and in 1988, the so-called gag rule that prevented staff at any federally funded clinic from discussing abortion with their patients, even when the woman's life was endangered by the pregnancy, was introduced by executive order through the Health and Human Services Department.[8]

---

[6]Sylvia Law, "Rethinking Sex and the Constitution," *University of Pennsylvania Law Review* 132 (1984): 955–1040, 1016–1017. See also Sally Markowitz, "Abortion and Feminism," in this volume, pp. 194–202.

[7]For further discussion of the relative merits of the privacy and the equality approach, see Ruth Colker, *Abortion and Dialogue: Prochoice, Prolife, and American Law* (Bloomington and Indianapolis: Indiana University Press, 1992).

[8]The Supreme Court upheld the constitutionality of the gag rule in *Rust v. Sullivan* (1991). In January 1993, President Clinton signed an executive order overturning the gag rule and four other restrictions on abortion established and upheld during the Reagan and Bush administrations.

Over the years, several states have introduced legislation imposing a variety of restrictions on a woman's right to choose abortion. Examples o f these measures are: a spousal notification requirement; a mandatory twenty-four-hour waiting period; mandatory counseling about fetal development and abortion; and a parental consent requirement for minors.

In evaluating the constitutionality of these restrictions, the Court has distinguished between legislation that places obstacles in the path of women seeking abortion and legislation that merely realizes the state's refusal to facilitate abortion. Since *Roe*, the Court has emphasized states' legitimate interests in protecting the potentiality of human life and has ruled that states may make a value judgment favoring childbirth over abortion and implement this judgment by allocating funds differentially, effectively paying for live births and not paying for abortions.[9] In its 1989 *Webster* decision, the Court upheld a Missouri statute that prohibits the use of public facilities for the purpose of performing abortions, disallows the use of public funds for abortion, and requires physicians to establish whether any fetus of twenty weeks or older is viable. The *Webster* decision, whether or not it was explicitly intended as such by the Court, was widely interpreted as a sign that states could permissibly legislate a variety of restrictions on abortion. Certainly, many states reacted this way.[10] For example, Louisiana declared all abortion illegal except when the life of the woman is in danger or in cases of rape and incest, provided the violation is rapidly reported to the police. Pennsylvania instituted a mandatory twenty-four-hour waiting period, counseling, and a spousal notification requirement. By contrast, fearing that *Webster* signaled the imminent overruling of *Roe*, other states (for example, New York, New Jersey, and Florida) looked to their state constitutions to justify liberal access to abortion.

Despite the significant criticisms leveled at *Roe* since 1973, that decision has not been overturned. In the Court's most recent important decision concerning abortion (*Planned Parenthood of Southeastern Pennsylvania v. Casey* [1992]), a plurality—consisting of Justices Kennedy, Souter, and O'Connor—reaffirmed what they called the central holding in *Roe*,[11] namely, that the state has an interest in protecting and preserving both maternal and fetal health and life, that the state may not unduly interfere with the right of a woman to choose to have an abortion prior to viability, and that the state may prohibit abortion after viability if it allows for exceptions when the pregnancy threatens the woman's life or health. In the second part of its opinion, the plurality in *Casey* essentially rejected the trimester framework developed in *Roe* and argued that the

---

[9]A very recent policy of this kind has been proposed in Utah as part of a welfare reform package. The Utah plan is that unwed pregnant women would be paid $3,000 by the state to bring their unwanted pregnancies to term and to put the child up for adoption. See Timothy Egan, "Take This Bribe, Please, for Values to Be Received," in *New York Times*, Sunday, November 12, 1995, E5.

[10]In 1990, no fewer than 465 abortion-related bills were introduced by state legislatures, representing a threefold increase over the previous year. See "State Legislation on Reproductive Health in 1990: What Was Proposed and Enacted," *Family Planning Perspectives*, March–April, 1992.

[11]The plurality was joined in this first part of its decision by Justices Blackmun and Stevens. Justices Rehnquist, White, Scalia, and Thomas dissented here but concurred in the second part of the plurality's decision, which rejected the trimester framework set out in *Roe*. See the Annotated Chronology of cases for details.

appropriate standard for assessing the constitutionality of restrictions on abortion should be whether the legislation constitutes an undue burden for a woman seeking an abortion. On this ground, the Court upheld a range of provisions, including mandatory counseling by a physician followed by a twenty-four-hour waiting period. However, it invalidated Pennsylvania's requirement that a married woman notify her spouse before obtaining an abortion. Arguing that many women are vulnerable to physical and psychological violence at the hands of their husbands, the Court deemed that this provision imposes an undue burden on married women seeking abortions.

Opposition to abortion has been organized and sometimes violent. In March 1993, Doctor David Gunn, a physician in Pensacola, Florida, who performed abortions, was shot and killed during a demonstration by a member of a pro-life group called Rescue America. Later that year, Doctor George Tiller was shot and wounded in Wichita, Kansas. In 1994 we saw the murder of Doctor Bayard, again in Pensacola; the wounding of Doctor Garson Romalis in Vancouver; and the murder of Shannon Lowney and Leanne Nichols, two employees at a Brookline, Massachusetts, clinic and the wounding of five others at the same clinic.

Abortion clinics have continued to be the site of pro-life demonstrations. In an effort to curb the effects of these protests, which often prevent women who are seeking abortions from entering a clinic, supporters of the right to abortion and operators of abortion clinics have attempted a variety of legal remedies. In one instance, clinics sued demonstrators under the so-called Ku Klux Klan Act, which prohibits conspiratorial action whose purpose is to deprive a class of people of equal protection of the law. However, in *Bray v. Alexandria* (1993), the Supreme Court ruled that clinics cannot bring suit against abortion protesters under this rubric, because the activities of the protesters are directed at the protection of fetal life, not at the deprivation of women's rights on the basis of their gender. In another case, abortion clinics and their supporters brought action against abortion demonstrators under the Racketeer Influenced Corrupt Organization (RICO) statutes. The Supreme Court considered this matter in *National Organization for Women v. Scheidler* (1994) and ruled that the clinics can indeed bring suit against abortion protestors under RICO if such protestors conspire in a pattern of racketeering activity against the clinics, their staff, or their clientele.[12]

Canada

In sharp contrast with the United States, the Canadian Supreme Court has considered the abortion issue only four times in recent history. The earliest statutory prohibition against attempting to procure an abortion is the 1869 "Act respecting Offences against the Person," which made the abortion of a "quick fetus" a crime punishable by life imprisonment. This prohibition entered the Canadian Criminal Code in 1892, and the provision survived (relatively unaltered) as part of the Code until 1969. In that year, under pressure from the medical community, the relevant section of the Code (section 251) was amended to allow for therapeutic exceptions to the outright ban on abortion. The

---

[12]See the Annotated Chronology of cases for further details.

revised section 251 set out the conditions under which an abortion would be legal: the procedure had to be carried out by a licensed medical practitioner in an accredited or approved hospital on the written advice of a three-member therapeutic abortion committee to the effect that the continuation of the pregnancy endangered the pregnant woman's life or health. The new law clearly made some abortions legal, but it did not make access to abortion uniform across the country. Hospitals were not required by law to establish therapeutic abortion committees, so many women were unable even to make the necessary requests. More important, whether a pregnant woman could undergo an abortion was wholly contingent upon the committee's assessment of the threat the pregnancy posed to her health or life; a pregnant woman could not represent her case to such committees.

Dr. Henry Morgentaler has been, perhaps, *the* pivotal figure in the judicial history of the problem of abortion in Canada.[13] For nearly two decades, Morgentaler directly defied the criminal provisions against abortion, opening clinics in several provinces. He was charged several times under section 251 and spent time in jail. The immediately relevant aspect of Morgentaler's story concerns the results of his appeal to the Canadian Supreme Court in 1988. This case represents the first time the Supreme Court considered the abortion question in the context of the Canadian Charter of Rights and Freedoms, which came into effect in 1982. Prior to the adoption of the Charter, courts could strike down only that legislation that violated the separation-of-powers doctrine under the British North America Act. But with the Charter in place, legislation can be challenged on the grounds that it unjustifiably infringes on Canadians' rights as articulated in that document.

At issue in *R. v. Morgentaler* was whether the abortion provision of the Criminal Code violates women's rights to security of the person as expressed in section 7 of the Charter. Section 7 reads:

> Everyone has the right to life, liberty and security of the person and the right not to be deprived thereof except in accordance with the principles of fundamental justice.

Judicial review of legislation challenged on Charter grounds involves two steps. First, the Court decides whether the impugned legislation does in fact infringe some right guaranteed in the Charter. Second, if this is so, the Court must determine whether that infringement is justified under section 1 of the Charter, which reads:

> The Canadian Charter of Rights and Freedoms guarantees the rights and freedoms set out in it subject to reasonable limits prescribed by law as can be demonstrably justified in a free and democratic society.

This so-called section 1 analysis is somewhat similar to the notion of strict scrutiny employed by the U.S. Supreme Court. A piece of impugned legislation will survive section 1 analysis only if it can be demonstrated (1) that the objective of the legislation relates to substantial governmental concerns; (2) that the measures adopted to meet that objective are rationally connected to the objective in question (that is, are not arbitrary or un-

---

[13]See F. L. Morton, *Morgentaler v. Borowski: Abortion, the Charter and the Courts* (Toronto: McClelland and Stewart, 1992).

fair, but based on rational considerations); and (3) that the measures taken to meet the objective minimally impair the right at stake.[14]

In *Morgentaler*, the majority agreed that section 251 did indeed infringe on a pregnant woman's right to security of the person. Focusing on the requirement for therapeutic abortion committees, the Court declared that "forcing a woman, by threat of criminal sanction, to carry a foetus to term unless she meets certain criteria unrelated to her own priorities and aspirations, is a profound interference with a woman's body and thus a violation of security of the person." (32) While the Court ruled that the section 251 provisions unjustifiably infringed a woman's security of the person, it clearly established that not all restrictions on abortion would do so. Justice Bertha Wilson was explicit that section 1 allows for the imposition of reasonable limits on a woman's section 7 right. In particular, she suggested that abortion legislation that is sensitive to the developmental facts of pregnancy—for example, legislation that adopts a permissive attitude toward early-term abortions and a more restrictive attitude toward late-term abortions—would probably be constitutional.

The Supreme Court's decision in *R. v. Morgentaler* invalidated the only abortion law in Canada, and subsequent attempts by Parliament to introduce new legislation have been unsuccessful. The current situation, then, is one in which there is no abortion law in Canada. Nonetheless, access to and funding for abortion is not uniform across the country. With respect to the future of the legal status of abortion in Canada, several things are worth noting. First, the Canadian Supreme Court did not explicitly declare, as the U.S. Supreme Court did in *Roe*, that the right to abortion is a fundamental right. Second, the Court expressly said that the state has a legitimate interest in protecting fetal life: "[The] protection of the fetus is and . . . always has been, a valid objective in Canadian criminal law" (113); the Court also suggested that an abortion law somewhat less restrictive than section 251 would pass constitutional scrutiny. Third, the Court has never directly considered the question of the fetus' juridical personality, that is, the question of whether the fetus is included in the term *everyone* in section 7. One anti-abortion campaigner, Joseph Borowski, sought to challenge section 251 on the grounds that in allowing therapeutic abortions at all it violated fetus' rights to security of the person, but section 251 had already been invalidated by the time the Court considered Borowski's appeal.[15] Finally, it is arguable whether the *Morgentaler* decision is one that feminist advocates of choice would or should support. Unlike its counterpart in the United States, the Canadian Supreme Court did not speak of the right of privacy in overturning the abortion provisions. But in her remarks in *Morgentaler*, Justice Bertha Wilson stressed the connections among personal dignity, autonomy, and the existence of an essentially private sphere around each individual into which the state cannot trespass and implied that the decision to have an abortion is a private one for women. Thus, some of the pragmatically motivated feminist concerns, discussed above, about framing the legal problem of abortion in terms of privacy arise again. Construing pregnancy and abortion as issues of private choice

---

[14]See *R. v. Oakes* [1986] 1 S.C.R. 103.

[15]In a very different case (*Tremblay v. Daigle* [1989] 2 S.C.R. 530), the Court held that the fetus is not a person under the Quebec Charter of Rights and Freedoms. However, since that case concerned a dispute between two private individuals, the Court did not consider whether the fetus is included under "everyone" of section 7. See the Annotated Chronology of cases for details.

encourages the belief that childbearing and childrearing are also entirely private matters. A possible consequence of this attitude is that existing social policies that support childbearing and childrearing may no longer be seen as justified.[16] However, the Charter does appear to embody the resources to launch a sex-equality defense of liberal abortion laws,[17] so it will be interesting to see how the Canadian Supreme Court addresses the question of abortion on future occasions.

---

[16]For a Canadian perspective on the appropriateness of thinking of abortion in terms of privacy, see Margaret E. McCallum, "Men, Women, and the Liberal Ideal: An Historian's Reflections on the Morgentaler Case," in *Contemporary Moral Issues*, 3d ed., Wesley Cragg (Toronto: McGraw-Hill Ryerson Limited, 1990).

[17]See, for example, Sheilah Martin, "Canada's Abortion Law and the Canadian Charter of Rights and Freedoms," *Canadian Journal of Women and the Law* 1 (1986): 339–384.

Annotated Chronology of U.S. and Canadian Supreme Court Cases

Canada

1933 *Montréal Tramways v. Léveillé* [1933] S.C.R. 456
The Court holds that under civil law, a child, although not yet born at the time some fault is committed, is deemed to be born for the purposes of collecting compensation for any damage it suffers as a result. Thus, if after the accident occurs, it is born alive and viable, the fetus has all the rights of action it would have had if it had already been born when the accident occurred.

United States

1942 *Skinner v. Oklahoma*, 316 U.S. 535
The Court holds that a law permitting the sterilization of habitual criminals violates the equal protection clause of the Fourteenth Amendment. The Court describes the subject matter of the law—the right to bear children—as one of the basic civil rights of man, fundamental to the very existence of the human race.

1965 *Griswold v. Connecticut*, 381 U.S. 479
The Court holds that a Connecticut law prohibiting the use of contraceptives by married couples is unconstitutional. Justice Douglas argues that the "various guarantees [of the Bill of Rights] create zones of privacy" (484). The concept of personal "liberty" embodied in the due process clause of the Fourteenth Amendment "protects those personal rights that are fundamental, and is not confined to the specific terms of the Bill of Rights" (486). The right of privacy is fundamental because it cannot be denied without violating the fundamental principles of liberty and justice, which lie at the base of civil and political institutions. Connecticut does not advance a compelling interest to justify the infringement of a fundamental right. Justices Black and Stewart dissent, arguing that there is no constitutional right of privacy.

1971 *United States v. Vuitch*, 402 U.S. 62
The Court upholds a Washington, D.C., criminal law provision that prohibits a physician from performing an abortion unless it is necessary for the preservation

of the pregnant woman's life or health and is performed under the direction of a competent licensed practitioner of medicine.

1972 *Eisenstadt v. Baird*, 405 U.S. 438
The Court extends *Griswold* to unmarried people. It recognizes that the right of privacy includes "the right of the *individual*, married or single, to be free from unwarranted governmental intrusion into matters so fundamentally affecting a person as the decision whether to bear or beget children" (453).

1973 *Roe v. Wade*, 410 U.S. 113
The Court holds that a Texas law making it a crime to "procure an abortion" except where it is necessary to save the pregnant woman's life is unconstitutional because it violates the due process clause of the Fourteenth Amendment. Justice Blackmun, for the majority, argues that, although the Constitution does not explicitly mention the right to privacy, zones of privacy do exist and the roots of the right have been found in the First, Fourth, Fifth, Ninth, and Fourteenth Amendments. (See *Griswold* above.) The right of privacy is broad enough to encompass a woman's decision whether or not to terminate her pregnancy, but "this right is not unqualified and must be considered against important state interests in regulation" (154). The state has legitimate interests in protecting the health of the pregnant woman and the fetus. The state's interest in maternal health becomes compelling only at the end of the first trimester, because until that point, the mortality rate for abortion is lower than that for childbirth. Therefore, the state may not enforce regulations that create obstacles to women's right to obtain an abortion until the end of the first trimester, and then it can do so only to the extent that the regulation reasonably relates to the preservation and protection of maternal health. The state's interest in potential life becomes compelling at the point of viability, the point at which the fetus is potentially able to live outside the womb. At that point, the state may proscribe abortion, except when necessary to preserve the life or health of the pregnant woman. The Court also notes that the unborn are not persons within the meaning of the Fourteenth Amendment. In dissent, Justice White calls the majority opinion an "exercise of raw judicial power" (222). Along with Justice Rehnquist, White denies that there is constitutional warrant for a woman's right to terminate her pregnancy. He argues that the issue of abortion, "over which reasonable men may easily and heatedly differ, . . . should be left with the people and to the political processes the people have devised to govern their affairs" (222). Rehnquist concedes that, if "privacy" means no more than freedom from unwanted state regulation of consensual transactions, then it may be a form of liberty protected by the Fourteenth Amendment. But he emphasizes that this liberty may be infringed by the state if it can be shown that such restriction is rationally related to a valid state objective. The fact that most states legislate against abortion is indicative that the right to terminate a pregnancy is not so fundamental, and as such the Texas law should not be subject to strict scrutiny.

1976 *Planned Parenthood of Central Missouri v. Danforth*, 428 U.S. 52
At issue are provisions of a Missouri law that prohibit the saline amniocentesis procedure for abortions performed after twelve weeks and that require (1) a woman's written consent to an abortion; (2) spousal consent to an abortion; (3)

parental consent as a condition for abortion of an unmarried minor during the first twelve weeks of pregnancy; (4) the keeping of certain records; and (5) physicians' exercise of reasonable care and skill and an attempt to save the fetus on penalty of manslaughter. Justice Blackmun, for the majority, upholds the written consent provision. Although the state may not restrict the abortion decision in the first trimester, it may try to ensure that the woman is aware of the significance of the decision. The spousal and parental consent provisions are invalidated because they give third parties veto power over the woman's abortion decision. The provision prohibiting the saline amniocentesis procedure is also invalidated. Although *Roe* permits the state to regulate with respect to maternal health after the first trimester, the provision is not reasonably related to the preservation and protection of maternal health because the method in question is common and safer for the woman than childbirth. The record-keeping provision is upheld as long as the requirements add no restrictions to abortion in the first trimester. The reasonable care and skill provision is invalidated because it does not exclude nonviable fetuses.

Canada

1976 *R. v. Morgentaler* [1976] 1 S.C.R. 616
Chief Justice Laskin holds that section 251 of the Criminal Code is not an invasion of the provincial power to legislate in relation to hospitals and to the regulation of the profession of medicine. The purpose of section 251 is related to the preservation of public peace, order, security, health and morality, and so section 251 meets the test of the valid use of the criminal law set by Justice Rand. The Court also holds that section 251 does not violate section 1 of the Canadian Bill of Rights, which prohibits discrimination by reason of sex. Justice Pigeon holds for the majority that the common law defense of necessity, codified in part by section 45 of the Criminal Code, can be applied with respect to abortion under two conditions: (1) the person providing the abortion believes in good faith that the continuation of the pregnancy poses an immediate threat to the pregnant woman's life or health; and (2) any reasonable consideration of the facts of the situation will make it impossible to obey the law. (The defense of necessity is a rule that exonerates from criminal responsibility a person who, in a particular situation, has no other option but to break the law in order to avoid worse consequences.)

United States

1977 *Carey v. Population Services International*, 431 U.S. 678
The Court invalidates a New York law prohibiting the sale of contraceptives to minors. Justice Brennan argues that "the decision whether or not to beget or bear a child is at the very heart of [the] . . . cluster of constitutionally protected choices [denoted by the concept of privacy]" (685), and this protection extends to minors as well as to adults. Restrictions on the distribution of contraceptives clearly burden the freedom to make these choices. If regulation by the state is burdensome, the state must have a sufficiently compelling interest, and the

regulation must be narrowly drawn to express only that interest. The compelling interest advanced by the state, that of protecting health, is unrelated to the law with respect to nonhazardous contraceptives.

1977 *Beal v. Doe*, 432 U.S. 438

Justice Powell, writing for the majority, holds that Pennsylvania is permitted to exclude nontherapeutic abortions from Medicaid coverage because the state has a valid and important interest in encouraging childbirth. Although the state's interest does not become compelling until the third trimester, it remains significant throughout the course of a pregnancy. Justice Marshall, in a strong dissent, argues that "in the present case, in its evident desire to avoid strict scrutiny—or indeed any meaningful scrutiny—of the challenged legislation, which would almost certainly result in its invalidation, the Court pulls from thin air a distinction between laws that absolutely prevent the exercise of the fundamental right to abortion and those that 'merely' make its exercise difficult for some people" (457). Justice Blackmun claims that the Court is allowing states to do indirectly what the Court said in *Roe* they could not do directly.

1977 *Maher v. Roe*, 432 U.S. 464

Justice Powell, writing for the majority, holds that Connecticut is permitted to exclude nontherapeutic abortions from Medicaid coverage while paying for the expenses incurred by childbirth. Although *Roe* protects women from unduly burdensome interference with the freedom to decide whether or not to end their pregnancies, it does not limit the authority of a state to make a value judgment favoring childbirth over abortion and to implement that judgment through the allocation of public funds. As such, the law does not violate a fundamental right protected by the Constitution. In dissent, Justice Brennan argues that the fundamental right established by *Roe* is impaired by bringing financial pressures on indigent women that force them to bear children they would otherwise not have. He adds that, in the past, the Court has found laws to be unconstitutional when their effect was an absolute ban on the right in question. He argues that the test of a compelling state interest applies to the regulation and that Connecticut has failed to satisfy the test.

1979 *Collautti v. Franklin*, 439 U.S. 379

The Court invalidates a provision of the Pennsylvania Abortion Control Act which provides that a person who performs an abortion must determine that the fetus is not viable. If it is viable, the person must exercise the same care to preserve the fetus' health and life as would be required in the case of a fetus intended to be born alive and to use the technique appropriate to this goal. The provision is held to be too vague, because the meaning of viability differs from that set forth in *Roe* and in *Danforth,* and the nature of the physician's duty to both the patient and the fetus is left unclear.

1979 *Bellotti v. Baird*, 443 U.S. 622

The Court invalidates the provision of a Massachusetts statute requiring parental consent for an abortion performed on an unmarried minor. On the basis of *Danforth,* the parental consent provision cannot give parents veto power over their daughter's abortion decision. If the state decides to require a pregnant minor to obtain one or both parents' consent, it must also have an alternative procedure in place so that authorization for the abortion can be obtained even if the parents refuse to consent. The woman is entitled to show either that she is mature enough to make the decision (in consultation with her doctor) or that the abortion would be in her best interests.

1980 *Harris v. McRae*, 448 U.S. 297

A majority upholds the Hyde Amendment, which bars the use of federal Medicaid funds for abortions except where the woman's life is in danger or in cases of rape or incest. The due process clause protects against unwarranted governmental interference with the freedom of choice, but it does not guarantee women the funds to realize the advantages of the freedom. The Hyde Amendment places no governmental obstacles in the path of a woman who chooses to terminate her pregnancy. It merely encourages an alternative activity. The majority argues that "the financial constraints that restrict an indigent woman's ability to enjoy a full range of constitutionally protected freedom of choice are the product not of governmental restrictions on access to abortion, but rather of her indigency" (315). The Hyde Amendment does not violate the equal protection clause of the Fifth Amendment, because the guarantee of equal protection is the right to be free from individual discrimination in statutory classifications, and under *Maher*, an indigent woman desiring an abortion does not come within the limited category of disadvantaged classes for the purposes of showing discrimination. "Where, as in this case, Congress has neither invaded a substantive constitutional right or freedom, nor enacted legislation that purposely operates to the detriment of a suspect class, the only requirement of equal protection is that congressional action be rationally related to a legitimate governmental interest" (326). The Hyde Amendment is rationally related to the legitimate governmental objective of protecting the life of the fetus.

1981 *H. L. v. Matheson*, 450 U.S. 398

The Court upholds a Utah statute that requires the physician to "notify, if possible" parents of minors upon whom an abortion is to be performed. As applied to unemancipated minors living with their parents, the statute serves important state interests, is narrowly drawn to protect only those interests, and does not violate any constitutional guarantees.

Canada

1981 *Canada (Minister of Justice) v. Borowski* [1981] 2 S.C.R. 571

The Court holds that Joseph Borowski, as an interested citizen, has standing to bring before the Court the issue of whether section 251 violates the rights of the fetus under the Canadian Bill of Rights. But the Court is silent on the question of whether fetuses can in fact claim the protection of the Bill of Rights.

United States

1983 *Akron v. Akron Center for Reproductive Health (Akron I)*, 462 U.S. 416

The majority invalidates the provisions of an Ohio statute that: (1) prohibit the performance of second-trimester abortions in outpatient facilities that are not part of acute-care, full-service hospitals; (2) require parental notification and consent for an abortion to be performed on an unmarried minor without an alternative procedure allowing the minor to demonstrate maturity to make the decision or that an abortion is in her best interests; (3) require a physician—and no one else, such as a counselor—to give women detailed information about abortion in order to have informed consent; (4) require a twenty-four waiting period before an abortion can be obtained; and (5) require that fetal remains be disposed of in a humane manner. In dissent, Justice O'Connor argues that the regulations imposed on lawful abortions are not unconstitutional unless they unduly burden the right to seek an abortion. Claiming that *Roe*'s trimester framework "is clearly on a collision course with itself" (458), she argues that the "unduly burdensome" standard be applied without reference to the different trimesters as articulated in *Roe*. If the fundamental right is not unduly burdened, then the evaluation is limited to whether a regulation is rationally related to a legitimate state purpose. She argues that the point of viability is entirely arbitrary and that "the state's interest in protecting potential human life exists throughout pregnancy" (459).

1983 *Planned Parenthood Association of Kansas City, Missouri v. Ashcroft*, 462 U.S. 476

Justices Powell, Blackmun, Brennan, Marshall, and Stevens hold to invalidate the provision of Missouri statutes requiring second-trimester abortions to be performed in a hospital. Also, Justices Powell, Burger, O'Connor, White, and Rehnquist uphold the provisions of the statute requiring: (1) a second physician to be present during abortions performed after viability; (2) a pathology report for each abortion performed; and (3) parental or judicial consent. In her concurring judgment, Justice O'Connor argues that the state has a compelling interest in protecting and preserving fetal life throughout pregnancy and that the provisions do not impose an undue burden on the limited right to have an abortion. She further argues that the validity of the legislation is not contingent on the trimester of pregnancy in which it is imposed.

1983 *Simopolous v. Virginia*, 462 U.S. 506

The Court upholds a Virginia statute that requires second-trimester abortions to be performed at licensed hospitals or clinics. The Court distinguishes this statute from the Missouri statute in *Ashcroft* because the Virginia statute does not require that such abortions be performed exclusively in full-service hospitals but permits their performance in licensed outpatient clinics. Although the state's discretion in outlining standards for the licensing of medical facilities does not permit it to adopt abortion regulations that depart from accepted medical practice, the Virginia regulations on their face are compatible with accepted medical standards governing outpatient second-trimester abortions. Justice O'Connor concurs, again expressing the view that the constitutional validity of the statute does not depend on the trimester on which it is imposed and that the requirement is not an undue burden on the decision to undergo an abortion.

1986 *Thornburgh v. American College of Obstetricians and Gynecologists*, 476 U.S. 747

The Court invalidates certain provisions of the Pennsylvania Abortion Control Act. The following are held to be unconstitutional: (1) the provision that defines "informed consent" as requiring the woman to be given certain information, including printed material from the state describing the anatomical characteristics of the fetus and alternatives to abortion; (2) the provision that requires reports from the physicians explaining the basis for a judgment of medical emergency or nonviability; (3) the provision that requires physicians to use a degree of care to preserve the life and health of the unborn and to use the technique that would provide the best opportunity for the child to be aborted live; and (4) the provision that requires a second doctor to be present where viability is possible with no exception for a medical emergency. The Act wholly subordinates constitutional privacy interests and concerns with maternal health in an effort to deter women from making a decision that is theirs to make. Justice Brennan argues that "the states are not free, under the guise of protecting maternal health or potential life, to intimidate women into continuing pregnancies" (759). In dissent, Justices Burger and White urge that *Roe* be overruled.

Canada

1988 *R. v. Morgentaler* [1988] 1 S.C.R. 30

The majority holds that section 251 violates section 7 of the Charter because it is an infringement on women's security of the person that is not in accordance with the principles of fundamental justice. The violation stems from the fact that the administrative structure and procedure set out in section 251 effectively deny the majority of Canadian women access to abortion services. The provision cannot be justified as a reasonable limit in a free and democratic society under section 1 of the Charter because it fails to satisfy the tests set out in *R. v. Oakes*. Although the objective of the law is pressing and substantial, the measures are not rationally connected to the objective, they do not impair the right as little as possible, and the effects of the provision are not proportional to the objective of the law. Justice Wilson, speaking for herself, agrees that section 251 is a violation of the security of the person that cannot be justified under section 1 of the Charter. However, her characterization of the central issue is whether the right to liberty in section 7 confers on the pregnant woman the right to decide for herself whether or not to have an abortion. She argues that section 7 guarantees every individual a degree of personal autonomy over important decisions intimately affecting his or her private life, and she concludes that the decision of a woman to terminate a pregnancy falls within this class of protected decisions.

1989 *Borowski v. Canada (Attorney-General)* [1989] 1 S.C.R. 342

Because the question of whether section 251 of the Criminal Code violates the rights of the fetus under sections 7 and 15 of the Charter has been rendered obsolete, Borowski no longer has standing before the Court. The Court refuses to address the issue of whether the fetus falls within the scope of "everyone" in section 7.

1989 *Tremblay v. Daigle* [1989] 2 S.C.R. 530

The Court holds that the Civil Code of Lower Canada does not view the fetus as a person. Any recognition in the Civil Code of the juridical personality of the fetus is a fiction of the civil law (see *Montréal Tramways*, above). Because the

Civil Code is used to interpret the Quebec Charter, the fetus is not considered a person under the Quebec Charter either. The Court refuses to rule on whether the fetus is within the scope of "everyone" in section 7 of the Canadian Charter of Rights and Freedoms. The Charter is intended to limit government action, but the dispute before the Court is one between private individuals.

United States

1989 *Webster v. Reproductive Health Services*, 492 U.S. 490
The majority refrains from addressing the constitutionality of the preamble of the Missouri statute, which sets forth "findings" that the life of each human being begins at conception and that unborn children have protectable interests in life, health, and well-being. The majority states that the preamble does not itself regulate abortion and that the state has the authority to make a value judgment favoring childbirth over abortion. The provision restricting the use of public employees and facilities for the performance of nontherapeutic abortions is upheld. The Court argues that the due process clause generally confers no affirmative right to governmental aid, even when such aid might be necessary to secure life, liberty, or property interests of which the government may not deprive the individual. Missouri's decision to use public facilities to encourage childbirth over abortion places no governmental obstacle in the path of a woman who chooses to terminate her pregnancy. Rather, it leaves her with the same choices she would have had if the state had decided not to operate any hospitals at all. The Court upholds the provision specifying that physicians must ascertain whether the fetus is viable prior to performing an abortion on any woman whom they believe is more than twenty weeks pregnant. This provision permissibly furthers the state's interest in protecting potential human life. In upholding this provision, four of the five justices of the majority would reconsider or explicitly overrule *Roe*.

1990 *Ohio v. Akron Center for Reproductive Health*, 497 U.S. 502
The Court upholds an Ohio statute that makes it a crime to perform an abortion on an unmarried, unemancipated minor unless the physician gives notice to her parents, or a juvenile court issues an order authorizing the minor to consent (judicial bypass). The bypass procedure meets the requirements identified in *Danforth, Bellotti, Ashcroft,* and *Akron I:* (1) the minor must be permitted to show her maturity; (2) the juvenile court must authorize consent when it is in the minor's best interest or when she is permitted to show that it is in her best interests; (3) anonymity must be ensured; and (4) time limitations on judicial action must satisfy the requirement that a bypass procedure be conducted quickly.

1990 *Hodgson v. Minnesota*, 497 U.S. 417
The Court upholds a Minnesota statute that prohibits an abortion to be performed on an unmarried minor until forty-eight hours after both parents are notified, unless the minor states that she is a victim of parental abuse or neglect and notice of this is given to the proper authorities. The two-parent notice is effective unless the court orders the abortion to proceed without notice on proof that the

minor is mature or that the abortion is in her best interests. However, the Court cannot agree in general about the constitutionality of the two-parent notice with or without judicial bypass. Justices Kennedy, Rehnquist, White, and Scalia would uphold any two-parent notice provision, with or without a judicial bypass procedure in place; Justices Stevens, Marshall, Brennan, and Blackmun would invalidate any two-parent notice provision, with or without a judicial bypass procedure in place. Justice O'Connor would uphold a two-parent notice provision only where there is a judicial bypass procedure in place.

1991 *Rust v. Sullivan*, 500 U.S. 173
The Court upholds provisions of the Public Health Service Act, which specify that no federal funds designated for family planning can be used where abortion is a method of family planning. The new regulations prohibit any federally funded projects from engaging in counseling concerning referrals for and activities advocating abortion as a method of family planning. Under *Maher*, the government is permitted to make a value judgment favoring childbirth over abortion and to implement that judgment through the allocation of funds. Under *Harris*, the differential allocation of funds places no governmental obstacle in the path of a woman seeking to terminate her pregnancy and leaves her with the same choices she would have had if the government had chosen not to fund anything.

1992 *Planned Parenthood of Southeastern Pennsylvania v. Casey*, 120 L. Ed. 2d 674
This case is intended to be the last word on the legal status of abortion in the United States. Justices O'Connor, Kennedy, and Souter write a joint opinion with which all the other justices concur and dissent in part. The first part of the joint opinion, in which Justices Stevens and Blackmun concur, reaffirms the "central ruling" in *Roe,* which is (1) the recognition of the right of a woman to choose to have an abortion previability and to obtain it without undue interference from the state; (2) confirmation of the state's power to restrict abortions after fetal viability, as long as the restrictions make exceptions for pregnancies that endanger the woman's life and health; (3) the recognition of the state's legitimate interest from the outset of pregnancy in protecting the health of the woman and the life of the fetus. It is argued that constitutional protection for the abortion decision derives from the due process clause of the Fourteenth Amendment and that the Constitution promises that there is a realm of personal liberty into which the government may not enter. Pennsylvania's spousal notification requirement is invalidated because it is likely to prevent a significant number of women from obtaining an abortion. The second part of the joint opinion, in which Justices Rehnquist, White, Scalia, and Thomas agree in result, overrules the trimester framework set out in *Roe*. They argue that the trimester framework undervalues the state's interest in potential life. Only where the state regulation imposes an undue burden on a woman's ability to make the abortion decision does the power of the state reach into the heart of the liberty protected by the due process clause. "A finding of an undue burden is a shorthand for the conclusion that a state regulation has the purpose or effect of placing a substantial obstacle in the path of a woman seeking an abortion of a nonviable fetus" (715). On the basis of the undue burden standard, the statute's definition of medical

emergency is upheld. The informed consent provision, which requires that the physician give the woman undergoing an abortion specific information including printed materials, is upheld. *Akron I* and *Thornburgh* are expressly overruled to the extent that the plurality finds no constitutional violation when the government requires the giving of truthful, nonmisleading information about the nature of the procedure, the attendant health risks and those of childbirth, and the "probable gestational age" of the fetus. *Akron I* is also overruled with respect to the physician providing information to the patient and the twenty-four-hour waiting period. The joint opinion argues that neither of these requirements imposes an undue burden on a woman seeking an abortion. They uphold the record-keeping requirements and the parental consent provisions as long as there is a judicial bypass procedure in place. Justice Rehnquist, with whom Justices White, Scalia, and Thomas concur, argues that the right to decide whether or not to terminate a pregnancy is not constitutionally protected because (1) the Constitution says nothing about abortion, and (2) it has been a long-standing American tradition to permit abortion to be legally proscribed.

1993   *Bray v. Alexandria Women's Health Clinic,* 122 L. Ed. 2d. 34
Abortion clinics sued to prohibit an anti-abortion organization from conducting demonstrations at clinics, claiming a conspiracy for the purpose of depriving a class of persons of equal protection. The Court argues that no federal cause of action is provided against persons obstructing access to abortion clinics. The clinic did not show that opposition to abortion qualifies as discrimination of a class for the purpose of the equal protection clause. The focus must be on women by reason of their sex, but the demonstrations are not directed at women. Rather, they are intended to protect the victims of abortion, to stop its practice, and to reverse its legalization.

Canada

1993   *R. v. Morgentaler* [1993] 3 S.C.R. 463
The Court invalidates regulations that prohibit the performance of an abortion anywhere other than in a place approved as a hospital under the Nova Scotia Hospitals Act and those that deny medical service insurance coverage for abortions performed outside a hospital. Such regulations are outside the provincial legislative power. The Court argues that "the legislation's central purpose and dominant characteristic is the restriction of abortion as a socially undesirable practice which should be suppressed or punished" (494). This infringes on the criminal law power of the federal government.

United States

1994   *National Organization for Women v. Scheidler,* 114 S. Ct. 798
At issue in this case is whether abortion clinics may bring suit against abortion protestors under the Racketeer Influenced Corrupt Organization (RICO) chapter of the Organized Crime Act of 1970 (18 USCS §§1961–1968). Any person associated with an enterprise that is engaged in, or with the activities of which affect, interstate or foreign commerce is prohibited by section 1962(c) from

conducting the affairs of the enterprise through a pattern of racketeering activity. Clinic operators and their supporters argue that abortion protesters participate in a pattern of racketeering activities, including extortion and threatened or actual violence designed to induce employees of abortion clinics to leave their jobs and patients to forgo their right to receive medical services. They also argue that these activities injure the business and property interests of the clinics. Previous attempts to bring suit under RICO had been dismissed by several lower courts on the grounds that the petitioners could not show that the activities of the abortion protesters were motivated by considerations of profit. The Court holds, unanimously, that a showing of economic motive is not required by any part of the RICO statute, and so rules that clinics may bring such action against abortion protesters. The Court does not address the question of whether abortion protesters actually engage in racketeering activity.

Excerpts from Opinion in *Roe v. Wade*

Majority Opinion

. . . A recent review of the common law precedents argues . . . that even post-quickening abortion was never established as a common law crime. This is of some importance because while most American courts ruled, in holding or dictum, that abortion of an unquickened fetus was not criminal under their received common law, others followed Coke in stating that abortion of a quick fetus was a "misprison," a term they translated to mean "misdemeanor." That their reliance on Coke on this aspect of the law was uncritical and, apparently in all the reported cases, dictum (due probably to the paucity of common law prosecutions for post-quickening abortion), makes it now appear doubtful that abortion was ever firmly established as a common law crime even with respect to the destruction of a quick fetus. . . .

It is thus apparent that at common law, at the time of the adoption of our Constitution, and throughout the major portion of the 19th century, abortion was viewed with less disfavor than under most American statutes currently in effect. Phrasing it another way, a woman enjoyed a substantially broader right to terminate a pregnancy than she does in most States today. At least with respect to the early stage of pregnancy, and very possibly without such a limitation, the opportunity to make this choice was present in this country well into the 19th century. Even later, the law continued for some time to treat less punitively an abortion procured in early pregnancy. . . .

Three reasons have been advanced to explain historically the enactment of criminal abortion laws in the 19th century and to justify their continued existence.

It has been argued occasionally that these laws were the product of a Victorian social concern to discourage illicit sexual conduct. Texas, however, does not advance this justification in the present case, and it appears that no court or commentator has taken the argument seriously. . . .

A second reason is concerned with abortion as a medical procedure. When most criminal abortion laws were first enacted, the procedure was a hazardous one for the woman. This was particularly true prior to the development of antisepsis. Antiseptic techniques, of course, were based on discoveries by Lister, Pasteur, and others first announced in 1867, but were not generally accepted and employed until about the turn of the century. Abortion mortality was high. Even after 1900, and perhaps until as late as the development of antibiotics in the 1940's, standard modern techniques such as dilation and curettage were not nearly so safe as they are today. Thus it has been argued that a State's real concern in enacting a criminal abortion law was to protect the pregnant woman, that is, to restrain her from submitting to a procedure that placed her life in serious jeopardy.

Modern medical techniques have altered this situation. Appellants and various *amici* refer to medical data indicating that abortion in early pregnancy, that is, prior to the end of first trimester, although not without its risk, is now relatively safe. Mortality rates for women undergoing early abortions, where the procedure is legal, appear to be as low as or lower than the rates for normal childbirth. Consequently, any interest of the State in protecting the woman from an inherently hazardous procedure, except when it would be equally dangerous for her to forgo it, has largely disappeared. Of course, important state interests in the area of health and medical standards do remain. The State has a legitimate interest in seeing to it that abortion, like any other medical procedure, is performed under circumstances that insure maximum safety for the patient. This interest obviously extends at least to the performing physician and his staff, to the facilities involved, to the availability of after-care, and to adequate provision for any complication or emergency that might arise. The prevalence of high mortality rates at illegal "abortion mills" strengthens, rather than weakens, the State's interest in regulating the conditions under which abortions are performed. Moreover, the risk to the woman increases as her pregnancy continues. Thus the State retains a definite interest in protecting the woman's own health and safety when an abortion is performed at a late stage of pregnancy.

The third reason is the State's interest—some phrase it in terms of duty—in protecting prenatal life. Some of the argument for this justification rests on the theory that a new human life is present from the moment of conception. . . .

Parties challenging state abortion laws have sharply disputed in some courts the contention that a purpose of these laws, when enacted, was to protect prenatal life. Pointing to the absence of legislative history to support the contention, they claim that most state laws were designed solely to protect the woman. Because medical advances have lessened this concern, at least with respect to abortion in early pregnancy, they argue that with respect to such abortions the laws can no longer be justified by any state interest. There is some scholarly support for this view of original purpose. The few state courts called upon to interpret their laws in the late 19th and early 20th centuries did focus on the State's interest in protecting the woman's health rather than in preserving embryo and fetus. . . .

The Constitution does not explicitly mention any right of privacy. In a line of decisions, however, going back perhaps as far as *Union Pacific R. Co. v. Botsford,* 141 U.S. 250, 251 (1891), the Court has recognized that a right of personal privacy, or a guarantee of certain areas or zones of privacy, does exist under the Constitution. In varying contexts the Court or individual Justices have indeed found at least the roots of that right in the First Amendment, . . . in the Fourth and Fifth Amendments . . . in the penumbras of the Bill of Rights . . . in the Ninth Amendment . . . or in the concept of liberty guaranteed by the first section of the Fourteenth Amendment. . . .These decisions make it clear that only personal rights that can be deemed "fundamental" or "implicit in the concept of ordered liberty," . . . are included in this guarantee of personal privacy. They also make it clear that the right has some extension to activities relating to marriage, . . . procreation, . . . contraception, . . . family relationships, . . . and child rearing and education. . . .

This right of privacy, whether it be founded in the Fourteenth Amendment's concept of personal liberty and restrictions upon state action, as we feel it is, or, as the District Court determined, in the Ninth Amendment's reservation of rights to the people, is broad enough to encompass a woman's decision whether or not to terminate her pregnancy. . . .

. . . Appellants and some *amici* argue that the woman's right is absolute and that she is entitled to terminate her pregnancy at whatever time, in whatever way, and for whatever reason she alone chooses. With this we do not agree. Appellants' arguments that Texas either has no valid interest at all in regulating the abortion decision, or no interest strong enough to support any limitation upon the woman's sole determination, is unpersuasive. The Court's decisions recognizing a right of privacy also acknowledge that some state regulation in areas protected by that right is appropriate. As noted above, a state may properly assert important interests in safe-guarding health, in maintaining medical standards, and in protecting potential life. At some point in pregnancy, these respective interests become sufficiently compelling to sustain regulation of the factors that govern the abortion decision. The privacy right involved, therefore, cannot be said to be absolute. . . .

We therefore conclude that the right of personal privacy includes the abortion decision, but that this right is not unqualified and must be considered against important state interests in regulation.

We note that those federal and state courts that have recently considered abortion law challenges have reached the same conclusion. . . .

Although the results are divided, most of these courts have agreed that the right of privacy, however based, is broad enough to cover the abortion decision; that the right, nonetheless, is not absolute and is subject to some limitations; and that at some point the state interests as to protection of health, medical standards, and prenatal life, become dominant. We agree with this approach.

The appellee and certain *amici* argue that the fetus is a "person" within the language and meaning of the Fourteenth Amendment. In support of this they outline at length and in detail the well-known facts of fetal development. If this suggestion of personhood is established, the appellant's case, of course, collapses, for the fetus' right to life is then guaranteed specifically by the Amendment. The appellant conceded as much on reargument. On the other hand, the appellee conceded on reargument that no case could be cited that holds that a fetus is a person within the meaning of the Fourteenth Amendment.

All this, together with our observation, *supra,* that throughout the major portion of the 19th century prevailing legal abortion practices were far freer than they are today, persuades us that the word "person," as used in the Fourteenth Amendment, does not include the unborn. . . . Indeed, our decision in *United States v. Vuitch,* 402 U.S. 62 (1971), inferentially is to the same effect, for we there would not have indulged in statutory interpretation favorable to abortion in specified circumstances if the necessary consequence was the termination of life entitled to Fourteenth Amendment protection.

. . . As we have intimated above, it is reasonable and appropriate for a State to decide that at some point in time another interest, that of health of the mother or that of potential human life, becomes significantly involved. The woman's privacy is no longer sole and any right of privacy she possesses must be measured accordingly.

. . . We need not resolve the difficult question of when life begins. When those trained in the respective disciplines of medicine, philosophy, and theology are unable to arrive at any consensus, the judiciary, at this point in the development of man's knowledge, is not in a position to speculate as to the answer.

It should be sufficient to note briefly the wide divergence of thinking on this most sensitive and difficult question. There has always been strong support for the view that life does not begin until live birth. This was the belief of the Stoics. It appears to be the predominant, though not the unanimous, attitude of the Jewish faith. It may be taken to represent also the position of a large segment of the Protestant community, insofar as that can be ascertained; organized groups that have taken a formal position on the abortion issue have generally regarded abortion as a matter for the conscience of the individual and her family. As we have noted, the common law found greater significance in quickening. Physicians and their scientific colleagues have regarded that event with less interest and have tended to focus either upon conception or upon live birth or upon the interim point at which the fetus becomes "viable," that is, potentially able to live outside the mother's womb, albeit with artificial aid. Viability is usually placed at about seven months (28 weeks) but may occur earlier, even at 24 weeks. . . .

In areas other than criminal abortion the law has been reluctant to endorse any theory that life, as we recognize it, begins before live birth or to accord legal rights to the unborn except in narrowly defined situations and except when the rights are contingent upon live birth. . . . In short, the unborn have never been recognized in the law as persons in the whole sense.

In view of all this, we do not agree that, by adopting one theory of life, Texas may override the rights of the pregnant woman that are at stake. We repeat, however, that the State does have an important and legitimate interest in preserving and protecting the health of the pregnant woman, whether she be a resident of the State or a nonresident who seeks medical consultation and treatment there, and that it has still *another* important and legitimate interest in protecting the potentiality of human life. These interests are separate and distinct. Each grows in substantiality as the woman approaches term and, at a point during pregnancy, each becomes "compelling."

With respect to the State's important and legitimate interest in the health of the mother, the "compelling" point, in the light of present medical knowledge, is at approximately the end of the first trimester. This is so because of the now established medical fact . . . that until the end of the first trimester mortality in abortion is less than mortality in normal childbirth. It follows that, from and after this point, a State may regulate the abortion procedure to the extent that the regulation reasonably relates to the preservation and protection of maternal health. Examples of permissible state regulation in this area are requirements as to the qualifications of the person who is to perform the abortion; as to the licensure of that person; as to the facility in which the procedure is to be performed, that is, whether it must be a hospital or may be a clinic or some other place of less-than-hospital status; as to the licensing of the facility; and the like.

This means, on the other hand, that, for the period of pregnancy prior to this "compelling" point, the attending physician, in consultation with his patient, is free to determine, without regulation by the State, that in his medical judgment the patient's pregnancy should be terminated. If that decision is reached, the judgment may be effectuated by an abortion free of interference by the State.

With respect to the State's important and legitimate interest in potential life, the "compelling" point is at viability. . . . State regulation protective of fetal life after viability thus has both logical and biological justifications. If the State is interested in protecting fetal life after viability, it may go so far as to proscribe abortion during that period except when it is necessary to preserve the life or health of the mother. . . .

To summarize and repeat:

1.   A state criminal abortion statute of the current Texas type, that excepts from criminality only a *life saving* procedure on behalf of the mother, without regard to pregnancy stage and without recognition of the other interests involved, is violative of the Due Process Clause of the Fourteenth Amendment.

(a) For the stage prior to approximately the end of the first trimester, the abortion decision and its effectuation must be left to the medical judgment of the pregnant woman's attending physician.

(b) For the stage subsequent to approximately the end of the first trimester, the State, in promoting its interest in the health of the mother, may, if it chooses, regulate the abortion procedure in ways that are reasonably related to maternal health.

(c) For the stage subsequent to viability the State, in promoting its interest in the potentiality of human life, may, if it chooses, regulate, and even proscribe, abortion except where it is necessary, in appropriate medical judgment, for the preservation of the life or health of the mother.

2.   The State may define the term "physician," as it has been employed in the preceding numbered paragraphs of this Part XI of this opinion, to mean only a physician currently licensed by the State, and may proscribe any abortion by a person who is not a physician as so defined.

. . . The decision leaves the State free to place increasing restrictions on abortion as the period of pregnancy lengthens, so long as those restrictions are tailored to the recognized state interests. The decision vindicates the right of the physician to administer medical treatment according to his professional judgment up to the points where important state interests provide compelling justifications for intervention. Up to those points the abortion decision in all its aspects is inherently, and primarily, a medical decision, and basic responsibility for it must rest with the physician. If an individual practitioner abuses the privilege of exercising proper medical judgment, the usual remedies, judicial and intraprofessional, are available. . . .

Dissent

At the heart of the controversy in these cases are those recurring pregnancies that pose no danger whatsoever to the life or health of the mother but are nevertheless unwanted for any one or more of a variety of reasons—convenience, family planning, economics, dislike of children, the embarrassment of illegitimacy, etc. The common claim before us is that for any one of such reasons, or for no reason at all, and without asserting or claiming any threat to life or health, any woman is entitled to an abortion at her request if she is able to find a medical advisor willing to undertake the procedure.

The Court for the most part sustains this position: During the period prior to the time the fetus becomes viable, the Constitution of the United States values the convenience, whim or caprice of the putative mother more than the life or potential life of the fetus; the Constitution, therefore, guarantees the right to an abortion as against any state law or policy seeking to protect the fetus from an abortion not prompted by more compelling reasons of the mother.

With all due respect, I dissent. I find nothing in the language or history of the Constitution to support the Court's judgment. . . . As an exercise of raw judicial power, the Court perhaps has authority to do what it does today; but in my view its judgment is an improvident and extravagant exercise of the power of judicial review which the Constitution extends to this Court.

The Court apparently values the convenience of the pregnant mother more than the continued existence and development of the life or potential life which she carries. . . .

It is my view, therefore, that the Texas statute is not constitutionally infirm because it denies abortions to those who seek to serve only their convenience rather than to protect their life or health. . . .

Excerpts from Opinion in
Planned Parenthood of Southeastern Pennsylvania v. Casey

Joint Opinion of Justices Kennedy, O'Connor, and Souter

Liberty finds no refuge in a jurisprudence of doubt. Yet 19 years after our holding that the Constitution protects a woman's right to terminate her pregnancy in its earliest stages, *Roe v. Wade*, 410 U.S. 113, that definition of liberty is still questioned. . . .

After considering the fundamental constitutional questions resolved by *Roe*, principles of institutional integrity, and the rule of *stare decisis*, we are led to conclude this: the essential holding of *Roe v. Wade* should be retained and reaffirmed.

It must be stated at the outset and with clarity that *Roe*'s essential holding, the holding we reaffirm, has three parts. First is a recognition of the right of the woman to choose to have an abortion before viability and to obtain it without undue interference from the State. Before viability, the State's interests are not strong enough to support a prohibition of abortion or the imposition of a substantial obstacle to the woman's effective right to elect the procedure. Second is a confirmation of the State's power to restrict abortions after fetal viability, if the law contains exceptions for pregnancies which endanger a woman's life or health. And third is the principle that the State has legitimate interests from the outset of pregnancy in protecting the health of the woman and the life of the fetus that may become a child. These principles do not contradict one another; and we adhere to each. . . .

Men and women of good conscience can disagree, and we suppose some always shall disagree, about the profound moral and spiritual implications of terminating a pregnancy, even in its earliest stage. Some of us as individuals find abortion offensive to our most basic principles of morality, but that cannot control our decision. Our obligation is to define the liberty of all, not to mandate our own moral code. The underlying constitutional issue is whether the State can resolve these philosophic questions in such a definitive way that a woman lacks all choice in the matter, except perhaps in those rare circumstances in which the pregnancy is itself a danger to her own life or health, or is the result of rape or incest. . . .

Our law affords constitutional protection to personal decisions relating to marriage, procreation, contraception, family relationships, child rearing, and education. . . . Our cases recognize "the right of the *individual*, married or single, to be free from unwarranted governmental intrusion into matters so fundamentally affecting a person as the decision whether to bear or beget a child." *Eisenstadt v. Baird*, 405 U.S. 438, 453. . . . These matters, involving the most intimate and personal choices a person may make in a lifetime, choices central to personal dignity and autonomy, are central to the liberty protected by the Fourteenth Amendment. At the heart of liberty is the right to define one's own concept of existence, of meaning, of the universe, and of the mystery of human life. Beliefs about these matters could not define the attributes of personhood were they formed under compulsion of the State.

These considerations begin our analysis of the woman's interest in terminating her pregnancy but cannot end it, for this reason: though the abortion decision may originate within the zone of conscience and belief, it is more than a philosophic exercise. Abortion is a unique act. It is an act fraught with consequences for others: for the woman who must live with the implications of her decision; for the persons who perform and assist in the procedure; for the spouse, family, and society which must confront the knowledge that these procedures exist, procedures some deem nothing short of an act of violence against innocent human life; and, depending on one's beliefs, for the life or potential life that is aborted. Though abortion is conduct, it does not follow that the State is entitled to proscribe it in all instances. That is because the liberty of the woman is at stake in a sense unique to the human condition and so unique to the law. The mother who carries a child to full term is subject to anxieties, to physical constraints, to pain that only she must bear. That these sacrifices have from the beginning of the human race been endured by woman with a pride that ennobles her in the eyes of others and gives to the infant a bond of love cannot alone be grounds for the State to insist that she make the sacrifice. Her suffering is too intimate and personal for the State to insist, without more, upon its own vision of the woman's role, however dominant that vision has been in the course of our history and our culture. The destiny of the woman must be shaped to a large extent on her own conception of her spiritual imperatives and her place in society. . . .

While we appreciate the weight of the arguments made on behalf of the State in the case before us, arguments which in their ultimate formulation conclude that *Roe* should be overruled, the reservations any of us may have in reaffirming the central holding of *Roe* are outweighed by the explication of individual liberty we have given combined with the force of *stare decisis*. We turn now to that doctrine.

. . . [W]hen this Court reexamines a prior holding, its judgment is customarily informed by a series of prudential and pragmatic considerations designed to test the consistency of overruling a prior decision with the ideal of the rule of law, and to gauge the respective costs of reaffirming and overruling a prior case. Thus, for example, we may ask whether the rule has proved to be intolerable simply in defying practical workability . . . ; whether the rule is subject to a kind of reliance that would lend a special hardship to the consequences of overruling and add inequity to the cost of repudiation . . . ; whether related principles of law have so far developed as to have left the old rule no more than a remnant of abandoned doctrine . . . ; or whether the facts have so changed or come to be seen so differently, as to have robbed the old rule of significant application or justification. . . .

So in this case we may inquire whether *Roe*'s central rule has been found unworkable; whether the rule's limitation on state power could be removed without serious inequity to those who have relied upon it or significant damage to the stability of the society governed by the rule in question; whether the law's growth in the intervening years has left *Roe*'s central rule a doctrinal anachronism discounted by society; and whether *Roe*'s premises of fact have so far changed in the ensuing two decades as to render its central holding somehow irrelevant or unjustifiable in dealing with the issue it addressed. . . .

The sum of precedential inquiry to this point shows *Roe*'s underpinnings unweakened in any way affecting its central holding. While it has engendered disapproval, it has not been unworkable. An entire generation has come of age free to assume *Roe*'s concept of liberty in defining the capacity of women to act in society, and to make reproductive decisions; no erosion of principle going to liberty or personal autonomy has left *Roe*'s central holding a doctrinal remnant; *Roe* portends no developments at odds with other precedent for the analysis of personal liberty; and no changes of fact have rendered viability more or less appropriate as the point at which the balance of interest tips. Within the bounds of normal *stare decisis* analysis, then, and subject to the considerations on which it customarily turns, the stronger argument is for affirming *Roe*'s central holding, with whatever degree of personal reluctance any of us may have, not for overruling it. . . .

Our analysis would not be complete, however, without explaining why overruling *Roe*'s central holding would not only reach an unjustifiable result under principles of *stare decisis*, but would seriously weaken the Court's capacity to exercise the judicial power and function as the Supreme Court of a Nation dedicated to the rule of law. . . .

. . . Where, in the performance of its judicial duties, the Court decides a case in such a way as to resolve the sort of intensely divisive controversy reflected in *Roe* and those rare, comparable cases, its decision has a dimension that the resolution of the normal case does not carry. It is the dimension present whenever the Court's interpretation of the Constitution calls the contending sides of a national controversy to end their national division by accepting a common mandate rooted in the Constitution.

The Court is not asked to do this very often, having thus addressed the Nation only twice in our lifetime, in the decisions of *Brown* and *Roe*. But when the Court does act in this way, its decision requires an equally rare precedential force to counter the inevitable efforts to overturn it and to thwart its implementation. Some of those efforts may be mere unprincipled emotional reactions; others may proceed from principles worthy of profound respect. But whatever the premises of opposition may be, only the most convincing justification under accepted standards of precedent could suffice to demonstrate that a later decision overruling the first was anything but a surrender to political pressure, and an unjustified repudiation of the principle on which the Court staked its authority in the first instance. So to overrule under fire in the absence of the most compelling reason to reexamine a watershed decision would subvert the Court's legitimacy beyond any serious question. . . .

The Court's duty in the present case is clear. In 1973, it confronted the already divisive issue of governmental power to limit personal choice to undergo abortion, for which it provided a new resolution based on the Fourteenth Amendment. Whether or not a new social consensus is developing on that issue, its divisiveness is no less today than in 1973, and pressure to overrule the decision, like pressure to retain it, has grown only more intense. A decision to overrule *Roe*'s essential holding under the existing circumstances would address error, if error there was, at the cost of both profound and unnecessary damage to the Court's legitimacy, and to the Nation's commitment to the rule of law. It is therefore imperative to adhere to the essence of *Roe*'s original decision, and we do so today. . . .

The very notion that the State has a substantial interest in potential life leads to the conclusion that not all regulations must be deemed unwarranted. Not all burdens on the right to decide whether to terminate a pregnancy will be undue. In our view, the undue burden standard is the appropriate means of reconciling the State's interest with the woman's constitutionally protected liberty. . . .

A finding of an undue burden is a shorthand for the conclusion that a state regulation has the purpose of placing a substantial obstacle in the path of a woman seeking an abortion of a nonviable fetus. A statute with this purpose is invalid because the means chosen by the State to further the interest in potential life must be calculated to inform the woman's free choice, not to hinder it. And a statute which, while furthering the interest in potential life or some other valid state interest, has the effect of placing a substantial obstacle in the path of a woman's choice cannot be considered a permissible means of serving its legitimate ends. . . .

Section 3209 of Pennsylvania's abortion law provides, except in cases of medical emergency, that no physician shall perform an abortion on a married woman without receiving a signed statement from the woman that she has notified her spouse she is about to undergo an abortion. . . .

. . . In well functioning marriages, spouses discuss important intimate decisions such as whether to bear a child. But there are millions of women in this country who are the victims of regular physical and psychological abuse at the hands of their husbands. Should these women become pregnant, they may have very good reason for not wishing to inform their husbands of their decision to obtain an abortion. Many have justifiable fears of physical abuse, but may be no less fearful of the consequences of reporting prior abuse to the Commonwealth of Pennsylvania. Many may have a reasonable fear that notifying their husbands will provoke further instances of child abuse; these women are not exempt from §3209's notification requirement. Many may fear devastating forms of psychological abuse from their husbands, including verbal harassment, threats of future violence, the destruction of possessions, physical confinement to the home, the withdrawal of financial support, or the disclosure of the abortion to family and friends. These methods of psychological abuse may act as even more of a deterrent to notification than the possibility of physical violence, but women who are the victims of the abuse are not exempt from §3209's notification requirement. And many women who are pregnant as a result of sexual assaults by their husbands will be unable to avail themselves of the exception for spousal assault, . . . because the exception requires that the woman have notified law enforcement authorities within 90 days of the assault, and her husband will be notified of her report once an investigation begins. . . . If anything in this field is certain, it is that victims of spousal sexual assault are extremely reluctant to report the abuse to the government; hence, a great many spousal rape victims will not be exempt from the notification requirement imposed by §3209.

The spousal notification requirement is thus likely to prevent a significant number of women from obtaining an abortion. It does not merely make abortions a little more difficult or expensive to obtain; for many women, it will impose a substantial obstacle. We must not blind ourselves to the fact that the significant number of women who fear for their safety and the safety of their children are likely to be deterred from procuring an abortion as surely as if the Commonwealth had outlawed abortion in all cases.

Dissent

The joint opinion, following its newly minted variation on *stare decisis*, retains the outer shell of *Roe v. Wade*, but beats a wholesale retreat from the substance of that case. We believe that *Roe* was wrongly decided, and that it can and should be overruled consistently with our traditional approach to *stare decisis* constitutional cases. We would adopt the approach of the plurality in *Webster v. Reproductive Health Services*, 492 U.S. 490, and uphold the challenged provisions of the Pennsylvania statute in their entirety. . . .

In *Roe v. Wade*, the Court recognized a "guarantee of personal privacy" which "is broad enough to encompass a woman's decision whether or not to terminate her pregnancy." 410 US, at 152–153. We are now of the view that, in terming this right fundamental, the Court in *Roe* read the earlier opinions upon which it based its decision much too broadly. Unlike marriage, procreation and contraception, abortion "involves the purposeful termination of potential life." *Harris v. McRae*, 448 US 297, 325. The abortion decision must therefore "be recognized as sui generis, different in kind from the others that the Court has protected under the rubric of personal or family privacy and autonomy." *Thornburgh v. American College of Obstetricians and Gynecologists*, [476 US 747], 792. One cannot ignore the fact that a woman is not isolated in her pregnancy, and that the decision to abort necessarily involves the destruction of a fetus. . . .

Nor do the historical traditions of the American people support the view that the right to terminate one's pregnancy is "fundamental." . . .

We think, therefore, both in view of this history and of our decided cases dealing with substantive liberty under the Due Process Clause, that the Court was mistaken in *Roe* when it classified a woman's decision to terminate her pregnancy as a "fundamental right" that could be abridged only in a manner which withstood "strict scrutiny." . . .

. . . In assuming that the Court is perceived as "surrender[ing] to political pressure" when it overrules a controversial decision, . . . the joint opinion forgets that there are two sides to any controversy. The joint opinion asserts that, in order to protect its legitimacy, the Court must refrain from overruling a controversial decision lest it be viewed as favoring those who oppose the decision. But a decision to *adhere* to prior precedent is subject to the same criticism, for in such a case one can easily argue that the Court is responding to those who demonstrated in favor of the original decision. The decision in *Roe* has engendered large demonstrations, including repeated marches on this Court and on Congress, both in opposition to and in support of that opinion. A decision either way on *Roe* can therefore be perceived as favoring one group or the other. But this perceived dilemma arises only if one assumes, as the joint opinion does, that the Court should make its decisions with a view toward speculative public perceptions. If one assumes instead, as the Court surely did in both *Brown* and *West Coast Hotel*, that the Court's legitimacy is enhanced by faithful interpretation of the Constitution irrespective of public opposition, such self-engendered difficulties may be put to one side. . . .

The sum of the joint opinion's labors in the name of *stare decisis* and "legitimacy" is this: *Roe v. Wade* stands as a sort of Potemkin Village, which may be pointed out to passersby as a monument to the importance of adhering to precedent. But behind the facade, an entirely new method of analysis, without any roots in constitutional law, is imported to decide the constitutionality of state laws regulating abortion. . . .

We have stated our belief that the Constitution does not subject state abortion regulations to heightened scrutiny. Accordingly, we think that the correct analysis is that set forth by the plurality opinion in *Webster*. A woman's interest in having an abortion is a form of liberty protected by the Due Process Clause, but States may regulate abortion procedures in ways rationally related to a legitimate state interest.

Bibliography

The papers in this volume focus on philosophical thinking about abortion, but it is clear that the problem of abortion raises a host of questions for other disciplines as well, including law, public policy, feminism, and religion. This selective bibliography is designed as a starting point for further (interdisciplinary) research.

I. Philosophical Perspectives

A. Books

Brody, Baruch. *Abortion and the Sanctity of Human Life*. Cambridge, Mass.: M.I.T. Press, 1975.

Callahan, Daniel. *Abortion: Law, Choice, and Morality*. New York: Macmillan, 1970.

Dworkin, Ronald. *Life's Dominion: An Argument About Abortion, Euthanasia and Individual Freedom*. New York: Alfred A. Knopf, Inc., 1993.

Glover, Jonathan. *Causing Death and Saving Lives*. Harmondsworth, Middlesex: Penguin Books, 1977.

Hursthouse, Rosalind. *Beginning Lives*. Oxford: Basil Blackwell, 1987.

Kamm, Frances M. *Creation and Abortion*. New York: Oxford University Press, 1992.

Sumner, L. W. *Abortion and Moral Theory*. Princeton: Princeton University Press, 1981.

Tooley, Michael. *Abortion and Infanticide*. Oxford: Oxford University Press, 1983.

B. Articles

Baker, John. "Philosophy and the Morality of Abortion." *Journal of Applied Philosophy* 2 (1985): 261–270.

Bigelow, John, and Robert Pargetter. "Morality, Potential Persons and Abortion." *American Philosophical Quarterly* 25 (1988): 173–181.

Brandt, Richard B. "The Morality of Abortion." *The Monist* 56 (1972): 503–526.

Cooney, William. "The Fallacy of All Person-Denying Arguments for Abortion." *Journal of Applied Philosophy* 8 (1991): 161–165.

Cudd, Ann E. "Sensationalized Philosophy: A Reply to Marquis's 'Why Abortion Is Immoral.'" *Journal of Philosophy* 87 (1990): 262–264.

Davis, Michael. "Foetuses, Famous Violinists and the Right to Continued Aid." *Philosophical Quarterly* 33 (1983): 259–278.

Davis, Nancy. "Abortion and Self defense." *Philosophy & Public Affairs* 13 (1984): 175–207.

Davis, Nancy (Ann). "The Abortion Debate: The Search for Common Ground, Part 1." *Ethics* 103 (1993): 516–539.

———. "The Abortion Debate: The Search for Common Ground, Part 2." *Ethics* 103 (1993): 731–778.

Dixon, Nicholas. "Abortion, Moral Neutrality, and Feminism." *The Philosophical Forum* 26 (1995): 315–330.

Dore, Clement. "Abortion, Some Slippery Slope Arguments and Identity over Time." *Philosophical Studies* 55 (1989): 279–291.

English, Jane. "Abortion and the Concept of a Person." *Canadian Journal of Philosophy* 5 (1975): 233–243.

Finnis, John. "The Rights and Wrongs of Abortion: A Reply to Judith Thomson." *Philosophy & Public Affairs* 2 (1973): 117–145.

Fischer, John M. "Abortion and Self-Determination." *Journal of Social Philosophy* 22 (1991): 5–13.

Gallagher, Kenneth. "Abortion and Choice." *Public Affairs Quarterly* 7 (1993): 13–17.

Gomberg, Paul. "Abortion and the Morality of Nurturance." *Canadian Journal of Philosophy* 21 (1991): 513–524.

Gould, James. "Abortion: Privacy versus Liberty." *Journal of Social Philosophy* 21 (1990): 98–106.

Hare, R. M. "A Kantian Approach to Abortion." *Social Theory and Practice* 15 (1989): 1–14.

Harris, George W. "Fathers and Fetuses." *Ethics* 96 (1986): 594–603.

Lomasky, Loren. "Being a Person—Does It Matter?" In *The Problem of Abortion*, 2nd ed., ed. Joel Feinberg. Belmont, Calif.: Wadsworth Publishing Company, 1984.

Lombardi, Louis. "The Legal versus the Moral on Abortion." *Journal of Social Philosophy* 17 (1986): 23–29.

McConnell, Terrance. "Permissive Abortion Laws, Religion and Moral Compromise." *Public Affairs Quarterly* 1 (1987): 95–109.

McInerney, Peter. "Does a Fetus Already Have a Future-Like-Ours?" *Journal of Philosophy* 87 (1990): 264–268.

McMahan, Jeff. "The Right to Choose an Abortion." *Philosophy & Public Affairs* 22 (1993): 331–348.

Meyers, Christopher. "Maintaining the Violinist: A Mother's Obligations to the Fetus She Decides to Keep." *Journal of Social Philosophy* 23 (1992): 52–64.

Norcross, Alastair. "Killing, Abortion, and Contraception: A Reply to Marquis." *Journal of Philosophy* 87 (1990): 268–277.

Pahel, Kenneth R. "Michael Tooley on Abortion and Potentiality." *Southern Journal of Philosophy* 25 (1987): 89–107.

Porter, Elizabeth. "Abortion Ethics: Rights and Responsibilities." *Hypatia* 9 (1994): 66–87.

Purdy, Laura. "Are Women Fetal Containers?" *Bioethics* 4 (1990): 273–291.

Quinn, Warren. "Abortion: Identity and Loss." *Philosophy & Public Affairs* 13 (1984): 24–54.

Ross, Steven. "Abortion and the Death of the Fetus." *Philosophy & Public Affairs* 11 (1982): 232–245.

Smith, Holly. "Intercourse and Moral Responsibility for the Fetus." In *Abortion and the Status of the Fetus*, ed. W. B. Bondeson, H. T. Englehardt, Jr., S. F. Spicker, and D. Winship. Dordrecht: D. Reidel, 1983.

Warren, Mary Ann. "The Moral Signifigance of Birth." *Hypatia* 4 (1989): 46–65.

Wertheimer, Roger. "Understanding the Abortion Argument." *Philosophy & Public Affairs* 1 (1971): 67–95.

Winkler, Earl R. "Abortion and Victimisability." *Journal of Applied Philosophy* 1 (1984): 305–318.

Zaitchik, Alan. "Viability and the Morality of Abortion." *Philosophy & Public Affairs* 10 (1981): 18–26.

C. Anthologies

Baird, Robert, and Stuart Rosenbaum, eds. *The Ethics of Abortion*. Rev. ed. Buffalo, N.Y.: Prometheus Books, 1993.

Bondeson, W. B., H. T. Englehardt, Jr., S. F. Spicker, and D. Winship, eds. *Abortion and the Status of the Fetus*. Dordrecht: D. Reidel, 1983.

Callahan, Sidney, and Daniel Callahan, eds. *Abortion: Understanding Differences*. New York: Plenum Press, 1984.

Cohen, Marshall, Thomas Nagel, and Thomas Scanlon, eds. *Rights and Wrongs of Abortion*. Princeton: Princeton University Press, 1974.

Feinberg, Joel, ed. *The Problem of Abortion*. 2nd ed. Belmont, Calif.: Wadsworth Publishing Company, 1984.

Noonan, John T., Jr., ed. *The Morality of Abortion: Legal and Historical Perspectives*. Cambridge, Mass.: Harvard University Press, 1970.

Pojman, Louis P., and Francis J. Beckwith, eds. *The Abortion Controversy*. Boston: Jones and Bartlett Publishers, 1994.

II. Legal Perspectives

A. United States

Colker, Ruth. *Abortion and Dialogue: Prochoice, Prolife, and American Law*. Bloomington and Indianapolis: Indiana University Press, 1992.

Craig, Barbara Hinkson, and David M. O'Brien. *Abortion and American Politics*. Chatham, N.J.: Chatham House Publishers, Inc., 1993.

Drucker, Dan. *Abortion Decisions of the Supreme Court, 1973–1989*. Jefferson, N.C.: McFarland & Company, Inc., Publishers, 1990.

Ely, John Hart. "The Wages of Crying Wolf: A Comment on *Roe v. Wade*." *Yale Law Journal* 82 (1973): 920–949.

Faux, Marian. Roe v. Wade: *The Untold Story of the Landmark Supreme Court Decision That Made Abortion Legal.* New York: Macmillan, 1988.

Garrow, David. *Liberty and Sexuality: The Right to Privacy and the Making of* Roe v. Wade. New York: Lisa Drew Books, Macmillan Publishing Co., 1994.

Ginsberg, Ruth Bader. "Some Thoughts on Autonomy and Equality in Relation to *Roe v. Wade.*" *North Carolina Law Review* 63 (1985): 375–386.

Glendon, Mary Ann. *Abortion and Divorce in Western Law: American Failures, European Challenges.* Cambridge, Mass.: Harvard University Press, 1987.

Goldstein, Robert. *Mother-Love and Abortion.* Berkeley, Calif.: University of California Press, 1988.

Horan, Dennis J., Edward R. Grant, and Paige Cunningham, eds. *Abortion and the Constitution: Reversing* Roe v. Wade *through the Courts.* Washington, D.C.: Georgetown University Press, 1987.

Karlan, Pamela S, and Daniel R. Ortiz. "In a Diffident Voice: Relational Feminism, Abortion Rights, and the Feminist Legal Agenda." *Northwestern University Law Review* 87 (1993): 858–896.

Law, Sylvia. "Rethinking Sex and the Constitution." *University of Pennsylvania Law Review* 132 (1984): 955–1040.

Rubin, Eva R., ed. *The Abortion Controversy: A Documentary History.* Westport, Conn.: Greenwood Press, 1994.

Tribe, L. *Abortion: The Clash of Absolutes.* New York: Norton, 1990.

Wenz, Peter. *Abortion Rights as Religious Freedom.* Philadelphia: Temple University Press, 1991.

B. Canada

Brodie, M. Janine. *The Politics of Abortion.* Toronto: Oxford University Press, 1992.

Gentles, Ian, ed. *A Time to Choose Life: Women, Abortion and Human Rights.* Toronto: Stoddart, 1990.

Kay, Barry J., Ronald D. Lambert, and Steven D. Brown. "Single-Issue Interest Groups and the Canadian Electorate: The Case of Abortion in 1988." *Journal of Canadian Studies* 26 (1991):142–154.

Morton, F. L. *Morgentaler v. Borowski: Abortion, the Charter and the Courts.* Toronto: McClelland and Stewart, 1992.

———. *Pro-Choice vs. Pro-Life: Abortion and the Courts in Canada.* Norman, Okla.: University of Oklahoma Press, 1993.

III. Feminism and Abortion

A. Feminist Defenses of Abortion

Gatens-Robinson, Eugenie. "A Defense of Women's Choice: Abortion and the Ethics of Care." *Southern Journal of Philosophy* 30 (1992): 39–66.

Jaggar, Alison. "Abortion and a Woman's Right to Decide." In *Philosophy and Sex*, ed. by Robert Baker and Frederick Elliston. Buffalo, N.Y.: Prometheus Books, 1975.

Overall, Christine. *Ethics and Human Reproduction: A Feminist Analysis*. Boston: Allen and Unwin, 1987.

———. *Human Reproduction: Principles, Practices, Policies*. Toronto: Oxford University Press, 1993.

Sherwin, Susan. "Abortion through a Feminist Ethics Lens." *Dialogue* 30 (1991): 327–342.

B. Pro-Life Feminism

Callahan, Sidney. "Abortion and the Sexual Agenda: A Case for Prolife Feminism. *Commonweal* 123 (1986): 232–238.

McDonnell, Kathleen. *Not an Easy Choice: A Feminist Reexamines Abortion*. Boston: South End Press, 1984.

Maloney, Anne M. "Cassandra's Fate: Why Feminists Ought to Be Pro-Life." In *Abortion: A New Generation of Catholic Responses*, ed. Stephen J. Heaney. Braintree, Mass.: The Pope John Center, 1992.

Sweet, Gail Greiner. *Pro-Life Feminism*. Lewiston, N.Y.: Life-Cycle Books, 1985.

C. General Discussion of Feminism and Abortion

Anderson, Susan. "Criticisms of Liberal/Feminist Views on Abortion." *Public Affairs Quarterly* 2 (1987): 83–96.

Cornell, Drucilla. *The Imaginary Domain: Abortion, Pornography and Sexual Harassment*. New York: Routledge, 1995.

Cudd, Anne. E. "Enforced Pregnancy, Rape, and the Image of Woman." *Philosophical Studies* 60 (1990): 47–59.

Dworkin, Ronald. "Feminism and Abortion." *The New York Review of Books*, June 10, 1993, 27–29.

Kaplan, Laura. *The Story of Jane: The Legendary Underground Feminist Abortion Service*. New York: Pantheon, 1996.

King, C. R. "Calling Jane: The Life and Death of a Woman's Illegal Abortion Service." *Women and Health* 20 (1993): 75–93.

MacKinnon, Catharine A. "Privacy v. Equality: Beyond *Roe v. Wade*." In *Feminism Unmodified*. Cambridge, Mass.: Harvard University Press, 1987.

Mahowald, Mary. "Feminism and Abortion Arguments." *Kinesis* 11 (1982): 57–68.

Petchesky, Rosalind. *Abortion and Woman's Choice: The State, Sexuality, and Reproductive Freedom*. Rev. ed. Boston: Northeastern University Press, 1990.

Shrage, Laurie. *Moral Dilemmas of Feminism: Prostitution, Adultery and Abortion*. New York: Routledge, 1994.

D. Feminist Ethics

Addelson, Kathryn Pyne. *Impure Thoughts: Essays on Philosophy, Feminism, and Ethics*. Philadelphia: Temple University Press, 1991.

Frazer, Elizabeth, Jennifer Hornsby, and Sabina Lovibond, eds. *Ethics: A Feminist Reader*. Cambridge, Mass.: Blackwell, 1992.

Gilligan, Carol. *In a Different Voice.* Cambridge, Mass.: Harvard University Press, 1982.

Greeno, Catherine G., and Eleanor E. Maccoby. "How Different Is the 'Different Voice'?" *Signs* 11 (1986): 310–316.

Kittay, Eva Feder, and Diana T. Meyers, eds. *Women and Moral Theory.* Totowa, N.J.: Rowman and Littlefield, 1987.

Noddings, Nel. *Caring: A Feminine Approach to Ethics and Moral Education.* Berkeley, Calif.: University of California Press, 1984.

Ruddick, Sara. *Maternal Thinking: Towards a Politics of Peace.* Boston: Beacon Press, 1989.

Smith, Janet. "Abortion and Moral Development: Listening with Different Ears." *International Philosophical Quarterly* 28 (1988): 31–51.

Tong, Rosemarie. *Feminine and Feminist Ethics.* Belmont, Calif.: Wadsworth Publishing Company, 1993.

Walker, Margaret Urban. "Moral Understandings: Alternative 'Epistemology' for a Feminist Ethics." *Hypatia* 4 (1989): 15–28.

E. Feminist Legal Theory

Bartlett, Katharine T., and Rosanne Kennedy, eds. *Feminist Legal Theory: Readings in Law and Gender.* Boulder, Colo.: Westview Press, 1991.

Smith, Patricia G., ed. *Feminist Jurisprudence.* New York: Oxford University Press, 1993.

IV. Sociological and Political Perspectives

Blanchard, Dallas A. *The Anti-Abortion Movement and the Rise of the Religious Right.* New York: Twayne Publishers, 1994.

Blanchard, D., and T. J. Prewitt. *Religious Violence and Abortion.* Gainesville, Fla.: University Press of Florida, 1993.

Condit, Celeste Michelle. *Decoding Abortion Rhetoric: Communicating Social Change.* Urbana, Ill.: University of Illinois Press, 1987.

Fung, Archon. "Making Rights Real: *Roe*'s Impact on Abortion Access." *Politics and Society* 21 (1993): 456–504.

Ginsberg, Faye D. *Contested Lives: The Abortion Debate in an American Community.* Berkeley, Calif.: University of California Press, 1989.

Luker, Kristin. *Abortion and the Politics of Motherhood.* Berkeley, Calif.: University of California Press, 1984.

Lunneborg, Patricia. *Abortion: A Positive Decision.* New York: Bergin and Garrey, 1992.

McKeegan, Michelle. *Abortion Politics: Mutiny in the Ranks of the Right.* New York: The Free Press, 1992.

Mensch, Elizabeth, and Alan Freeman. *The Politics of Virtue—Is Abortion Debatable?* Durham and London: Duke University Press, 1993.

Peach, Lucinda. "Feminist Cautions about Casuistry: The Supreme Court's Abortion Decisions as Paradigms." *Policy Sciences* 27 (1994): 143–160.

V. International Perspectives

Berer, Marge. "Abortion in Europe from a Woman's Perspective." In *Progress Postponed: Abortion in Europe in the 1990s.* International Planned Parenthood Europe Region, 1993.

Funk, Nanette, and Magda Mueller, eds. *Gender Politics and Post-Communism: Reflections from Eastern Europe and the Former Soviet Union.* New York: Routledge, 1993.

Hadley, Janet. "God's Bullies: Attacks on Abortion." *Feminist Review* 48 (1994): 94–113.

Jankowska, Hanna. "The Reproductive Rights Campaign in Poland." *Women's Studies International Forum* 16 (1993): 291–296.

LaFleur, William R. *Liquid Life: Abortion and Buddhism in Japan.* Princeton, N.J.: Princeton University Press, 1992.

Muldoon, Maureen. *The Abortion Debate in the US and Canada.* New York: Garland, 1991.

Stephenson P., M. Wagner, M. Badea, and F. Serbanescu, "Commentary: The Public Health Consequences of Restricted Induced Abortion—Lessons from Romania." *American Journal of Public Health* 82 (1992):1328–1331.

VI. Religious Perspectives

Byrnes, Timothy A., and Mary C. Segers. *The Catholic Church and the Politics of Abortion: A View from the States.* Boulder, Colo.: Westview Press, 1992.

Campbell, Liz. "Abortion: A Christian Feminist Perspective." *New Blackfriars* 61 (1980): 370–377.

Coward, Harold G., Julius Lipner, and Katherine K. Young. *Hindu Ethics: Purity, Abortion, and Euthanasia.* Albany, N.Y.: State University of New York Press, 1989.

Davis, Dena S. "Abortion in Jewish Thought: A Study in Casuistry." *Journal of the American Academy of Religion* 60 (1992): 313–324.

Feldman, David. *Birth Control in Jewish Law.* New York: New York University Press, 1968.

Harrison, Beverley Wildung. *Our Right to Choose.* Boston: Beacon Press, 1983.

Heaney, Stephen J., ed. *Abortion: A New Generation of Catholic Responses.* Braintree, Mass.: The Pope John Center, 1992.

Larson, David R. *Abortion: Ethical Issues and Options.* Loma Linda, Calif.: Loma Linda University Center for Christian Bioethics, 1992.

Lundblad, Barbara K. "Abortion: The Lutherans' Turn." *Christianity and Crisis* 51 (1991): 382–383.

Steffen, Lloyd. *Life/Choice: The Theory of Just Abortion.* Cleveland, Ohio: The Pilgrim Press, 1994.

VII. General Interest

Davis, Nanette. *From Crime to Choice: The Transformation of Abortion in America.* Westport, Conn.: Greenwood Press, 1985.

Rodman, Hyman, Betty Sarvis, and Joy Walker Bonar. *The Abortion Question.* New York: Columbia University Press, 1987.

Rosenblatt, Roger. *Life Itself: Abortion in the American Mind.* Random House, 1992.

Weddington, Sarah. *A Question of Choice.* New York: Grosset/Putnam, 1992.

VIII. Facts and Statistics

Blendon, Robert J., John M. Benson, and Karen Donelan. "The Public and the Controversy over Abortion." *Journal of the American Medical Association* 270 (1993): 2871–2875.

Daley, D., and R. B. Gold. "Public Funding for Contraceptive, Sterilization and Abortion Services, Fiscal Year 1992." *Family Planning Perspectives* 25 (1993): 244–251.

Forrest, J. D., and S. K. Henshaw. "Providing Controversial Health Care: Abortion Services since 1973." *Women's Health Issues* 3 (1993):152–157.

Henshaw, S. K. "Induced Abortions: A World View, 1990." *Family Planning Perspectives* 22 (1990): 76–89.

———. "The Accessibility of Abortion Services in the United States." *Family Planning Perspectives* 23 (1991): 246–252.

Henshaw, S. K., and J. Van Vort. "Abortion Services in the United States, 1991 and 1992." *Family Planning Perspectives* 26 (1994): 100–106.

Jacobson, Jodi L. *The Global Politics of Abortion.* Washington, D.C.: Worldwatch Institute, 1990.

Marsiglio, W., and C. L. Shehan. "Adolescent Males' Abortion Attitudes: Data from a National Survey." *Family Planning Perspectives* 25 (1993): 162–169.

Sachdev, Paul, ed. *International Handbook on Abortion.* New York: Greenwood Press, 1988.